Wade McClusky
and
the Battle of Midway

OSPREY
PUBLISHING

WADE McCLUSKY
AND THE BATTLE OF
MIDWAY

DAVID RIGBY

OSPREY PUBLISHING
Bloomsbury Publishing Plc
PO Box 883, Oxford, OX1 9PL, UK
1385 Broadway, 5th Floor, New York, NY 10018, USA
E-mail: info@ospreypublishing.com
www.ospreypublishing.com

OSPREY is a trademark of Osprey Publishing Ltd

First published in Great Britain in 2019

This paperback edition was first published in Great Britain in 2020 by Osprey Publishing.

ISBN: HB 9781472834737; PB 9781472848239; eBook 9781472834720; ePDF 9781472834713; XML 9781472834744

20 21 22 23 24   10 9 8 7 6 5 4 3 2 1

Typeset in Sabon LT Std by Deanta Global Publishing Services, Chennai, India
Printed and bound in Great Britain by CPI (Group) UK Ltd, Croydon CR0 4YY

Front and back cover: A squadron of US Douglas SBD-3 Dauntless dive bombers in flight as they patrol the coral reefs off Midway Island, Midway Islands, 1942. (Photos by Frank Scherschel/The LIFE Picture Collection/Getty Images).
Inside back cover: Wade McClusky pictured as a captain in 1946. (US Navy Photo. Phil McClusky collection).

Osprey Publishing supports the Woodland Trust, the UK's leading woodland conservation charity.

In Memory of Lt Charles Rollins Ware, USN

Dive-bomber pilot (VS-6)
Killed in action at Midway

CONTENTS

PREFACE

During the Battle of Midway in June 1942, US Navy pilot Wade McClusky proved himself to be one of the greatest pilots and combat leaders in American history, but his story has never been told – until now.

The grand strategy involved in the Battle of Midway is well known and does not need retelling. What is needed in the literature on the Battle of Midway is a book chronicling the contributions to American victory made by then Lt Cdr C. Wade McClusky, Jr, air group commander of the USS *Enterprise* (CV-6). It was Wade McClusky who remained calm when the Japanese fleet was not where he expected it to be. It was McClusky who made the counterintuitive choice to then search to the north instead of to the south. It was also McClusky who took the calculated risk of continuing to search even though he knew that the 32 pilots in his two squadrons of dive-bombers were all running dangerously low on fuel and that even if they found the enemy, his boys would barely have enough fuel left to make it back to the *Enterprise*. McClusky's ability to remain calm under enormous pressure enabled him to find the Japanese fleet, which in turn enabled the pilots under his direct command to deliver the attacks that destroyed two of the four Japanese aircraft carriers sunk at Midway.

Every book about the Battle of Midway mentions Wade McClusky, but usually only in passing, as if his actions on June 4, 1942 were somehow "ordinary." McClusky's immediate superiors, by contrast, knew differently. Just after the Battle of Midway, USS *Enterprise* captain George D. Murray, Task Force 16 commander R Adm Raymond Spruance, and Commander-in-Chief of the US Pacific Fleet Adm Chester W. Nimitz all stated that Wade McClusky had made the single most important contribution to American victory in one of the most utterly decisive naval battles in all of history. Somehow over time, however, these early accolades became forgotten so that by the time of his death in 1976, Wade McClusky had faded into obscurity.

It is my sincere hope that this book will change all that by breathing life into a man who is treated in other accounts of the Battle of Midway as a shadowy background figure. Being one of the oldest pilots in the Navy in 1942 gave McClusky the gravitas to handle unexpected situations. It also made him one of the most experienced pilots in the US Navy in terms of the hours of "hands-on" flying time he had logged. Having completed his flight training more than a decade prior to Pearl Harbor meant that McClusky was experienced in, and familiar with the characteristics of, every type of aircraft in the naval inventory of the time – dive-bombers, fighter planes, and torpedo planes.

There was something serendipitous about the timing of Wade McClusky's entry into naval service. Graduating from the US Naval Academy in 1926, he went on active duty just one year before the US Navy received its first two true aircraft carriers, USS *Lexington* (CV-2) and USS *Saratoga* (CV-3). Thus, when he underwent flight training in late 1928 and early 1929, McClusky was getting in on the "ground floor" of naval aviation, which, as history has shown, was where the Navy's future lay.

There have been accusations made in recent literature on the Battle of Midway to the effect that Wade McClusky was supposedly "unfamiliar" with dive-bombing doctrine and that he therefore supposedly "bungled" the dive-bombing attacks made against the Imperial Japanese Navy (IJN) aircraft carriers *Akagi* and *Kaga*. I intend to disprove these fallacies. There is a wealth of information available to refute these inaccurate accusations, beginning with the fact that both of the targets Wade McClusky selected for his group of pilots to attack were in fact destroyed in the attack McClusky led. How can he then have "bungled"? It is hard to argue with success.

Most of all, this is a story about destiny; about how, as stated by historian George J. Walsh, Wade McClusky's story is the story of "the right man in the right place at the right time"[1] to make the calm, rational decisions that enabled the Americans to win the Battle of Midway. Wade McClusky was that man.[2] This book is his story.

---

[1] Lt Cdr George G. Walsh USNR (Ret.) "Lt. Cmdr. Wade McClusky Hero of the Battle of Midway." Blog, 12 May 2012. http://mccluskymidwayhero.blogspot.com/.
[2] Ibid.

I

June 4, 1942 – The Search Begins

Right now Wade McClusky had a problem. In fact, he had several problems. It was 9.30am on the morning of June 4, 1942. McClusky was flying at 19,000ft in a Douglas SBD-3 Dauntless dive-bomber at the head of two squadrons of USS *Enterprise* dive-bombers, Scouting Six (VS-6) and Bombing Six (VB-6); 33 aircraft in all, including the one he and his rear seat gunner/radio operator Walter G. Chocalousek were riding in. McClusky's group had been in the air for two-and-a-half hours. The fuel situation was becoming critical for everyone. McClusky and his two wingmen, Ensigns Bill Pittman and Dick Jaccard, had attached themselves to Scouting Six for the day's mission. Every aircraft in VS-6, including those of McClusky, Pittman, and Jaccard, was carrying a 500lb bomb affixed to the belly of the airplane. In addition to the 500lb bomb, nine of the 15 aircraft in VS-6 were also each carrying two 100lb bombs; one under each wing. McClusky and his wingmen carried just one 500lb bomb each. All of the 15 pilots of Bombing Six carried one 1,000lb bomb each.[1] All of this ordnance would be useless, however, unless Wade McClusky could solve his biggest problem – figuring out where the enemy was.

As air group commander of USS *Enterprise* (CV-6), McClusky was in charge of all of the aircraft from that carrier: dive-bombers,

---

[1]John B. Lundstrom, *The First Team: Pacific Air Combat from Pearl Harbor to Midway* (Annapolis: Naval Institute Press, 1984): p335.

torpedo planes, and fighters. Yet, because of delays during that morning's launch, McClusky had been ordered to proceed to the target with just his dive-bombers. McClusky thus had no idea where his torpedo planes and his fighter aircraft were. And he knew that he and his dive-bombers would have to face Japanese fighter planes without any American fighter escort. The SBD Dauntless would on this day prove itself to be the finest dive-bombing aircraft type in the world, but the prospect of attacking the Japanese fleet without fighter escort must have been sobering to say the least. The Americans were well aware by now of the high quality of the Japanese Mitsubishi A6M2 "Zero" or "Zeke" fighters planes and the prowess of the Imperial Japanese Navy (IJN) pilots who were certain to be flying combat air patrol (CAP) over the target McClusky was determined to find and attack.

That target was the Japanese aircraft carrier striking force, often referred to by its Japanese name – *Kido Butai* – under the command of V Adm Nagumo Chuichi, which had been tasked with spearheading the Japanese invasion of Midway atoll, 1,300 miles northwest of Pearl Harbor. Invading Midway was a campaign that the Japanese hoped would lure the US Pacific Fleet into a decisive naval battle that the Japanese had every reason to believe would result in the destruction of the American Pacific Fleet aircraft carriers; ships that had been absent from Pearl Harbor on December 7, 1941.

Having flown out on a southwesterly heading for over an hour and a half, McClusky had reached the interception point as calculated from a contact report that had been radioed back to Midway from an American PBY Catalina flying boat early that morning. The problem was that there was nothing in sight below him other than an empty expanse of ocean.

The idea of turning left and searching to the south must have been very tempting to McClusky. After all, in that direction lay the two islets of Midway atoll itself, the Japanese objective. Perhaps the Japanese had made better speed than expected on their southeasterly course toward Midway and had gotten past the interception point? Turning south also would have provided the soothing reassurance that whether or not he found the enemy, McClusky's aircraft, already low on fuel, could conceivably land and refuel on Midway (as several dive-bombers from the USS *Hornet* would do that day). But McClusky did not turn left. That sixth sense that is possessed by great military commanders told him that the Japanese were not going too fast, but too slow. They must have been held up somehow and still be to his north.

What he did next prompted the late historian Gordon Prange to write of Wade McClusky that: "What he brought to his job was a gift for command, composed in equal parts of personal fearlessness and the ability to feed unexpected data into his brain cells and click out a prompt, intelligent answer. [Admiral Raymond A.] Spruance, who never tossed adjectives around recklessly, called McClusky 'terrific.'"[1] To provide for the eventuality that Nagumo might have turned west, McClusky flew on to the southwest for five more minutes.[2] Then at 9.35am he took the counterintuitive path by leading his squadrons in a turn to the right on to a northwesterly heading. When he did that, Wade McClusky made what was arguably the most important single decision by any American commander during the entirety of World War 2 in the Pacific.

Wade McClusky was a reticent man. He wrote a bare-bones after action report, which after the war he expanded to the length of a scholarly article, which sadly remained unpublished. He never wrote a full-length memoir. Indeed, after the war McClusky rarely spoke of the battle in which he had played such an utterly decisive role, even to his family. It is therefore difficult to know exactly what he was thinking when he reached the interception point and found nothing but empty ocean, but it certainly never occurred to McClusky that he and his pilots had done their best and that it would be all right to turn around and return to the *Enterprise* at this point in order

---

[1]Gordon W. Prange, Donald M. Goldstein, and Katherine V. Dillon, *Miracle at Midway* (New York: McGraw Hill, 1982): p259.

[2]Wade McClusky, "The Midway Story" Unpublished manuscript, p4. Walter Lord Papers. Operational Archives. Naval History and Heritage Command (NHHC). Washington Navy Yard. Washington, DC.

to refuel. Wade McClusky was all about getting the job done, not just doing one's best. He was certain that he needed to improvise; to come up with a contingency plan of his own without being swayed by panic or anger. Somebody else had been supposed to find the enemy. McClusky's job was to lead an attack, not a search. But what was supposed to happen did not matter now. Something had gone wrong and it was up to Wade McClusky to make the decisions that would rectify the situation. Pacific Fleet commander Adm Chester W. Nimitz had ordered his two flag officers on the scene, R Adms Frank Jack Fletcher and Raymond A. Spruance, to operate in the coming battle under "the principle of calculated risk."[1] That is exactly what Wade McClusky now did. He would have been well aware that the fuel situation was especially critical for the aircraft in Bombing Six, each of which was lugging a bomb weighing half a ton. McClusky not only made the right call by turning north, not south, but he also accepted the calculated risk in searching for the Japanese of taking his pilots beyond the safe margin of fuel endurance his pilots needed to ensure that they would all be able to make it back to the *Enterprise*.

When asked during the war how he decided which colonels should be promoted and made into generals, US Army Chief of Staff Gen George C. Marshall gave an answer that describes many of the qualities possessed by Wade McClusky. Marshall stated that when choosing senior commanders for the Army: "the most important factor of all is character, which involves integrity, unselfish and devoted purpose, a sturdiness of bearing when everything goes wrong and all are critical, and a willingness to sacrifice self in the interest of the common good."[2] The sort of situations faced by senior commanders that Gen Marshall meant, are, for instance:

[1]Nimitz orders to Fletcher and Spruance, as quoted in E.B. Potter, *Nimitz*. (Annapolis: Naval Institute Press, 1976, 1987): p87.

[2]Larry I. Bland, ed., and Sharon Ritenour Stevens, Associate Ed, *The Papers of George Catlett Marshall*. Vol. 4. *Aggressive and Determined Leadership: June 1, 1943–December 31, 1944* (Baltimore: Johns Hopkins University Press, 1996): p345.

what would a hypothetical commander of an artillery battery do upon learning in the middle of a battle that some fool in a rear area supply dump had sent him the wrong ammunition for his guns? Would he sit down and cry like a baby or would he think quickly and improvise to find a solution?[1] By Gen Marshall's criterion, Wade McClusky would have scored quite highly, particularly in regard to his ability to remain calm and adapt when things went badly awry.

Wade McClusky improvised and he did indeed find a solution. McClusky risked everything when he realized that the Japanese fleet was not where it was supposed to be. An Annapolis graduate and a career naval officer, McClusky had no civilian career that he could return to if things in the Navy did not work out. If he had turned in the wrong direction and had not found the Japanese fleet, the striking power represented by the Japanese aircraft carriers likely would have ensured the destruction of all three of the American aircraft carriers at Midway. Indeed, Adm Nagumo was preparing *Kido Butai* to launch a massive air strike against the American carriers just as McClusky's dive-bombers appeared overhead at 10.20am (local time) on June 4, 1942. Wade McClusky's ability to think on his feet, to improvise, is reminiscent of another sailor who, 30 years earlier, had also made all the right moves under intense pressure: Arthur Rostron, who had been captain of the Cunard liner *Carpathia*, the ship that rescued the survivors of the *Titanic* disaster. In describing the very first actions taken by Arthur Rostron in the early hours of April 15, 1912, upon his being informed of the distress signals from the *Titanic* that the *Carpathia* had received via wireless (ie radio), the dean of *Titanic* historians Walter Lord writes that:

> "at 12.35 A.M., . . . Harold Cottam, the *Carpathia*'s wireless operator, burst into the Captain's quarters to report that the *Titanic* had struck a berg and urgently needed help. Rostron's

[1]Forrest C. Pogue, *George C. Marshall*. Vol. 2. *Ordeal and Hope: 1939–1942* (New York: Viking, 1966): p97, pp103–104.

reaction was completely in character. He immediately ordered the *Carpathia* turned around then asked Cottam if he was sure. Nine out of ten captains would have done it the other way around."[1]

Japanese naval officers in World War 2 excelled at following a carefully scripted plan, but the Japanese showed at Midway that they were not good at improvising when the plan went awry.[2] Without meaning any disrespect to the Japanese pilots who fought bravely at Midway, I believe that a Japanese squadron leader (and probably nine out of ten American squadron leaders), faced with the problem McClusky faced, would have turned his group around and headed back to his carrier to refuel and to get new orders before continuing a search for an enemy fleet. McClusky knew there was no time for that. Like Arthur Rostron in Walter Lord's analogy, Wade McClusky *was that tenth man*. (It is probably no accident that as a historian, Walter Lord would choose to write books that mention the accomplishments of both men, Arthur Rostron *and* Wade McClusky.) McClusky realized that there was only going to be one chance, and that he just *had* to succeed. In fact, Wade McClusky was determined to locate the Japanese carriers even if all of his planes ran out of fuel after making their attacks.[3] Finding the enemy and making the attack was all that mattered to McClusky. Finding the enemy required cool, calm, rational decision-making under intense pressure. His turn to the north at 9.35am, when almost any other commander would have turned south or turned back, proves that despite his relatively low rank at the time, Wade McClusky was one of the greatest American combat leaders of World War 2.

[1]Walter Lord, *The Night Lives On* (New York: Avon Books, 1986, 1987): p126.

[2]Jonathan Parshall and Anthony Tully, *Shattered Sword: The Untold Story of the Battle of Midway* (Washington, DC: Potomac Books, 2007): p400, pp411–414.

[3]Edward Stafford, *The Big E: The Story of the U.S.S. Enterprise* (Annapolis: Naval Institute Press, 1962, 2002): p99.

2

BACKGROUND OF A BATTLE – AND OF A LEADER

The Japanese were actively beaten in the Battle of Midway, a fact at odds with much recent literature on the battle that claims that the Americans did not so much win the Battle of Midway, but rather that the Japanese lost it.[1] In fact, the American victory at Midway was far from being a passive victory won "by default." Japanese mistakes and lackadaisical planning were not nearly enough to hand victory to the Americans. It was positive action, such as Wade McClusky's ability to keep cool and improvise when things went wrong, that won the battle for the Americans. Chance did play a role in the battle, but it is grossly inaccurate to say that Midway was an accidental victory for the Americans.

To prove this point, an overview of the battle and of the role of Lt Cdr C. Wade McClusky, Jr in it, is essential. The significance of what McClusky and the dive-bomber pilots under his command accomplished in the Battle of Midway cannot be overstated. As of 10.00am on the morning of June 4, 1942, after six months of war, the United States was losing the war in the Pacific. One half hour later, at 10.30am on June 4, 1942, the United States was winning.[2] In that half hour occurred the pivotal events of an

---

[1]Jonathan Parshall and Anthony Tully, *Shattered Sword: The Untold Story of the Battle of Midway* (Washington, DC: Potomac Books, 2007): p414.

[2]Craig L. Symonds, *The Battle of Midway* (New York: Oxford University Press, 2011, 2013): pp3–4 .

utterly decisive battle that brought to a crashing halt the hitherto seemingly unstoppable Japanese advance in the Pacific. The Imperial Japanese Navy (IJN) that had launched the Pearl Harbor attack had followed that stunning blow by providing the muscle with which Japanese forces were able to seize American Pacific possessions, such as Wake Island, Guam, and the Philippines; and to stage landings in the Bismarck archipelago in the southwest Pacific – the last being uncomfortably close to Australia. The Battle of Midway put a very sudden end to such expansionist moves by the Japanese. The most decisive phase of the Battle of Midway was the ten-minute attack commencing at 10.20am (local time) by American dive-bombing aircraft from the carriers *Enterprise* (CV-6) and *Yorktown* (CV-5). That attack transformed the Japanese carriers *Akagi*, *Kaga*, and *Soryu* into blazing, exploding hulks. That afternoon, in a second dive-bombing attack, American pilots would put four bombs through the flight deck of the fourth Japanese carrier, *Hiryu*. The destruction of these four fine aircraft carriers and their elite air groups in one day was a stunning blow to the Imperial Japanese Navy and to the entire Japanese war effort – a blow from which the Japanese never recovered.

There are many books that describe the events of the critical ten minutes of the morning attack that decided the Battle of Midway. All of them mention Wade McClusky who, in his role as air group commander of the USS *Enterprise*, led two squadrons of Douglas SBD Dauntless dive-bombing aircraft in the attack. The pilots under McClusky's command destroyed Adm Nagumo's flagship *Akagi* and its consort in IJN Carrier Division One, the *Kaga*. The *Soryu* was destroyed by bombs dropped by a squadron of American dive-bomber pilots from the *Yorktown*, who were led by McClusky's Annapolis classmate Lt Cdr Maxwell Leslie. Despite his critical role, the bulk of the literature on the Battle of Midway persists in describing Wade McClusky's actions in the battle as being "routine," as something not much different from the activities of, say, plane handlers on the American aircraft carriers who fueled and armed aircraft prior to take-off; essential work, yes, but routine. There are even unfounded allegations that Wade McClusky made critical errors during the battle due to a supposedly incomplete understanding on his part of dive-bombing doctrine.

McClusky's role in the battle was anything but "routine" and he had first strapped himself into the cockpit of a dive-bomber in 1930, when many of the pilots who would fly with him at Midway were children in middle school. By 1942, there was very little that Wade McClusky *didn't* know about dive-bombers and dive-bombing doctrine; by June of that year he had amassed more than 2,900 total hours of flying time in 13 years as a Navy pilot. He had spent just over 400 of those hours flying dive-bombers in the 1930s – the Curtiss F8C-4 and the Vought SBU-1, which were biplanes that had been retired from front-line duty prior to Pearl Harbor.[1] McClusky's time in the SBD Dauntless, the type of dive-bomber he would fly at Midway, was sharply limited. However, his extensive experience in the older dive-bomber types made it easy for McClusky to transition to the SBD in spring 1942 because he was already thoroughly versed in the art of dive-bombing. In addition, he had also by that time flown just about every type of aircraft in the naval inventory. In short, Wade McClusky and his Annapolis (1926) classmate Maxwell Leslie, who were both to play such critical roles at Midway, were two of the most versatile pilots the US Navy has ever produced.

The misunderstandings about Wade McClusky's role in the Battle of Midway are quite unfair to his legacy. The aircraft carriers that McClusky's pilots destroyed, IJN *Akagi* and *Kaga*, were the pride of Japan's navy and in terms of gross tonnage were the largest aircraft carriers in the world at the time. Despite having an excellent claim to being the most important single factor in the American victory at Midway, Wade McClusky

---

[1] Compilation of dive-bombing hours provided by Philip McClusky from analysis of his father's pilot logbooks. Email communication, Philip McClusky to me, March 6, 2016 and March 14, 2016. Wade McClusky tally of his total flying hours from his pilot logbook entry page for June 1942. Philip McClusky collection.

remains a surprisingly obscure figure – always mentioned, but only in passing, and often wrongly accused of incompetence.

McClusky had been with the *Enterprise* since before Pearl Harbor. He had been assigned to fly with the Big E's Fighting Squadron Six in June 1940 and became the commander of that squadron a year later. All accounts agree that McClusky's handling of the *Enterprise* fighter group in the first six months of the war was superb, and just prior to Midway he was awarded the Distinguished Flying Cross for those efforts.

Wade McClusky was popular with his brother pilot officers in the naval aviation community. He was a quiet man, never one for back-slapping gregariousness, but there is no evidence whatsoever that he had any martinet tendencies. He was ambitious, but then what Navy pilot isn't? However, something about McClusky's promotion to air group commander in March 1942,[1] his decision to give up his fighter plane and go back to flying dive-bombers as air group commander, and the prominence he gained by leading the *Enterprise* dive-bombers at Midway seems to have riled some of his fellow pilots at the time and continues to anger many historians.

At the time of McClusky's promotion in March 1942, no Americans outside of a small group of code breakers at Pearl Harbor had as yet any inkling of an impending Japanese thrust toward Midway. Thus, it is utterly impossible that any kind of "fix" was "in" to give McClusky a plum assignment and so the "why" part of the jealousy evinced by some of his fellow pilots at the time and by many historians since the war at the merit-based elevation of McClusky to the position of commander of Air Group Six remains a mystery. This unfathomable attitude, coupled with several other reasons – such as that he remains almost completely unknown to the American public at large – demonstrate why

[1]Lundstrom, John B., *The First Team: Pacific Air Combat from Pearl Harbor to Midway* (Annapolis: Naval Institute Press, 1984): p137. Tillman, Barrett, *The Dauntless Dive Bomber of World War Two* (Annapolis: Naval Institute Press, 1976): p55.

an attempt to tell the story of the Battle of Midway from the perspective of Wade McClusky is long overdue.

Perhaps the best way to begin solving the mystery of why Wade McClusky is generally disliked by historians is to debunk the idea that he was some sort of time server; that any reasonably experienced pilot could have led the *Enterprise* dive-bomber squadrons with the same degree of success. To prove the fallacy of this line of reasoning it is necessary to reiterate that the American victory at Midway did not happen "by default." The Japanese had to be actively beaten at Midway – and they were. Wade McClusky's actions on June 4, 1942 were a vital component of the positive, energetic actions that made the American victory at Midway happen.

At the time, the Americans had to deal with many materiel shortages. On the plus side of the ledger, however, they had top-notch aviators available: valiant torpedo plane pilots such as John Waldron, George Gay, Thomas Eversole, Pablo Riley, Eugene Lindsey, Albert Winchell, and Lem Massey; fighter pilots such as John S. "Jimmy" Thach, who utilized his famous "Thach Weave" tactic for grappling with Japanese fighter planes for the first time at Midway, and Roger Mehle, who flew countless combat air patrol (CAP) missions high above the aircraft carrier USS *Enterprise* (CV-6) during the battle. But it would be the American dive-bomber pilots who delivered the mortal blows that destroyed four irreplaceable Japanese aircraft carriers at Midway. Many American dive-bomber pilots, such as Richard Best, Charles R. Ware, Earl Gallaher, Norman "Dusty" Kleiss, and Maxwell Leslie performed brilliantly at Midway. However, the greatest performance by an American dive-bomber pilot at Midway was turned in by Wade McClusky. Even though the 500lb bomb he himself dropped on the *Kaga* was a near miss, McClusky's ability to keep cool and make decisions without being swayed by emotion remains the most critical aspect of the battle. The *Enterprise* dive-bomber pilots who did score hits on the *Akagi* and the *Kaga* probably would never have found the enemy without McClusky to lead them in a search that proved to be maddeningly difficult and that required a leader with ice water in his veins and possessed of the tracking abilities of a bloodhound.

The brief overview of McClusky's actions on June 4, 1942 in Chapter 1 shows how McClusky's ability to keep calm under immense pressure enabled him to find the Japanese fleet. It is worth repeating that if, when his initial search coordinates yielded no targets, McClusky had turned left and searched to the south, the Americans would have lost the battle. But he did not turn left. McClusky had a hunch that the Japanese fleet was off to the north and so he turned to the right and 30 minutes later located the Japanese fleet, which included the four large aircraft carriers *Akagi*, *Kaga*, *Hiryu*, and *Soryu*. No novelist could ever imagine a plot more exciting than what McClusky and his pilots actually did during that ten-minute attack.

It is also worth noting that if, when he realized that the Japanese fleet was not where it was supposed to be, Wade McClusky had turned left and searched to the south instead of to the north, many of his planes almost certainly would have run out of fuel. In such a scenario, putting his planes and pilots into the water coupled with *not* finding the enemy could well have resulted in McClusky being court-martialed had he survived. McClusky risked everything, and the risk paid off.

Although their approach had been undetected by the Japanese, after pulling out of their dives the American dive-bomber crews experienced the full wrath of their enemy in the form of antiaircraft fire from Japanese ships and vigorous attacks by Japanese fighter planes. Wade McClusky's plane had 55 bullet holes in it when he landed back aboard the *Enterprise* at approximately 11.46am local time.[1] He himself had bullet wounds in his left arm. (Some

---

[1] Time of landing calculated from Wade McClusky's flight log entry for June 4, 1942, where McClusky recorded the flight as lasting four hours and 36 minutes. Philip McClusky collection. See also, Stephen L. Moore, *Pacific Payback: The Carrier Aviators Who Avenged Pearl Harbor at the Battle of Midway* (New York: NAL Caliber, 2014): p180, and Robert J.

accounts say "shrapnel," but in a 1972 radio interview with WMCA/New York, McClusky himself said he had "bullets" in his left arm.)[1] To boot, upon his return to the ship after the morning attack on June 4, 1942, there were just two gallons of gasoline left in the fuel tank of McClusky's badly shot-up SBD when its tail hook caught an arrester wire on the aft end of the *Enterprise* flight deck.[2]

Lt Cdr Maxwell Leslie arrived over the Japanese fleet at the head of a squadron of 17 *Yorktown* dive-bombers, Bombing Three (VB-3), coincidentally at the same time as did McClusky, but a faulty electrical arming device had resulted in four VB-3 pilots (Leslie included) accidentally jettisoning their bombs when they pushed the arming switch. Thus, when VB-3 arrived over the target, only 13 of the *Yorktown* dive-bombers still had their bombs. Max Leslie's *Yorktown* group did destroy the *Soryu*, but without McClusky's large *Enterprise* air group available to destroy the *Akagi* and the *Kaga*, the Japanese would have had three carriers left with which to launch a counterattack against the Americans, instead of just one (*Hiryu*).

As with any large battle in history, a great many people contributed to the American victory in the Battle of Midway. The brilliant linguist and cryptanalyst Cdr Joseph Rochefort headed a team of extremely talented code breakers at Pearl Harbor's radio interception and decryption "station Hypo." Working marathon shifts in a cramped bunker-like basement office, Rochefort's group had cracked enough of the Japanese Naval Code, JN 25, to be able to piece together the outline plan for the coming Japanese

Cressman, Steve Ewing, Barrett Tillman, Mark Horan, Clark Reynolds, and Stan Cohen, *A Glorious Page in Our History: The Battle of Midway, 4–6 June 1942.* (Missoula, Montana: Pictorial Histories Publishing Co, Inc, 1990): p86, for approximate time of take-off.

[1]Podcast of Wade McClusky 1972 interview with radio station WMCA. Courtesy of Philip McClusky.

[2]Edward P. Stafford, *The Big E: The Story of the U.S.S. Enterprise* (Annapolis: Naval Institute Press, 1962, 2002): p103.

attack on Midway.[1] Specifically, Rochefort and his team became convinced that the Japanese planned to invade Midway atoll and to concurrently destroy the American Pacific Fleet in an open-ocean naval battle. Adm Chester Nimitz, as commander-in-chief, US Pacific Fleet and the Allied theater commander for the Pacific Ocean Areas, wisely chose to trust the code breakers enough to take their advice that the main Japanese offensive for the summer of 1942 would be an attack against Midway. That the fleet commander believed the decoded information to be accurate enabled Nimitz's fleet intelligence officer, Lt Cdr Edwin T. Layton, to mold the raw intelligence data provided by Rochefort into a remarkably accurate prediction as to when and how the Japanese attack against Midway would unfold.[2] Rochefort and Layton made an excellent team, both having spent time in Japan before the war learning the language. Nimitz acted on the intelligence data provided to him in a positive and energetic manner. In making this decision to place his trust in the data provided by code decrypts, Nimitz had to keep calm and ignore all of the other, largely unwanted, advice that he was getting, such as that the next Japanese move was certain to be a landing in California, in mainland Alaska, on Oahu, or in Australia.[3] The American people, and many other peoples around the world, were still quite rattled by the stunning success of the devastating Japanese attack on Pearl Harbor.

It is difficult in the 21st century to imagine that the United States could ever have been in desperate straits during a war. It is important, therefore, to remember that the first six months of 1942 were indeed a fraught time for the Allied cause the world over. In the weeks following the Pearl Harbor attack, Japanese forces seized Guam and Wake islands and landed troops in

[1]Symonds, *The Battle of Midway*, p141.

[2]E. B. Potter., *Nimitz* (Annapolis: Naval Institute Press, 1976, 1987): p83, p87.

[3]Samuel Eliot Morison to Walter Lord, February 10, 1966. Walter Lord Papers, Operational Archives. Naval History and Heritage Command (NHHC), Washington Navy Yard. Washington, DC.

the Philippines. Japanese troops advancing down the Malayan peninsula, then a British possession, captured Kuala Lumpur on January 11, 1942 and by the end of the month had forced the army of British lieutenant Gen Sir Arthur Percival out of Malaya and back on Singapore. On February 15, Singapore itself would fall to the Japanese. At that time, a handful of German submarines were wreaking havoc out of all proportion to their numbers off the East Coast of the United States by torpedoing dozens of American merchant ships. The U-boats had easy pickings in American coastal waters because, unlike transatlantic cargo ships, merchant vessels traveling up and down the East Coast of the United States were not organized into easily defensible convoys until midsummer, 1942. In North Africa, German Gen Erwin Rommel was having an impact out of all proportion to *his* numbers as his small German/Italian army pressed the British Eighth Army eastward back toward the British stronghold at the port city of Tobruk in northeastern Libya, which Rommel would capture on June 21, 1942. In Russia, German troops had advanced to within 12 miles of downtown Moscow before being thrown back in a desperate and heroic Russian counterattack that began in early December 1941. The ability of the Russian Army to be reconstituted, phoenix-like, from the ashes of the terrible mauling it had received at the hands of the advancing German Army during the summer and fall of 1941 did mean that the quick collapse of Russian resistance that Hitler had counted on when he ordered the invasion of the Soviet Union was not going to happen. However, the Russian military situation was still desperate in the spring of 1942, with German armies occupying a large swath of Russian territory and Hitler preparing to renew the offensive there in the summer.[1]

Refusing to be discouraged by this backdrop of Allied defeats, Adm Nimitz at Pearl Harbor moved quickly in May 1942 to send troops and aircraft to reinforce the defenses on Midway

[1]Symonds, *The Battle of Midway*, pp3–4.

itself should a Japanese landing there actually be attempted. He directed all of his available submarines to patrol the likely Japanese approach routes, and he ordered that long-range air searches be conducted by aircraft out of Midway beginning on May 30 so that the approaching Japanese fleets could be spotted as soon as possible.[1] Shipyard workers at the Pearl Harbor Navy Yard worked feverishly and heroically to repair the aircraft carrier USS *Yorktown*, disabled by a bomb hit in the Battle of the Coral Sea, in record time so that Nimitz could send three rather than two American aircraft carriers out to do battle with the Japanese at Midway. To command the counterstroke that he was planning to unleash against the Japanese in the upcoming Midway battle, Adm Nimitz appointed R Adm Frank Jack Fletcher (overall commander) and Raymond A. Spruance; two men who deserve considerable credit for the American victory.

The energetic activity described above exemplifies the undeniable fact about the Midway battle mentioned by historians Jonathan Parshall and Anthony Tully that "the Americans simply 'wanted the win' more than their opponents."[2] Gordon W. Prange also stressed that the American victory at Midway was an active, not a passive, affair. While the Americans did fight defensively at Midway, reacting to Japanese moves on a schedule set by the Japanese, the battle was far from a matter of the Americans simply sitting back and watching the Japanese defeat themselves through the many mistakes inherent in their battle plan. Prange writes that "Midway was a positive American victory, not merely the avoidance of defeat."[3] Trying to win is a far more active form of behavior than is merely trying not to lose. Gordon Prange is somewhat rare among historians in believing that the Japanese

[1] Potter, *Nimitz*, pp79–80, p88. Cressman, *A Glorious Page in Our History*, pp35–36.

[2] Parshall and Tully, *Shattered Sword*, p66. See also p67 and p94 in the same text for more on the American "will to win."

[3] Gordon W. Prange, Donald M. Goldstein, and Katherine V. Dillon, *Miracle at Midway* (New York: McGraw-Hill, 1982): p383.

were outfought at Midway and not simply unlucky. Carl Cavanagh Hodge is another historian who supports this view. Writing in the Winter 2015 edition of the *Naval War College Review* of the outcome of the Battle of Midway Hodge states that:

"A culture of learning, arising from experience rather than theory and shared in the weeks between Coral Sea and Midway at every level of the U.S. Navy's carrier task forces, meant that ultimately victory was earned by the Americans rather than thrown away by the Japanese."[1]

Craig L. Symonds also supports the view that the Japanese were beaten, and not merely unlucky, at Midway. Symonds writes that "certainly chance – or luck – played a role at Midway, but the outcome of the battle was primarily the result of decisions made and actions taken by individuals who found themselves at the nexus of history at a decisive moment."[2]

Perhaps the biggest mistake the Japanese made in the weeks leading up to the Battle of Midway was to ever think that the Americans, after the string of defeats they had suffered in early 1942, were practically finished. In fact, as Hitler was finding out by spring 1942 to his intense consternation regarding the Russians, there is such a thing as an enemy who simply refuses to *feel* beaten, no matter what. Such an enemy makes an extremely dangerous adversary. In the US Navy, and completely unbeknown to the Japanese, this feeling permeated all ranks, not just the American high command. On the eve of the Battle of Midway, morale was high aboard the *Enterprise*, something that would have come as a great surprise to the Japanese naval general staff. *Enterprise* biographer Edward Stafford writes, making a reference to the carrier USS *Lexington* that had been sunk in the

[1] Carl Cavanagh Hodge, "The key to Midway: Coral Sea and a culture of learning" *Naval War College Review,* 68.1 (Winter 2015): p119.

[2] Symonds, *The Battle of Midway*, p5.

Battle of the Coral Sea a month prior to Midway, that aboard *Enterprise* in the days before Midway:

> "The feeling throughout the ship was one of confidence. Pearl Harbor was beginning to fade from memory and the *Enterprise* sailors who had not actually seen the *Lex* go down, remembered best the recent successful strikes against the enemy bases when attacks on the Big E herself had been rare and always unsuccessful."[1]

While eager to fight, the Americans faced temporary tactical limitations in the spring and early summer of 1942. Namely, fighting defensively was the only option open to the Americans in the early summer of 1942 because the United States was not yet the overwhelmingly powerful military juggernaut it would be two years later. By the summer of 1944 the Americans would choose the times and the places where battles in the Pacific would be fought. In 1942, however, its as-yet incomplete mobilization for war and the shock of early Japanese successes had thrown the Americans temporarily on to the defensive, which is why the Japanese were able to choose the arena and the timetable for the Battle of Midway. Ever the fighter, however, Adm Nimitz definitely saw the upcoming battle as an opportunity to destroy the enemy's aircraft carriers, and he intended to do just that despite the constraints under which he was forced to operate.[2]

The Japanese battle plan was complex and vague. Nimitz ensured that the American battle plan was tight and focused. Adm Yamamoto would be trying to orchestrate the movements of four distinct Japanese surface fleets, among which, including himself, there were 28 flag officers. Adm Nimitz expected his modest force of American ships to remain close together and he had only two

[1]Edward Stafford, *The Big E: The Story of the U.S.S. Enterprise* (Annapolis: Naval Institute Press, 1962, 2002): p94.

[2]Potter, *Nimitz*, p83.

admirals, Fletcher and Spruance, on the scene. Despite the need to fight from a defensive posture, there was nothing passive or complacent in the way the Americans approached the upcoming battle. Indeed, within the arena chosen by the Japanese for battle, the Americans threw everything into the scales in their determination to win at Midway.[1]

There is a wealth of evidence attesting to the complacency and poor planning with which the Japanese approached the Midway battle. For instance, the four widely dispersed Japanese fleets involved in the Midway operation were scattered over far too wide an area to make any kind of mutual support possible should one of those fleets encounter difficulties – as one of them certainly did on June 4.[2] Throughout the war, the Japanese proved to be first-rate fighters but poor planners. Regarding the Japanese naval high command's fondness for overly complex plans, Samuel Eliot Morison writes that Japanese naval leaders: "overvalued surprise, which had worked so well at the beginning, and always assumed they could get it. They loved diversionary tactics – forces popping up at odd places to confuse the enemy and pull him off base."[3]

The Japanese fast carrier striking force (*Kido Butai*), which was the key to the entire operation, had sailed from Japan with just four aircraft carriers instead of its usual six. *Zuikaku* remained in port in Japan during the Midway battle because of heavy losses of its planes and pilots sustained in the Coral Sea battle. Its sister carrier *Shokaku* was in dockyard hands at the Kure Naval Arsenal

---

[1]Parshall and Tully, *Shattered Sword*, p51, pp66–67, p94. David Rigby, *No Substitute for Victory: Successful American Military Strategies from the Revolutionary War to the Present Day* (New York: Carrel Books, 2014): p23. Thaddeus V. Tuleja, *Climax at Midway* (New York: Jove/Norton, 1983, 1960): p53.

[2]Parshall and Tully, *Shattered Sword*, p405.

[3]Parshall and Tully, *Shattered Sword*, pp52–57. Samuel Eliot Morison, *History of United States Naval Operations in World War II*. Vol. 4. *Coral Sea, Midway and Submarine Actions: May 1942–August 1942* (Boston: Little, Brown and Company, 1954): p78.

having damage from three American bombs that had struck home in the Coral Sea battle repaired. It would have been very difficult to get the heavily damaged *Shokaku* ready in time for it to sortie for the Midway battle – although Midway historian Robert E. Barde felt that it could have been done. There is much less doubt about what could have been done with *Zuikaku*. Had Japanese planning been infused with even a modest amount of urgency and willingness to improvise in the matter of finding replacement planes and pilots – perhaps borrowing planes and pilots from *Shokaku*'s relatively intact air group – *Zuikaku* could easily have sailed with its *Kido Butai* cohorts for the Midway confrontation.[1] That *Zuikaku* was left behind was a significant factor in Japan's defeat at Midway. Indeed, historians Jonathan Parshall and Anthony Tully have noted the marked contrast between the Japanese leaving *Zuikaku* behind and the Americans sparing no effort to repair the bomb-damaged *Yorktown* and to find enough replacement aircraft and pilots so that the *Yorktown* could be ready in time to fight at Midway. *Yorktown* and *Zuikaku* had just come from the same battle: Coral Sea. Both ships needed replacement pilots and aircraft, but the Americans faced the added difficulty that because of the bomb hit at Coral Sea, there was structural damage to *Yorktown*'s internal compartments that had to be repaired – something that was not an issue for the undamaged *Zuikaku*.[2]

In order that there be no delay in getting *Yorktown* into dry dock, the masonry blocks upon which her keel would rest in the dry dock at Pearl Harbor had been put in place on the evening of May 26, before the ship had even arrived back in port. Upon arrival on the afternoon of May 27, *Yorktown* was immediately moved into the dry dock. Making the necessary repairs to the

---

[1] Robert E. Barde, "The Battle of Midway: A Study in Command" Ph.D. dissertation. University of Maryland, 1971, p49.

[2] Parshall and Tully, *Shattered Sword*, pp19–22, pp53–56, pp64–69, p94. Barde, "The Battle of Midway: A Study in Command," p89.

damaged carrier was a priority, all-hands operation. Some 1,400 repair specialists from half a dozen specialties, such as welding and electrical, toiled in three shifts around the clock to get *Yorktown* back on its feet again. They made their deadline. The patched-up carrier was able to depart Pearl on May 30.[1] The contrast with *Zuikaku*, which arrived back in Japan at about the same time but was simply warped to a pier at Kure and idled even though all it needed was replacement pilots and aircraft, is startling. The Japanese could have, and should have, made *Zuikaku* ready in time for the Midway battle.[2] That she was not symbolizes the overconfidence and laziness (and perhaps even the criminal negligence) with which the planning for the Midway battle was carried out by senior Japanese naval officers; factors that were to loom large in the outcome of the coming battle.

All of the *Enterprise* and *Yorktown* dive-bomber pilots who had participated in the morning attack on June 4, 1942 – the attacks that destroyed the *Akagi*, *Kaga*, and *Soryu* – had been amazed while pushing over into their dives that there had been no interference from Japanese fighter planes. The lack of any high-altitude combat air patrol and radar on Japanese warships was symptomatic of two prominent features of the Imperial Japanese Navy – namely, that the IJN was focused entirely on offense and that its high command regarded Americans as a soft and unwarlike people from whom there was little to fear. Jonathan Parshall and Anthony Tully have written that going into the Battle of Midway Adm Nagumo and his staff harbored "a bone-deep contempt for American naval aviation."[3] The lack of respect for the fighting abilities of the Americans makes it difficult to avoid the conclusion that as his ships approached Midway, Nagumo never even expected to be attacked by American aircraft, much

---

[1]Potter, *Nimitz*, p85. Morison, *Coral Sea, Midway and Submarine Actions*, p81.

[2]Parshall and Tully, *Shattered Sword*, pp19–22, pp53–56, pp64–69, p94. Barde, "The Battle of Midway: A Study in Command," p89.

[3]Prange, et al, *Miracle at Midway*, p225.

less brought to ruin by American naval aviators. In planning the Midway battle, Nagumo and Yamamoto thought only in terms of best-case scenarios for Japan, rather than in terms of the US Navy's true capabilities.[1]

The Japanese experience in the first six months of the war had reinforced this feeling, so that by the time of Midway a sense of invincibility seems to have thoroughly permeated the ranks of *Kido Butai*, among both the officers and ordinary sailors. Nagumo and his staff were not present at the Battle of the Coral Sea, a month prior to Midway. Had Nagumo participated in this engagement he certainly would have gained a healthier respect for American fighting abilities. There, IJN Carrier Division 5 (*Shokaku* and *Zuikaku*) – under the command of R Adm Hara Tadaichi – had been vigorously attacked by American dive-bomber pilots, who scored three bomb hits on *Shokaku*. In addition to being the first naval battle in history in which the opposing fleets never came within visual sighting distance of each other, Coral Sea was also significant because there for the first time the Americans succeeded in destroying a major Japanese warship,[2] the light carrier *Shoho*, which exploded and sank at noon on May 7, 1942 under a hail of American bomb and torpedo hits.

Nagumo and the rest of the IJN high command heard about Japanese losses in the Coral Sea, but not being there to see with their own eyes the Americans fighting well meant that the low opinion of American fighting abilities remained strong in the minds of Nagumo, Yamamoto, and the latter's nominal superior, Adm Nagano Osami, chief of the naval general staff in Tokyo. It therefore came as quite a surprise to Nagumo when at approximately 7.00am (local time) on the morning of June 4, before his own aircraft had even returned from their strike against Midway, his force came under attack by the first of what would be wave after wave of American land-based and carrier-based

---

[1]Parshall and Tully, *Shattered Sword*, p408.

[2]Morison, *Coral Sea, Midway and Submarine Actions*, p5.

aircraft, culminating in the devastatingly successful attacks by *Enterprise* and *Yorktown* dive-bombers. This first American counterattack, by six Grumman TBF torpedo planes that had flown out from Midway, was easily dispatched by fleet antiaircraft fire and by the guns of Japanese fighter planes. Following closely on the TBFs came four Army B-26 twin-engined medium bombers, also from Midway and also carrying torpedoes. All of the torpedoes missed and five TBFs and two of the B-26s were shot down. However, despite missing their targets, the American pilots had gotten close enough to make decent drops, meaning that Nagumo's ships were forced to take evasive action to avoid the torpedoes in the water. The determination of these American pilots came as a profound shock to Nagumo and his staff. One of the B-26 bombers did not pull away after its torpedo had been dropped. With its pilots perhaps already killed by antiaircraft fire, this plane passed within a few feet of *Akagi*'s bridge before crashing into the water alongside the ship.[1]

Nagumo's chief-of-staff, R Adm Ryūnosuke Kusaka, spoke of this encounter with the American B-26 when he was interviewed by Walter Lord in the 1960s: "A shaken Kusaka found himself strangely moved. He thought only Japanese pilots did things like that. He had no idea who this steadfast American was, but there on the bridge of the *Akagi* he silently said a prayer for him."[2]

Prior to Midway, Adm Nagumo's carriers had never come under heavy, sustained aerial attack.[3] Between Pearl Harbor and Midway, Nagumo's carriers had been almost continuously employed, steaming more than 10,000 miles and pummeling American, British, and Dutch shore bases and shipping in the South West Pacific Area and in the Indian Ocean. For instance, on February 19, 1942, aircraft from *Akagi*, *Kaga*, *Hiryu*, and *Soryu* bombed the port city of Darwin in northern Australia. During this

---

[1] Symonds, *The Battle of Midway*, p236. Parshall and Tully, *Shattered Sword*, p149–152.

[2] Walter Lord, *Incredible Victory* (New York: Harper & Row, 1967): p118.

[3] Parshall and Tully, *Shattered Sword*, p145.

time, Nagumo's aviators added to the Allied naval woes that had begun with the carnage at Pearl Harbor by doing considerable damage to the Royal Navy's Far Eastern Fleet. During air strikes against Colombo and Trincomalee, respectively, in Ceylon (Sri Lanka) in April, Nagumo's pilots sank the British heavy cruisers *Dorsetshire* and *Cornwall*, as well as the old aircraft carrier HMS *Hermes* and its escorts, the British corvette HMS *Hollyhock* and the Australian destroyer HMAS *Vampire*.[1] While carrying out these bold and confident air strikes, in the six months between Pearl Harbor and Midway, Adm Nagumo's carriers had only come under aerial attack once, on April 9, 1942, during the raid on Trincomalee, when nine land-based British Bristol Blenheim twin-engined bombers had attacked *Akagi*. All of the British bombs missed and the attacking aircraft suffered heavy losses.[2] This attack did nothing to improve Nagumo's opinion of the fighting abilities of the Allied nations, although perhaps it should have. The attacking British aircraft were not detected by the crews of the Japanese ships or by the Japanese pilots flying combat air patrol until they were less than 10 miles away.[3] Parshall and Tully have pointed out that this attack, although unsuccessful, was an early illustration of the ignorance displayed by the Japanese naval high command regarding the importance of strong and vigilant air defense measures.[4]

It is quite easy and quite natural for students of naval history to place too much emphasis on the role of admirals in deciding the outcome of naval battles. Be that as it may, in regard to the

[1]Samuel Eliot Morison, *History of United States Naval Operations in World War II*. Vol. 3. *The Rising Sun in the Pacific, 1931–April 1942* (Boston: Little, Brown and Company, 1948, 1954): pp383–385. Walton L. Robinson, "Akagi," in *U.S. Naval Institute Proceedings*, Vol. 74: May 1948, pp584–585.

[2]Morison, *The Rising Sun in the Pacific*, pp383–385. Robinson, "Akagi," in *U.S. Naval Institute Proceedings*, Vol. 74: May 1948, pp584–585.

[3]Robinson, "Akagi," in *U.S. Naval Institute Proceedings*, Vol. 74: May 1948, p585.

[4]Parshall and Tully, *Shattered Sword*, p145.

respective opposing high commands at Midway, there is no doubt that Adm Yamamoto Isoroku, commander of the Japanese Combined Fleet, was thoroughly outgeneraled by his opposite number Adm Nimitz. Brilliant as his code breakers were, even they could not give Nimitz the complete Japanese order of battle. Rochefort's team did, however, give Nimitz enough of it so that the American fleet commander had a very clear idea of his enemy's intentions while Yamamoto completely misread and underestimated American intentions.[1] Yamamoto and his staff were complacently convinced that the Japanese carrier-launched airstrikes to be made against Midway atoll on June 4 would come as a complete surprise to the Americans. According to the Japanese plan, only then would the American Pacific Fleet sortie from Pearl Harbor and head for Midway. Yamamoto and Nagumo thought it would take at least two days from the time the Japanese announced their presence by pounding Midway's defenses from the air for the Americans to get their fleet into position in the vicinity of Midway; plenty of time for the Japanese to prepare for the fleet action that they were certain would finish the Americans – and the war. The reality, that a fully alerted Nimitz would spring a trap on Nagumo's fast carrier striking force, was an idea that never occurred to Yamamoto and when it happened was a shock of such magnitude that Yamamoto almost certainly never recovered his psychological equilibrium in the ten months that remained before he was killed when American fighter planes (guided by the same type of code decrypts that had proved so disastrous for Japan at Midway) shot down the plane Yamamoto was traveling in over Bougainville on April 18, 1943.[2] Adm Nagumo, too, was a broken man after Midway, committing suicide in a cave on Saipan in the Mariana Island chain in the western Pacific on July 6, 1944, as Saipan was about to fall to the American marines and infantry who had landed there three weeks earlier.

[1] Parshall and Tully, *Shattered Sword*, pp53–57.
[2] Parshall and Tully, *Shattered Sword*, pp53–57, p408. Tuleja, *Climax at Midway*, p54.

There were two main causes of the laziness and haphazard nature of Japanese planning for Midway. By late spring 1942, Japanese forces had won the natural resources and regional hegemony – the objectives that had persuaded Japan's leaders to start a war with the Americans in the first place. Japan was now master of the Dutch East Indies and the rich oil fields there, as well as of Malaya, Burma, and the Philippines. In addition, in the weeks following the Pearl Harbor attack, Japanese forces had seized Wake Island, the Gilbert Islands, and Guam (the last of these cementing Japan's control of the Mariana Island group). These territories, when added to the Marshall and Caroline Island groups that had been mandated to Japan following World War 1, had greatly expanded Japan's hold on the Central Pacific Area. The speed with which Dutch, American, and British overseas possessions had been seized by the Japanese came as a rude jolt to the Allies. Less well known is that the speed of the Japanese advance in early 1942 had been almost as much of a surprise to the Japanese high command. By late March 1942, Japan's leaders were in a bit of a quandary, trying to figure out what to do next.[1]

Complicating the vacillation of the Japanese military high command at that time was the fact that all of Japan's conquests, while certainly impressive in scale, represented short-term objectives. Japan never had a long-term strategy, and indeed had never envisioned that the war against the United States would be lengthy. After winning its short-term objectives, "Japanese war aims consisted of little more than digging in to fortify Japan's newly captured island empire and hoping that its navy could serve as enough of a deterrent to keep the Americans away while Japan used its newly acquired resources to strengthen its domestic economy and its military machine."[2] The only question

[1]Richard Overy, *Why the Allies Won* (New York: Norton, 1995, 1997): p33. Parshall and Tully, *Shattered Sword*, pp19–22.

[2]David Rigby, *Allied Master Strategists: The Combined Chiefs of Staff in World War II* (Annapolis: Naval Institute Press, 2012): p94.

for the Japanese was when to start "digging in" and go over on to the defensive. History has made it abundantly clear that Japan's leaders would have been far wiser to halt offensive operations in the Pacific after the Coral Sea battle in early May 1942 at the latest.

The second cause of the slipshod work of Japanese planning staffs in regard to the Midway operation was the strange paradox that while Japanese soldiers and sailors proved time and again during the war that they would fight to the last man during an individual battle – saving the last bullet for themselves instead of enduring the humiliation of surrender and captivity – Japan's leaders had no conception whatsoever of the American strategy of total war. Japanese soldiers on the ground in Pacific Area battlegrounds such as New Guinea, Tarawa, and Saipan fought with a ferocity and determination that has with considerable justification been classified as fanaticism. That "fight to the finish" mentality of Japanese troops in the field was, however, very different from the attitude of the government in Tokyo. There, Japan's leaders were fighting for limited objectives, after which they expected a negotiated peace settlement by which the Americans would recognize Japanese hegemony in the western Pacific and in Asia.[1] The military junta in Tokyo headed by Gen Tōjō Hideki hoped for a repeat of the Russo-Japanese War of 1904–1905 in which Japanese victories in a few sharp land and sea battles had enabled Japan to win important but limited objectives against a much larger nation (Imperial Russia), which was then a major world power. Like Adm Yamamoto completely misreading American intentions in the weeks prior to the Battle of Midway, the Japanese did not understand that from the moment the first bombs and torpedoes struck home at Pearl Harbor on December 7, 1941 the Americans were fighting a total war that would not end until Japan's navy and air force were annihilated; its cities lay in ruins due to American bombing – both conventional and nuclear;

[1]Morison, *The Rising Sun in the Pacific*, p81.

and Japanese leaders agreed to surrender unconditionally and to accept the occupation of mainland Japan by American troops. There would be no negotiated peace. Believing that there ever could be offers convincing evidence that Japan's leaders failed at every level – tactical, strategic, military, diplomatic, and political – to heed Sun Tzu's dictum that in war one must "know" one's enemy.[1]

The fact that the Americans were determined to utterly destroy Japanese military power and would never negotiate could no longer be hidden from the Japanese people once the Americans breached Japan's inner defensive perimeter by invading the Mariana Islands in the summer of 1944. The loss of the Marianas resulted in a "palace coup" in Tokyo in which General Tōjō was ousted in July 1944.[2] He was replaced as prime minister by Kuniaki Koiso, another Army general. Under Gen Koiso, the Japanese government became radicalized, adopting desperate tactics, such as the use of kamikaze suicide attacks against American shipping. Thus, from the summer of 1944 onward, the Japanese government adopted the nihilistic outlook that characterized the Hitler regime in Germany. No longer trying to win, Japan from mid-1944 had altered its war aims to an attempt to stave off defeat at all costs, using any means necessary. Now, the mood in Tokyo matched the "fight to the finish" mentality that Japanese soldiers at the front had always shown. But the transformation of the government into a group of men willing to see their country destroyed rather than surrender took longer in Tokyo than it had in Berlin. Hitler and his most fanatical underlings such as Goebbels and Himmler had known by December 1942 at the latest, with the German Sixth Army marooned at Stalingrad, that their war was lost. The disappearance of any kind of logic to a continuation of the war took longer to manifest itself in Tokyo than it had in Berlin.

[1] Rigby, *No Substitute for Victory*, pp185–186. Sun Tzu, *The Art of War*, Lionel Giles, trans. (New York: Barnes & Noble, 2012): pp43–45.

[2] Rigby, *No Substitute for Victory*, pp185–186. Sun Tzu, *The Art of War*, pp43–45.

The fury felt by the American people over the Japanese attack on Pearl Harbor was exacerbated by the fact that American public opinion had already been anti-Japanese for several years prior to Pearl Harbor due to the occupation of Manchuria by Japanese troops in 1931, an act that was expanded in 1937 into a full-scale Japanese invasion of China. At that time, China was a weak nation for which Americans felt great sympathy.[1] President Roosevelt summed up the national mood toward Japan in a radio broadcast to the American people on December 9, 1941 – two days after the Pearl Harbor attack and one day after he had asked for and received from the US Congress a declaration of war against Japan. In that broadcast, FDR detailed the aggressions committed by Japan, Germany, and Italy, respectively. He correctly assumed that it was only a matter of time (in point of fact a very *short* time – just 48 hours after this broadcast) before the United States would be at war with Germany and Italy as well as with Japan. The tone of the broadcast was that FDR felt the Pearl Harbor attack to be completely in keeping with the manner in which lawless dictatorial regimes had been behaving since the early 1930s. The President presciently took the broad view that Japan's invasion of China and the attack on Pearl Harbor were motivated by the same contempt for international law that characterized the regimes of Hitler, Mussolini, and of Spain's Franco in Europe. FDR began his December 9 radio address to the American people by stating that "the sudden criminal attacks perpetrated by the Japanese in the Pacific provide the climax of a decade of international immorality."[2] Shrewd reader of public opinion that he was, President Roosevelt correctly ascertained that the American people were in no mood for partial victory or for a

---

[1] Parshall and Tully, *Shattered Sword*, pp32–33, pp53–54. Rigby, *No Substitute for Victory*, pp100–101.

[2] FDR radio broadcast. December 9, 1941, transcript thereof as printed in Franklin Watts, ed, *Voices of History: Great Speeches and Papers of the Year 1941* (New York: Franklin Watts, Inc, 1942): p563.

"negotiated" peace settlement. Indeed, later in the same broadcast, and more than a year before the Casablanca Conference at which he would state the Allied war aim of unconditional surrender in a more formal setting, the President stated unequivocally that for Americans this would be a total war. In that December 9, 1941 radio broadcast, with the oily black smoke of burning, wrecked battleships still clouding the skies above Pearl Harbor, FDR told his listeners that "the United States can accept no result save victory, final and complete."[1]

Thus, in spring 1942 the Americans had many short-term problems, such as shortages of weapons, supplies, and trained personnel, but they always enjoyed a critical advantage in having a clear-cut long-term war aim: the complete and total defeat of the armed forces of Japan and Germany, respectively. By contrast, in early 1942, Japan had short-term advantages that included "the aura of invincibility"[2] that followed from the early Japanese victories, but lacked a long-term, coherent, strategic war plan.

In addition to its lack of clear war aims, there is other evidence that Japan was not prepared for a long war. Namely, its economy was never fully mobilized for one. Meanwhile, by the summer of 1940 at the latest, the United States was well on its way to full mobilization for war even though it was not yet a formal combatant. An example from the naval sphere alone is that in July 1940 the US Congress passed and President Roosevelt signed into law the Two-Ocean Navy Act, which made possible a massive build-up in American naval strength, which bore fruit very quickly as a fully mobilized American economy saw factories and shipyards working three shifts per day. By late 1944, funding from the Two-Ocean Navy Act and the hard labor of highly motivated war workers who fully supported the American war effort meant that more than 200 new destroyers had joined the US fleet, as had a dozen new *Essex* Class aircraft carriers, four

---

[1]FDR radio broadcast. December 9, 1941, in Watts, ed, *Voices of History*, p568.

[2]Parshall and Tully, *Shattered Sword*, p41.

Iowa Class battleships, several dozen cruisers, and more than 100 submarines. The Navy's pilot training programs were vastly and successfully expanded without any lowering of standards. By war's end, the US Navy's aircraft carriers and shore installations would between them be operating some 41,000 aircraft and there would be just over 60,000 trained pilots available to fly them.[1] Japan was totally unprepared to fight against an antagonist like the United States that would mobilize all of its resources for war.[2]

That the United States had consistent, clear, and logical war aims right from the outset of hostilities was a critical factor in the American victory in the war against Japan. Nevertheless, severe shortages of weapons, supplies, and trained personnel would plague the Americans throughout 1942. Even though the American mobilization for war had begun well before Pearl Harbor, it had not begun early enough to avoid a situation in which American military commitments and priorities exceeded available resources until early 1943.[3] Consequently, in May 1942 the Americans had to scramble to cobble together a plan to defend Midway from invasion and to lay a trap for the Japanese aircraft carrier striking force that would spearhead that invasion. Evidence of the necessarily hasty planning for the upcoming Midway battle is that Wade McClusky and other senior pilots were not even told the outlines of the impending battle until after the *Enterprise* and the rest of Task Force 16 (*Enterprise*, *Hornet*, and their escorts) had put to sea from Pearl Harbor on May 28, 1942, headed for a position northeast of Midway where the three available American aircraft carriers, *Enterprise*, *Hornet*, and *Yorktown*, would lie in wait for the approaching Japanese. Thus,

[1] Rigby, *Allied Master Strategists*, pp103–105. Thomas Wildenberg, *Destined for Glory: Dive Bombing, Midway, and the Evolution of Carrier Airpower* (Annapolis: Naval Institute Press, 1998): pp162–163. Clifford Lord and Archibald Turnbull, *History of United States Naval Aviation*, (New Haven: Yale University Press, 1949): p322.

[2] Symonds, *The Battle of Midway*, p360.

[3] Rigby, *Allied Master Strategists*, p78.

McClusky had only a few days in which to acclimate himself to the fact that he was expected to play a leading role in what he had to have immediately surmised could be, and in fact was, the most important naval battle of the war.[1]

The lack of time for senior pilots to prepare detailed battle plans was regrettable because it was obvious that all of the hard work of code breakers, planning staffs, and admirals would have been for nothing without great pilots to carry out the air strikes that would be necessary to destroy the Japanese aircraft carrier striking force.[2] The Coral Sea and Midway battles would prove that the US Navy did indeed have great pilots. American naval pilots in 1942 were of the prewar generation who had to hold the line while new pilots could be trained and made available to replace losses and, from early 1943, to man the new planes on the new aircraft carriers of a rapidly expanding fleet.

Wade McClusky exemplifies the extremely high level of skill and motivation of that prewar generation of naval aviators who manned the US Navy's combat squadrons in 1942. When given cursory mention, what McClusky did on June 4, 1942 can sound easy and straightforward. The reality was far from this. He did not panic when the combined attack plan came unraveled and he had to proceed to the target with only his dive-bombers, independently of his fighter and torpedo planes. He did not panic when the Japanese fleet was not where he had been told it would be. It would have been so easy to panic. Which way should he turn? Would the 32 aircraft he was leading, after two-and-a-half hours in the air already, have enough fuel to search for the elusive enemy, then attack, then make the long return flight to the *Enterprise*? After making the counterintuitive decision to search to the north instead of the south, and being rewarded by finding the

---

[1]Stephen L. Moore, *Pacific Payback: The Carrier Aviators Who Avenged Pearl Harbor at the Battle of Midway* (New York: NAL Caliber, 2014): p168.

[2]Carl Cavanagh Hodge, "The key to Midway: Coral Sea and a culture of learning" *Naval War College Review*, 68.1 (Winter 2015): p119.

enemy fleet, McClusky then had to be sure that it *was* the enemy, and that he was not attacking his own (ie American) fleet. By not panicking, and by making all the right decisions under extremely difficult conditions, Wade McClusky was himself arguably the most important single factor in the American victory in the Battle of Midway. The late Edward P. Stafford showed himself to be somewhat rare among historians of the battle in that he states this fact outright:

"If one man can be said to win a battle and change the course of a war, Wade McClusky, by deciding to search beyond the range of his aircraft and correctly calculating the direction of that search, won the Battle of Midway and turned the war against Japan. He led against the enemy air power the force that in three minutes destroyed half of it and changed the odds in America's favor for the first time."[1]

Despite the fact that the Americans fought with the utmost determination, there is no denying that their performance at Midway was uneven in quality. Adm Spruance did not send out any search planes from Task Force 16 on the morning of June 4, instead leaving it to scouting aircraft from Adm Fletcher's Task Force 17 and to Midway-based PBY Catalinas to locate the Japanese for him. That was a potentially disastrous oversight by Spruance. Lt Jim Gray, the commander of the *Enterprise* squadron of fighter planes (VF-6), was the first to find the Japanese fleet on the morning of June 4. However, it did not occur to him to radio a contact report back to the *Enterprise* until he and his squadron of fighter planes had been circling high above the Japanese fleet for almost an hour. Gray assumed that his superior officers back on the *Enterprise* must be aware of everything he himself knew. Wade McClusky made no such assumptions, breaking radio silence as soon as he found the

[1]Stafford, *The Big E,* pp109–110.

Japanese. He knew it was imperative to get a contact report back to the *Enterprise* in case he did not survive the attack he and his group of dive-bombers were about to make. Jim Gray acted like a person who witnesses a mugging in the street but does nothing because he cannot believe and process what he is seeing. Wade McClusky was very different in nature and realized fully the significance of what was happening on June 4, 1942: that he was watching history unfold and that he himself was a key player in making that history. McClusky was decisive; he acted. He did not wait for others to tell him what to do.

Wade McClusky was also an intensely modest man. When everything went wrong on June 4, 1942, he responded by keeping a clear head and making the correct decisions. In so doing, he displayed unique and superb qualities of leadership, yet his modesty seems to have prevented him from realizing just how rare the particular qualities of leadership he displayed really are.[1] Indeed, McClusky was somewhat like the character of Davies in Erskine Childers's classic espionage novel *The Riddle of the Sands*. At one critical point in that novel, Childers's two British heroes, Carruthers and Davies, have to row some 10 miles in a small dinghy in order to reconnoiter a secret German naval installation in the Frisian Islands off Germany's North Sea coast. The two men use a heavy fog to hide their approach, but the fog also means they cannot see where they are going – the book is set around 1900, long before the advent of radar. While Carruthers rows, Davies uses his expert navigational skills to guide the dinghy using only a compass, a sounding weight, a map of the Frisian Islands area, and a pocket watch. Davies adds to these basic material tools his exact knowledge of the currents, tides, and channels in and among the Frisian Islands to guide the two men safely to their destination and back without being discovered

[1] Captain Chris Johnson, "Clarence W. McClusky: Intuition" in Joseph J. Thomas, ed. *Leadership Embodied: The Secrets to Success of the Most Effective Navy and Marine Corps Leaders*, 2nd Edition (Annapolis: Naval Institute Press, 2013): pp81–82.

by their German adversaries. Afterward, Carruthers marvels at the fact that Davies did not seem to be aware that his brilliant feat of navigation had been at all unusual or that he himself was in any way special.[1] Likewise, Wade McClusky did not seem to see his actions on June 4, 1942 as anything other than what any competent Navy pilot would have done.[2]

Of course, trained Navy pilots do not always measure up. A classic example from the Battle of Midway is Cdr Stanhope Ring, the *Hornet* air group commander. Ring was unable to locate the enemy on the morning of June 4, and that unfortunately meant that the 35 dive-bombers launched by the *Hornet* did not participate in the morning attacks on the Japanese carriers at all.[3] All four of the Japanese aircraft carriers were sunk by dive-bombers from the *Enterprise* and the *Yorktown*. The absence of the *Hornet's* dive-bombers presents tantalizing questions for Monday morning quarterbacks. If Ring had found the enemy that morning, would the added punch of the *Hornet's* dive-bombers have ensured that all four of the Japanese carriers would be destroyed in the morning attack? If so, the USS *Yorktown* would have survived the battle because the Japanese would not have had the *Hiryu* available to launch a counterattack. Indeed, in his after action report to Adm Nimitz, Adm Spruance blamed the poor performance of the *Hornet's* dive-bombers on the morning of June 4 for the loss of the *Yorktown*. Even when taking into account the understated language that characterized all official US Navy reports in World War 2, one can sense Adm Spruance's anger when he wrote: "*Hornet* dive-bombers failed to locate the target and did not participate in this attack. Had they done so,

---

[1]Erskine Childers, *The Riddle of the Sands* (Mineola, New York: Dover Publications, Inc, 1903, 1976, 1999): pp146–173.

[2]Johnson, "Clarence W. McClusky: Intuition" in Thomas, ed. *Leadership Embodied*, pp81–82.

[3]Johnson, "Clarence W. McClusky: Intuition" in Thomas, ed. *Leadership Embodied*, pp81–82.

the fourth carrier could have been attacked and later attacks made on *Yorktown* by this carrier prevented."[1]

A quick comparison between the actions of the *Enterprise* and *Hornet* air groups at Midway demonstrates the crucial role Wade McClusky performed in the battle. As a full commander, Stanhope Ring outranked Wade McClusky. The *Hornet* and the *Enterprise* both began launching their strike aircraft at 7.00am on June 4, 1942. In his after action report, McClusky indicates that he thought it odd that: "although the HORNET GROUP COMMANDER was senior, no command relationship or co-ordination was prescribed. No information was received as to how the YORKTOWN GROUP was to participate."[2] While the *Yorktown*'s air group, which began launching later, did navigate extremely well, Stanhope Ring's faulty navigation for the *Hornet* group made it a blessing in disguise that McClusky's *Enterprise* dive-bombers headed off to find the enemy alone, without Ring, whose rank would have put him in overall command had the aircraft from the *Enterprise* and *Hornet* headed out together as one group.[3] Ring, flying a dive-bomber, instead led the entire *Hornet* air group in the wrong direction, either too far north or too far south. Opinions vary as to just where Ring flew that day; the only point of agreement about Ring's "flight to nowhere" is that he failed to find the enemy. Lt Cdr John C. Waldron,

[1]Battle of Midway: 4–7 June 1942, Online Action Reports: Commander, Task Force SIXTEEN, Serial 0144A of 16 June 1942. Commander, Task Force SIXTEEN to Commander-in-Chief, U.S. Pacific Fleet, June 16, 1942. Archives of Naval History and Heritage Command, Washington, DC. Available online at: www.midway42.org/Midway_AAR/RAdmiral_Spruance.aspx. Accessed August 13, 2016.

[2]Personal Report. LCDR Wade C. McClusky. Air Group Commander. Enterprise Air Group. Battle of Midway, 4–6 June, 1942. P1. Courtesy National Naval Aviation Museum, Pensacola, Florida.

[3]Robert J. Cressman, Steve Ewing, Barrett Tillman, Mark Horan, Clark G. Reynolds, and Stan Cohen, *A Glorious Page in Our History: The Battle of Midway, 4–6 June 1942* (Missoula, Montana: Pictorial Histories Publishing Co, Inc, 1990): p84.

commanding the *Hornet*'s squadron of torpedo planes (VT-8), grew disgusted with Ring's faulty navigation and ordered his squadron on to a new course that did lead VT-8 to the enemy. All 15 of the *Hornet*'s torpedo planes were shot down in their valiant attack on the Japanese fleet, with only one of the 30 men in the squadron surviving the encounter. By contrast, Stanhope Ring's dive-bombers, as well as the *Hornet*'s fighter planes, never sighted the enemy during the morning attack on June 4.[1] Thus, despite outranking McClusky and Maxwell Leslie, the latter being the leader of the *Yorktown*'s dive-bombing squadron (VB-3), it is extremely fortunate that Stanhope Ring was *not* in command of the *Enterprise* and *Yorktown* dive-bombers, whose pilots would win the battle for the Americans.

Before proceeding to the specifics of the dive-bombing attack McClusky led at Midway, some background is in order, describing how Wade McClusky came to be leading the *Enterprise* dive-bombers into battle on June 4, 1942.

---

[1]Parshall and Tully, *Shattered Sword*, pp271–274. Morison, *Coral Sea, Midway and Submarine Actions,* pp116–121, Symonds. *The Battle of Midway*, pp245–265. Symonds uses the expression "Flight to Nowhere", as does Moore, *Pacific Payback*, p196.

3

The McCluskys of Buffalo

Clarence Wade McClusky, Jr was born in Buffalo, New York on June 1, 1902, the second oldest of five children, three boys and two girls, in the household of his father and namesake and of his mother, Mary Anastasia Stearns McClusky. Mary was almost always referred to as "May" by family members. Both parents had been born in Pennsylvania but lived their entire adult lives in Buffalo. The children were close in age, Wade's older brother Frank being born in 1901 and the baby of the family, sister Evelyn, arriving in 1910. It had to have been difficult and hectic for May to be taking care of so many active young children.

The family moved several times within the city of Buffalo, suggesting that they probably rented. In 1910 the McCluskys resided at 360 Normal Avenue. The household must have been especially busy that year; in addition to the arrival of baby Evelyn, the Federal Census of 1910 shows that May's brother Robert Stearns and his wife, also named May, were then living with the seven McCluskys. Wade, Sr was a senior accountant at the Mann Brothers Linseed Oil manufacturing firm in Buffalo. A handsome man, he had wavy brown hair, wore steel-rimmed glasses, and had a cleft chin.[1]

---

[1] Generic Ancestry.com citation: http://trees.ancestry.com/tree/32878307/person/ 18347994059. See also, World War I Draft Registration Card for Clarence Wade McClusky, Sr Registration State: *New York*; Registration County: *Erie*; Roll: *1712049*; Draft Board: *02*.

Both parents could trace their lineage to the British Isles, where the wars of religion had ended in July 1690 when William III defeated the Catholic Army of James II at the Battle of the Boyne in Ireland. In the McClusky household, however, the English Reformation was still being fought out. Wade, Sr was of Protestant Scotch–Irish stock, most likely Presbyterian. May, on the other hand, was Irish Catholic to the core. Wade, Sr was adamant that the McClusky children would not be brought up in the Catholic faith. Not only that, but May herself was forbidden from attending Catholic Mass while her husband was alive, though she did resume her life as a practicing Catholic after the tragic death of Wade, Sr in 1928. Understandably, the children ended up being somewhat conflicted regarding religion. After she returned to the Catholic Church, May was able to convince at least one of Wade, Jr's sisters to convert to Catholicism. Wade, Jr himself emerged from this religious turmoil as an Episcopalian.[1]

Wade, Sr was killed in a horrific automobile crash just after midnight on Sunday, October 8, 1928. Everything about the accident was bizarre, beginning with the fact that McClusky, Sr was not even supposed to be in the car that crashed. He had been out walking very late that night on Elk Street in Buffalo when he was offered a ride home by a friend, an off-duty police officer named James Reville, who happened to be driving after finishing work and left the Louisiana Street police station just after midnight. Within minutes of picking McClusky up, Reville

Ancestry.com. *U.S., World War I Draft Registration Cards, 1917–1918* [database online]. Provo, UT, USA: Ancestry.com Operations Inc, 2005.

Original data: United States, Selective Service System. *World War I Selective Service System Draft Registration Cards, 1917–1918*. Washington, DC: National Archives and Records Administration. M1509, 4,582 rolls. Imaged from Family History Library microfilm.

[1] Email communication, Philip McClusky to me, March 8, 2015. Wade McClusky obituary; *The Baltimore Sun*, June 29, 1976, pA13.

lost control of the vehicle at the intersection of Elk and Van Rensselaer Streets. The car went through a guard rail and fell 30ft into a viaduct, evidently landing nose first. McClusky was thrown from the vehicle on to the concrete of the viaduct and was killed instantly, having suffered massive trauma to the head. Somehow, even though the accident occurred in the pre-seatbelt, pre-airbag era, James Reville was not thrown from the vehicle and survived with only minor injuries. Reville later claimed that he had been sideswiped by a vehicle traveling in the same direction, which struck his rear fender, propelling Reville's car off the road and through the guard rail, but there were apparently no other witnesses – except the driver of the other vehicle, if there was another vehicle.[1]

At the time of Wade, Sr's death the family resided at 1519 Abbott Road, approximately 2 miles from the crash site. What was Wade's father doing out walking after midnight on a Saturday night so far from his home? Most likely, he had worked late, although working until midnight on a Saturday shows an unusual level of diligence. The accident site lies just under a mile east of the Mann Brothers factory, which was then located at 352 Ohio Street. Supporting the idea that Wade, Sr may have been walking home from his place of work is that Elk Street, where Reville picked him up, would have been one of the most direct routes between Mann Brothers and the McClusky household.[2]

When his father was killed, Wade, Jr was at Pensacola in the midst of his formal training to become a fully qualified naval aviator. He was given leave to go home for the funeral. Passenger air service in the United States was then in its infancy. As such, Wade, Jr was able to fly north from Florida to Washington, DC.

[1]*Buffalo Evening News*, October 8, 1928, p34. (Buffalo) *Courier Express*, October 8, 1928, Section 2, p1, Column 1 and Ibid, Section 2, p20. Courtesy Buffalo & Erie County Public Library, 1 Lafayette Square, Buffalo, NY, 14203.

[2](Buffalo) *Courier Express*, October 8, 1928, Section 2, p1, Column 1.

From there, he took a train to Buffalo. The family delayed the funeral until young Wade arrived back home.[1]

Father and son got their middle name from Wade, Jr's paternal grandmother, Rachael Wilson Wade. Since neither man liked his first name, Clarence, it is a bit odd that Wade, Sr and May did not simply dispense with the "Clarence" altogether when naming their second child, who always signed his name "C. Wade McClusky, Jr."[2] Rachael Wilson Wade's husband, Samuel McClusky, had been born in Pennsylvania in November 1846. The couple moved to New York state soon after the birth of Wade, Sr., one of five children, in 1875. By 1880 the family was living in Westfield, New York. A decade later they had settled in Buffalo, where Samuel worked as a plumber. In the 19th century, the family name was sometimes spelled "Mccloskey", "McCluskey", or "Mcclusky" with two lowercase "c" letters. It seems to have been Wade, Sr who decided on the permanent spelling of "McClusky."[3]

Samuel's father – Wade, Jr's great grandfather – Thomas McCluskey (sic), had emigrated to New York from Ireland sometime before the Civil War. Thomas served as a private in Company E of the 139th New York Regiment of Infantry during the Civil War and was captured by Confederate forces on May 16, 1864 during a failed attempt by Union forces to capture a fortress at Drewry's Bluff, Virginia. Thomas had the terrible misfortune as a prisoner of war of being sent to the notorious Andersonville Prison Camp

[1](Buffalo) Courier Express, October 8, 1928, Section 2, p1, Column 1.

[2]E-mail communication, Philip McClusky to me, March 8, 2015.

[3]US Federal Census, 1880. Westfield, Chautauqua, New York. Roll 816; Family History Film 1254816, p128D; Enumeration District 074, image 0616. Via Ancestry.com. See also, US Federal Census, 1900. Buffalo; Ward 22; Erie, New York. Roll 1031, p6B. Enumeration District 0184, FHL microfilm: 1241031. Via Ancestry.com. See also, Ancestry.com. Buffalo, New York Directory, 1890 [database online]. Provo, UT. USA. Ancestry.com Operations, Inc, 2000. Original Data: Buffalo City Directory: 1890. Buffalo, NY, USA, Courier, Co, 1890. Via Ancestry.com.

in Georgia, where he died on September 9, 1864, thus becoming one of the 13,000 Union prisoners to die there of abuse, neglect, and disease. In the Andersonville records the cause of death for Thomas was listed as "Diarrhea." In view of the conditions, it is far more likely that dysentery was the real culprit.[1] Confederate Army Capt Henry Wirz, who presided over this humanitarian disaster as commander of Andersonville, went on to be hanged as a war criminal on November 10, 1865.

Wade, Jr seems to have had a happy childhood. He was a gifted and diligent student, graduating from South Park High School in Buffalo in 1918, when he was just 16 years old. It seems that he did not originally plan on going to college, perhaps due to the family's meager financial resources. Buffalo being an important rail hub meant that railroad work was an alternative. According to his son Philip, Wade's first job after high school was scrubbing oil and other chemical sludge from the inside walls of railroad tanker cars. The acrid fumes and, depending upon the type of chemical that had most recently been carried, the threat of immolation should there be a spark within the confines of a tank car, caused Wade to hate the job. According to Philip: "He told me once that it was a miserable job and as a result he was determined to go to college or the academy!"[2]

Since accounts of the Battle of Midway usually mention only the bare outlines of what McClusky did on June 4, 1942, some personal information about the man is in order. Wade McClusky stood 5ft 10in tall and had "steel blue" eyes. In his Annapolis years, he weighed 150lb. Like most people, he gained some weight as the years went by; in retirement he weighed approximately 190lb.

[1]Email communication, Philip McClusky to me, March 8, 2015. See also, Ancestry. com. Andersonville Prisoners of War [database online] Provo, Utah, USA. Ancestry. com Operations, Inc, 1999. Original data: Andersonville, GA: Andersonville Prisoner of War Database. Andersonville, GA, USA. National Park Service. Andersonville National Historic Site.

[2]Email communication, Philip McClusky to me, February 15, 2015.

He had dark brown hair. In photographs, he is rarely smiling but always looks as if he is about to break out into a smile.[1] Regarding his hobbies and habits as an adult, McClusky enjoyed long walks. He also played golf as a young man, but tennis was his favorite sport and he played superbly throughout his life.[2] The incredible eye-hand coordination and lightning-fast reflexes that had enabled McClusky to fly with the Nine High Hats, the Navy's first aerobatics squadron; to become a marksman as a fighter pilot; and to be a superb dive-bomber pilot kept his tennis game razor sharp up through his 70th birthday. Wade's son Philip recalls that as a teenager, when Wade was in his late 60s, father and son would often play tennis. Wade always won. In fact he didn't "just" win – young Philip would be blown off the court by his father. An ankle injury finally forced Wade finally to give up tennis just a few years before his death.[3]

According to Philip, Wade: "drank bourbon and water in the winter and gin or vodka and tonic in the summer. He would have an occasional beer after a tennis match or working outside but I don't believe he favored a particular brand. Like many of his generation he liked his cocktails! That seemed to apply to all those old navy pilots!"[4] Wade never smoked cigarettes, cigars, or pipes, which was unusual for a man of his generation.[5]

In June 1944 Wade, now a war hero, returned to Buffalo to lend his name and presence to a War Loan rally. It was probably with some reluctance that he undertook this particular duty, since it meant being treated like a celebrity for a few days – something that would have taken a reticent man like Wade far outside his personal comfort zone. The Navy wanted him there, however.

[1] Email communication, Philip McClusky to me, March 1, 2015.

[2] Email communication, Philip McClusky to me, March 1, 2015 and June 5, 2017, respectively.

[3] Email communication, Philip McClusky to me, March 1, 2015.

[4] Email communication, Philip McClusky to me, March 1, 2015.

[5] Interviews with Philip McClusky, December 27 and December 29, 2016.

His orders to participate in the Buffalo event came direct from the office of V Adm Randall Jacobs, the chief of the Navy's Bureau of Personnel.[1] The city was delighted at the return of the local son who had made good. The *South Buffalo News* printed an article on McClusky on June 15, 1944 headlined "Midway Battle Hero Returning to Native South Buffalo to Aid Fifth War Loan Drive." Wade would have had the chance to visit with some of his family during this trip. At that time, his mother May was still living in Buffalo, on Tuscarora Road, in the home of one of Wade's sisters.[2]

Wade had absolutely no desire to settle in Buffalo after the war. He had never liked the town and his naval career had broadened his horizons considerably. While serving in Washington, DC during the mid-war period on the staff of V Adm Frederick J. Horne, Wade and his first wife, Millicent King, had either bought or rented a house in nearby Chevy Chase, Maryland. Wade found suburban Maryland to be much to his liking. After his retirement from the Navy in 1956, he and his second wife, Ruth Goodwin Mundy, moved to Ruxton, Maryland, a suburb of Baltimore, where Wade would live for the rest of his life.

---

[1] Order signed by Jacobs to McClusky, June 10, 1944. Philip McClusky collection.

[2] "Midway Battle Hero Coming Back to Native South Buffalo to Aid Fifth War Loan Drive" *South Buffalo News*, June 15, 1944.

4

ANNAPOLIS AND A NAVY IN TRANSITION

Founded in 1845, the United States Naval Academy at Annapolis was a well-established institution when Wade McClusky arrived as a midshipman for his plebe year in the summer of 1922. By then, the Academy had taken on much of its modern architectural form. The master plan for a revised and expanded campus drawn up by the prominent New York architect Ernest Flagg in the 1890s had been largely implemented by 1910. The perfect man for the job of conceiving a college campus, Flagg loved to design large, functional buildings, an excellent example of which was his 47-story Singer Building in Manhattan, which was completed in 1908.

Included in Flagg's plan for the Naval Academy were two majestic buildings that still dominate the campus: Bancroft Hall and the Chapel. The former is named in honor of George Bancroft, a noted historian who served as the secretary of the Navy under President James K. Polk. George Bancroft is widely credited with doing more than any other single individual to see to it that the Navy would have a suitable and permanent campus for the training of its officers. In 1845, Secretary Bancroft was able to convince the Army to grant the Navy permission to build a training academy on the grounds of the by then abandoned Fort Severn, located where the Severn River drains into Annapolis harbor.

As for the building named in his honor, Bancroft Hall is a sprawling but stately five-story granite structure completed in

1906. It was, and remains, large enough to house the entire complement of midshipmen in the hundreds of rooms that open off the long corridors within its very long wings. The original mansard roof cupolas above the main entrance and at the corners were very much in the Second Empire Baroque style, with which Ernest Flagg had become enamored as a young man while studying architecture at the École des Beaux-Arts in Paris, where he had arrived in 1889 to begin a two-year course of study. The vast, elegant, marble-floored main foyer was large enough to provide a comfortable venue when young ladies were invited to the then all-male campus for dances, or "hops," as they were called in McClusky's day. Over time and as additions were added, some of the ornamentation of the roofing was removed, which was probably a good thing because the original roof cupolas were a bit gaudy. Ernest Flagg was a fine architect but Second Empire as a style was beginning to look a bit dated by 1900. Toning down the ornamentation of the roofing made Bancroft Hall an extremely handsome building.

Already an enormous edifice when first built, Bancroft Hall has had new wings added several times. As the result of those added during World War 1, Bancroft Hall in Wade McClusky's day had more than 1,000 rooms and could house 2,200 midshipmen, which made it one of the largest, if not *the* largest, dormitory at any institution of higher learning in the United States.[1] The 1926 edition of the Academy yearbook, *The Lucky Bag*, describes what it was like for a plebe to enter Bancroft Hall for the first time:

> "One's first impression is a sense of the size of this structure and, as a lowly plebe, one's first act is to get hopelessly lost in the maze of corridors and rooms. Then the plebe grasps the

[1] Jack Sweetman and Thomas J. Cutler, *The U.S. Naval Academy: An Illustrated History* 2nd Edition. (Annapolis: Naval Institute Press, 1979, 1995): pp142–144, p169.

systematic scheme of arrangement and in due time his own little apartment with bare buff walls, white iron bed, hard bottomed chair, and green topped study table becomes endowed with a personality which distinguishes it from a thousand similar rooms."[1]

The chapel, completed in 1908, has a beautiful Italian Renaissance-style dome. Initially, short knaves extended outward from the base of the dome in the shape of an Orthodox Christian Cross. In 1940, the east knave was extended considerably in length, giving the building the shape of a Western Christian Cross.[2] The original knaves are very much in the High Church Anglican and Lutheran tradition, with large stained-glass windows. The newer, extended knave is more Low Church, with large windows of clear glass. Below the clear glass windows in the new wing, however, there are small stained-glass panels, which were donated by various classes, including one from the class of 1926. The inscription on the 1926 panel is from St. Mathew VIII: 27 – "What manner of man is this that even the winds and the sea obey him." The altar is flanked on both sides by the tall brass pipes of a magnificent organ, the keyboard of which is situated behind the pulpit. The remains of John Paul Jones have since 1913 resided in a crypt in the chapel's basement.

Although Wade McClusky had always been a good student, the competition for openings at the Naval Academy was highly competitive in 1922. McClusky's nomination letter from the Naval Academy invites him to submit his credentials as "First Alternate

---

[1]*The Lucky Bag: Nineteen-Twenty-Six. The Annual of the Regiment of Midshipmen,* (Rochester, NY: The Du Bois Press, 1926): p17.

[2]Jack Sweetman and Thomas J. Cutler, *The U.S. Naval Academy: An Illustrated History* 2nd Edition (Annapolis: Naval Institute Press, 1979, 1995): p144 and photo caption on p145.

to Principal Kenneth Rosengren."[1] Whoever Kenneth Rosengren was, he did his country a great service by deciding not to enroll at Annapolis, thereby making room for Wade McClusky. That everyone was calling McClusky "Wade" by then was no accident. According to his son Philip, "my father hated the name Clarence. He always signed his name C. Wade McClusky."[2] Indeed, the 1922 nomination letter from the Naval Academy is addressed to "Mr. Wade McClusky."[3] The McClusky family was living at 29 Girard Street in Buffalo when Wade arrived at Annapolis to begin his plebe year in the summer of 1922.[4]

Despite the fact that he was initially considered an alternate, McClusky had received a good education at South Park High and the Navy was pleased with the subjects he had studied and with the grades he had earned there. The acceptance letter Wade received from the Academy, dated May 17, 1922, reveals much about how the Navy selected its officer candidates in the 1920s. At that time, academic credentials submitted to the Naval Academy were evaluated according to a 14-point scale of required units. A candidate needed all 14 points to be accepted unconditionally – without the need for further evaluation, such as taking the Academy's entrance exam. Eight of the points were for required subjects, which included algebra, plane geometry, grammar and composition, literature, and history. The other six points were for academic subjects outside these areas, but still in accordance with a Naval Academy list of approved subjects. McClusky scored eight of eight in the required subjects and exceeded the

---

[1] Navy Department; Bureau of Navigation letter to Wade McClusky, Jr. March 30, 1922. Philip McClusky papers.

[2] Email communication, Philip McClusky to me, March 8, 2015.

[3] Navy Department, Bureau of Navigation, Washington, DC. Clarence McGregor to McClusky. March 30, 1922. Philip McClusky collection.

[4] Navy Department; Bureau of Navigation letter to Wade McClusky, Jr. March 30, 1922. Philip McClusky collection.

requirements in optional subjects by scoring seven and one-half points there.[1]

Wade played football during his first two years at Annapolis, until he was sidelined with a shoulder injury.[2] As a midshipman, he got into just enough trouble to be respectable, but not enough to endanger his naval career. The record shows that Wade acquired five demerits during his time at Annapolis. The records of his exact offenses have not survived but may have had something to do with the fact that Wade met and fell in love with a 20-year-old Baltimore beauty named Millicent King during his plebe summer at Annapolis.[3] Many midshipmen found ways to sneak off campus for a few hours to visit their sweethearts, a maneuver known as "Frenching Out." Wade would have received one or more demerits if he had tried to "French Out" to visit Millicent and been caught. His Academy nicknames were "Mac" and "Wade." The Annapolis yearbook, *The Lucky Bag*, prophetically concludes its entry on McClusky by noting that with Wade McClusky in the Navy "we all think the Navy will be the winner and civilian life the loser."[4]

In addition to his injury-shortened football career, McClusky enjoyed spending time on the Academy firing range, where he earned the designation of "expert rifleman."[5] The fact that he was a good shot would help McClusky to excel as a fighter pilot years later. McClusky's commission as an ensign is dated June 3, 1926.[6] Wade and Millicent were married that same day, Wade being

[1] Naval Academy acceptance letter to Wade McClusky, May 17, 1922. Philip McClusky collection.

[2] Email communication, Philip McClusky to me, May 16, 2016.

[3] *The Lucky Bag: Nineteen-Twenty-Six*, p361. "Baltimoreans Who Wedded Midshipmen." *The Baltimore Sun*. June 4, 1926. p3. Available online at: www.newspapers.com/image/215712119/?terms=Wade%2BMcClusky. Accessed September 18, 2016.

[4] *The Lucky Bag: Nineteen-Twenty-Six*, p361.

[5] *The Lucky Bag: Nineteen-Twenty-Six*, p361.

[6] McClusky Commission, June 3, 1926. Philip McClusky collection.

one of 13 midshipmen from his class to do so; this was also the first day that the rules prohibiting midshipmen from marrying expired.[1]

The Naval Academy allowed McClusky to broaden his horizons considerably. In addition to receiving a top-notch classroom education, he got to travel and was introduced to the potential inherent in a then new phenomenon called naval aviation. While this was a new subject at the Academy in Wade's day, the summer training cruise for Academy midshipmen was a long-established tradition by the 1920s. In the summer following both McClusky's first and second years, the entire regiment of midshipmen was assigned to a squadron of battleships that crossed the Atlantic and made goodwill visits at several European ports. The midshipmen were spread out among several battleships, which for McClusky's first transatlantic cruise in the summer of 1923 comprised the dreadnoughts *Arkansas*, *Delaware*, *North Dakota*, and *Florida* for a crossing that was slow and rough. The battleships and the young "mids" endured a force 10 gale with 40ft waves off the Virginia Capes. The battleships had regular officers as department heads and navigators as well as a core of seasoned enlisted men to staff the critical departments, such as engine room and galley. The midshipmen were on hand to observe and to learn by doing. McClusky and his fellow midshipmen heaved coal, holystoned decks, participated in gunnery exercises, and served as lookouts. The fleet docked in Scotland at Pentland Firth on June 18, after a 13-day crossing, and also visited Copenhagen before heading for the Iberian Peninsula where *Arkansas* and *Florida* visited Lisbon

---

[1] "Society in Navy Circles" *Honolulu Star-Bulletin*, June 11, 1932. P24. (Notice of Wade and Millicent's sixth wedding anniversary). Available online at: www.newspapers.com/image/274960635/?terms=Wade%2BMcClusky. Accessed September 16, 2017. "Baltimoreans Who Wedded Midshipmen" *The Baltimore Sun*. June 4, 1926. P3. Available online at: www.newspapers.com/image/215712119/?terms=Wade%2BMcClusky. Accessed September 18, 2016.

while *North Dakota* and *Wyoming* visited Cadiz. All four of the battleships stopped at Gibraltar in late July. The cadets even saw a bit of Africa when the fleet crossed the straits of Gibraltar for a brief stop at Tangier.[1]

For the 1924 summer cruise to Europe the midshipmen were again divided between four battleships, this time *Arkansas*, *Wyoming*, *New York*, and *Texas*. The Navy continued its practice of using older battleships that had not yet been converted to burn oil for these training cruises. So, the midshipmen loaded coal during port calls and shoveled it into hungry furnaces when the ships were underway. There were more gunnery drills and more scrubbing of decks. The first port of call on June 19 was Torquay in Devonshire, England – a port rich in history. It was there, in November 1688, that the agreeably Calvinist William III, Stadholder of the Netherlands, having been invited to "invade" England by British Parliamentary leaders who were fed up with the "Catholic King" James II, had landed with a small army of Dutch troops during the Glorious Revolution.[2]

During the 1924 cruise, the American dreadnoughts were in Britain long enough for the midshipmen to travel to London and see the sights. By June 30, the fleet had crossed the English Channel and had docked at Brest, France, then the group was temporarily divided into two units in mid-July. *Arkansas* and *Wyoming* proceeded to Rotterdam while *New York* and *Texas* docked at Antwerp. Again, allotted liberty time was generous and the midshipmen had time to see the sights and enjoy the nightlife

[1] *The Lucky Bag: Nineteen-Twenty-Six*, pp73–82. *Annual Register of the United States Naval Academy: Annapolis, MD: 1923–1924* (Washington, DC: Government Printing Office, 1923): p25. Available online at: https://archive.org/details/annualregiste19231924unse/page/24.

[2] *Annual Register of the United States Naval Academy: 1924–1925: Annapolis, MD* (Washington, DC: Government Printing Office, 1924): p25. Available online at: https://archive.org/details/annualregiste19241925unse/page/24.

in Paris and Brussels. Once reunited, the fleet once again visited Gibraltar before heading home in late August.[1]

R Adm Henry B. Wilson served as superintendent during most of McClusky's time at Annapolis. Wilson was a superb administrator whose four years as superintendent are considered to have been highly successful. Wilson worked hard to eliminate one of the Academy's biggest problems: hazing. It was during McClusky's first two years at Annapolis, his "plebe" and "youngster" years, respectively, that Adm Wilson formally instituted a system of regulations intended to gently remind underclassmen, officially, of their "place" in the hope that this would deter the juniors and seniors (second classmen and first classmen, respectively) from *unofficially* reminding the younger students of their lowly status via a hazing regimen that was often quite violent; paddling the backside of an underclassman using a broomstick handle swung like a baseball bat being one of the favorite hazing techniques. According to naval historians Jack Sweetman and Thomas J. Cutler, the new rules put in place by Adm Wilson meant that:

"Plebes were to report to formations on the double; to keep off the benches sacred to first and second classmen; to answer upper classmen's questions; to refrain from using certain walks reserved for upper classmen; to memorize notices posted on the bulletin boards in Bancroft Hall; and to observe innumerable other time-honored customs."[2]

Hazing may have declined as a result of the measures taken to fight it during Wilson's tenure as superintendent, though it did not disappear entirely at Annapolis until the mid-1970s.[3]

---

[1] *The Lucky Bag: Nineteen-Twenty-Six*, pp87–96. *Annual Register of the United States Naval Academy: Annapolis, MD: 1924–1925*, p25. Available online at: https://archive. org/details/annualregiste19241925unse/page/24. Accessed July 3, 2020. Interviews with Philip McClusky, December 27 and December 29, 2016.

[2] Sweetman and Cutler, *The U.S. Naval Academy*, p180.

[3] Sweetman and Cutler, *The U.S. Naval Academy*, p180, p238.

The 1920s was a transformational time for the United States Navy. The biggest changes being thrust upon it during those years were due to the great potential of aircraft used in military roles that had been demonstrated during World War 1. Important geostrategic issues strengthened the hand of American naval officers who were the early proponents of naval aviation in the 1920s. Indicative of this trend is that in the summer of 1921 the US Navy acquired a new Bureau of Aeronautics – an organization that would eventually handle all administrative matters relating to fleet aviation.[1]

Tensions between the United States and Japan had been rising ever since the United States took control of the Philippines and Guam as a result of the Spanish-American War in 1898. The 1920s would see the formulation of the "Orange" Plans at the Naval War College in Newport, Rhode Island, the blueprints for what would eventually become the war-winning island-hopping campaigns of the Central Pacific Drive in World War 2. Also in the 1920s, the Navy's General Board was grappling with the consequences of the Washington Naval Treaty of 1922, which, among other things, contained a "fortification clause" that prohibited the United States and Japan from fortifying the island bases each controlled in the central and western Pacific. Banned from building elaborate military bases on Wake or Guam or from expanding existing bases in the Philippines, the US Navy recognized quite early on the importance of the tactical flexibility that aircraft carriers would give to the fleet,[2] though the naval high command in the 1920s still saw the battleship as the premier naval weapon, with the aircraft carrier in a supporting

---

[1] Cdre Dudley W. Knox, USN (Ret), "The United States Navy Between World Wars" – printed as the Introduction to Samuel Eliot Morison, *History of United States Naval Operations in World War II*. Vol. 1. *The Battle of the Atlantic, September 1939–April 1943* (Boston: Little, Brown and Company, 1947): li.

[2] John T. Kuehn, *Agents of Innovation: The General Board and the Design of the Fleet that Defeated the Japanese Navy* (Annapolis: Naval Institute Press, 2008): pp31–33, pp42–44.

role. However, the fortification clause of the Washington Treaty meant that, even in support, the aircraft carrier would play a critical role.

Most high-ranking American naval officers in the 1920s felt that in a potential war against Japan, the US Navy's battleships would first win a Trafalgar-style victory against the Japanese in the western Pacific. Then, owing to the restrictions put in place by the Washington Naval Treaty's fortification clause, American aircraft carriers would have to be rushed out to the western Pacific to provide floating airfields until landing strips on islands in the Mariana and Caroline island groups could be developed. Despite what American admirals had thought in the 1920s, however, when the Central Pacific Campaign actually began in November 1943, it would be American aircraft carriers, not battleships, that spearheaded the operation.[1]

The timing of Wade McClusky's entry into active duty as a naval officer in 1926 and his subsequent decision to become a pilot meant that he witnessed first-hand the beginnings of the bitter administrative turf battle within the US Navy, between the "Gun Club" (ie battleship officers) and the "Young Turks" of the then nascent naval aviator community over which group and which weapon system – the big gun battleship or the aircraft carrier – would control the Navy's future. That dispute would continue well into World War 2.

At the Academy itself, aviation received a boost when, upon Adm Wilson's retirement in February 1925, R Adm Louis M. Nulton was tapped to be the new superintendent of the Naval Academy. Although he himself had graduated from Annapolis 14 years before the Wright Brothers flew at Kitty Hawk, Adm Nulton was quick to see the potential value of aviation to the fleet. As superintendent, he was determined to make sure that every midshipman who graduated on his watch was made fully aware of the possibilities of naval air power.

---

[1]Kuehn, *Agents of Innovation*, pp98–101.

Immediately upon taking up his duties as superintendent, Adm Nulton set about integrating aviation into the curriculum. Pilots were added to the faculty. The Department of Marine Engineering and Naval Construction was reorganized and renamed the "Department of Engineering and Aeronautics." Similarly, the Department of Seamanship became the "Department of Seamanship and Flight Tactics." Among the faculty of the latter department during Wade McClusky's senior (first class) year was a youngish lieutenant commander and early naval aviator named George D. Murray.[1] In 1942, McClusky would again serve under George Murray, this time when Murray was captain of the USS *Enterprise* while Wade McClusky served as that carrier's air group commander. By the time McClusky graduated from the Naval Academy in May 1926, the US Navy had won a critical administrative victory in that it was clear by then that the planes and pilots of the Navy would remain under naval control.

Keeping naval aviation under Navy control owed much to the deliberations and recommendations of an investigatory and advisory body convened by President Calvin Coolidge in September 1925 under the leadership of the distinguished lawyer and investment banker Dwight W. Morrow – a man whose ties to aviation history became permanent a few years later when his beautiful daughter, Anne, married Charles Lindbergh. The immediate catalysts for the creation of the Morrow Board were the crash of the Navy dirigible *Shenandoah* and the subsequent public accusation by the always outspoken Army pilot William "Billy" Mitchell that the War and Navy departments were incompetent and negligent, particularly in the management of

---

[1] *The Lucky Bag: Nineteen-Twenty-Six*, p45, p48. *Annual Register of the United States Naval Academy: Annapolis, MD: 1926–1927* (Washington, DC: Government Printing Office, 1926): pp18–19. *Annual Register of the United States Naval Academy: Annapolis, MD: 1924–1925*, pp17–18. *Annual Register of the United States Naval Academy: Annapolis, MD: 1925–1926* (Washington, DC: Government Printing Office, 1925): pp17–18.

military aircraft. Mitchell's enthusiasm for openly criticizing his superiors regarding what he saw as foot dragging in the matter of developing an independent air force that was truly ready for war had already resulted in his demotion in the Army Air Service from the rank of brigadier general to colonel in April 1925. Now Mitchell was court-martialed for his outburst following the *Shenandoah* disaster.[1]

The Morrow Board has been widely praised for its thorough investigation and for the wisdom of its recommendations. Among the latter was that naval aviation should remain under the control of the Navy and that aircraft carriers should be commanded by naval officers who were qualified pilots. Some duplication of effort regarding procurement issues and research and development would be accepted in maintaining two distinct administrative structures for American military aviation. The Army would handle the land-based air force; a situation that continued until the creation of an independent Air Force in September 1947. The Navy would control all carrier-based aviation as well as the seaplanes (and even some landplanes) that would perform maritime patrol duties. Indeed, the Morrow Board wisely predicted that a healthy spirit of competition between American Army and Navy aviators would be a good thing for the overall readiness of the nation's armed forces.[2]

The wisdom of keeping naval aviation under naval control is easily demonstrated by a comparison with the corresponding situation in Great Britain. There, the placement of Royal Navy Fleet Air Arm aircraft and crews under the operational control

[1]Archibald D. Turnbull and Clifford L. Lord, *History of United States Naval Aviation* (New Haven: Yale University Press, 1949): pp249–258. *Encyclopædia Britannica Online*, s. v. "William Mitchell", accessed June 12, 2016, www.britannica.com/biography/William-Mitchell. Accessed June 12, 2016.

[2]Cdre Dudley W. Knox, USN (Ret), "The United States Navy Between World Wars" – printed as the Introduction to Morison, *The Battle of the Atlantic*, li. Turnbull and Lord, *History of United States Naval Aviation*, pp249–258.

of the land-based Royal Air Force (RAF) from 1919–1939 was a disastrous move, particularly as regards the matter of procuring high-quality naval aircraft types. British *Illustrious* Class aircraft carriers in World War 2 were excellent ships that had enclosed "hurricane" bows and armored flight decks, but the airplanes they carried, such as the much-loved but hopelessly obsolete Fairey Swordfish torpedo plane, were a generation behind American and Japanese naval aircraft and could only avoid being slaughtered when they faced no enemy fighter plane opposition. British pilots who flew from carriers in World War 2 demonstrated that they had plenty of fighting spirit and they did score some spectacular successes early in the war. The most notable of these was the November 11, 1940 raid on the Italian fleet base at Taranto in southern Italy by Swordfish flying from HMS *Illustrious*. In this brilliantly executed attack, three Italian battleships were sunk in the harbor after being struck by aerial torpedoes. Nevertheless, the neglect of naval aviation between the wars was highly detrimental to the Royal Navy, particularly when that Navy faced an enemy, like Japan, that had aircraft carriers, first-rate naval aircraft, and highly skilled naval pilots – three things lacking in the navies of Britain's European opponents, Germany and Italy.[1]

As the Americans would discover with their obsolescent TBD Devastator torpedo planes at Midway, a British Swordfish torpedo bomber would never have been able to get anywhere near a Japanese fleet carrier due to the vulnerability of the Swordfish to attack by modern fighter planes such as the Mitsubishi Zeros that flew combat air patrol over Japanese aircraft carriers. On February 12, 1942, during the famous "Channel Dash" in which the German cruisers *Scharnhorst*, *Gneisenau*, and *Prinz Eugen* made a high-speed run under a heavy escort of Luftwaffe fighter planes, including Messerschmitt 109s, through the English Channel from Brest to Wilhelmshaven, six Swordfish attempted

---

[1]Clark G. Reynolds, *The Fast Carriers: The Forging of an Air Navy* (New York: McGraw-Hill, 1968): pp303–305.

a torpedo attack and all six were quickly shot down without inflicting any damage on the German ships.

The Royal Navy in World War 2 did not have a single flag officer who was a fully qualified pilot, but some British admirals had completed the equivalent of an American Naval Aviation Observer course, which meant that they had some time in the cockpit but that they had never soloed and probably could not handle either a take-off or a landing. The fact that until late in the war, the Royal Navy simply was not ready or able to utilize naval airpower to its true potential can be traced directly to the identity crisis that Britain's Fleet Air Arm had been forced to endure during the 1930s when it had been under RAF control.[1] The late historian Clark G. Reynolds has written that at the time of Pearl Harbor, "British Naval aircraft were by all standards inferior to those of the RAF, Japan, and the United States."[2] The most promising attempt to rectify this situation was the development of a naval version of the Supermarine Spitfire with an arrester hook for carrier landings. The Spitfire was one of the war's finest fighter planes, but the naval version, called the "Seafire," was not entirely satisfactory as a naval fighter due to its narrow undercarriage and limited range. The narrow undercarriage meant that Seafires suffered the same instability problems during carrier landings as the ones that plagued the American Grumman F4F Wildcat. The Spitfire undercarriage also just did not have the strength required for carrier landings. Extra strength is necessary so that the wheel and strut assembly of a naval aircraft will have the ability to absorb the shock of hard landings, which are the norm rather than the exception on aircraft carriers as opposed to airfields on land. It is difficult for even the best pilots to make a perfect landing on the pitching and very confined surface of an aircraft carrier deck – a deck that might suddenly be thrust upward in a heavy sea just as an aircraft is touching down.

[1]Reynolds, *The Fast Carriers*, pp303–305.
[2]Reynolds, *The Fast Carriers*, p303.

By the middle of World War 2, and thanks to the Lend-Lease policy, most British aircraft carriers operated American naval aircraft.[1]

The US Navy embraced air power during the interwar years far more vigorously than did the British. Not satisfied with merely having aviation matters discussed in the classroom, one of Adm Nulton's first decisions upon taking over as superintendent of the Naval Academy in February 1925 was that the regiment would get hands-on exposure to aircraft. America's first two full-sized aircraft carriers, USS *Lexington* and it sister ship USS *Saratoga*, were then under construction and it was clear that the Navy was going to need more pilots. Nulton decided that on his watch all midshipmen would receive basic flight training. This decision to teach every midshipman the basics of how to fly was one of the most profound upheavals ever in the Academy's curriculum. To accomplish his task, Nulton made a drastic alteration to the itinerary for the first classmen (returning seniors) in the summer of 1925.

The summer cruise planned for 1925 called for the midshipmen to travel with the battleship training squadron down the East Coast, through the Panama Canal, and on to ports along the West Coast of the United States.[2] However, in 1925, Nulton decided that not all of the first classmen would make this trip. In a complete break with tradition, it was announced in early May of Wade's second class (ie third) year that one-third of his class would remain at Annapolis that summer in order to learn how to fly. To accomplish this ambitious task, a half-dozen F-5-L flying boats, with instructor pilots and ground crews for servicing, arrived at Annapolis in July 1925. The planes, designed to take off from and land on water, were moored on the Severn River.[3]

---

[1]Reynolds, *The Fast Carriers*, p305. Alan Shepard and Deke Slayton, with Jay Barbree, *Moon Shot: The Inside Story of America's Apollo Moon Landings* (New York: Open Road, 2011): p47.

[2]*The Lucky Bag: Nineteen-Twenty-Six*, pp101–110.

[3]*The Lucky Bag: Nineteen-Twenty-Six*, pp111–115, text and photos.

The F-5-L, large for its day, was a joint British-American twin-engined biplane design that entered service on both sides of the Atlantic in 1918. The American versions were built in Buffalo by Curtiss-Wright (then known as "The Curtiss Aeroplane and Motor Company") and by the US Naval Aircraft Factory in Philadelphia, respectively. This startling change to the Naval Academy curriculum must have deepened Wade McClusky's desire to become a pilot and he had to have been frustrated at not being among the 150 midshipmen chosen for the 1925 flight-training course. Nulton's plan was that one-third of the incoming first class (ie seniors) would take their flight training in the summer of 1925. The remaining two-thirds of the class would remain at Annapolis for several months after their spring 1926 graduation to take their flight training then.[1] That is how Wade McClusky came to remain at Annapolis for several months after graduating in 1926 so that he could take that year's course of aviation instruction. This flight training at Annapolis was not a full-fledged naval aviator training program. Time was short and the midshipmen were many. The F-5-L carried a crew of four, so none of the midshipmen would get to go solo, but they would all get time in the air.

While he almost certainly would have preferred to take his basic flight training with the first group in 1925, McClusky instead found himself back on a battleship for that summer's cruise. After clearing the Panama Canal, the first West Coast port of call for the battleship training squadron was San Pedro, California, where the fleet stayed for the first week of July 1925. During the layover at San Pedro, the midshipmen visited Hollywood and were taken on a tour of the MGM movie studio, which was becoming the premier studio in the rapidly expanding film industry.[2] Although only recently formed via a series of mergers, MGM in 1925 already occupied an impressive 43-acre campus in Culver City.

[1]Turnbull and Lord, *History of United States Naval Aviation*, p268.
[2]*The Lucky Bag: Nineteen-Twenty-Six*, pp101–110.

Talking films were still two years in the future, but silent films were raking in enormous profits by the mid-1920s. While on the MGM lot, the midshipmen may have run into such famous movie stars as Norma Shearer, John Gilbert, ZaSu Pitts, and a rising young talent named Lucille LeSueur – soon to become much more well known to the world as Joan Crawford.[1] Heading north, the dreadnoughts, which for this trip included the *Utah* and the *New York*, received a very warm welcome in San Francisco, where they remained for a week. On July 23, the battleships nosed into the Columbia River and docked at Astoria. The midshipmen did not get to see much of Oregon, however, since this was apparently a brief stop in which no shore leave was given. By July 28, the fleet had docked in Seattle, where the mids did get to go ashore. On the way home, refueling stops were made at San Diego and in Panama.[2]

By the time Wade McClusky took his basic flight training in 1926, there were more aircraft available in a wider variety of types. Also, because the students were now commissioned ensigns who did not have to return to the classroom at the end of the summer, the 1926 flight program at Annapolis was extended well into the fall. McClusky began recording his first rides in F-5-Ls in July 1926 in the first of the eight logbooks in which he recorded each and every flight he made during his 30-year naval career. This first logbook is practically empty, however. He filled up a page or two describing his first flights in July 1926, during which he served, respectively, as an "Observer," "Navigator," and "Radio Operator" in an F-5-L. He also rode in another Curtiss machine, again developed with British assistance, the H-16 – essentially a slightly smaller version of the F-5-L. Wade seemed to feel that

[1]MGM Studio Tour 1925. Silent short film. Available online at: https://www.youtube.com/watch?v=Trni2JBzDaE&t=60s.

[2]*The Lucky Bag: Nineteen-Twenty-Six*, pp101–110. *Annual Register of the United States Naval Academy: Annapolis, MD: 1925–1926*, p25.

his real flight training did not begin until the fall, specifically on October 26, 1926. He began a new logbook that day, one that he would fill up with details of every flight he made for the next three years, up through his formal pilot training at Pensacola and his assignment to the fleet as a qualified naval aviator. As for the significance of October 26, 1926, he had now been in the flight program for several months. After his early orientation flights in July, Wade had presumably spent the rest of the summer performing the ground portion of the basic aviation program. In addition to classroom instruction in the basic principles of flight, he would have received hands-on training in how to assemble and disassemble aircraft engines and in how to send and receive Morse code. By October, he had perhaps begun to consider himself a useful member of the crew, as someone who could help to operate the aircraft, rather than just being an observer along for the ride.[1]

For the October 26 flight, Wade went up with a pilot named "Elmore" in an aircraft denoted in the logbook with the abbreviation "DH." This was probably a de Havilland DH-4B, a British design that was built under license in the United States during World War 1. The DH-4B was a two-seat, open-cockpit biplane bomber; not fast, not elegant, but reliable, sturdy, and forgiving – the perfect aircraft in which to train new pilots. His logbook remarks, always brief to the point of being cryptic, indicate that he practiced navigation on this flight.

For the remainder of October and through November 1926 Wade would fly with different pilots in the DH-4B and in two other biplane types: the Boeing NB-1 and the Vought UO-1. Wade's logbook indicates that he was working hard during this period, learning "Navigation," "Bombing," "Radio," "Gunnery,"

---

[1]Wade McClusky logbook entries, July, October, and November 1926. Philip McClusky collection. Anonymous. *Aloha: Class of 1926: United States Naval Academy*. Written by an unnamed 1926 class member or members to commemorate the 55th class reunion. (Privately printed, 1982): pp5–7.

"Spotting," "Free Gun," and "Photo." On November 12, he began a series of entries labeled "Dual." He was now apparently helping the pilot to actually fly the plane, but he did not solo during his time in the Annapolis flight program. His last flight there occurred on November 26, 1926 when he practiced aerial photography from an NB-1 flown by a pilot named "Forsyth."[1]

The calm personality that would, at Midway, enable Wade McClusky to make good decisions under pressure without panicking was apparent to his Academy classmates as soon as he arrived at Annapolis in 1922. According to *The Lucky Bag*: "Mac's philosophy of life is never to let anything interfere with pleasure, because you are young only once. It took him a long time to decide to dedicate his life to the Service, but to hear him talk of Buffalo, with its many wonders, it is hard to see how he ever tore himself away from the old homestead."[2] The first part of that description, about enjoying being young, was accurate. The second part was satirical. Wade undoubtedly told his Academy classmates what it was like to clean the inside of railroad tank cars and how glad he had been to get away from Buffalo. Philip McClusky confirms that his father harbored no great love for his hometown.[3]

Wade's academic performance at Annapolis was solid, but not stellar. He finished almost exactly one-third of the way down his class list – 159th in a graduating class of 456 members.[4] Being an Academy graduate automatically made Wade a member of an elite fraternity. In the pre-World War 2 Navy it was very difficult to become an officer if one had not graduated from Annapolis. There was a definite hierarchical system. Up through the end

---

[1]Wade McClusky pilot logbook entries for October and November 1926. Philip McClusky collection.

[2]*The Lucky Bag: Nineteen-Twenty-Six*, p361.

[3]Interviews with Philip McClusky, December 27 and December 29, 2016.

[4]*Annual Register of the United States Naval Academy: Annapolis, MD: 1926–1927*, pp27–37. Available online at: https://archive.org/details/annualregiste19261927unse/page/26.

of World War 2, any naval officer who was not an Annapolis graduate was considered a reservist, even if he was on full-time active duty. After the war that gradually began to change, but even as the Navy began to allow college graduates who had not attended Annapolis to become regular line officers, it remained very difficult to gain promotion if one was not an Academy graduate. As late as 1958 only three of the 245 admirals then on active duty had *not* graduated from Annapolis.[1] Wade showed himself to be something of a reformer after the war by criticizing this situation. In an undated five-page document he wrote after the war, perhaps as the rough draft for a paper at the National War College where he was a student in 1949–1950, McClusky stated that he felt the route to flag rank in the Navy was too dependent upon an old-boy network, politics, and social climbing, with far too much emphasis on an Annapolis education. Summing up his opposition to this situation, Wade wrote that: "it is my opinion that the method of selection to flag rank should be changed."[2]

[1]"Non-Academy Graduates to Get Navy Jobs" Associated Press article published in the *New York Times*, February 3, 1985. Online at: www.nytimes.com/1985/02/03/us/non-academy-graduates-get-to-navy-jobs.html?mcubz=1. Accessed September 13, 2017.

[2]Wade McClusky, undated post-World War 2 manuscript criticizing the Navy's method for promoting officers. Philip McClusky collection.

5

NAVAL AVIATOR

Wade McClusky had been determined to become a pilot from the moment he graduated from the Naval Academy, if not earlier. He and Millicent remained at Annapolis for the summer and fall of 1926 so that Wade could take the introductory course of flight training that had been mandated by Adm Nulton for all midshipmen before being assigned as a line officer to his first ship, the battleship USS *Pennsylvania*.[1] In the 1920s and 1930s, Naval Academy graduates who wanted to be pilots had to first put in two years of general duty in surface ships before they could apply for full-scale flight training. But Adm Nulton's emphasis at Annapolis on the possibilities of aviation had struck a chord among the class of 1926, no fewer than 78 of whom would go on to become Navy pilots.[2]

As the flagship of Battleship Division Three, the *Pennsylvania* was based on San Pedro, California. Wade served as assistant communications officer. After ten months aboard, McClusky was transferred in June 1927 to the USS *Williamson*, a *Clemson* Class four-stack destroyer that had entered service in 1920, for an 18-month tour. The *Williamson* was based in the Atlantic.

---

[1] Philip McClusky breakdown of flying time from Wade's logs, 1926–1942. Email communication, Philip McClusky to me, March 6, 2016.

[2] Anonymous, *Aloha: Class of 1926: United States Naval Academy*. Written by an unnamed 1926 class member or members to commemorate the 55th class reunion (Privately printed, 1982): p7.

It, and the young ensign McClusky, alternated between three main ports, Newport, Rhode Island, Hampton Roads, Virginia, and Guantanamo Bay, Cuba, with Wade serving as assistant gunnery officer and assistant engineer officer.[1] A six-month course of instruction in the intricacies of torpedoes at the Naval Torpedo Station in Newport was McClusky's last general duty assignment before he began training to be a fully qualified Navy pilot.[2]

Still an ensign when he arrived at Naval Air Station (NAS) Pensacola for flight training in June 1928, McClusky's course of instruction there lasted for one year, from June 29, 1928 to June 11, 1929. Wade proved to be a born pilot. His final grade report from Pensacola lists him as a "Qualified Catapult Pilot" and states that McClusky is "Recommended for Combat Duty." The report showed that McClusky was fully trained in "Primary Landplanes" as well as "Primary Seaplanes" during his time at Pensacola.[3] The seaplane training would come in handy in the mid-1930s when Wade found himself flying a catapult-launched scouting floatplane from the battleship USS *Maryland*.

After 1920, all American battleships and heavy cruisers were equipped with catapults with which to fling their observation aircraft into the air, initially for scouting beyond the horizon and later, after radios began to be placed in aircraft, to radio corrections back to the ship's gun crews after spotting "fall of shot" from the air when the home ship's big guns were being fired. Battleship floatplanes were equipped with a main pontoon under the fuselage and a stabilizing "outrigger" float under the

---

[1]Wade McClusky 1956 resumé, p4. Philip McClusky collection.

[2]*Register of Commissioned and Warrant Officers of the United States Navy and Marine Corps*, July 1, 1943 (Washington, DC: Government Printing Office, 1943): p10, p54 for the titles of Wade's postgraduate courses of instruction. Available at: https://babel.hathitrust.org/cgi/mb?a=listcs&colltype=featured. Accessed July 4, 2020.

[3]US Naval Air Station: Pensacola, Florida, "Final Report of Training for MCCLUSKY, Clarence W., jr.", June 1929. Philip McClusky collection.

tip of each lower wing.[1] After a battleship observation pilot had made a water landing, he would taxi alongside the ship, whereupon aircraft and pilot would be hoisted by a crane back aboard. Wade's final grade report from Pensacola also indicates that the training there was quite comprehensive, with McClusky flying torpedo planes, fighters, bombers, and observation planes.[2]

NAS Pensacola had been a busy place during World War 1 but by the summer of 1928, when Wade McClusky arrived, the area had reverted to being a bit of a sleepy southern town, but a pretty one with miles of beautiful beaches and the ruins of Spanish fortresses – evidence of the region's first European settlers. The aviators-in-training worked hard, but they also found ways to relax. A commemorative volume published in 1982 that was written by an anonymous member, or members, of the Academy class of 1926 to celebrate the 55th reunion of surviving members of that class describes the manner in which the young naval officers learning to fly at Pensacola procured alcohol:

"These were the days of Prohibition, and our libations for the weekend festivities had to be obtained from the piney countryside. Sam Clipper provided 'shinny,' basically corn whiskey. Sam was not a bootlegger, but a gentleman distiller who was venerated by all prominent citizens in the town. The

---

[1]*Register of the Commissioned and Warrant Officers of the United States Navy and Marine Corps.* January 1, 1934 (Washington, DC: Government Printing Office, 1934): p142. University of Michigan copy available online at: https://babel.hathitrust.org/cgi/pt?id=mdp.39015036626334;view=1up;seq=13. Accessed June 13, 2017.

US Naval Air Station: Pensacola, Florida. "Final Report of Training for MCCLUSKY, Clarence W., jr.", June 1929. Philip McClusky collection.

Philip McClusky breakdown of Wade's time in various aircraft types based on Wade's logbooks. Email communication, Philip McClusky to me, March 6, 2016.

[2]US Naval Air Station: Pensacola, Florida. "Final Report of Training for MCCLUSKY, Clarence W., jr.", June 1929. Philip McClusky collection.

procedure was to drive out to his estate, wait at his front door while he toured the pine forest for certain markings on the trees. He then dug and produced a five gallon charred keg which he delivered by hand to his thirsty customers at the front door. We also made home brew."[1]

The fledgling pilots may not have considered "Sam" to have been a bootlegger, but the ease with which Mr Clipper was able to keep the Navy in corn shows that most Americans who voted in favor of Prohibition thought of the measure as being necessary to keep other people in check and had no intention whatsoever of ceasing their own drinking.

At Pensacola, Wade trained primarily in the Consolidated NY-2, the Vought O2U-2 (SU-2), and the Curtiss F6C-4. All three types were biplanes. The Curtiss F6C-4 was an operational fighter plane. Wade's qualification as a "catapult pilot" derives from the fact that he made at least two catapult launches at the controls of a Vought UO-1 biplane while at Pensacola. He may also have made catapult launches in other types – other planes he flew at Pensacola, such as the Boeing NB-1, the O2U-2, and the NY-2, were each produced in both landplane (wheeled) and pontoon-equipped amphibious versions. The amphibious versions of these aircraft types were suitable for catapult launches.

The first few weeks of flight training were devoted to ground school. Wade's pilot logbooks claim that he soloed for the first time on July 24, 1928, which seems odd since this was also his first flight since beginning his flight training. The mystery is cleared up on the next page of his logbook. After flying almost every day in late July and into August, Wade's comments in the "Remarks" area of his logbook for August 20th read "Solo *Alone*."[2] So the August 20, 1928 flight was his first true solo flight

---

[1] *Aloha: Class of 1926*, p8.

[2] Wade McClusky, pilot logbook entries for July and August 1928. Philip McClusky collection. My italics.

in which he took an NY-2 up, circled the airfield a few times, then landed all on his own with nobody else in the airplane. His earlier flights labeled "Solo" were flights in which he was accompanied by an instructor pilot but in which Wade did all of the flying. The instructor was along as insurance.

The pace of the training was rigorous. Wade continued to fly almost every day; about half the time as the pilot and half the time observing as an instructor pilot flew the plane. On December 19, 1928, Wade practiced bombing while at the controls of a big Martin T3M torpedo plane. He made several more flights in a T3M that month. Practice bombing missions complete his entries for the month of December. Wade made some "torpedo runs" in early January 1929, and he also practiced formation flying during this period. He actually dropped a practice torpedo on two separate flights on January 10. For most of the month of April 1929, Wade practiced to master the art of communicating by radio while airborne. Although voice radio had made its debut by then at radio stations on the ground, the radio communication that Wade was using at this time was almost certainly the old-fashioned dot-dash Morse code type. On May 10, Wade endured five high g-force catapult launches in a Vought UO-1 biplane. During two of these launches he was the pilot. For the other three he observed other pilots handling this difficult maneuver. Wade's logbook entries show that his last month of pilot training, June 1929, was devoted entirely to aerial gunnery while at the controls of an F6C-4 fighter plane.[1]

Although his first assignment after earning the golden wings of a naval aviator was to a fighter squadron, Wade would get more practice in the T3M and its successor, the T4M, in the early 1930s. These large Martin machines were the first American torpedo planes that were designed to be launched from aircraft carriers. Wade's successful qualification as a pilot

---

[1]Wade McClusky, pilot logbook entries, August 1928–June 1929. Philip McClusky collection.

was accompanied by promotion to lieutenant, junior grade, effective June 3, 1929.[1]

It was an exciting time to be a young pilot. The NY-2 type that Wade flew at Pensacola achieved aircraft immortality status in September 1929 when another great pilot, Jimmy Doolittle, used a landplane version of an NY-2 to prove that an aircraft could be flown from take-off through landing solely on instruments, with no visual aid. Doolittle's historic flight with a canvas hood covering the cockpit so that all he could see were his instruments meant that, in the future, flying would no longer be restricted to the hours of daylight and good weather.

The high marks Wade had earned at Pensacola earned him a spot as a pilot with the Nine High Hats, formally known as Fighting Squadron ONE-B, flying Boeing F2B fighter planes from the USS *Saratoga*. It was a good omen for Wade's future as a combat pilot that the elite High Hats was his first squadron assignment after qualifying as a naval aviator. The Nine High Hats squadron was a precision flying team that was the precursor to the Blue Angels of today. As with the Blue Angels, the Nine High Hats accepted only the best pilots. Performances of the High Hats consisted of acrobatics carried out by nine F2B biplanes flying in three elements of three aircraft each. The three planes in

---

[1]*Register of the Commissioned and Warrant Officers of the United States Navy and Marine Corps.* January 1, 1934, p142. Ancestry.com. *U.S., Select Military Registers, 1862-1985* [database on-line]. Provo, UT, USA: Ancestry.com Operations, Inc, 2013. This collection was indexed by Ancestry World Archives Project contributors.

Original data: *United States Military Registers, 1902–1985.* Salem, Oregon: Oregon State Library.

US Naval Air Station: Pensacola, Florida. "Final Report of Training for MCCLUSKY, Clarence W., jr.", June 1929. Philip McClusky collection.

Breakdown of aircraft types prepared from Wade's logbooks by Philip McClusky. Courtesy Philip McClusky. Email communication, Philip McClusky to me, March 6, 2016. My own analysis of Wade's pilot logbook entries for the 1928–1933 period. Philip McClusky collection.

each element were actually tied together by ropes, so that in the words of McClusky's son Philip, "If they broke formation they lost their wings!"[1] Even if they didn't break formation, flying with the High Hats was incredibly dangerous. One airplane suffering engine failure would take two other planes down with it. The Nine High Hats performed at a variety of venues, including the 1929 Cleveland Air Races.[2] The end of McClusky's tour in the High Hats in May 1931 coincided with a decision by the Navy that F2Bs were now obsolete and were to be scrapped. Before his own plane was discarded, McClusky cut out the patch of fabric from the fuselage containing the High Hat logo. This included a small letter "M," which indicated that McClusky's gunnery skills had earned him the label of "expert marksman."[3] This gunnery prowess would serve McClusky well later when he commanded Fighting Squadron Six aboard the USS *Enterprise* (CV-6).

It was as a member of the Nine High Hats that Wade made his first carrier landings on July 16, 1929. On that day Wade, flying an F2B-1, made several landings on the USS *Langley* (CV-1), the US Navy's first aircraft carrier. The *Langley* was a small, experimental carrier that had been created by placing a flight deck atop the hull of a collier. Wade's natural reticence often made his logbook comments somewhat cryptic, but it seems that he made his first landing on the *Saratoga*, his first true "home" carrier, on August 16, 1929.[4] By October 31, 1929, Wade

[1]Email communication, Philip McClusky to me, February 15, 2015.

[2]"LIEUTENANT COMMANDER CLARENCE W. MCCLUSKY, JR., USN" – a brief career summary prepared by the Navy Department after Midway and dated November 12, 1942, p1. From the McClusky "Jacket" on file at the Naval Academy, "McClusky, Clarence Wade, Jr." Jacket Number 8306. Special Collections & Archives Department, Nimitz Library, United States Naval Academy.

[3]Email with photo sent by Philip McClusky to me, February 15, 2015.

[4]Wade McClusky logbook entries for July and August, 1929. Philip McClusky collection.

had made 17 carrier landings.[1] The young pilot made a good impression on the *Saratoga*'s commanding officer, then captain Frederick J. Horne. Later, after Horne had attained flag rank, Wade would serve two tours as Horne's aide and chief-of-staff, respectively. Frederick Horne had completed the Naval Aviation Observer's course at Pensacola in 1926 at age 45.[2] Naval aviation observers were not full-fledged pilots; they had far fewer hours of flying time than did a true naval aviator. Observers never soloed and they did not have to learn the intricacies of taking-off and landing. They would observe somebody else conducting those difficult maneuvers and could confine their activities to taking the controls for a time while the plane was airborne. Having qualified as a naval aviation observer gave Frederick Horne the minimum qualifications mandated by the Morrow Board for command of an aircraft carrier.

For almost a year after his tour with the Nine High Hats, from July 1930 to May 1931, McClusky would divide his flying time between the Vought O2U-2, a scouting aircraft, and the Curtiss F8C-4. The F8C series were the first true dive-bombers to serve in the US Navy. The fact that he spent considerable time flying an F8C-4 ten years prior to Pearl Harbor, when many of the young pilots who would fly with him at Midway had not even reached their teen years, proves that Wade McClusky was not "new" to dive-bombers in 1942. Indeed, even while working as aide and flag lieutenant to Adm Horne between 1935 and 1938, Wade was able to get in plenty of flying time, no doubt encouraged in this by Adm Horne, himself part of the naval aviation community.

[1]Summary at end of McClusky pilot logbook covering the period November 1929 to October 1931. Philip McClusky collection.

[2]Biography of Frederick J. Horne prepared by the Navy Department's Office of Public Relations and dated January 31, 1945, p2. A copy of this is in the Horne "Jacket" on file at the Naval Academy. "Horne, Frederick J." Alumni Jacket. Special Collections & Archives Department, Nimitz Library, United States Naval Academy.

Regarding his experience in dive-bombers, Wade spent the 18 months from June 1936 to January 1938 alternating between the Vought SBU-1, a far more advanced dive-bomber than the F8C-4, and the Grumman F3F-1 fighter plane.[1] Wade's pilot logbooks show that he compiled more than 400 hours in dive-bombers during the 1930s – most of it in the F8C-4, in which he logged 294.95 hours, to which he would later add 113.9 hours at the controls of an SBU-1.[2] In addition, while the Curtiss F6C-4 that Wade had flown during his flight training at Pensacola was built as a fighter, its robust construction made it a viable dive-bomber, albeit with only a light bomb load. The F6C series from Curtiss were apparently the first American naval aircraft that could make the kind of nearly vertical dives that American pilots would employ with such great success years later in their SBD Dauntlesses in the Battle of Midway.[3] It is thus quite possible that Wade made his first dive-bombing flights in the F6C-4 back in 1929, even before he flew the F8C-4 and the SBU-1 purpose-built dive-bombers. The fact that McClusky had more than 400 hours in dive-bombers (not counting his time in the F6C-4) prior to Pearl Harbor means that every statement in the literature to the effect that Wade McClusky was "new to" or "unfamiliar with" dive-bombers at the time of Midway is quite simply wrong. What is true is that Wade's time in the particular *type* of dive-bomber that he would fly in the Battle of Midway, the Douglas SBD-3 Dauntless, was sharply limited.

Wade's logbooks show that his first flight in an SBD Dauntless took place on March 20, 1942. Despite having well over 2,900 hours of total flying time under his belt by then, Wade had only

---

[1]Email communication, Philip McClusky to me, March 6, 2016 and March 14, 2016. Information compiled from Wade's logbooks.

[2]Compilation of dive-bombing hours provided by Philip McClusky from analysis of his father's pilot logbooks. Email communication, Philip McClusky to me, March 14, 2016.

[3]Thomas Wildenberg, *Destined for Glory: Dive Bombing, Midway, and the Evolution of Carrier Airpower* (Annapolis: Naval Institute Press, 1998): pp31–33.

been able to fit in 11 hours and 24 minutes flying an SBD before he took off in one from the *Enterprise* to lead the most important air strike in US naval history on June 4, 1942.[1] Dive-bomber technology had advanced greatly in the ten-year period following Wade's first flights in an F8C-4. While the Vought SBU-1 was far more advanced than the F8C-4, both types were biplanes. The SBD Dauntless was a quantum leap forward in dive-bombing capability. An all-metal monoplane with an enclosed cockpit and a retractable landing gear, the Dauntless also had slatted dive brakes along the trailing edge of the wing, which, when open, slowed the plane sufficiently to allow the pilot to dive at a 70-degree angle without tearing the wings off the airplane. While the SBD was a superb bomb-aiming platform, a dive in a Dauntless was far from easy. It was not uncommon for a Dauntless pilot to experience a g-force level of nine during pullout from a long, steep dive. That SBD pilots routinely returned safely from missions involving such nine-g pullouts is a testimony to the ruggedness of the airplane – and of the pilots who flew it.

During the six months following the Pearl Harbor attack, almost all of Wade's flying time had been in the cockpit of an F4F Wildcat fighter plane flying from the *Enterprise* as the commander of Fighting Squadron Six (VF-6). While McClusky's introduction to the SBD Dauntless was delayed by his time spent commanding a fighter squadron, it should be remembered that at the time of American entry into the war, the SBD Dauntless was a brand new aircraft type. Thus, every dive-bomber pilot in the Navy who had completed his flight training prior to December 1940 had had to undergo the awkward process of transitioning to the SBD from older dive-bomber types. Wade's ability to take to the Dauntless easily after his promotion to air group commander, to make a good dive, and to near-miss the *Kaga* with his 500lb bomb at Midway undoubtedly owed much

---

[1] Wade McClusky logbook entries for March, April, and May 1942. Also, Wade McClusky logbook entry of total hours as of June 1, 1942. Philip McClusky collection.

to his experience in the older model dive-bombers that he had often flown during the 1930s. It also owed much to his natural versatility as a pilot and to the wonderful variety of his prewar piloting experiences.

In fact, during the 1930s, Wade seems to have flown just about every type of aircraft in the naval inventory, including at least three different types of flying boat. One of these was the sleek Douglas RD-3, the art deco lines of which earned it the nickname "Dolphin." Wade also flew the Consolidated P2Y-2, a large flying boat with a 100ft wingspan and a crew of five. The P2Y-2 was Consolidated's predecessor to its legendary PBY Catalina. He also spent some time in the Keystone PK-1, larger than the Dolphin but not quite as large as the P2Y-2.[1] All of the flying boats Wade flew were twin-engined machines that were large enough that he had a copilot sitting next to him. The flying boats also gave him a taste of command. In both the P2Y-2 and the PK-1, Wade was in command of a five-man crew. The Dophin was primarily used for carrying passengers, of which Wade might have half a dozen at a time.

The intense rivalry between American naval aviators and the "Gun Club" officers who were still wedded to the big-gun battleship alluded to in Chapter 4 meant that when McClusky qualified as a pilot in 1929, the naval aviation community, being new, definitely felt it had something to prove. In the late-1920s and early 1930s, the two big new carriers *Lexington* and *Saratoga* competed against each other regularly in fleet exercises, such as "Fleet Problem XIII" conducted in the waters off Hawaii in the spring of 1932. The crews and air groups of the two carriers developed a competitive intensity that was undoubtedly good for the fleet.[2] During Fleet Problem XIII, the *Lexington* was commanded by a bad-tempered, hard-drinking, tart-tongued but undeniably brilliant rising star named Ernest J. King, then a

[1]Philip McClusky analysis of Wade's logbooks via an email to me, March 6, 2016.
[2]Wildenberg, *Destined for Glory*, p96.

captain. King would later attain five-star rank as commander-in-chief, US Fleet and chief of naval operations during World War 2. As for King's view of his rivals in such fleet exercises – the crew and air group of the *Saratoga* – historian Thomas Wildenberg writes that: "King always wanted to win, and it was said that 'he would change the rules or do anything to insure victory."[1] Indeed he would. In those days, ensuring that the *Lexington* defeated the *Saratoga* in every conceivable category seemed to be Ernest J. King's reason for living. This included intramural athletic events between the ships. King would consider it a personal affront if, when the two carriers were in port together, the *Lexington*'s football team should lose to the *Saratoga* team on the playing field.[2]

The competitive rivalry between the *Lexington* and the *Saratoga* meant that the umpires who adjudicated the results of mock engagements such as Fleet Problem XIII often found themselves as vilified for "bad calls" as has been any Major League Baseball umpire in a modern World Series game. The naval officers who served as umpires in the fleet exercises were supposed to be neutral, and they tried hard to be just that. Sometimes, however, they were overly generous to one side or the other so as to keep the exercises going. The umpires were thus always reluctant to declare either of the two big carriers to be "sunk." The *Saratoga*'s captain, Frank R. McCrary, was therefore enraged during Fleet Problem XIII in 1932 when Adm Frank H. Shofield, as chief umpire, had declared the *Lexington* to be still "operational" even though *Saratoga* pilots had made a brilliantly executed mock attack that, if the planes had been carrying real bombs, would most likely have dumped seven tons of bombs on to the *Lexington*'s flight deck.[3]

[1]Wildenberg, *Destined for Glory*, p97.

[2]Thomas B. Buell, *Master of Sea Power: A Biography of Fleet Admiral Ernest J. King* (Boston: Little, Brown and Company, 1980): p92.

[3]Wildenberg, *Destined for Glory*, pp96–97.

The healthy rivalry that had developed between the crews of the US Navy's first two truly operational aircraft carriers, and the fleet exercises those ships participated in during the 1928–1933 period, had amply demonstrated that while aircraft carriers had great offensive potential, they were also extremely vulnerable to attack. The *Lexington* versus *Saratoga* war games had also inculcated into the thinking of the Navy's pilots, ten years before the Battle of Midway, that the first order of business in any naval battle was to find and destroy the enemy's aircraft carriers. The side that strikes first would be the side that wins; a fact of carrier warfare that the Americans would demonstrate in spectacular fashion at Midway.[1]

The intense rivalry already apparent in the US Navy by the early 1930s between battleship officers and the upstart naval aviators undoubtedly delayed the acceptance by the former group of the seriousness of the threat to any warship posed by naval airpower. However, after the Pearl Harbor attack removed any lingering doubts as to the vulnerability of battleships to carrier-based air attack, it was easy for those surface admirals like Chester Nimitz who had the good sense to not be "bitter clingers" to the battleship-versus-battleship Jutland-style gunnery duel viewpoint to accept the idea that it was vital to find and destroy the most potent force in the Imperial Japanese Navy – namely, its big carriers.

It seems strange that the Japanese, who were experimenting with their first two large carriers, *Akagi* and *Kaga*, in the late 1920s and early 1930s – at the same time the *Lexington* and *Saratoga* were fighting mock "battles" against each other – did not quite reach the same conclusion as had the American naval aviators. After brilliantly demonstrating the capabilities of naval airpower in the Pearl Harbor attack, Adm Yamamoto, in his preparations for the invasion of Midway, oddly reverted to his own background as a battleship admiral. Yamamoto's highly complex scheme for invading Midway showed that he

[1]Wildenberg, *Destined for Glory*, p84, pp96–98, pp126–128.

hoped that the fleet action he was planning would allow for a major role, perhaps *the* major role, for his battleships. Adm Nagumo's *Kido Butai* fast carrier striking force was supposed to soften up Midway's defenses. After that, Yamamoto had hoped to have at least seven battleships on the scene by the time (according to Yamamoto's plan) the American fleet arrived. Yamamoto, the man who had so spectacularly demonstrated the offensive punch that could be delivered by naval airpower, seemed to hope that the destruction of the American fleet at Midway would be accomplished primarily by the big guns of his battleships. It is telling that Adm Yamamoto did not travel with Nagumo's fast carrier striking force, but instead made the new battleship *Yamato*, trailing far behind Nagumo, his flagship for the Midway battle.

Despite the devastation wrought at Pearl Harbor, half of the large fleet of American battleships had not been in Hawaiian waters on December 7, 1941. Thus, the Americans still had seven old undamaged battleships in commission in early 1942 as well as five new ones. Some of the older battleships, such as the USS *New York* and its sister the *Texas*, had served in World War 1. These ships were too slow to operate with fast carriers and while they had the big guns necessary for a surface battle, they were short on the small-caliber light antiaircraft (AA) weapons that would be so important for defense against air attack in World War 2. The modern battleships *North Carolina* and *Washington* had joined the fleet in 1941 and three of the new *South Dakota* Class battleships were commissioned in early 1942. These ships were fast enough to operate with aircraft carriers and carried adequate AA armament. However, at the time of the Battle of Midway these five new battleships were still in the Atlantic; either on other duty or completing their shakedown cruises.[1]

[1]David Rigby, *No Substitute for Victory: Successful American Military Strategies from the Revolutionary War to the Present Day* (New York: Carrel Books/Skyhorse Publishing, 2014): p6.

Six of the old American battleships were in San Francisco Bay in the weeks leading up to the Battle of Midway. While this battleship force under V Adm William S. Pye did do some patrolling off the West Coast of the United States during the battle, Adm Nimitz had made it clear that he did not want the old battleships to be anywhere near Midway.[1] Nimitz correctly foresaw, far more than did Yamamoto, that "Midway was to be a carrier battle in which naval air power would reign supreme."[2]

Earning his pilot's wings in 1929 meant that Wade McClusky got in on the ground floor of naval aviation, and its attendant controversies. The number of Navy pilots who graduated from the pilot training program at Pensacola grew steadily enough during the 1930s that the US Navy had 2,965 pilots on its roster in June 1940.[3] The vast majority of these men were in the junior commissioned ranks (ensigns; lieutenants, junior grade; and full lieutenants) while some were enlisted men. The Navy's high command continued to be dominated by non-aviator battleship admirals, much to the chagrin of the pilots. A glance at the proportion of pilots to non-pilots among American flag officers at the outbreak of war demonstrates this fact handily. Of the 84 admirals in the US Navy in July 1941, only ten were pilots. Eight of these men – John H. Towers, Arthur B. Cook, Charles A. Blakely, Leigh Noyes, Arthur L. Bristol, Jr, John S. McCain, John H. Hoover, and Aubrey Fitch – were rear admirals. Only two Navy pilots, V Adms Ernest J. King and William F. Halsey, Jr, had advanced beyond two-star rank by

[1]Samuel Eliot Morison, *History of United States Naval Operations in World War II*. Vol. 4. *Coral Sea, Midway and Submarine Actions. May 1942–August 1942* (Edison, NJ: Castle Books, 2001): pp82–83, text and notes.

[2]Rigby, *No Substitute for Victory*, p6.

[3]Clifford Lord and Archibald Turnbull, *History of United States Naval Aviation* (New Haven: Yale University Press, 1949): p313.

that time.[1] There were also a few "Naval Air Observers" like the now V Adm Frederick J. Horne among the flag officers. Another "Observer," Adm Harry Yarnell, would be called out of retirement in November 1941. Three other Navy pilots – Ernest D. McWhorter, Patrick N. L. Bellinger, and Richmond Kelly Turner – were scheduled for promotion to flag rank but were still officially captains in July 1941. Some Navy captains who would go on to become some of the most celebrated carrier admirals of the war, such as Alfred E. Montgomery, DeWitt C. Ramsey, Arthur C. Davis, John W. Reeves, Marc Mitscher, and Frederick C. (Ted) Sherman, had not even been put on the list for promotion to flag rank as of July 1941.[2] If anything, being a naval aviator in the 1930s was an impediment, as opposed to a boost, to one's chances of promotion.

The officer corps of the US Navy, both the pilots and the surface officers, had been kept to a bare minimum during the lean years of the Great Depression. All that changed with the approach of war. Evidence of the exponential expansion in naval pilot training programs during the war is that in the four-and-a-half years from mid-1940 to January 1945, well over 50,000 trained pilots would join the fleet.[3] Many factors made this meteoric expansion from a core of less than 3,000 naval pilots in 1940 possible: money suddenly became available; new airfields were built for training; and the building of aircraft was transformed from a craft practiced by artisans into an assembly line process.

[1]*Register of Commissioned and Warrant Officers of the United States Navy and Marine Corps, July 1, 1941* (Washington, DC: Government Printing Office, 1941): p7, p8, p14, p16, p18, p20. Available online at: www.ibiblio.org/hyperwar/USN/ref/BuPers/USN-USMC-1941.pdf. Accessed July 17, 2016.

[2]*Register of Commissioned and Warrant Officers of the United States Navy and Marine Corps, July 1, 1941* (Washington, DC: Government Printing Office, 1941): p7, p8, p14, p16, p18, pp20–28. Available online at: www.ibiblio.org/hyperwar/USN/ref/BuPers/USN-USMC-1941.pdf. Accessed July 17, 2016.

[3]Turnbull and Lord, *History of United States Naval Aviation*, p321.

Something more was needed, however, to allow such a massive expansion in the ranks of naval aviators without lowering standards. That something was specialization.[1] Overnight, several requirements that Navy pilots of McClusky's generation had had to satisfy were scrapped. No longer did naval officers have to put in two years of surface duty before they could be accepted for flight training. By the time of Pearl Harbor, young men, some just out of high school, could be accepted for flight training as long as they were at least 18 years of age, intelligent, and physically fit. Unlike the Navy pilots of McClusky's generation who had heaved coal on those summer training cruises during their Academy days and who later, as commissioned officers, had stood watches on the bridges of destroyers and battleships, the new young wartime pilots would earn their commissions as ensigns simply by completing their flight training. Their job was to fly. They knew nothing about ship-handling. Tending to the engines of a ship at sea, standing watch on the bridge, or evaluating radar data in the darkened confines of a warship's Combat Information Center (CIC) was for other people. What's more, Navy pilots trained during World War 2 were not expected to learn to fly every type of aircraft in the naval inventory. They would focus on mastering one type of airplane – a dive-bomber, a torpedo plane, a fighter plane, or a patrol plane – but not all four. These thousands of young men trained as Navy pilots after Pearl Harbor may never have even set foot on a ship until they had completed their flight training from land bases and then began to make the five arrested landings on the deck of an aircraft carrier that were, and are, the "final exam," the successful completion of which qualifies one as a naval aviator.[2]

Navy pilots like McClusky from the prewar generation of aviators also saw themselves first and foremost as pilots. Yet because the older pilots also understood how ships worked they

[1]Turnbull and Lord, *History of United States Naval Aviation*, pp311–312.
[2]Turnbull and Lord, *History of United States Naval Aviation*, pp311–316.

were especially valuable in the wartime Navy. As we shall see, as small escort carriers (CVE) began to join the fleet in 1942, there would be a great need for pilots with ship-handling experience to serve as commanding officers in what was rapidly becoming an "air navy."[1]

---

[1]For the label "air navy," see Clark G. Reynolds, *The Fast Carriers: The Forging of an Air Navy* (New York: McGraw-Hill, 1968): *passim.*

6

THE 1930S – ORIGINS OF A TROUBLESHOOTER

Wade's versatility and ability to handle unexpected situations began to appear in the 1930s. During that decade, he began to acquire a reputation in the Navy as an officer who could put out bureaucratic fires on a moment's notice. Doing so kept him on the move. Wade's orders show that he began to be detached from wherever he was stationed for a week or two to travel to a different location for some sort of special duty. Thus, the period 1940–1942 while he was part of the *Enterprise* air group represented one of relatively few periods of stability in Wade's career in which he could not be reassigned with little notice for special duty. After Midway, however, Wade's orders show that he was often forced back into the role of visiting fireman during the middle period of the war.[1]

Perhaps becoming a family man helped Wade to become adept at handling crises. Wade and Millicent were constantly moving during the 1930s. On May 9, 1931 Millicent and Wade boarded a Los Angeles Steamship Company liner, the SS *Calawaii* – a handsome 13,500-ton white-hulled steamer – at Wilmington, California for passage to Honolulu and Wade's first posting to Pearl Harbor. His official title in this billet was aviation aide to the staff commander, Minecraft, Battle Force (R Adm George T. Pettengill). The couple arrived in Honolulu on May 16. The Los Angeles Steamship Company was a rival to the famous Matson

---

[1]Wade McClusky, orders received; *passim*. Philip McClusky collection.

Line whose elegant white-hulled steamships dominated travel between California and Hawaii in the 1920s and 1930s. One hopes the seas were calm on this particular trip since Millicent was seven months pregnant.[1] Wade Sanford McClusky, the couple's only child, was born in Hawaii on July 21, 1931.

Wade Sanford, whom his parents called "Pat," was determined from an early age to follow in his father's footsteps by becoming a Navy pilot. An overachiever like Wade, Pat would graduate from the elite Principia school in St Louis, where he had been a boarding student. Principia provided stability as well as an excellent education for Pat. No matter how many times Wade and Millicent had to move for Wade's duty postings, Principia

---

[1] SS *Calawaii* brochure, at http://cruiselinehistory.com/wp-content/uploads/2012/10/Screen-shot-2012-10-10-at-11.47.49-AM1.png. National Archives and Records Administration (NARA); Washington, DC; *Passenger Lists of Vessels Arriving at Honolulu, Hawaii, compiled 02/13/1900 - 12/30/1953*; National Archives Microfilm Publication: *A3422*; Roll: *114*; Record Group Title: *Records of the Immigration and Naturalization Service, 1787 - 2004*; Record Group Number: *RG 85*.

Ancestry.com. *Honolulu, Hawaii, Passenger and Crew Lists, 1900-1959* [database online]. Provo, UT, USA: Ancestry.com Operations, Inc, 2009. Original data: *Passenger Lists of Vessels Arriving or Departing at Honolulu, Hawaii, 1900–1954.* NARA Microfilm Publication A3422, 269 rolls; A3510, 175 rolls; A3574, 27 rolls; A3575, 1 roll; A3615, 1 roll; A3614, 80 rolls; A3568 & A3569, 187 rolls; A3571, 64 rolls; A4156, 348 rolls. Records of the Immigration and Naturalization Service, Record Group 85. National Archives, Washington, DC.

Passenger and Crew Manifests of Airplanes Departing from Honolulu, Hawaii, 12/1957-9/1969. NARA Microfilm Publication A3577 56 rolls. Records of the Immigration and Naturalization Service, 1787-2004, Record Group 85. National Archives, Washington, DC.

"LIEUTENANT COMMANDER CLARENCE W. MCCLUSKY, JR., USN" – a brief career summary prepared by the Navy Department after Midway and dated November 12, 1942, p1. From the McClusky "Jacket" on file at the Naval Academy. "McClusky, Clarence Wade, Jr." Jacket Number 8306. Special Collections & Archives Department, Nimitz Library, United States Naval Academy.

meant that from eighth grade on, Pat was always able to attend the same school. Pat played basketball and tennis at Principia. He earned Bachelor and MBA degrees at Stanford and he did indeed earn his wings as a Navy pilot in 1956.[1]

Wade, Sr's first tour of duty at Pearl Harbor lasted exactly two years, from May 1931 to May 1933. Pearl Harbor was not yet nearly as busy and bustling a place as it would be during World War 2; it would not be until May 1940 that President Roosevelt would move the Pacific Fleet from the West Coast of the United States out to Pearl Harbor. Nonetheless, Pearl was an important American outpost in 1931. It was also an idyllic setting for a young couple. Wade and Millicent lived in the fashionable Pacific Heights neighborhood of Honolulu. Perhaps because Pearl Harbor was a much smaller establishment than it would be in World War 2, the naval community there in the early 1930s was very close knit.[2] As such, the McCluskys were active on the social circuit, hosting dinners and bridge parties. Their guests were usually other naval officers and their wives.[3]

---

[1]Obituary, *Baltimore Sun*. August 30, 1986. P9A. Email communication, Philip McClusky to me, September 10, 2017. *The Times* (San Mateo). December 5, 1962. P19. *The Times* (San Mateo). December 5, 1962. P21. *St. Louis Post-Dispatch* (Tennis Scores). May 6, 1949. P7 D. Telephone conversation with Carole McClusky-Pewthers, September 28, 2017.

[2]Telephone conversation with Carole McClusky-Pewthers, September 28, 2017.

[3]"Navy & Marine Corps Social Notes" *Honolulu Sunday-Advertiser*. April 3, 1932. P8 of Society Section. Available online at: www.newspapers.com/image/259238238/?terms= Wade%2BMcClusky. Accessed September 14 and September 16, 2017. "Society in Navy Circles." *Honolulu Star-Bulletin*. March 19, 1932. P10. Available online at: www.newspapers. com/image/274956584/?terms=Wade%2BS.%2BMcClusky. Accessed September 14, 2017. "Society in Navy Circles" *Honolulu Star-Bulletin*. April 2, 1932. P4 of Second Section. Available online at: www.newspapers.com/image/275042117/?terms=Wade%2BMcClusky. Accessed September 14 and September 16, 2017. "Society in Navy Circles" *Honolulu Star-Bulletin*. June 11, 1932. P4 of Second Section. Available online at: www.newspapers. com/image/274960635/?terms=Wade%2BMcClusky. Accessed September 14 and September 16, 2017.

As an aide to Adm Pettengill, Wade was a staff officer, and it seems that staff duties took up most of his time during his first year in Hawaii. During that time, he would fly from four to seven hours per month. As usual, Wade flew a variety of different aircraft types, including the Vought O2U-3 scout and the big Martin T3M and T4M torpedo planes. From August 1932 until the end of the year, his first tour in Hawaii, Wade flew a Douglas PD-1 as a member of Patrol Squadron 4F (VP-4F). Upon joining VP-4F, Wade now did less staff work and a lot more flying; sometimes on 16 or 17 days a month, compiling 20 or 30 hours in the air – a lot of flying for one month, especially in peacetime. The PD-1 was a large, twin-engined, open-cockpit biplane flying boat – essentially a more modern version of the old F-5-Ls that Wade had ridden in during his introductory flights back at Annapolis in the fall of 1926.[1]

Wade received orders on May 24, 1933 detaching him from VP-4F and ordering him back to the mainland. For some reason, the family could not travel together for this trip. Wade sailed from Pearl on June 22 aboard the USS *Henderson*, a troopship that had been built for the Navy during World War 1. Millicent and two-year old Wade Sanford were waiting for him when he arrived in California. They had arrived in San Francisco on June 3 aboard the Matson Line's brand new SS *Lurline*, having departed Honolulu a week earlier.[2] The family did not stay

[1]Orders from Bureau of Navigation to McClusky, May 24, 1933. Philip McClusky collection. Wade McClusky pilot logbook entries May 1931 to May 1933. Philip McClusky collection.

[2]Ancestry.com. *Honolulu, Hawaii, Passenger and Crew Lists, 1900-1959* [database online]. Provo, UT, USA: Ancestry.com Operations, Inc, 2009.

National Archives and Records Administration (NARA); Washington, DC; *Passenger Lists of Vessels Departing from Honolulu, Hawaii, compiled 06/1900 - 11/1954*; National Archives Microfilm Publication: *A3510*; Roll: *098*; Record Group Title: *Records of the Immigration and Naturalization Service, 1787 - 2004*; Record Group Number: *RG 85*

Original data: *Passenger Lists of Vessels Arriving or Departing at Honolulu, Hawaii, 1900–1954.*

in California for long. That summer, the McCluskys traveled cross-country because Wade, then still a lieutenant (junior grade), had been ordered back to Annapolis for the 1933–1934 academic year for postgraduate study. Officially, he would be taking what was known as the "Post Graduate Course in General Line Duties." In fact, he mainly studied advances in aviation. This year at Annapolis was the equivalent of earning a Master's degree and was a sure sign that McClusky was being groomed for promotion and its attendant increases in responsibility.[1]

Wade spent most of his postgraduate year at Annapolis attending lectures and seminars. Even though the focus was on aviation, Wade did far less flying back at Annapolis than he had been doing in Hawaii. At Annapolis, Wade was careful to always get in his minimum of four hours per month in the air so that he could continue to collect the hazardous duty bonus pay that the Navy paid, and still pays, to its aviators and its submariners, but he was not an instructor pilot during this time and the aircraft he was flying were not cutting edge; that year, he almost always flew a Vought O2U Scout, a plane in which he had already logged many hours. He nevertheless characterized most of his flights for the year as "Familiarization." By the time he finished his studies in May 1934 Wade must have been quite "familiar" with the

NARA Microfilm Publication A3422, 269 rolls; A3510, 175 rolls; A3574, 27 rolls; A3575, 1 roll; A3615, 1 roll; A3614, 80 rolls; A3568 & A3569, 187 rolls; A3571, 64 rolls; A4156, 348 rolls. Records of the Immigration and Naturalization Service, Record Group 85. National Archives, Washington, DC.

[1] "LIEUTENANT COMMANDER CLARENCE W. MCCLUSKY, JR., USN" – brief career summary, p1, from the McClusky "Jacket" on file at the Naval Academy. See also, Orders from Bureau of Navigation to McClusky, May 24, 1933. Philip McClusky collection. *Register of Commissioned and Warrant Officers of the United States Navy and Marine Corps.* July 1, 1943. (Washington, DC: Government Printing Office, 1943): p10, p54 for the title of Wade's post-graduate course of instruction.

O2U, since he had rarely flown anything else during the previous nine months.[1]

Perhaps choosing an O2U in which to get in his required flying time while back at Annapolis was more than chance. Wade may have known that his next assignment after his postgraduate year at Annapolis was going to be as a scout pilot with a battleship squadron. Accordingly, at the end of the academic year, Wade was assigned to Observation Squadron (VO) 4B, which was headquartered at Naval Air Station (NAS), San Diego. As such, Wade would become one of five pilots who would fly Vought's successor to the O2U series, the O3U-1, from the battleship USS *Maryland*. The battleship's aircraft were pontoon-equipped and launched from a catapult. Wade reported aboard the battleship in late June 1934.[2] While he flew from the *Maryland*, Wade and the ship's other observation pilots observed fall of shot during firing practice and radioed corrections for the *Maryland* and sometimes for other battleships as well when *Maryland* was operating as part of a task force.[3]

Millicent and young Wade Sanford dutifully followed McClusky to San Diego. Again, Wade made the trip first, and alone. Millicent seemed to prefer ships to trains when it came to traveling. Mother and son sailed from New York to San Diego on the Panama Pacific Line's SS *California* – an interesting 13-day voyage via the Panama Canal. In the manifest the young mother and her son were labeled like freight to be delivered "c/o Lt. McClusky, North Island, San Diego, Calif."[4]

[1] Wade McClusky pilot logbook entries, December 1932 to May 1934. Philip McClusky collection.

[2] Bureau of Navigation to McClusky, April 11, 1934. Wade McClusky logbook entries for July 1935. Both, Philip McClusky collection.

[3] Commander Battleships, Battle Force to Commanding Officer, U.S.S. MARYLAND. Standing of OBSERVATION WING pilots and observers in Main Battery Spotting Practices – 1934–1935. April 8, 1935. Philip McClusky collection.

[4] Ancestry.com. *California, Passenger and Crew Lists, 1882-1959* [database online]. Provo, UT, USA: Ancestry.com Operations Inc, 2008.

Evidence of Wade's growing abilities as a troubleshooter and special assignment man is that he was detached from the *Maryland* in early January 1935 for temporary duties back at NAS San Diego, although he was still considered to be a part of *Maryland*'s crew. He made a quick visit back to the battleship on February 27, but flew back to San Diego the following day. At NAS San Diego, his work involved testing a gun camera that had been mounted in an O3U-3 version of the Vought floatplane. While he did plenty of flying in January and February in O3U-3s, he first tested the gun camera in the air on March 12. He was returned to full-time duties aboard the *Maryland* five months later, by which time the *Maryland* itself had received the upgraded O3U-3 type.[1]

By the time he rejoined *Maryland* in early summer 1935, Wade had already been informed that his next billet after completing his tour aboard *Maryland* was going to be that of aide and flag lieutenant to R Adm Frederick J. Horne, who was then

Original data: *Selected Passenger and Crew Lists and Manifests.* National Archives, Washington, DC.

On Wade being sent back to Annapolis in 1934, see *Register of the Commissioned and Warrant Officers of the United States Navy and Marine Corps*, January 1, 1934, (Washington, DC: Government Printing Office, 1934): p142. Available at: https://babel. hathitrust.org/cgi/pt?id=mdp.39015036626334;view=1up;seq=152. Accessed February 3, 2018.

US Naval Air Station: Pensacola, Florida. "Final Report of Training for MCCLUSKY, Clarence W., Jr.", June 1929. Philip McClusky collection.

[1] Headquarters US Fleet, Battle Force, San Pedro via the commanding officer (CO), USS. *Maryland* to McClusky, January 7, 1935. CO *Maryland* to McClusky, June 10, 1935. Bureau of Navigation to McClusky, May 11, 1935 and February 28, 1936, respectively. Commander, Battleships; Battle Force, April 8, 1935. Philip McClusky collection. Wade McClusky logbook entries October 1934 through March 1935. Philip McClusky collection. "LIEUTENANT COMMANDER CLARENCE W. MCCLUSKY, JR., USN" – a brief career summary prepared by the Navy Department, p1, from the McClusky "Jacket" on file at the Naval Academy. Wade McClusky, logbook entries, January to May, 1935. Philip McClusky collection.

serving as commander aircraft, Base Force. Earlier, as a captain, Frederick Horne had commanded the USS *Saratoga* during the period when Wade served aboard as a member of the Nine High Hats squadron. Horne's flagship now was considerably less glamorous – the seaplane tender USS *Wright*. Nevertheless, Wade was moving up. This tour of duty with Adm Horne would last for the next three years and it kept Wade at the forefront of naval aviation. During those years, Adm Horne was promoted to commander, Aircraft Battle Force in June 1936, at which time he transferred his flag to the carrier USS *Saratoga*; a homecoming for both men. Horne's new duties were accompanied by promotion to vice-admiral. Wade was now working for the man in charge of all fleet aviation.[1] Having a high-ranking boss, however, did not stop the Navy from continuing to use Wade in the role of roving troubleshooter. For instance, Wade was loaned out to NAS Norfolk, Virginia for unspecified temporary duty in September 1937.[2]

In February 1936, during a visit of the *Wright* to Ecuador, Wade was forced to endure the time-honored ritual of being transformed from the "pollywog" to a "shellback" as he crossed the equator for the first time. In his papers is a "Subpoena and Summons Extraordinary" from "The Royal High Court of the Raging Main." This charge sheet explains the need for the ceremony thus:

---

[1] Headquarters US Fleet, Battle Force, San Pedro via the commanding officer (CO), USS *Maryland* to McClusky, January 7, 1935. CO *Maryland* to McClusky, June 10, 1935. Bureau of Navigation to McClusky, May 11, 1935 and February 28, 1936, respectively. Commander, Battleships; Battle Force, April 8, 1935. Philip McClusky collection. Wade McClusky logbook entries October 1934 through March 1935. Philip McClusky collection. "LIEUTENANT COMMANDER CLARENCE W. MCCLUSKY, JR., USN" – a brief career summary prepared by the Navy Department, p1, from the McClusky "Jacket" on file at the Naval Academy. Ernest J. King and Walter Muir Whitehill, *Fleet Admiral King: A Naval Record* (New York: Norton, 1952): p266, p277.

[2] Orders, Horne to McClusky, September 7, 1937. Philip McClusky collection.

102

"Whereas; the good ship WRIGHT, bound southward for Guayaquil, Ecuador, is about to enter my domain carrying a large and slimy cargo of landlubbers, beachcombers, sea-lawyers, politicians, lounge-lizzards [sic], parlor-dunnigans, plow-deserters, box-car tourists, hitch-hikers, park-bench warmers . . . falsely masquerading as seaman [sic], of which low order you are a member, having never appeared before me."[1]

This summons was signed by "Davy Jones." Wade's orders for the ceremony were to stand watch on the flag bridge and to supervise the activities of the unfortunate pollywogs who had been assigned duty as lookouts whose job was to "look" for the equator. Wade was to enter each "sighting" in the ship's log. His uniform for the day was outlined in precise detail in his orders:

"a. Cocked Hat
 b. Frock Coat
 c. Dress and service equilettes
 d. No pants, socks or shoes."[2]

The appointment to serve with Adm Horne was accompanied by promotion to full lieutenant. The commission is dated February 12, 1937, but the promotion was made retroactive to June 30, 1936.[3] Wade and Adm Horne were with the *Saratoga* until December 1937, at which time Adm Horne was relieved as commander, Aircraft Battle Force by the irascible Ernest J. King, himself now a rear admiral. Adm Horne's next billet was to serve

---

[1]Subpoena and Summons Extraordinary: The Royal High Court of the Raging Main. The Trusty Shellbacks Versus C. W. McClusky, Lieutenant (jg), US Navy. February 2, 1936. Philip McClusky collection.

[2]"The Royal Realm" to McClusky, undated, but probably February 2, 1936. Philip McClusky collection.

[3]R Adm Adolphus Andrews, Chief of the Bureau of Navigation, to McClusky, February 17, 1937. Philip McClusky collection.

as part of the Navy's General Board – the body that supervised the design of new naval warships as well as the procurement of anything else the Navy needed. The General Board had needed an aviator. As such, Adm Horne was kept busy for the next three years supervising the design of naval aircraft and the training of new pilots.[1]

During his time on the USS *Wright*, Wade almost always flew an O3U-3. After Horne's promotion and the move to the *Saratoga*, Wade flew the SBU-1 dive-bomber. Several entries in Wade's logbook show that during his time as flag secretary he often carried Adm Horne as a passenger when flying. Indeed, for 4.3 of the 8.1 hours McClusky spent flying an SBU-1 dive-bomber during the month of July 1936 he had been accompanied by Horne. Perhaps Adm Horne, who himself had qualified as an "Aviation Observer" but was not quite a pilot, had wanted to observe dive-bombing operations at first hand, or perhaps the admiral just needed a ride somewhere and was using McClusky as his chauffeur.[2] The most likely reason for Horne to be riding as a passenger with McClusky is that McClusky's duties as Horne's aide probably included keeping the admiral aloft for at least four hours per month so that Horne could collect his own hazardous duty stipend. Adm Horne, having completed only the Naval Aviation Observer's course, would have needed a fully qualified pilot like Wade McClusky to accompany him whenever he was in the air. In those July 1936 flights with Horne, Wade's logbooks show that McClusky flew the plane as the pilot of record. Horne was along only for the ride. Keeping one's hazardous duty stipend was vitally important, particularly during the lean years of the Depression. Indeed, whenever Wade was ordered ashore for staff duty, his orders always included the phrase "for duty involving flying," which enabled him to set aside at least four hours a month

[1]King and Whitehill, *Fleet Admiral King*, p277, p295.

[2]Wade McClusky logbook entries for July 1935 through October 1935 and for June and July 1936. Philip McClusky collection.

104

to fly.[1] Maintaining his flight status while stationed ashore meant more than just the money to Wade: it also kept his flying skills sharp enough that he could eventually go back to sea, which is where he greatly preferred to be.

McClusky saw himself first and foremost as a pilot.[2] However, the fact that he also excelled as a staff officer made it impossible for Wade to escape shore duty. As such, Wade returned to Annapolis in 1938 as an instructor. Interestingly, his appointment to the faculty of the Academy's Department of Seamanship and Navigation would seem more suited to a line officer than a pilot. This would be Wade's last posting before he went back to sea as a member of Fighting Six (VF-6) in the summer of 1940. Although his Annapolis assignment officially placed him as a classroom instructor, Wade found plenty of excuses to fly during his tour there. His pilot logbook entries for March and April 1938 frequently mention "Mid Train" – that is, he was taking groups of midshipmen up in a Consolidated P2Y-2 flying boat for the same type of initial indoctrination into basic flight tactics that had been such an important motivator for Wade himself to become a pilot when he had taken his first rides in an F-5-L back in the summer of 1926. The midshipmen that McClusky took aloft in 1938 benefited from the fact that the P2Y-2 was a much more advanced flying boat than was the old F-5-L. For one thing, riding in the fully enclosed P2Y-2 did not require shivering in an open cockpit.[3]

While teaching at Annapolis, Wade was still being called upon to put out bureaucratic fires. For instance, the Navy's patrol

---

[1]An example of this language appears in the orders issued to McClusky by the Bureau of Personnel via Commander Fleet Air, Alameda, R Adm William. W. Smith, dated May 10, 1943, transferring McClusky to Washington. Philip McClusky collection.

[2]Interviews with Philip McClusky, December 27 and December 29, 2016.

[3]Wade McClusky pilot logbook entries for March and April 1938. Philip McClusky collection. See also McClusky career overview, p1, in the McClusky "Jacket." Special Collections & Archives Department, Nimitz Library, United States Naval Academy.

squadrons were in need of experienced old hands in the late 1930s. Accordingly, in April 1939 Wade was assigned to fly with Patrol Wing Five as extra duty in addition to his work as an instructor at Annapolis.[1] Although he was now getting extra flying time, Wade had to have been relieved when, at the end of his second full year as an instructor, he was detached from the Annapolis faculty and sent back to a carrier-based combat squadron.

[1]Orders, R Adm Wilson Brown (Superintendent of Annapolis) to McClusky, April 4, 1939. Philip McClusky collection.

7

FIGHTING SIX

June 1940 was a busy month for Wade. Against a backdrop of grim events overseas, most particularly the shocking surrender of France after a six-week lightning German invasion, Wade underwent the formal process of examination and evaluation for promotion to lieutenant commander while he was in the process of being detached from the faculty at the Naval Academy so that he could take up his new assignment to join Fighting Squadron Six (VF-6) aboard the USS *Enterprise* (CV-6).[1] Wade's examination for promotion was coordinated by the Navy's Bureau of Navigation, an office that would soon be renamed the "Bureau of Personnel" – a much more accurate description of its activities. The Navy's personnel manager in 1940 was R Adm Chester W. Nimitz, whose stewardship of the Bureau of Navigation would be his last assignment prior to his promotion and appointment just after Pearl Harbor to the office of commander-in-chief, US Pacific Fleet.

It is ironic that in June 1940 Nimitz, the man who two short years later would pin the Distinguished Flying Cross on to Wade's uniform, and who a few weeks after that would describe

[1] R Adm Chester W. Nimitz, Chief of the Bureau of Navigation, to McClusky, June 27, 1940. Philip McClusky collection. John B. Lundstrom, *The First Team: Pacific Air Combat from Pearl Harbor to Midway* (Annapolis: Naval Institute Press, 1984): p8.

McClusky's role in the Battle of Midway as "decisive,"[1] actually harbored some doubts about Wade's suitability for promotion. Nimitz wrote Wade on June 27, 1940 regarding the Examining Board's preliminary assessment of Wade's suitability for promotion to lieutenant commander that:

> "The Naval Examining Board which reviewed your professional examination found you mentally and morally fitted to perform all your duties at sea but owing to deficiency in the subjects of Strategy and Tactics and Communications, as shown by your written examination papers, your professional fitness has not been so established.
>
> By direction of the Secretary of the Navy no action will be taken on the report of the Supervisory Naval Examining Board in your case. You will be ordered to report for such further examination as may be necessary to determine your fitness for promotion."[2]

Being left in suspended animation by this somewhat ambiguous report from Nimitz must have been unbearable for an overachieving perfectionist like Wade McClusky. The next few months had to have been a very stressful time for him. When word came down that his promotion was stalled, Wade had already been with Fighting Six and the *Enterprise* for several weeks. Going to sea again as a member of a carrier squadron must have been exhilarating for a man who always thought of himself as a pilot first and a sailor second,[3] but his happiness would have been tempered by the delay in his promotion. In the pre-Pearl Harbor Navy, Annapolis graduates who were going to

[1]Adm Chester W. Nimitz. Battle of Midway After Action Report. Cincpac File No.A16 01849. Available at www.ibiblio.org/hyperwar/USN/rep/Midway/Midway-CinCPac.html. Accessed December 20, 2015. See Paragraph 30.

[2]Nimitz to McClusky, June 27, 1940. Philip McClusky collection.

[3]Interviews with Philip McClusky, December 27 and 29, 2016.

be promoted tended to receive their promotions all at about the same time as others in their respective classes, a situation that would change once the nation was at war. In the summer of 1940 it must have been agonizing for Wade to think that he might be left behind on the promotion ladder by his friends in the Academy class of 1926.

Whatever "further examination" Nimitz had in mind for McClusky was cleared up by late November. Wade's promotion came through on November 29, 1940 and, interestingly, was made retroactive to July 1, the date that it would have taken effect had there been no delay. He formally took the Oath of Office as a lieutenant commander on December 17, 1940 on board the *Enterprise* in a ceremony witnessed by his new commanding officer, Lt Cdr Howard Young, then the commanding officer of Fighting Six.[1] Incidentally, in the official roster of Navy and Marine Corps officers covering that period, Wade's name is followed by "(B) (F)," indicating that in summer 1940 he was fully qualified as a dive-bomber pilot as well as a fighter pilot. It also states that he had by then "completed postgraduate course in general line duties" (the 1933–1934 academic year he had spent at Annapolis) and had "completed course in torpedo instruction" (the six months he had spent at the Naval Torpedo Factory in Newport in 1928).[2] Joining Fighting Six began McClusky's association with that squadron's famous home, the aircraft carrier USS *Enterprise*, a ship that would earn the greatest combat record in the history of the US Navy.

The carrier Wade McClusky flew from was itself central to American victory at Midway, but this book is not another

---

[1]Bureau of Navigation to McClusky, November 29, 1940. Oath of Office form, dated and signed December 17, 1940. Philip McClusky collection.

[2]*Register of Commissioned and Warrant Officers of the United States Navy and Marine Corps.* July 1, 1943. (Washington, DC: Government Printing Office, 1943): p10, p54 for the titles of Wade's postgraduate courses of instruction. Available at: https://babel. hathitrust.org/cgi/pt?id=mdp.39015036626284&view=1up&seq=66&size=150.

biography of the legendary *Enterprise*. There are already two of those in print – Edward Stafford's classic 1962 account *The Big E: The Story of the USS Enterprise*, and Barrett Tillman's more recent *Enterprise: America's Fightingest Ship and the Men Who Helped Win World War II*. However, there is no doubt that there was something special about that ship; about serving aboard *Enterprise*, a ship that seemed to breed excellence. Her wartime captains, such as George D. Murray, Osborne B. Hardison, Arthur C. Davis, and Matthias B. Gardner, usually went on to attain flag rank.

Osborne Hardison typifies the extremely high quality of the commanding officers *Enterprise* was blessed with during the war. It was Hardison who was pacing the bridge of the Big E on October 26, 1942 during the fast and furious action that characterized the Battle of the Santa Cruz Islands.[1] The *Enterprise* spent the middle of that highly eventful day maneuvering at high speed while under attack by enemy dive-bombers and torpedo planes. While the ship was damaged by three bomb hits, Capt Hardison gave a clinic-like demonstration on how to evade torpedoes. From the bridge wings, Hardison watched the approach of fast Japanese Nakajima B5N "Kate" torpedo planes whose pilots were intent on lining up their aircraft so that the deadly Type 91 torpedo slung under the belly of each plane would, when dropped into the water from low altitude, run straight and true into the hull of the *Enterprise*. Observing the track of each approaching torpedo, Hardison calmly gave orders to the helmsman for the evasive high-speed turns that enabled the *Enterprise* to turn parallel to the track of each of the rapidly approaching "fish."[2] In fact,

[1] Edward P. Stafford, *The Big E: The Story of the U.S.S. Enterprise* (Annapolis: Naval Institute Press, 1962, 2002): pp200–203.

[2] Stafford, *The Big E*, 200–203. Barrett Tillman, *Enterprise: America's Fightingest Ship and the Men Who Helped Win World War II* (New York: Simon & Schuster, 2012): p127. My additional thanks to Barrett Tillman for reminding me just how superb Osborne Hardison's ship-handling was. Email communication, Barrett Tillman to me, February 4, 2015.

the *Enterprise* dodged no fewer than nine torpedoes that day, a spectacular display of ship-handling for which Capt Hardison was awarded the Navy Cross.[1] Another *Enterprise* captain, Arthur Davis, would become chief-of-staff to Adm Spruance late in the war when Spruance was commanding the Fifth Fleet during the Central Pacific Drive. The *Enterprise* participated in every major naval battle in the Pacific War with the exception of Coral Sea, earning 20 battle stars and a Presidential Unit Citation in the process.

Wade fit in well with Fighting Six and got on well with the squadron's commanding officer, Lt Cdr Howard Young. As Wade's immediate superior, Young would sign Wade's pilot logbook each month verifying that Wade's record of hours flown was accurate.[2] A ruggedly handsome New Yorker, Howard Young had been tagged with the inevitable nickname "Brigham" at least as far back as his Academy days. A 1923 Annapolis graduate, Young had qualified as a naval aviator in 1926.

Fighting Six was still flying Grumman F3F biplane fighters when Wade McClusky joined the outfit in 1940. His flying skills, vast experience, and his seniority enabled McClusky to move up fast, and he was quickly advanced to be Young's executive officer. Just under a year after joining Fighting Six, Wade was promoted on orders from *Enterprise* commanding officer Capt George D. Murray to be the squadron's commanding officer effective April 19, 1941.[3] The occasion was "Brigham" Young's advancement to the post of commander, *Enterprise* Air Group. Capt Murray's choice of Wade McClusky to fill the vacancy as commanding officer, Fighting Six was confirmed a few weeks later

---

[1] Tillman, *Enterprise*, p127.

[2] Wade McClusky logbook covering the years 1940–1951, passim. Philip McClusky collection.

[3] Orders, George D. Murray promoting McClusky from executive officer to commanding officer, Fighting Squadron Six, April 19, 1941. Philip McClusky collection.

by Adm Nimitz, who at that time was still chief of the Bureau of Navigation.[1]

At the outset of the war, it was the intention of the naval high command that air groups form a very strong bond with the carrier on which they served. Until late 1942, Navy pilots were generally not seen merely as "guests" who could be moved around from one carrier to another. Up until the Battle of Midway, carrier air groups were intended to be organic to the carrier on which they served to the extent that the squadrons adopted the hull number of the carrier they flew from. Hence, Fighting Six flew from the deck of CV-6 (*Enterprise*). This bonding process between air groups and ships contributed to the fact that the prewar carriers, such as *Lexington*, *Enterprise*, and *Yorktown* tended to be very "happy" ships. The exigencies of war quickly put a strain on this bonding system, however. For instance, for the Battle of Midway, the *Yorktown* needed replacement pilots and aircraft in a hurry due to losses sustained during the Battle of the Coral Sea. Thus, during its brief stopover at Pearl Harbor in late May 1942, the *Yorktown* embarked Bombing Squadron Three (VB-3), whose pilots were refugees from the USS *Saratoga* (CV-3) who had been left in Hawaii in January when the *Saratoga* returned to the West Coast for repairs after being torpedoed by a Japanese submarine. Later in the war, with the Navy growing by leaps and bounds and new carriers rapidly entering service, it became impossible to keep the air groups organic to one carrier. Thus the number designations between air groups and carrier hulls began to diverge as a matter of routine. By the time of the Battle of Santa Cruz, the *Enterprise* had embarked the completely new Air Group Ten.[2]

While he was a great fighter pilot, Wade did have a few rough moments in Fighting Six. One of them occurred on July 11, 1940

---

[1] Nimitz (as chief of the Bureau of Navigation) to McClusky, June 12, 1941. Philip McClusky collection.

[2] Stafford. *The Big E*, p174.

when, after a training flight, he came in a bit high on landing, missed the arresting wires, and crashed into the barrier – a series of cables stretched across the Big E's flight deck amidships and high enough to snag the propeller of any landing aircraft that got that far forward. This crash landing is preserved in all its ignominy in a slow-motion black-and-white silent training film, in which Wade is misidentified as "Lt. McCousky." The barrier did stop the airplane, but the shock of stopping suddenly stood the F3F on its nose. Wade walked away with only his pride damaged. He mentions the event discreetly in his logbook under the heading "Remarks" where he recorded the purpose for and details of each flight: "Tactics (Hit Barrier)."[1] Even the best pilots had occasional mishaps. The same training film contains footage of Earl Gallaher, who would go on to score the first bomb hit on *Kaga* at Midway, snapping off his landing gear and making a belly landing on the *Enterprise* in September 1940.[2] Nevertheless Wade, who was in the words of his son Philip "a consummate professional,"[3] must have been mortified with embarrassment to have made a bad landing in full view of his shipmates and squadron mates.

McClusky and the other VF-6 pilots traded in their F3Fs for the new monoplane Grumman F4F-3 Wildcat fighter plane in April 1941,[4] traveling to the Grumman factory in Bethpage, New York to pick up their new airplanes in person. Wade's pilot logbook shows that he left San Diego, where the *Enterprise* was docked,

[1]Wade McClusky logbook entry, July 11, 1940. Philip McClusky collection. For the landing, see US Navy Training Film "Landing Crashes of 1940: U.S.S. *Enterprise*" Available on Youtube at: www.youtube.com/watch?v=ZriGDd0RtFo. Accessed January 7, 2017.

[2]"Landing Crashes of 1940: U.S.S. *Enterprise*" Accessed January 7, 2017.

[3]Interviews with Philip McClusky, December 27 and 29, 2016.

[4]Philip McClusky breakdown of flying time from Wade's logs, 1926–1942. Email communication, Philip McClusky to me, March 6, 2016. Lundstrom, *The First Team*, p8.

on April 19, 1941 and flew a zigzag route cross-country in his F3F, stopping in Tucson; El Paso; Abilene; Barksdale Field near Shreveport, Louisiana; Jackson, Mississippi; Pensacola; Orlando; and finally Miami, where he arrived on April 21. He apparently left the F3F in Florida, perhaps taking the train from there to Long Island.[1]

The next logbook entry is dated a week later. On April 28, 1941, Wade picked up an F4F-3A Wildcat at Floyd Bennett Field in Brooklyn. Having been replaced as New York City's air terminal in 1940 by the recently completed La Guardia Airport, Floyd Bennett had been redesignated as a Naval Air Station in 1941. Floyd Bennett Field was the first stop for all Grumman aircraft after they were flown off the airstrip at the company's factory at Bethpage on Long Island. It was close enough to Bethpage that any kinks in a new airplane could be easily worked out. During his first flight in a Wildcat, serial number 3907, Wade familiarized himself with the new airplane and then flew it to Bethpage, probably for adjustments at the factory. Later the same day he flew back to Floyd Bennett, but returned to Bethpage the next day.[2]

On April 29, 1941, his new aircraft deemed ready for action, Wade headed back to San Diego. Again he flew a zigzag course. His first stop after leaving Bethpage was Anacostia Naval Air Station near Washington, DC, where he spent the night. The next day he flew west, stopping in Cleveland and Chicago, respectively. Wade's next log entry, on May 1, reads "Chicago to Barlington." The latter is perhaps a misspelling of "Burlington," Indiana. He flew on to Kansas City and then Amarillo that day. From Texas, Wade flew to Albuquerque, New Mexico on May 4. He finally made San Diego two days later, after additional stops in Winslow and Kingman, Arizona.[3]

[1]Wade McClusky logbook entries for April and May, 1941. Philip McClusky collection.

[2]Wade McClusky logbook entries for April and May, 1941. Philip McClusky collection.

[3]Wade McClusky logbook entries for April and May, 1941. Philip McClusky collection.

Wade had been landing on aircraft carriers since July 1929 when, as a member of the Nine High Hats, he had first set a Boeing F2B fighter plane down on the deck of the old *Langley*.[1] Nevertheless, May 12, 1941 marked a milestone in his career in that it was the first time he had landed a *monoplane* on a carrier. The *Enterprise* had departed San Diego on May 8, arriving at Pearl Harbor on the 11th. New aircraft, like Wade's F4F, had apparently been hoisted aboard by crane at the pier in San Diego. The air group did not fly aboard when the ship was at sea, as was customary. For this trip, the pilots went aboard in a much less dramatic fashion – they walked up the gangway while the ship was tied to a pier in San Diego. Wade's carrier landing in his new F4F on May 12 would have taken place in Hawaiian waters with the *Enterprise* steaming a few miles offshore.[2] He was now flying a different F4F-3 than the one he had picked up in Bethpage. This machine, serial number 3906, would become his regular plane until just before Pearl Harbor.

The F4F Wildcat was only the second monoplane to be accepted as a US Navy fighter, the first being the Brewster F2A Buffalo. The Wildcat was a better airplane than was the Buffalo, but both types left much to be desired when compared to other fighters that entered service at approximately the same time, such as the German Messerschmitt Bf 109; the British Hawker Hurricane and Supermarine Spitfire designs; and most importantly from the standpoint of US Navy pilots, Japan's Mitsubishi A6M2 "Zero" or "Zeke." The Messerschmitt, the Hurricane, the Spitfire, and the Zero were all low-wing monoplanes with slender lines and with undercarriage wheels and struts that retracted into the underside of the wing. The Buffalo and the Wildcat, on the other hand, had short, chubby fuselages with generally poor

---

[1]Wade McClusky logbook entries for July 1929. Philip McClusky collection.

[2]For confirmation of the whereabouts of the *Enterprise* in May 1941, see N. Jack "Dusty" Kleiss, *Never Call Me a Hero: A Legendary American Dive-Bomber Pilot Remembers the Battle of Midway* (New York: William Morrow, 2017): pp75–77, p83.

aerodynamic lines. The Grumman Corporation had been a pioneer among American aircraft manufacturers when it came to designing combat aircraft with wheels that could be retracted during flight, thereby reducing drag considerably. In a series of biplane fighters that it supplied to the Navy during the 1930s, Grumman had perfected an undercarriage that retracted into the fuselage just behind the engine. While certainly an advance over a fixed landing gear, the Grumman undercarriage, by retracting into the body of an aircraft instead of into the wing, necessitated a fuselage that has been accurately described as "pot-bellied" and "thick-waisted."[1] The best fighter planes in World War 2, such as the North American P-51 Mustang, had wheels that retracted into the wings, which allowed the fuselage to be slender and aerodynamic. Being a short, fat airplane was just one of the many problems to plague the F4F Wildcat in combat.

In early spring 1942, the F4F-3s of Fighting Six and other American carrier squadrons were replaced by a newer version of the Wildcat, the F4F-4, in what was supposed to be an upgrade. Both variants of the Wildcat were outclassed in terms of speed, maneuverability, and rate of climb by the Mitsubishi A6M2 Zero fighter flown by pilots of the Imperial Japanese Navy (IJN). The F4F-4 version of the Wildcat was a well-intentioned attempt by Grumman to do something about the deficiencies of the Wildcat's basic design. The results of the "upgrade" from the F4F-3 to the F4F-4 were, however, a mixed blessing at best. The F4F-4 was armed with six .50 caliber machine guns instead of the four carried in the F4F-3. In addition, the F4F-4 was equipped with armor plate on the back of the pilot's seat, self-sealing fuel tanks, and folding wings. The self-sealing tanks and the armor enabled the Wildcat to withstand more punishment than could the A6M2 Zero. Wings that could be folded were a great aid in stowing aircraft in the cramped spaces available

[1]Thomas Wildenberg, *Destined for Glory: Dive Bombing, Midway, and the Evolution of Carrier Airpower* (Annapolis: Naval Institute Press, 1998): p111.

on an aircraft carrier, especially in the hangar deck just below the flight deck. However, the armor plate, the rubber-lined fuel tanks that sealed themselves when a bullet passed through them, and the extra guns added considerable weight that slowed the Wildcat down. The extra weight also caused the F4F-4 to burn more fuel than had its predecessor, which considerably reduced the plane's combat radius. Most unfortunately, in an effort to save weight somewhere, the designers at Grumman decided that the F4F-4 would carry fewer rounds for its guns than had the F4F-3. This was an especially poor decision since the F4F-4 had six guns to feed instead of four. Thus, instead of 450 rounds per gun in the F4F-3, the 1,440 rounds of ammunition carried in the F4F-4 would enable the pilot to fire only 240 rounds from each of his six guns. Apparently, at least two of the six guns in the F4F-4 could be fired independently of the other four, meaning that a prudent pilot could conserve some of his ammunition. Nevertheless, 240 rounds per gun meant far shorter bursts of fire than had been possible in the F4F-3. Historian John B. Lundstrom has done the math and has concluded that a .50 caliber machine gun with only 240 rounds will run out of ammunition after being fired for exactly 18 seconds. With 450 rounds, however, a "fifty" can be fired for almost twice as long.[1] Thus, while the armor and the self-sealing fuel tanks in the F4F-4 version of the Wildcat were welcome defensive safety features, there is no doubt that the plane represented a definite step backward in terms of its offensive capabilities when compared to the F4F-3. Needless to say, this retrograde step did not inspire confidence in the pilots who would have to fly the F4F-4 in combat against the Japanese A6M2.

US Navy pilots would not get a truly great fighter plane until the Wildcat was replaced in front-line combat service during 1943 by the Grumman F6F Hellcat – an entirely new airplane, not an upgrade to an existing design. The F6F Hellcat was a low-wing

---

[1]Lundstrom, *The First Team*, p15, p173, p560. Tillman, *Enterprise*, p126.

monoplane with a powerful Pratt & Whitney R-2800 radial engine that delivered 2,000hp, and with landing gear struts and wheels that retracted into the wing, not the fuselage. In addition to allowing for a more slender fuselage, an undercarriage that retracted into the wing allowed for the wheels of the F6F to be much more widely spaced than those of the Wildcat, making the F6F much more stable during take-off and landing. While still not as slender as it perhaps could have been, the lines of the F6F were far more clean and aerodynamic than were those of its Wildcat forebear. With a 65 percent increase in horsepower over the Wildcat, the F6F Hellcat was fast and was blessed with plenty of ammunition for its six guns. Unfortunately, it was mid-1943 before enough Hellcats had been built to enable the F6F to become the standard front-line fighter plane on all of the US Navy's fleet carriers.[1]

The grave deficiencies in the Douglas TDB Devastator torpedo plane with which the US Navy began the war have been described in great detail elsewhere; and since Wade McClusky flew fighter planes and dive-bombers during the war, the tragic history of the deathtrap TBD Devastator need not be repeated here. Regarding the two aircraft types that McClusky did fly during the first year of the war, the mediocrity of the F4F Wildcat fighter plane stands in stark contrast to the superb qualities of the Douglas SBD Dauntless dive-bomber, the latter being the type that McClusky would fly at Midway.

There were a number of political, budgetary, and doctrinal reasons to explain why the development of a first-class fighter plane for the US Navy lagged far behind the development process that led to the SBD dive-bomber; a plane that in 1942 proved itself to be the world's finest dive-bomber and the premier aerial shipkilling weapon then in existence. Prewar US Navy fighter plane development had been hampered by flawed designs and by the effects of the Great Depression in forcing the Navy to operate

[1]Lundstrom, *The First Team*, p14, p561.

within extremely tight budgets during the 1930s. The most critical factor in explaining the mediocrity of the F4F Wildcat fighter, however, was that the US Navy's Bureau of Aeronautics displayed in the decade prior to Pearl Harbor a marked and surprising degree of confusion when it came to defining to everyone's satisfaction just exactly *what* the role of fighter planes in naval service was supposed to be. Indeed, historian Thomas Wildenberg states that without this prewar doctrinal confusion about the role of fighter planes in naval service:

> "the U.S. Navy could have entered World War II with a better fighter than the overburdened F4F-4, which suffered a degradation in performance when additional ordnance, armor plate, and self-sealing tanks were added to the plane after it had entered production."[1]

During the 1930s, some high-ranking American naval officers had the right idea and urged that the US Navy's fighters should be high-altitude interceptors designed for speed, rate of climb, and firepower so as to be well suited to the combat air patrol (CAP) role of protecting the home carrier at all costs from attacking enemy aircraft. Such a fighter would also be well suited to tangling with enemy fighter planes when escorting American torpedo planes and dive-bombers in attacks against enemy shipping. The proponents of speed and firepower above all else squared off with other American naval aviators who felt that naval fighters should be a multi-role aircraft able to carry out bombing attacks against enemy shipping while protecting American dive-bombers and torpedo planes while those types made their attacks. Many of the multi-role advocates even thought the Navy's fighters should be two-seater aircraft with a pilot and a radioman/gunner. Unfortunately, the multi-role advocates, who had no qualms about adding weight to the Navy's fighters, held the upper hand

[1]Wildenberg, *Destined for Glory*, p142.

during the 1930s. As a result, US Navy fighters during the 1930s were consistently overweight and underpowered.[1]

The true potential of American naval fighters in World War 2 would not become fully apparent until the Navy re-equipped with the aforementioned Grumman F6F Hellcat in 1943. In the F6F Hellcat, the US Navy had a fighter plane that could do everything that was needed. During the Central Pacific Drive that began with the American invasion of the Gilbert Islands in November 1943, carrier-based Hellcats had the speed and the firepower to perform superbly in the combat air patrol role of protecting the fleet. But they could, and did, do far more. In the island campaigns of the Central Pacific advance, Hellcat fighters were usually sent in first to attack land targets before American dive-bombers and horizontal bombers arrived. More than a match for the A6M2 Zero, Hellcats could shoot down any enemy fighter aircraft in the air and then strafe those that had not yet taken off.[2] F6F Hellcats were also ideal in the role of escorts, protecting American dive-bombers and torpedo planes during attacks against Japanese shipping.

In 1944, the Navy received another top-notch fighter plane: the Vought F4U Corsair, a type that had initially been assigned to land-based Marine fighter squadrons due to the fact that, unlike the Hellcat, the Corsair was not an easy plane to land on a carrier. Even faster than the F6F, the Corsair was simply too good an airplane to remain ashore, however. With six .50 caliber machine guns and a very fast – by World War 2 standards – top speed of 400mph, the Corsair was a fearsome opponent in a dogfight. In addition, the rugged and versatile Corsair could also carry a 500lb bomb beneath the fuselage and/or underwing rockets, making it a superb ground attack platform as well. After some modifications to the aircraft and adjustments in the training of the pilots who

---

[1]Wildenberg. *Destined for Glory*, p114, pp141–142, pp146–148.
[2]Stafford, *The Big E*, pp330–334.

would land the plane on aircraft carriers, the Corsair became a very welcome addition to the fleet in 1944.[1]

Wade's personal life was hectic in the months leading up to the Pearl Harbor attack. The family's zigzag journeys back and forth across the United States at the whim of the Navy Department were probably why Wade and Millicent chose to send young Wade Sanford (Pat) to a private high school, Principia, where he could board. In the decade prior to Pearl Harbor, the frequent changes of station never abated for the family. Shortly before Pearl Harbor, Millicent, with the now ten-year-old Pat, would again follow her husband out to Pearl Harbor in 1941, arriving in Honolulu from Los Angeles on the *Matsonia* on September 3.[2] Mother and son would only stay three months. The deteriorating international situation may have contributed to this decision. War with Japan seemed to be unavoidable and the tempo of Wade's training picked up. During the month of November 1941, Wade flew almost every day, practicing bombing and gunnery, making 14 carrier landings (including his first night-time carrier landing), and logging a total of 43 hours and 30 minutes of flying time for the month.[3]

[1]Wildenberg, *Destined for Glory*, p154.

[2]National Archives and Records Administration (NARA); Washington, DC; *Passenger Lists of Vessels Arriving at Honolulu, Hawaii, compiled 02/13/1900 – 12/30/1953*; National Archives Microfilm Publication: *A3422*; Roll: *233*; Record Group Title: *Records of the Immigration and Naturalization Service, 1787–2004*; Record Group Number: *RG 85*Ancestry.com. *Honolulu, Hawaii, Passenger and Crew Lists, 1900-1959* [database on-line]. Provo, UT, USA: Ancestry.com Operations, Inc, 2009.

Original data: *Passenger Lists of Vessels Arriving or Departing at Honolulu, Hawaii, 1900–1954.*

NARA Microfilm Publication A3422, 269 rolls; A3510, 175 rolls; A3574, 27 rolls; A3575, 1 roll; A3615, 1 roll; A3614, 80 rolls; A3568 & A3569, 187 rolls; A3571, 64 rolls; A4156, 348 rolls. Records of the Immigration and Naturalization Service, Record Group 85. National Archives, Washington, DC.

[3]Wade McClusky, pilot logbook entries for November 1941. Philip McClusky collection.

The *Enterprise*, flying the three star flag of V Adm William F. Halsey, Jr, set sail from Pearl Harbor on November 28, 1941. Its mission was to deliver a squadron of Marine fighter planes and their pilots to Wake Island, an American possession 2,000 miles west of Oahu. If Wade was in any doubt as to how close war was, those doubts would have been removed shortly after the air group landed on the Big E's flight deck that day. He and every other *Enterprise* pilot was handed a written order signed by *Enterprise* captain George D. Murray and by Adm Halsey that read:

> "1. The Enterprise is now operating under war conditions.
> 2. At any time, day or night, we must be ready for instant action.
> 3. Hostile submarines may be encountered."[1]

A week after Wade and *Enterprise* had set out for Wake Island, Millicent and young Pat put to sea themselves, headed in the opposite direction. Mother and son departed Hawaii aboard the Matson Line's *Lurline* on December 5, 1941, headed for California just two days prior to the Pearl Harbor attack. The *Lurline* was full to capacity in what one Hawaii newspaper called "the big Mainland Christmas rush."[2] The same paper continued: "The departure was a gala affair, and lei sellers did a land office business."[3] For most of the passengers, this capacity sailing of the *Lurline* was more than a "Christmas rush." It was, in fact the beginning of the evacuation of dependents from what would soon

[1]As quoted in Stafford, *The Big E*, p14.

[2]"Record Mail Goes Out When Lurline Departs" *Honolulu Advertiser*. December 6, 1941. P3. Available online at: www.newspapers.com/image/259703612/?terms=Wade%2BS.%2BMcClusky. Accessed September 16, 2017.

[3]"Record Mail Goes Out When Lurline Departs" *Honolulu Advertiser*. December 6, 1941. P3. Available online at: www.newspapers.com/image/259703612/?terms=Wade%2BS.%2BMcClusky. Accessed September 16, 2017.

be a war zone. Even Adm Nimitz left his wife stateside when he came to Pearl Harbor in late December 1941 to take over as the new commander of the US Pacific Fleet. As for why Wade Sanford and Millicent were heading back to the mainland at this time, Wade's daughter-in-law Carole McClusky-Pewthers claims that the scuttlebutt around Pearl Harbor at the time the *Enterprise* departed Pearl Harbor on November 28, 1941 was that the big carrier was headed for Bremerton in Washington state to be drydocked and overhauled. Millicent wanted to be there to greet Wade when the ship arrived. The Big E's actual destination, Wake Island to deliver Marine fighter aircraft and their pilots, was of course a closely guarded secret until after the ship set sail.[1]

In fact all seven of America's aircraft carriers were mercifully absent from Pearl Harbor on December 7, 1941, but the *Enterprise*, with Wade McClusky and Fighting Six embarked, did not entirely escape tragedy that day. Returning from Wake, the *Enterprise* was scheduled to dock at Pearl Harbor on December 8. Tension was high on board the *Enterprise* on the trip out to Wake. War with Japan seemed imminent, but nobody expected it to begin in Hawaii. American outposts further west, such as Wake, Guam, and the Philippines, seemed far more likely as first strike targets for the Japanese. The *Enterprise* and its escorts were approximately 200 miles west of Pearl Harbor, inbound, at dawn on December 7, 1941. With no idea that an attack on Pearl Harbor was imminent, but nonetheless operating on what was essentially a war footing, Adm Halsey ordered the launch of 18 *Enterprise* SBD dive-bombers shortly after 6.00am that fateful Sunday morning. The idea was for the *Enterprise* dive-bombers, under the command of "Brigham" Young, who had moved up to air group commander, to search for Japanese submarines ahead of the task force and then to fly on and land at NAS Ford Island in the middle of Pearl Harbor. Thus, Cdr Young's SBD pilots had the misfortune to find themselves over Pearl Harbor at the height

[1]Telephone conversation with Carole McClusky-Pewthers, September 28, 2017.

of the Japanese attack. American antiaircraft gunners afloat and ashore at Pearl were firing at any plane in the sky and four of the *Enterprise* dive-bombers were shot down, with two of the pilots and all four of the rear seat gunners killed (the first American "friendly fire" casualties of World War 2). A fifth badly shot-up *Enterprise* SBD made a wheels-up water landing in the harbor. Its pilot and gunner survived. When word reached the *Enterprise* by radio of the Japanese attack shortly after 8.00am, Wade McClusky and the 13 pilots under his command in Fighting Six were ordered to man their Wildcats and warm up the engines in preparation for take-off. Every pilot in the squadron was eager to seek out the attacking Japanese aircraft. Ultimately, however, Adm Halsey decided that in the absence of definite information as to the exact location of the Japanese aircraft carriers that had launched the attack it would be wiser to use his fighter planes to fly combat air patrol over his own ships rather than sending them to look for the attacking Japanese aircraft. The 14 Wildcats in Fighting Six were thus divided into small groups, which took turns flying CAP over the *Enterprise* for the remainder of the day. Wade McClusky flew his first combat mission of the war when he took off at approximately 12.30pm at the head of a four-strong section of F4Fs to fly the early afternoon CAP shift.[1]

Late in the afternoon, when the Japanese aircraft carrier striking force had recovered its aircraft and was well to the northwest of the Hawaiian Islands heading back across the north Pacific to Japan, an *Enterprise* dive-bomber pilot misidentified a small group of American cruisers and destroyers steaming south of Oahu as a Japanese fleet. This sighting began a chain of events that resulted in some of McClusky's fighter pilots themselves needlessly becoming friendly fire casualties after dark on December 7. On the basis of this erroneous contact report, Adm Halsey ordered a strike force of dive-bombers and torpedo planes to be sent out. While McClusky and seven other Fighting Six pilots

---

[1]Lundstrom, *The First Team*, pp18–20. Stafford, *The Big E*, pp20–24.

remained behind to fly CAP patrols, six *Enterprise* fighter planes under the command of Lt (junior grade) Francis Hebel took off to escort the strike force.[1] The American strike group, under the command of Torpedo Squadron Six (VT-6) commanding officer Lt Eugene Lindsey, who would perish six months later making a torpedo attack against the Japanese carrier *Kaga* at Midway, never found the "targets," thus fortuitously preventing a possible accidental attack by American aircraft against American ships. All of the dive-bombers and torpedo planes returned safely to the *Enterprise*. Unwisely, however, Adm Halsey had ordered the six fighter planes to land at Pearl Harbor and had a message to that effect radioed ahead to NAS Ford Island. Despite the radioed warning to expect "friendly" aircraft, and as "Brigham" Young's dive-bomber pilots had discovered earlier in the day, Pearl Harbor was absolutely the worst place in the world for any American pilot to attempt a landing on December 7, 1941. Making matters worse was that Hebel's group of F4Fs arrived over Pearl after dark. In the inevitable friendly fire shooting gallery that erupted over the harbor when Hebel's fighters tried to land, four of the planes were shot down and three of Wade McClusky's fighter pilots – Hebel, Ensign Herbert H. Menges, and Lt (junior grade) Eric Allen – were killed.[2]

McClusky himself got his first look at the devastation at Pearl Harbor on December 8, but from a distance. Adm Halsey was not going to have his pilots attempt any more landings at Pearl Harbor for the time being. Late in the afternoon of Monday, December 8, as the *Enterprise* prepared to enter Pearl Harbor, McClusky took off at the head of a flight of eight Wildcat fighters, which he led to Wheeler Field, an Army Air Forces fighter base approximately 10 miles north of Pearl Harbor. Wheeler had not been spared in the Japanese attack. Regarding the scene awaiting McClusky and the pilots with him, John B. Lundstrom writes that: "the visit to

[1]Stafford, *The Big E*, pp27–30.

[2]Stafford, *The Big E*, pp27–30. Lundstrom, *The First Team*, pp21–25.

Wheeler, once the pride of the Air Corps' pursuit forces, gave the VF-6 pilots . . . their first look at war. Wheeler was a shambles of bomb craters, over forty burnt fighters, bullet holes, and broken glass. After the comforts of life on board ship, war-torn Wheeler was a shock."[1] The *Enterprise* was in port for just ten hours, barely long enough to take on fuel and restock provisions. Early on the morning of the 9th, once the *Enterprise* had cleared the harbor entrance, McClusky led his squadron, now augmented by four additional F4Fs to a total of 12, on the short flight from Wheeler back to the deck of the *Enterprise*.[2]

The *Enterprise* spent most of the next month patrolling the waters north of Oahu to prevent a return of any Japanese striking force, with occasional brief visits to Pearl Harbor for refueling and resupply. McClusky and Fighting Six flew CAP missions as the *Enterprise* performed sentry duty, guarding the Hawaiian chain of islands, including Midway. It was on one of the ship's reprovisioning visits, on December 16, that the *Enterprise* air group landed at the NAS Ford Island for the first time since the attack instead of being diverted to places like Wheeler. McClusky and the other *Enterprise* pilots thus got their first close look at the actual devastation at Pearl Harbor itself.[3] The view was sobering. *Arizona*, its forward magazines having exploded, had settled to the bottom. Its decks awash, *Arizona*'s forward tripod mast was canted forward at an angle of 45 degrees. *Nevada* was still stranded at the side of the entrance channel where she had run aground after getting underway and attempting to clear the harbor mouth during the attack. Perhaps the sight most difficult to bear was that of the overturned hull of the *Oklahoma*, its port side having been ripped open by five torpedoes dropped by Nakajima B5N torpedo planes.

---

[1]Lundstrom, *The First Team*, pp28–29.

[2]Stafford, *The Big E*, pp33–34. Lundstrom, *The First Team*, pp28–29.

[3]Lundstrom, *The First Team*, pp29–30, p38, p39, p45, p55, p59. Stafford, *The Big E*, pp35–40.

On January 11, 1942, the *Enterprise* departed Pearl Harbor with an escort of cruisers and destroyers on its first true combat mission of the war. Once again, Adm Halsey was using the Big E as his flagship. The newly appointed Commander-in-Chief, US Fleet Adm Ernest J. King, had ordered the new Pacific Fleet commander, Adm Chester W. Nimitz, to reinforce a chain of island strong points that would enable communications to be maintained between Hawaii and Australia. Samoa was a vital link in that chain of outposts but its garrison of American marines was badly understrength. Accordingly, in early January 4,798 US Marines of the 2nd Brigade, along with construction equipment to be used for completing a new airfield on Tutuila, American Samoa's main island, were hastily loaded aboard ships at San Diego and dispatched to the South Pacific. This troop convoy sailed with a naval escort that included the aircraft carrier USS *Yorktown* (CV-5), an exact twin of the *Enterprise*. Aboard the *Yorktown* and in command of the force was R Adm Frank Jack Fletcher. The convoy arrived at Pago Pago harbor on January 19, 1942. The *Enterprise*, with its escort of cruisers and destroyers, had sailed separately and had arrived in Samoan waters a day earlier to help cover the unloading of the Marines and their equipment. On January 26, the *Yorktown* and *Enterprise* and their respective escorts were formed into one task force. Adm Halsey, senior to Adm Fletcher, assumed tactical command of the combined force and headed north. His orders were to begin, in a small way, offensive operations against the Japanese in the Pacific.[1]

Halsey's mission was to launch hit-and-run airstrikes against six Japanese-held atolls in the Gilbert and Marshall Island groups

---

[1]Lundstrom, *The First Team*, pp67–73. Stafford, *The Big E*, pp41–44. Frank O. Hough, Henry I. Shaw, and Verle E. Ludwig, *U.S. Marine Corps Operations in World War II*. Vol. 1. *Pearl Harbor to Guadalcanal* (Washington, DC: Historical Branch, G-3 Division, Headquarters, US Marine Corps, 1958): pp86–89. Available online at: www.ibiblio.org/hyperwar/USMC/I/USMC-I-II-3.html. Accessed May 1, 2016.

in the central Pacific. Later, beginning in November 1943, the Gilberts and Marshalls would become bloody battlegrounds when American marines and infantry, vigorously supported by naval and air forces that had grown exponentially stronger during the preceding 18 months, would wrest control of both island groups from the Japanese. In early 1942, however, the temporarily limited strength of American forces meant that for now, hit-and-run raids would have to do.

A few *Enterprise* pilots had already seen some combat action. Dive-bomber pilots from the *Enterprise* had attacked three Japanese submarines caught on the surface in Hawaiian waters on December 10, 1941, apparently sinking one of them. However, for Wade McClusky and for most of the *Enterprise* air group, the early raids in the Marshall Islands would be their baptism of fire in combat against enemy forces.

The *Yorktown* and its escorts were detached from the *Enterprise* task force on January 29 so that they could strike the more southerly targets. The two carriers would operate approximately 300 nautical miles apart from each other during the raids.[1] Adm Halsey chose February 1, 1942 as the day for the attacks. Wade McClusky's role in these attacks began early on the morning of February 1, 1942 when he led half a dozen VF-6 Wildcats in the role of fighter-bombers in a strike against Wotje Atoll in the Marshalls. For this mission, in addition to its .50 caliber machine guns, each Wildcat was carrying two 100lb bombs, slung on racks, one under each wing. One of the most important Japanese seaplane bases in the central Pacific, Wotje also had a 5,000ft runway for landplanes.[2] Wotje was

[1]Stafford, *The Big E*, p46. Lundstrom, *The First Team*, p80 (distance computed from map).

[2]Lundstrom, *The First Team*, pp78–79, p81. Samuel Eliot Morison, *History of United States Naval Operations in World War II*. Vol. 3. *The Rising Sun in the Pacific, 1931–April 1942* (Boston: Little, Brown and Company, 1948, 1954): p261, p263. Dirk H.R. Spennemann, "The Japanese Seaplane Base on Wotje Island, Wotje Atoll" 2000. URL:

close enough to the *Enterprise* and its escorts that the atoll was scheduled for a shelling from naval gunfire as well as an air attack. The airstrip was on the atoll's largest island (also called Wotje). It was there that McClusky's group dropped their bombs and then swept in low to strafe with their .50 caliber machine guns. The VF-6 pilots finished their work at approximately 7.15am. As McClusky's F4Fs headed back to the *Enterprise*, the heavy cruisers *Northampton* and *Salt Lake City*, under the command of then R Adm Raymond A. Spruance, opened fire with their 8in. guns on Japanese ships in Wotje's lagoon and against buildings on shore. Overall, the damage done to Wotje in the morning attacks was minimal due to the fact that the 100lb bombs carried by McClusky's pilots were too small to do much real harm and the gunners on Adm Spruance's cruisers had not yet mastered the art of shore bombardment. Clearly, Wotje would need more attention from *Enterprise* aircraft that day. Accordingly, shortly after noon nine bomb-carrying torpedo planes and eight dive-bombers led by *Enterprise* air group commander Howard Young swept in over Wotje. Carrying much heavier bombs than McClusky's fighters had, the dive-bombers and torpedo planes destroyed a Japanese cargo ship that had been anchored in the lagoon at Wotje and also bombed buildings near the Wotje airstrip.[1]

Although he was not assigned to accompany Young on the second air strike against Wotje, McClusky's day was not over yet. Late in the afternoon, while flying combat air patrol near the *Enterprise* with a dozen other fighter pilots, McClusky assisted

http://marshall.csu.edu.au/Marshalls/html/WWII/Wotje.html. Accessed June 7, 2016. Jonathan Parshall and Anthony Tully. *Shattered Sword: The Untold Story of the Battle of Midway*. (Washington, DC: Potomac Books, 2007): p50, p99.

[1] Lundstrom, *The First Team*, p77, pp81–82, p89, pp92–93. Stafford, *The Big E*, pp54–55, pp58–59. Stephen L. Moore, *Pacific Payback: The Carrier Aviators Who Avenged Pearl Harbor at the Battle of Midway* (New York: NAL Caliber, 2014): pp100–101. Tillman, *Enterprise*, p52. Thomas B. Buell, *The Quiet Warrior: A Biography of Admiral Raymond A. Spruance* (Annapolis: Naval Institute Press, 1974, 1987): pp114–118.

two of them, Lt (junior grade) James Daniels and Lt Roger Mehle, in shooting down a Japanese Mitsubishi G3M "Nell" twin-engined land-based bomber, one of two that had flown out from an airstrip on the island of Taroa, part of Maloelap Atoll, to attack the American ships. Jim Daniels did most of the work in bringing this aircraft down.[1] In his official report, Wade said his pilots also brought down a "twin float seaplane" at approximately 3.00pm local time.[2] Incidentally, by all accounts, Wade McClusky was well liked by the pilots who served under him in Fighting Six. Jim Daniels became a lifelong friend who would often stop by the McClusky household in Ruxton, Maryland after the war to have a drink and reminisce about the war with Wade.[3]

The pair of Mitsubishis were not the first land-based bombers to attack the *Enterprise* that day. Earlier in the afternoon, while he was taking a break back aboard the *Enterprise* between the morning mission he had flown against Wotje and the late-afternoon CAP shift he was scheduled to fly, Wade McClusky would have witnessed a spectacular episode in the career of the *Enterprise*, a ship that experienced many spectacular episodes during the war. Shortly before 2.00pm five other "Nells" from the Japanese airfield at Taroa found the *Enterprise* and made a bombing run. All of the bombs missed, but at least one exploded close enough alongside to mortally wound one American sailor and cause minor damage to the ship's hull. The plane that scored the near miss, flown by squadron leader Lt Nakai Kazuo, was badly damaged by the American fighters flying CAP. Instead of trying to escape with his comrades, Nakai turned his crippled aircraft back toward the *Enterprise* and tried to crash the flight deck. It would

---

[1]Lundstrom, *The First Team*, p77, p82, pp92–93. Stafford, *The Big E*, pp54–55, pp58–59. Moore, *Pacific Payback*, pp100–101. Tillman, *Enterprise*, p52.

[2]National Archives and Records Administration (hereinafter NARA). Record Group (hereinafter RG) 38. Records of the Office of the Chief of Naval Operations. WW II Action and Operational Reports. Box 966. Wade McClusky Action Report as CO of Fighting Six During the Marshalls Raid. Enclosure D. P1.

[3]Interviews with Philip McClusky, December 27 and 29, 2016.

not be until late 1944 that the idea of kamikaze suicide attacks would become a formal, officially sanctioned policy for Japanese pilots, but there were isolated earlier instances of Japanese suicide attacks and this was one. The defensive measures taken, consisting primarily of violent high-speed maneuvering ordered by *Enterprise* Capt George D. Murray and an intense curtain of antiaircraft fire thrown up by the ships of the task force, got an unexpected boost when a young aviation machinist's mate named Bruno Peter Gaido ran across the *Enterprise* flight deck and jumped into the rear seat of an SBD parked there and began firing away with that aircraft's twin .30 caliber machine guns at Nakai's incoming bomber.[1] This confrontation has been retold many times, never with more verve than by Edward Stafford, who writes that:

"In a final right turn the enemy pilot [Nakai] tried for a deck crash. His right wing tip sliced through Gaido's SBD, shearing its tail off three feet from where the mechanic furiously kept up his fire. The right wing of the enemy plane separated from the fuselage and skidded into the port catwalk, the fuel from its ruptured tanks drenching the ship forward to the island and up into the superstructure. The broken Dauntless was knocked far over to port on the extreme aft edge of the flight deck. In its rear seat Gaido stood to depress his guns, hammering their tracers into the wreckage of . . . [Nakai's] bomber as it settled into the sea astern."[2]

Three months later, on June 4, 1942 at Midway, the same Bruno Peter Gaido (who had been promoted one grade on the spot on February 1 by Adm Halsey, a witness to Gaido's duel with Nakai's aircraft) flew as the rear seat gunner in another *Enterprise* SBD, that of Ensign Frank O'Flaherty of Scouting Squadron Six

---

[1]Stafford, *The Big E*, pp57–58. Lundstrom, *The First Team*, p77, pp91–92.
[2]Stafford, *The Big E*, p58.

(VS-6). After participating in the attack that Wade McClusky led on the Japanese aircraft carriers *Kaga* and *Akagi* on June 4, 1942, O'Flaherty's Dauntless had run out of fuel and O'Flaherty was forced to ditch uncomfortably close to the Japanese fleet. O'Flaherty and Gaido were plucked from their liferaft by the crew of the Japanese destroyer *Makigumo*. Both men were interrogated (quite possibly under torture) and later, on June 15, murdered by their captors.[1]

The *Enterprise* received a rousing welcome upon its return to Pearl Harbor on February 5, 1942.[2] Even though the damage inflicted by *Enterprise* and *Yorktown* pilots in the February 1 air strikes against the Japanese central Pacific bases was minimal, the American people were delighted that the Navy was taking the fight to the enemy. Wade McClusky and the rest of the ship's company were able to unwind on Oahu for a week before the ship sailed on its next mission. The *Enterprise* and its escorts, now officially known as Task Force 16, the name that that group of ships would take into the Battle of Midway, sailed west from Pearl Harbor on February 14. The objective this time was Wake Island, 2,000 miles west of Hawaii.

An American possession, Wake had fallen to Japanese invading forces on December 23, 1941. The American Marine defenders on Wake, aided by civilian construction workers who had been sent to Wake shortly before the outbreak of war, had fought with a tenacity that had made the atoll a particularly tough nut to crack; it took the Japanese more than two weeks to overrun Wake. The Marines on Wake, including the fighter pilots that the *Enterprise* had delivered just prior to Pearl Harbor, had actually repulsed the first Japanese attempt to put troops ashore on December 11. The heroism of Wake's defenders was, like the February 1 airstrikes

---

[1]Stafford, *The Big E*, p58. Parshall and Tully, *Shattered Sword*, pp319–320. Robert E. Barde, "Midway: Tarnished Victory" *Military Affairs*. Vol. 47; No. 4. December 1983, pp188–192.

[2]Stafford, *The Big E*, p60.

against the Japanese bases in the Marshalls and Gilberts, a much-needed morale builder for the American people in the grim months immediately following the Pearl Harbor attack.[1] A relief mission in the form of a small task force built around the carrier *Saratoga* had departed Pearl Harbor on December 16 headed for Wake. That force was recalled and the mission cancelled on December 23 when it became clear that Wake was about to fall to the enemy and that the *Saratoga* task force was judged to be not powerful enough to attempt a reconquest of the atoll. The recall of the Wake relief force had been an especially bitter pill to swallow, both within the US Navy and among the American public at large.[2]

As in the February 1 raids, this attack on Wake was to be a combination of bombing delivered by carrier-based aircraft coupled with shelling by cruiser gunfire. At dawn on February 24, 1942, the *Enterprise* was in position off Wake and 52 aircraft took off for the attack. The brunt of the attack was to be delivered by SBD dive-bombers, along with some torpedo planes that were carrying bombs instead of torpedoes for the occasion. Wade McClusky, with five other VF-6 Wildcats, was tasked with protecting the group from any Japanese fighter planes that might be in the vicinity.[3]

No Japanese fighter planes were encountered, but the fighters did see some action. While the *Enterprise* bombers were pounding the most promising targets on Wake, which included blowing up a group of large storage tanks that the American pilots knew to be full of American 100 octane aviation fuel that had been delivered prior to Pearl Harbor,[4] McClusky was alerted by radio that a dive-bomber pilot had spotted a Japanese Kawanishi H6K Type 97 flying boat airborne at low altitude a few miles east of

[1]Stafford, *The Big E*, pp62–63.

[2]Lundstrom, *The First Team*, pp44–54.

[3]Stafford, *The Big E*, pp62–65.

[4]Stafford, The Big E, p66. Moore, *Pacific Payback*, p119.

the atoll.[1] The Kawanishi was an enormous four-engined airplane, nicknamed "Emily" by the Americans, with a crew of nine that proved superb for long-range maritime patrol but, being slow and sluggish to maneuver, was no match for a fighter plane, much less for a group of them. McClusky and two other VF-6 pilots displayed excellent teamwork in destroying the lumbering giant.[2] As Edward Stafford describes the attack:

"The skipper [McClusky] made the first run, silencing the enemy gunners and smoking the left outboard engine. B.H. Bayers was next, his tracers raking the fuselage and starting a second engine burning. Then, skinny, aggressive Roger Mehle bored in, firing in long, repeated bursts. Before his eyes the big plane blew apart. Ducking under the debris, Mehle saw the enemy pilot tumbling toward the sea."[3]

All of the American pilots were enjoying having the opportunity to strike back at the enemy to the extent that a bit of inter-squadron rivalry became apparent. After destroying the Kawanishi, McClusky and his VF-6 pilots happened upon a group of *Enterprise* dive-bombers that were bombing and strafing a Japanese patrol boat. McClusky and the fighter pilots were getting set up to help out by making strafing runs against the target when the dive-bomber pilots curtly informed McClusky by radio that this was *their* target. That they, the dive-bombers, had the situation well in hand and would McClusky please be so good as to take his fighter jockeys and kindly stay out of the way?[4]

The day after the Wake raid, Adm Nimitz radioed Halsey suggesting that the latter attack Marcus Island as well. Always

[1]Stafford, *The Big E*, p66.

[2]Tillman, *Enterprise*, p54

[3]Stafford, *The Big E*, p67.

[4]Lundstrom, *The First Team*, p142.

eager for a fight, Halsey was delighted with the idea and immediately headed for Marcus with the *Enterprise* and two cruisers. Marcus lies approximately 900 miles west-northwest of Wake and is less than 1,200 miles from Japan. A prewar Japanese possession, Marcus had a garrison of Japanese troops and an airstrip. The *Enterprise* air group, still under the command of "Brigham" Young, made its attack on March 4, 1942 with 32 dive-bombers. Wade McClusky's task, as at Wake, was to accompany and guard the bombers with a force of six fighter planes (including his own). No enemy aircraft attempted to interfere with the American dive-bombers as they delivered their payloads but antiaircraft fire from the ground was heavy. Because the attack was made at dawn under a heavy overcast weather front, the *Enterprise* dive-bomber pilots were unsure how much damage they had inflicted, but they thought they had blown up an oil tank and damaged some buildings.[1] For McClusky, the mission was routine, but one of his VF-6 pilots, Lt Jim Gray (who would take command of Fighting Six upon McClusky's promotion to air group commander) got lost and barely made it back to the *Enterprise* with just few gallons of gasoline left in the tanks of his F4F.[2]

The *Enterprise* arrived back at Pearl Harbor on March 10 and the pilots were given a week off to rest. Wade thus got to spend a week relaxing at the Royal Hawaiian Hotel located right on Waikiki Beach, a facility that had been taken over by the Navy for the duration as a rest and relaxation center. Wade would need the break since his return to duty on March 17 would bring vastly increased responsibilities.[3]

---

[1]Moore, *Pacific Payback*, pp126–133.

[2]Lundstrom, *The First Team*, pp145–149. Stafford, *The Big E*, pp67–72.

[3]Stafford, *The Big E*, p61, p72, p121. Lundstrom, *The First Team*, p149, pp170–171.

8

COMMANDER, AIR GROUP SIX

Wade McClusky was promoted to command of the entire *Enterprise* air group on March 21, 1942.[1] He had been hand-picked for the job by Adm Halsey himself. McClusky's orders to assume command of Air Group Six came from the office of Adm Nimitz, now Pacific Fleet commander. The orders are printed on letterhead bearing the header "United States Pacific Fleet: Flagship of the Commander-in-Chief" and are signed by Capt Harold C. Train, assistant chief-of-staff to Nimitz. Halsey's involvement in choosing Wade is stated clearly: "These orders are issued at the express request of the Commander Aircraft, Battle Force [ie Halsey]. The urgency of this change has prompted the Commander-in-Chief, U.S. Pacific Fleet, to issue these orders subject to confirmation by the Chief of the Bureau of Navigation."[2] Formal approval from the Bureau of Navigation of Nimitz's action in making McClusky commander of Air Group Six came through on April 23, 1942.[3] It had been mid-April before Joe

---

[1]John B. Lundstrom, *The First Team: Pacific Naval Air Combat from Pearl Harbor to Midway*. (Annapolis: Naval Institute Press, 1984): p137. Barrett Tillman, *Enterprise: America's Fightingest Ship and the Men Who Helped Win World War II* (New York: Simon & Schuster, 2012): p55.

[2]Capt Harold C. Train (as assistant chief-of-staff to Adm Nimitz) to McClusky, March 21, 1942. Philip McClusky collection.

[3]Chief, Bureau of Navigation (R Adm Randall Jacobs) to McClusky, April 23, 1942. Philip McClusky collection.

Rochefort had decoded enough Japanese naval radio traffic to enable him to inform Adms Nimitz and King that the Japanese were planning a major operation in the Central Pacific Area.[1] Thus, at the time of Wade's appointment as air group commander on March 21, neither Nimitz nor Halsey had any idea that in just a few short months there was going to be a major battle in the waters off Midway. The upcoming battle thus had nothing to do with Wade's appointment per se.

While they did not yet know about Japanese plans to invade Midway, Nimitz and Halsey *did* know by mid-March, however, that the remaining months of 1942 were going to be a very busy time for the US Pacific Fleet's aircraft carriers. For instance, the "urgency" referred to by Train in the orders to McClusky quoted above was almost certainly a reference to the fact that Nimitz and Halsey had just learned on March 19 of the plans for the Doolittle Raid on Tokyo. They had been asked by Capt Donald B. Duncan, who had traveled to Pearl Harbor on behalf of the joint chiefs-of-staff, to provide a second carrier to escort the USS *Hornet*, which would be laden with Col Doolittle's 16 Army B-25 bombers, into Japanese waters. Nimitz agreed to provide *Enterprise* as protection for *Hornet* and Halsey had agreed to command the combined task force.[2] Therefore, an important appointment such as choosing a successor to Howard Young as commander of the *Enterprise* air group at that critical time was a decision to be made with great care. Halsey and Nimitz had liked what they had seen in Wade's aggressive leadership of Fighting Six. With "Brigham" Young's tour as commander of Air Group Six coming to a close, Wade McClusky was the natural choice to succeed to the position.

As mentioned in Chapter 2, Wade's promotion to air group commander seemed to anger some of the pilots. Exactly why remains a mystery. Perhaps some of the dive-bomber pilots were

---

[1] E. B. Potter, *Nimitz* (Annapolis: Naval Institute Press, 1976, 1987): pp65–67.

[2] Potter, *Nimitz*, pp65–66.

angry that McClusky decided to switch from flying a fighter back to flying a dive-bomber as group commander, although Howard Young had done the same thing when he became air group commander without arousing any animosity. Just like Wade, Howard Young had commanded Fighting Six before being promoted. Also just like Wade, Young chose to fly a dive-bomber while he served as *Enterprise* air group commander.

It should be noted that there were *Enterprise* pilots who thought that Wade McClusky was the perfect choice for the role. Young Bill Pittman revered McClusky and was honored to be chosen to fly wing on the group commander at Midway.[1] Roger Mehle also admired McClusky. Mehle had enjoyed serving under McClusky's command in Fighting Six and never hesitated to say that he felt McClusky's performance at Midway was brilliant. During the research for his 1967 Midway classic, *Incredible Victory*, Walter Lord sent a standardized questionnaire to every veteran of the battle he could locate. The questionnaire he sent to Roger Mehle, who during the battle was executive officer to Jim Gray in Fighting Six, is undated, but is probably from 1966 or 1967. At the time, Mehle was a rear admiral in command of the Navy's Strike Warfare Division at the Pentagon. One of Lord's questions, and Roger Mehle's answer to it, are worth quoting in full:

From Walter Lord's questionnaire:

"In times of great stress, some people show unusual ingenuity and self-reliance; others do incredibly stupid things. Do you remember any outstanding examples of either? There was, for instance, the rear-seat man who somehow cradles a heavy machine gun in his arms when the mount broke [Floyd Atkins; rear-seat gunner in Bill Pittman's SBD] . . . and the pilot who splashed and rowed six miles back to his carrier in his rubber raft . . . and the Yorktown men who neatly arranged their shoes side-by-side before abandoning ship. Can you recall anything too?"

[1] Interview with Philip McClusky, December 29, 2016.

Roger Mehle's reply:

"Yes—The redoubtable resolve and brilliant leadership and airmanship of (then) LCDR C. Wade McClusky, Commander Air Group Six, who I am certain turned the tide of the Battle of Midway in his decision to seek out the Japanese carrier force, after having been unable to locate it in the position given him, even though some of his attack aircraft had reached the point of no return. The results of this particular attack, after fruitless and costly attacks by VT8 and VT6, eliminated three of the four Japanese carriers."[1]

Mehle errs in lumping the third carrier, *Soryu*, in with the ships destroyed by *Enterprise* dive-bombers in the morning attack. In fact, *Enterprise* SBD pilots destroyed the *Kaga* and the *Akagi* in the morning attack. *Soryu* was dispatched by Max Leslie's Bombing Three from the *Yorktown*. However, although he was a young man at the time of Midway, Roger Mehle was no naive novice. Rather, by June 4, 1942, Mehle was already a seasoned combat pilot whose views should not be dismissed lightly.

McClusky's decision that as air group commander, he should fly a dive-bomber, not a fighter, was perfectly natural. The SBD Dauntless had the longest range of any American carrier-based aircraft in the first half of 1942. Flying a Dauntless would allow McClusky to remain with Air Group Six at its maximum striking distance. The range handicap of the F4F-4 Wildcat fighter plane made that type totally unsuitable for an air group commander to fly. It is an understatement to say that the decision by McClusky to switch from Wildcat fighters to the cockpit of an SBD Dauntless dive-bomber was extremely fortunate for the American war effort. That switch put him in position to lead dive-bombers, the

---

[1]Undated 1960s questionnaire from Walter Lord, filled out and returned by Roger Mehle, then rear admiral and director, Strike Warfare Division, Navy Department. Page number not known. Walter Lord papers, Naval History and Heritage Command (NHHC), Washington Navy Yard. Washington, DC.

premier American shipkilling weapon of 1942, to the target at Midway.

Recent histories of the Battle of Midway have stated that McClusky was unfamiliar with dive-bombing tactics. That is quite inaccurate. As an older, prewar aviator, Wade McClusky was well trained in flying all types of naval aircraft – fighters, gunnery spotting battleship floatplanes, torpedo planes, and dive-bombers. McClusky's son Philip states that his father was an expert in dive-bombing, and in every other aspect of naval aviation.[1]

Nevertheless, there seemed to be a lingering feeling among some of the *Enterprise* dive-bomber pilots that somehow Wade McClusky just had not quite paid his dues as a dive-bomber pilot. Dusty Kleiss, an SBD pilot in VS-6, wrote of the flight out during the morning attack on June 4 that:

> "It pains me to say this, but our new air group commander made a decision that had grim consequences for our squadron. LCDR McClusky piloted his dive bomber as if it were a fighter. He barreled along at 190 knots instead of the normal cruising speed of 160 knots... His unorthodox cruising speed caused major problems. In each squadron, the trailing planes tended to burn more fuel because it was their responsibility to adjust and hold fast to the flight leader's course and altitude... Our trailing planes burned fuel faster, and at higher cruising speed the waste was greater than it should have been."[2]

In fact, McClusky was acutely aware of the fact that the planes he was leading would be forced to burn more fuel than he himself used as his pilots adjusted their throttle settings to maintain

---

[1] Email communication, Philip McClusky to me, February 15, 2015.
[2] N. Jack "Dusty" Kleiss, with Timothy and Laura Orr, *Never Call Me a Hero: A Legendary American Dive-Bomber Pilot Remembers The Battle of Midway* (New York: William Morrow, 2017): pp194–195.

station. He felt bad about it, but he regarded the situation as an unavoidable consequence of formation flying.[1]

Things had changed since McClusky's dive-bomber training, which began in 1930, very early in his career. The first dive-bomber McClusky flew, the Curtiss F8C-4 was a biplane that could make steep dives but was slow, overweight, and possessed of a poor rate of climb.[2] Later in the 1930s Wade flew the Vought SBU-1; more advanced, but still a biplane. McClusky compiled more than 400 hours in these older-model dive-bombers prior to Pearl Harbor.[3] In late 1940, US Navy dive-bomber squadrons began to receive the superb Douglas SBD Dauntless dive-bomber. The Dauntless was an all-metal monoplane with an enclosed cockpit, retractable landing gear, and sophisticated dive brakes consisting of split, slatted flaps that when extended up and down slowed the aircraft in steep dives. These flaps enabled Dauntless pilots to drop their bombs while in a 70-degree dive toward the target without accelerating. The arrival of the Dauntless into naval service occurred while McClusky was busily flying an F4F Wildcat fighter plane as the commander of Fighting Six. Thus, while McClusky was quite familiar with dive-bombing tactics, the Dauntless was a much higher-performance dive-bomber than he had ever flown before he returned to dive-bombers in March 1942.

The dive-bombers that he had flown in the 1930s were biplanes that had no dive brakes. The lack of dive brakes meant that while and F8C-4 or an SBU-1 could dive steeply, the pilot had to begin his pullout at a much higher altitude than was possible with an SBD because the speed in the dive was much greater, which also

[1]Podcast of Wade McClusky 1972 interview with radio station WMCA. Courtesy of Philip McClusky.

[2]Thomas Wildenberg, *Destined for Glory: Dive Bombing, Midway, and the Evolution of Carrier Airpower* (Annapolis: Naval Institute Press, 1998): pp43–46.

[3]Compilation of dive-bombing hours provided by Philip McClusky from analysis of his father's pilot logbooks. Email communication, Philip McClusky to me, March 6, 2016 and March 14, 2016.

made bomb-aiming more difficult. At Midway, and in an SBD, McClusky dropped his bomb at 1,800ft while in a 70-degree dive and was still able to pull out of his dive safely. Such a steep, low drop never would have been possible in an F8C-4 or an SBU-1. Unlike many of the dive-bomber pilots he would fly with at Midway, such as Dick Best, the commander of Bombing Squadron Six (VB-6), Wade McClusky had apparently never flown the Northrop BT-1, the aircraft that was the immediate predecessor of the SBD Dauntless. Dick Best had flown the BT-1 before himself transitioning to the SBD Dauntless. The BT-1 entered service in spring 1938 and was the Navy's first monoplane dive-bomber. It was also the first to use slatted dive brake flaps that opened both upward and downward during a dive, making it possible for pilots to dive at an angle of 70 degrees without continuing to accelerate – an absolutely essential element for accurate dive-bombing. Despite its advanced features, the BT-1 was not quite the dive-bomber the Navy needed, however, being underpowered and with a landing gear that was not fully retractable.

Like every other major corporation in the United States, Northrop had been hit hard by the Great Depression and was forced to undergo a major downsizing. While tough on Northrop, this upheaval turned out quite well for the US Navy. Northrop sold its El Segundo, California factory in which BT-1s were produced to Douglas Aircraft in spring 1938. With the factory, Douglas also purchased the rights to the BT-1 design as well as Northrop's dive-bomber contract with the Navy. Douglas also hired many of the designers who had been laid off by Northrop, including Ed Heinemann who as chief engineer at Northrop had designed the BT-1. Heinemann and the other Northrop veterans worked with the superb designers already at Douglas on an upgrade to the BT-1. They took the good features of the BT-1, eliminated the bad, and developed a new airplane: the legendary SBD Dauntless.[1]

---

[1]Wildenberg, *Destined for Glory*, pp128–129, pp136–139, pp160–161. Barrett Tillman, *The Dauntless Dive Bomber of World War Two* (Annapolis: Naval Institute Press, 1976): pp5–8.

Because the Northrop BT-1 had served as a stepping stone in the development process that led to the SBD Dauntless, it was an excellent training platform for pilots who would later fly the SBD Dauntless. Wade McClusky, on the other hand, had to make the transition from the relatively primitive F8C-4 and SBU-1 dive-bombers to the highly advanced SBD without being able to use the BT-1 for preparation.

McClusky began to practice flying an SBD-3 on March 20, 1942 – the day before he became air group commander. While he was getting used to the Dauntless, McClusky still made occasional flights in an F4F-4 Wildcat fighter.[1] For instance, on May 5 and 6, McClusky flew in an F4F, flights that he labeled in his logbook as "patrol." He was almost certainly helping out with combat air patrol duties while Adm Halsey raced south with *Enterprise* and *Hornet* in hopes of helping R Adm Frank Jack Fletcher's *Yorktown/Lexington* task force in the Battle of the Coral Sea. Halsey was not in time for that due to the delays incurred by the Doolittle Raid on Tokyo, for which the *Enterprise* stood guard duty for the *Hornet* as the two carriers and their escorts steamed to within 700 miles of the Japanese coast. *Enterprise* fighter pilots shouldered all of the CAP missions during the outward leg of the Doolittle Raid mission since the presence of 16 Army Air Forces B-25 bombers on the *Hornet*'s flight deck meant that the *Hornet*'s own fighters were stowed below in the hangar deck. McClusky was aboard the *Enterprise* for the Doolittle mission, but he did not fly any CAP missions during April 1942. Instead he was busy settling in as air group commander and putting in time in SBDs. As such, Wade flew only three times during April: once in an SBD-2 on April 4, and twice in an SBD-3 on April 8, the date that *Enterprise* and its escorts set out from Pearl for the Doolittle raid.[2] The first of these flights he labeled as "Patrol" in his logbook

---

[1] Email communication, Philip McClusky to me, March 5, 2016, reporting upon his review of Wade's logbooks.

[2] Potter, *Nimitz*, p66.

– probably an antisubmarine patrol, something for which SBDs were often used. The other two flights that month are labeled as "Ferry" and "Ferry to Ship," respectively.[1] The last of these flights would have been Wade as air group commander leading the entire air group out from Pearl to meet the *Enterprise* as the Big E hurried on its way to join up with the *Hornet* task force.

Col Doolittle's B-25 bombers took off from the *Hornet* for the famous Tokyo Raid on April 18, 1942. Doolittle's big Army bombers could never land on a carrier. Just *launching* twin-engined bombers, which each had a 67ft wingspan, from a carrier deck was certainly one of the greatest feats in 20th-century aviation history. The plan was for Doolittle's planes to fly on to China after unloading their bombs over Tokyo. Japanese picket boats had spotted Halsey's fleet early on the morning of April 18, when the Americans were still 700 miles from the Japanese coast. This was much further out than the intended launch point, but Halsey was compelled to order Doolittle to take off immediately since the Japanese were now alerted to the presence of two American aircraft carriers. All 16 of Doolittle's plane crews did succeed in dropping their bombs on Tokyo and other Japanese cities. Afterward, one of Doolittle's raiders landed at Vladivostock. Being short on fuel due to the increased range of their mission caused by the earlier than expected take-off, most of the crews were forced to bail out of their aircraft as the tanks ran dry just after they crossed the China coast. One crew made a water landing just off a Chinese beach. Unable to be of any assistance in landing Doolittle's aircraft, the *Enterprise* and *Hornet* turned around immediately after the launch and headed for Pearl Harbor.

Since they had a tanker with them for at-sea refueling, the two carriers perhaps could have made it down to the Coral Sea in time for the battle there if they had headed south immediately after launching the Doolittle raiders. However, the force had been ordered to return to Pearl Harbor first, both to reprovision and so

---

[1]Wade McClusky logbook entries for April 1942. Philip McClusky collection.

that the *Enterprise* could embark a squadron of Marine Corps F4F fighter planes, which were to be delivered to a Marine airfield on Efate in the New Hebrides, an island chain at the eastern edge of the Coral Sea that was a vital link in the chain of island strong points enabling the United States to maintain air and sea communications with Australia and New Zealand. The two carriers and their escorting cruisers and destroyers arrived back at Pearl Harbor on April 25.[1] The turnaround time in port was rather slow considering the urgency of the situation and it was not until April 30 that the *Enterprise/Hornet* task force departed Pearl Harbor and headed south.[2] Action in the Coral Sea was just a week away, but the theater of operations for that battle was more than 3,000 miles to the southwest of Pearl Harbor. The distance was simply too great and the time too short for the *Enterprise* and *Hornet* to get there in time to help Fletcher.

Too late for the Coral Sea battle, Halsey proceeded with his secondary mission: to deliver the Marine fighter planes and their pilots to the rapidly expanding American air and naval base at Efate. The incomplete runway there was apparently not yet fully paved, so Wade McClusky took off from the *Enterprise* in an SBD-3 on May 11, 1942 to ascertain whether F4Fs, with their narrow undercarriages, could safely land there. He describes this duty cryptically in his logbook as "Special Mission."[3] He was able to land and take off from the Efate airstrip without difficulty in his rugged Dauntless with its widely spaced undercarriage wheels, but he concluded that the runway would need more work before it could be used by Wildcat fighter planes. Based on McClusky's evaluation, Adm Halsey ordered the Marine fighters to fly to

[1]Thomas B. Buell, *The Quiet Warrior: A Biography of Admiral Raymond A. Spruance* (Annapolis: Naval Institute Press, 1974, 1987): p132.

[2]Edward P. Stafford, *The Big E: The Story of the U.S.S. Enterprise* (Annapolis: Naval Institute Press, 1962, 2002): pp83–86.

[3]Wade McClusky logbook entries for May 1942. Philip McClusky collection.

Noumea in New Caledonia instead.[1] On May 16, the task force turned north and headed back toward Pearl Harbor. By now, Adm Nimitz was convinced that his code breakers were right and that the Japanese were indeed preparing to invade Midway in early June. He needed all of his carriers back at Pearl to get ready. On May 17 he ordered Halsey to get back as quickly as possible.[2]

The greatly improved capabilities of the Dauntless dive-bomber undoubtedly did take some getting used to, but his versatility and the 400-plus hours he had already spent flying older-model dive-bombers enabled McClusky to master the SBD very quickly. As for a breakdown of McClusky's exact time in SBDs prior to Midway, he had made eight flights in an SBD totaling 11 hours and 24 minutes' flying time, including at least four carrier landings in the type, before he took off in an SBD-3, serial number 4618, on June 4, 1942 to lead the two squadrons of *Enterprise* dive-bombers in the attack that would make legends out of the plane, the ship, and many of the pilots.[3] Midway historian Robert E. Barde writes of Wade McClusky's limited experience with the SBD Dauntless that McClusky:

"knew the plane and how to take it off and bring it aboard, but by no stretch of the imagination was he an accomplished divebomber [sic] pilot. He had never dropped a bomb from a Dauntless and yet his leadership and appreciation of the situation on that morning of 4 June were to be a major factor in the American victory at Midway."[4]

---

[1]Lundstrom, *The First Team*, p368. Email communication, Philip McClusky to me, May 16, 2016. Stafford, *The Big E*, p86.

[2]Stafford, *The Big E*, p87.

[3]Wade McClusky logbook entries for March, April, and May 1942. Philip McClusky collection.

[4]Robert E. Barde, "The Battle of Midway: A Study in Command" PhD dissertation. University of Maryland, 1971, p234.

Barde had interviewed Wade McClusky on June 30, 1966 at Wade's home in Ruxton, Maryland.[1] Therefore, his claim that McClusky dropped his first bomb from an SBD in the actual battle may well be correct, but Barde was incorrect in claiming that McClusky was unfamiliar with dive-bombing. For some reason, the subject of Wade's extensive experience in older-model dive-bombers in the 1930s seems not to have come up in McClusky's interview with Barde. In addition to dropping bombs from the F8C-4 and the SBU-1 dive-bomber types during the 1930s, McClusky practiced dropping bombs from fighter planes during the seven months prior to the Pearl Harbor attack and he had dropped a pair of 100lb bombs from an F4F for real in action during the Wotje raid on February 1, 1942. While flying with Fighting Six, McClusky had trained hard in every aspect of fighter tactics, including dogfighting, gunnery, and flying at night. Between April 1941 and American entry into the war, McClusky's training in the Wildcat had included 27 hours using the plane in the role of fighter-bomber. Those hours, when added to his time in dive-bombers during the 1930s, show that Wade McClusky, while usually labeled as a fighter pilot, was no stranger to dropping bombs from airplanes.[2] As part of his practice in using the F4F as a fighter-bomber, on November 18, 1941, McClusky spent an hour in his F4F-3A bombing the old battleship USS *Utah*, which had been converted into a target ship. Later that month, just before the *Enterprise* put to sea on November 28, McClusky even did some night-time bombing in an F4F.[3]

---

[1] Barde, "The Battle of Midway: A Study in Command," p176, *n*. This interview took place on June 30, 1966.

[2] Philip McClusky analysis of Wade's time in F4Fs. Email communication, Philip McClusky to me, March 6, 2016.

[3] Wade McClusky logbook entries for November 1941. Philip McClusky collection.

9

LAST MINUTE PREPARATIONS

The American pilots who would actually win the Battle of Midway for the United States were the last ones to find out what the upcoming operation was all about. Adm Nimitz sent some information about the Midway operation by radio to Adms Halsey and Fletcher as the carriers *Enterprise*, *Hornet*, and *Yorktown* were making their way back to Pearl Harbor after the Coral Sea battle,[1] but he delayed giving a full briefing until he could see his commanders in person, to eliminate both the possibility of misunderstanding and the risk of putting such highly classified information out on radio airwaves, even in code. Joe Rochefort's success in cracking parts of the Japanese JN 25 code was a stark reminder to Adm Nimitz that nobody's codes were unbreakable. To brief Adms Fletcher and Spruance in person, Nimitz had to wait until the *Yorktown* and *Enterprise* task forces arrived back at Pearl Harbor from the South Pacific. The schedule was very tight. The *Enterprise* and its consort USS *Hornet*, with their escorts, arrived back at Pearl on May 26. The *Yorktown* task force did not arrive until the next day.

May 26, 1942 was a very busy day for R Adm Raymond A. Spruance, the commander of the cruisers that screened Halsey's carriers. Spruance had visited Adm Nimitz as soon as Task Force 16, of which Spruance's flagship the heavy cruiser USS *Northampton*

---

[1]Thomas B. Buell, *The Quiet Warrior: A Biography of Admiral Raymond A. Spruance* (Annapolis: Naval Institute Press, 1974, 1987): pp132–133.

was a part, had arrived back at Pearl Harbor. It was only then that Spruance learned three surprising pieces of information: that Bill Halsey was ill and had just been admitted to the hospital; that the Japanese fleet was bearing down on Midway with the intention of occupying the atoll; and that Nimitz had concurred in Halsey's recommendation that Spruance should take command of Task Force 16 (*Enterprise*, *Hornet*, and the cruisers and destroyers whose sole purpose was to protect the precious carriers) for the coming battle. Being placed in command of a carrier task force charged with hurling back an enemy invasion force was quite a change for Spruance. His previous assignment had been a supporting role as the commander of Cruiser Division Five, the four (sometimes three) heavy cruisers that accompanied Halsey's carrier task force on all of the latter's operations during the first six months of the war, such as the Marshalls raid in February 1942.[1] The heavy cruiser USS *Northampton* had been Spruance's flagship and home for months. But now, on the evening of May 26, Spruance stepped aboard the *Enterprise* as his two-star flag was unfurled and hoisted up the signal mast to snap in the breeze high above the carrier's flight deck and Spruance himself moved into the comfortably appointed cabin that had previously been occupied by Halsey. Adm Spruance would make some mistakes during the Battle of Midway, but his overall performance in that battle has generally been rated as brilliant. Midway was for Spruance the beginning of the journey that before the war was over would see his name enshrined as one of America's greatest seagoing warriors.[2]

The next 48 hours Task Force 16 spent at Pearl were extremely hectic as the ship was prepared for sea. Refueling

---

[1]Buell, *The Quiet Warrior*, pp99–101, pp110–111.

[2]Samuel Eliot Morison, *History of United States Naval Operations in World War II*. Vol. 4. *Coral Sea, Midway and Submarine Actions: May 1942–August 1942* (Boston: Little, Brown and Company, 1954; reissued in 2001 by Castle Books, Edison, NJ): p158.

and provisioning were the first orders of business. As usual, Air Group Six had flown ashore on the 26th as the *Enterprise* approached Oahu, landing at NAS Ford Island. Although he was now air group commander, it appears that McClusky did not fly ashore with the air group on the 26th, but rather that he remained aboard the *Enterprise* during the visit to Pearl. Wade was meticulous in recording each and every flight he made in his pilot logbooks, even the short hops from ship to shore and vice versa. For instance, his wartime logbook notes that on January 7, 1942 while commanding Fighting Six, Wade flew an F4F-3 "ENT TO KANEOHE." The same day he flew "KANEOHE TO EWA." On January 8, he flew "EWA TO FORD," and on January 11 "FORD TO ENT. 1CL" [ie one carrier landing]. Wade was proud of his carrier landings and he noted in his logbooks every time he made one. However, his logbook mentions no flights between May 12, 1942 when he landed an SBD back aboard the *Enterprise* after completing his examination of the new airstrip at Efate, a flight mentioned in Chapter 8, and June 4, 1942 when he took off from the *Enterprise* to lead the attack at Midway.[1]

The most likely reason that Wade remained aboard while the *Enterprise* was in port was that he was slated to receive the Distinguished Flying Cross (DFC) at a hastily prepared ceremony that was held on the flight deck of the *Enterprise* on May 27. Adm Nimitz, dressed in white, was piped aboard to do the honors. Among the awards, several pilots were being honored for their actions during the early hit-and-run raids against the Marshall Islands as well as Marcus and Wake. Although he was now air group commander, the DFC Wade was awarded was for his leadership of Fighting Six during the hit-and-run raids. While the ceremony was taking place, the

---

[1]Wade McClusky pilot logbook entries for May and June 1942. Philip McClusky collection.

ship was being busily reprovisioned and made ready for sea. The Midway battle was only a week away. McClusky's citation for the DFC reads:

> "For heroic conduct in aerial flight as commander of a Fighting Squadron in the initial attack on Wotje Atoll, Marshall Islands, on February 1, 1942 ... he repeatedly bombed and strafed objectives causing severe damage to the enemy. Later, while leading a combat air patrol over the task force, contact was made with two twin-engined bombers... He led his command in repeated aggressive attacks ... resulting in the destruction of one and serious damage to the other."[1]

Also receiving Distinguished Flying Crosses that day were Lts Roger Mehle and Wade's good friend Jim Daniels; both from Fighting Six and from VS-6, dive-bomber pilots Lts (junior grade) Cleo Dobson and Norman "Dusty" Kleiss.[2] The highest awards presented that day were five Navy Crosses, one of which was awarded to Doris (Dorrie) Miller, the first African-American to win one. On December 7, 1941, Dorrie Miller, an African-American man in a strictly segregated Navy, was attending to his duties as a cook and laundry attendant aboard the battleship USS *West Virginia*. During the Japanese attack, Miller carried the ship's mortally wounded captain, Mervyn Bennion, off the open deck to a sheltered area. Miller then manned a .50 caliber antiaircraft machine gun and shot down two Japanese aircraft; a feat all the more amazing in that African-American sailors at the

[1]"Rear Admiral C. Wade McClusky, Jr. United States Navy, Retired" Navy Biographies Section, OI-440, May 23, 1957, p2. Courtesy National Naval Aviation Museum, Pensacola, Florida.

[2]Edward P. Stafford, *The Big E: The Story of the U.S.S. Enterprise* (Annapolis: Naval Institute Press, 1962, 2002): p88.

time were used by the Navy strictly for menial chores and were not given any weapons training at all.[1]

Once the award ceremony was over, there was much for Adm Spruance to do as he tried to settle in to his new and entirely unexpected billet. Spruance, like Wade McClusky, was a reticent man – cerebral in the extreme. While working as chief-of-staff to Adm Nimitz at Pearl Harbor after the battle, Spruance worked at a stand-up desk in his office. In fact, that office contained no chairs whatsoever. Spruance had no time or interest in small talk and he actively discouraged visitors from lingering in his office.[2] He was the absolute antithesis of the gregarious Halsey. *Enterprise* put to sea again on Thursday May 28, 1942, exactly one week before her dive-bomber pilots would destroy Japan's two largest aircraft carriers and would help to destroy a third.

As Task Force 16 steamed towards "Point Luck," the spot northeast of Midway where Spruance and Fletcher would join up, Spruance had the following message blinkered to the force:

"An attack for the purpose of capturing Midway is expected. The attacking force may be composed of all combatant types including four or five carriers, transports and train vessels. If presence of Task Force 16 and 17 remains unknown to the enemy we should be able to make surprise flank attacks on enemy carriers from a position northeast of Midway. Further operations will be based on result of these attacks, damage inflicted by Midway forces, and information of enemy movements. The successful conclusion of the operation now commencing will be of great value to our country."[3]

[1] N. Jack "Dusty" Kleiss, with Timothy and Laura Orr, *Never Call Me a Hero: A Legendary American Dive-Bomber Pilot Remembers the Battle of Midway* (New York: William Morrow, 2017): p175.

[2] E. B. Potter, *Nimitz* (Annapolis: Naval Institute Press, 1976, 1987): p223.

[3] Buell, *The Quiet Warrior*, pp141–142.

Knowing the intentions of the Japanese prior to the battle was a stunning Intelligence coup for the United States, but the message Spruance shared with the fleet did not contain nearly enough information to enable senior pilots such as McClusky to formulate effective tactical plans. Spruance did give more information to the senior pilots in the days to come, but it seems that he never gave a comprehensive briefing to explain the American command setup and exactly how Spruance and Fletcher intended to destroy the Japanese aircraft carriers. Part of the reason for this, no doubt, is the last-minute nature of Spruance's appointment to command Task Force 16. It is highly unlikely that Raymond Spruance ever imagined in his wildest dreams that someday he would be placed in tactical command of an aircraft carrier task force. Spruance and Fletcher had only had time for one conference together with Nimitz to discuss the battle plan before the two American Task Forces sailed from Pearl, and carrier warfare was simply too new an activity for there to be anything like complete consensus regarding how it should be fought.

Although in hindsight it would have been advantageous for the pilots to have had more time to make plans for the Midway battle at squadron and group level, the brief visits of *Yorktown*, *Enterprise*, and *Hornet* to Pearl Harbor just a week before the battle began made it impossible to give senior pilots like Wade McClusky much time to make in-depth battle plans that could in turn be presented in detail to the pilots in the combat squadrons. In the first-person account he wrote after the war, McClusky provides insight into the hectic and hurried nature with which the final plans for the upcoming battle were hammered out. His account also shows that Adm Halsey's illness had been completely unexpected and that Adm Spruance was indeed a last-minute replacement as the commander of Task Force 16. On June 1, with the *Enterprise* at sea and shortly before the message quoted above was blinkered to the other ships in the force, McClusky and *Enterprise* Capt George D. Murray were summoned to the spacious cabin set aside for admirals located on the port side of *Enterprise*'s gallery deck just below the flight deck amidships.

A twin of the captain's cabin located next door, the admiral's cabin was large enough to have a conference table in the middle. Adjacent to the admiral's main cabin were a sitting room and a bath. McClusky was surprised to find Raymond Spruance, not Bill Halsey, occupying that cabin. This was the first McClusky had heard of the Halsey's illness and the consequent change in the command of Task Force 16.[1] Adm Spruance explained to McClusky and Murray that the Japanese were going to attempt a landing on Midway and that Adm Nimitz had ordered Adms Spruance and Fletcher to use the three available American aircraft carriers to ambush the Japanese fast carrier striking force that would soften up Midway and provide cover for Japanese troop landings. Spruance then gave McClusky permission to brief the air group. There was still much that McClusky did not know. He would later write: "What command relationship existed between Admiral Fletcher and Admiral Spruance remains unknown to the writer."[2] In point of fact, then R Adm Fletcher, with Task Force 17 (*Yorktown* and her escorts) would be in overall command.

Spruance and presumably Fletcher did allow senior pilots to read the text of the orders they had received from Adm Nimitz. These were encompassed in a document known as CinCPac Operation Plan No. 29–42. In addition to the plan of action, this document also contained everything that had been learned about the enemy's objectives and forces at hand. The extraordinary level of detail with which the enemy's intentions and order of battle had been laid bare made for breathtaking reading. The effect the document had on those allowed to read it is aptly

---

[1]Wade McClusky, "The Midway Story" Unpublished manuscript, p1. Lord Papers, Naval History and Heritage Command (NHHC). Washington, DC. Deck plans, USS *Yorktown* [sister ship of USS *Enterprise*, CV-6], from *Booklet of General Plans*, Newport News Shipbuilding and Drydock Company, Newport News, VA. Final blueprints drawn in 1939 and 1940 to accurately reflect the completed ship. Available online at: https://maritime. org/doc/plans/cv5.pdf.

[2]McClusky, "The Midway Story," p2. Lord Papers, NHHC.

summed up by E.B. Potter in his biography of Adm Nimitz. Of CinCPac Operation Plan No. 29–42 and its readers, almost all of whom were blissfully unaware of the sophisticated code-breaking operation going on at Pearl Harbor, Potter writes that:

"Officers qualified to read the bulky plan found it a fascinating and chilling document. Without revealing its sources of information, it stated in astonishing detail what enemy forces would attack Midway and when. Commander Richard Ruble, navigator of the *Enterprise*, evidently a reader of spy thrillers, could only mutter in wonder, 'That man of ours in Tokyo is worth every cent we pay him.'"[1]

---

[1]Potter, *Nimitz*, p87.

10

June 4, 1942 – Take-off

Wade McClusky's problems on June 4, 1942 began even before
he took off from the *Enterprise*. His rear-seat gunner that day,
Aviation Radioman 1st Class Walter Chocalousek, was a last-
minute replacement for his regular gunner, Chief Radioman
John M. O'Brien, who could not fly because he had broken his
eyeglasses after tripping on a bulkhead doorsill in a passageway
inside the carrier's island. McClusky was not actually overly
concerned about losing O'Brien. On the contrary, while O'Brien
was a good radio operator, McClusky had apparently been less
than thrilled with O'Brien's gunnery skills. Walter Chocalousek
had successfully checked out as a qualified gunner, but unlike
O'Brien, he had no combat experience as yet and his radio skills
were apparently somewhat rudimentary. The primitive dot-dash
radio at the rear-seat station of a Dauntless was somewhat
redundant since McClusky and the other SBD pilots had voice
radio in the front cockpit. There was, however, one radio task in
which rear-seat gunners had to be proficient. The SBD-3 featured
a new homing device called ZD (Zed) Baker, which aided pilots
in finding their home carrier after a mission. Since it was needed
only for the return leg of a mission, ZD Baker required the
rear-seat gunner to switch out certain coils in the voice radio
during a flight so that the homing signal being broadcast by
an American aircraft carrier could be received. Since McClusky
did use his ZD Baker device to find the *Enterprise* after the
morning attack, it seems that Chocalousek was able to handle
that part of his radio duties. Nevertheless, it had to have been

a bit nerve-wracking for Wade to fly with a gunner he did not know at all.[1]

Regarding the two skills – radio operation and gunnery – required of SBD rear-seat crewmen, McClusky regarded gunnery as by far the more important. He wanted an excellent gunner riding behind him – at the expense of radio skills if necessary. McClusky hoped that Chocalousek would be a better gunner than O'Brien – a wish that was to be granted in full; Chocalousek would not disappoint.[2]

Figuring out what somebody else was thinking at a given time is, at best, an endeavor of dubious accuracy. Nevertheless, when asked what his father would have been thinking about as he prepared to take off on June 4, 1942, knowing that he was going into battle, Phil McClusky relates that his father would have been methodically reviewing in his mind the technical aspects of the upcoming flight – fuel, bomb load, distance to target – but that there would have been no fear.[3]

Lt Jim Gray had taken up McClusky's old billet as the commander of Fighting Six. Gray's F4Fs were divided into two groups: one for combat air patrol (CAP) duty over Task Force 16 and the other a ten-strong contingent of Wildcats led by Gray, which was assigned to provide fighter escort for the *Enterprise* torpedo planes and dive-bombers of the striking force. The eight fighter planes assigned to CAP duty, including the one flown by McClusky's friend Roger Mehle, took off first that

[1]Wade McClusky, "The Midway Story" Unpublished manuscript, p3. Lord Papers, Naval History and Heritage Command (NHHC). Stephen L. Moore, *Pacific Payback: The Carrier Aviators Who Avenged Pearl Harbor at the Battle of Midway* (New York: NAL Caliber, 2014): pp175–176. N. Jack "Dusty" Kleiss, with Timothy and Laura Orr, *Never Call Me a Hero: A Legendary American Dive Bomber Pilot Remembers the Battle of Midway* (New York: Morrow, 2017): p154, p177, p199, p227.

[2]McClusky, "The Midway Story," p3. Lord Papers, NHHC. Moore, *Pacific Payback*, pp175–176.

[3]Interviews with Philip McClusky, December 27 and December 29, 2016.

morning, beginning just before 7.00am. McClusky's SBD, with a 500lb bomb tucked underneath the fuselage, trundled down the *Enterprise* flight deck and lifted into the air at 7.06am. He was followed by his wingmen, Pittman and Jaccard, then by Earl Gallaher and the SBDs of Scouting Six. The SBDs of Bombing Six were spotted aft so that they would have the longest take-off runs – essential since each SBD in VB-6 was carrying a bomb weighing 1,000lbs. They were to be followed by the ten fighter planes under Gray and then by the Torpedo planes of VT-6.[1]

Adm Spruance's decision on the morning of June 4, 1942 to send all of his Task Force 16 aircraft from *Enterprise* and *Hornet*, except a few CAP fighters, against the Japanese in one massive strike was undoubtedly the correct decision. Unfortunately, the Americans were as yet unfamiliar with the intricacies of launching full deckload strikes.[2] Therefore, while "bungled" may be too strong a word to describe the launch from Task Force 16, things definitely did not go smoothly. As such, McClusky and his dive-bombers ended up circling the Task Force for 40 minutes, burning much precious fuel, while they waited for the fighters and torpedo planes to get aloft. Finally, McClusky was ordered by signal lamp to proceed with the dive-bombers alone. McClusky was startled by this departure from doctrine, but this decision by Adm Spruance to send McClusky on his way without waiting for the torpedo planes or for fighter support was actually beneficial in the end.

Since junior and mid-ranking officers were not informed of the details of the mission until Task Forces 16 and 17 had put to sea, McClusky had had no chance to confer with the other

[1]John B. Lundstrom, *The First Team: Pacific Air Combat from Pearl Harbor to Midway* (Annapolis: Naval Institute Press, 1984): pp406–411, pp419–422. Craig L. Symonds, *The Battle of Midway* (New York: Oxford University Press, 2013): 274.

[2]Walter Lord, *Incredible Victory* (New York: Harper & Row, 1967): pp139–140. H. P. Willmott, *The Barrier and the Javelin: Japanese and Allied Pacific Strategies February to June 1942* (Annapolis: Naval Institute Press, 1983): pp401–403.

two air group commanders: Lt Cdr Oscar Pederson (Annapolis 1926) of *Yorktown* and Cdr Stanhope Ring of the *Hornet*. It is not entirely clear if McClusky held a preflight conference with his squadron commanders aboard the *Enterprise*: Lt Richard Best of Bombing Six (VB-6), Lt Earl Gallaher of Scouting Six (VS-6), Lt Jim Gray of Fighting Six (VF-6), and Lt Cdr Eugene Lindsey of Torpedo Six (VT-6).[1] If he didn't convene such a conference, he probably should have, although no preflight conference could possibly have prepared the Big E's pilots for the bizarre manner in which the battle actually unfolded.

Yorktown's captain, Elliott Buckmaster, did not allow *Yorktown* air group commander, Oscar Pederson, to fly with the *Yorktown* air group during the battle, much to Pederson's chagrin. Buckmaster wanted Pederson close at hand to advise him on air operations and to serve as fighter director officer coordinating the aerial defense of the flagship. *Hornet* air group commander Stanhope Ring did fly that day and Ring was a full commander who outranked McClusky and the *Yorktown*'s dive-bombing squadron leader Maxwell Leslie, the latter another 1926 Annapolis classmate of McClusky's. However, unlike McClusky, Ring had no previous combat experience and everyone agrees that Ring performed poorly at Midway; the *Hornet*'s dive-bombers, led by Ring, never even sighting the Japanese carriers on the morning of June 4.

McClusky had expected that all three American carriers would launch their dive-bombers simultaneously and that Ring, as the senior officer, would lead all of the American dive-bombers to the target. In light of the fact that Ring was unable to locate the enemy, the Americans would in fact have lost the battle if Stanhope Ring had been in command of all of the American dive-bombers on June 4. Thus, the fact that McClusky and Leslie each led the *Enterprise* and *Yorktown* dive-bombers independently to the target was a critical stroke of good fortune for the Americans.

[1] Lundstrom, *The First Team*, p408.

Max Leslie, commanding *Yorktown*'s Bombing Three (VB-3), had much in common with Wade McClusky. In addition to being a 1926 Annapolis classmate of McClusky's, he had also begun his flight training at Pensacola as soon as he possibly could after the completion of the then mandatory two years of duty with the surface fleet required of all naval officers upon graduation from Annapolis in the 1920s. Leslie qualified as a naval aviator in 1930, having arrived at Pensacola to begin his flight training in mid-1929. This put Leslie in the class of aviation cadets who began their flight training just after the members of Wade McClusky's 1929 class had won their wings. Like McClusky, Max Leslie was well versed in flying all types of naval aircraft. In terms of total flying hours, McClusky and Leslie were old hands by the time of Midway.[1]

The *Yorktown* and Task Force 17 operated independently of the other two American carriers, with its own flag officer aboard – R Adm Frank Jack Fletcher, the overall commander of American naval forces at Midway. Ten SBDs from the *Yorktown*'s Scouting Squadron Five (VS-5) had been sent out early in the morning to conduct a fan-shaped search to the north of the American carriers.[2] World War 2 aircraft carriers did not yet have angled flight decks, and the catapults located at the bows of American fleet carriers were used only infrequently during the war – usually

[1]*Navy Directory: Officers of the United States Navy and Marine Corps: July 1, 1929.* (Washington, DC: Government Printing Office, 1929): p51. Available online at https://archive. org/stream/navydirectoryof1929unit_1#page/50/mode/2up. *Navy Directory: Officers of the United States Navy and Marine Corps: October 1, 1929.* (Washington, DC: Government Printing Office): p50. Available online at https://archive.org/stream/ navydirectoryoff19294unit#page/50/mode/2up. *Navy Directory: Officers of the United States Navy and Marine Corps: October 1, 1930.* (Washington, DC: Government Printing Office, 1930): p52. Available online at https://archive.org/stream/navydirectoryof 1930unit_1#page/52/mode/2up. Lundstrom, *The First Team*, p169.

[2]Barrett Tillman, *The Dauntless Dive Bomber of World War Two* (Annapolis: Naval Institute Press, 1976, 2006): p63.

to launch fighters, the lightest of American World War 2 combat aircraft. As we will see, later in the war the small American escort carriers (CVE) would use their catapults for launches far more frequently than did the big fleet carriers. On fleet carriers such as the *Enterprise*, heavily laden American dive-bombers and torpedo planes usually took off under their own power and needed as much of the flight deck length as possible to do so. Thus, without angled flight decks, World War 2 aircraft carriers could not conduct take-offs and landings at the same time. Partly because he had to allow his search planes to land, Adm Fletcher did not begin launching the *Yorktown*'s strike aircraft until shortly before 9.00am, two hours after *Enterprise* and *Hornet* had begun launching their planes.

I I

June 4, 1942 – North or South?

McClusky and the *Enterprise* dive-bombers reached the interception point at 9.20am (local time). There was nothing but empty ocean as far as the eye could see in any direction. McClusky did not break radio silence to ask for guidance when he learned that the interception coordinates he had been given were out of date, which was just as well because Adm Spruance and his staff on the *Enterprise* were as yet unaware of the change of course made by Adm Nagumo's carrier striking force – a course change that had taken the Japanese fleet away from the interception point in a northeasterly direction. By the time Jim Gray, occupying McClusky's old billet as the commander of Fighting Six, very belatedly radioed in a contact report at approximately 10.00am after circling above the Japanese fleet for almost an hour, McClusky was on the verge of finding the enemy on his own anyway. Also, Gray's contact report seems to have included only that he was leaving the vicinity of the enemy fleet due to fuel shortage. Gray apparently did not report the coordinates of Nagumo's location. McClusky continued on to the southwest for 15 minutes beyond the anticipated interception point because there was a slim chance that the Japanese approach track toward Midway was further west than he had anticipated or that Nagumo may have turned west.

What followed was one of the most important decisions made by any American military commander in all of World War 2. Wade McClusky now displayed that sixth sense: the intuition shared by all great military commanders of having a gut feeling, even when the enemy was not in sight, as to what the enemy was actually doing – a gut feeling that in this case turned out to be dead on in terms of accuracy. A logical assumption would have been that the Japanese were making better than expected speed, and thus had gotten past McClusky and were now off to the south. McClusky was sure that this was not the case, which was a counterintuitive but quite accurate assessment. He sensed the truth: that persistent American air attacks from Midway-based aircraft and carrier-based torpedo planes, as well as a Japanese cruiser floatplane's sighting of one of the American task forces, had forced Nagumo to undertake course changes. The initial changes were evasive actions to avoid bombs and torpedoes dropped by attacking American aircraft. These maneuvers slowed Nagumo's southeasterly progress. Then, at 9.17am, Nagumo turned 90 degrees to port, on to a northeasterly heading, in order to close with the American surface ships so that he could launch a strike against them with his own dive-bombers and torpedo planes. McClusky did not know all of these details yet, but he was certain that something had delayed the Japanese and that the carriers of *Kido Butai* were north of him.

McClusky himself never thought it was intuition or guesswork that guided him during the battle. After the war, he always bristled if he read an account of the Battle of Midway that claimed that he had made a lucky guess in turning north. Wade told his family that there was no guesswork involved. According to Phil McClusky, on the relatively rare occasions when his father spoke about the battle, Wade always said that if the Japanese carriers had gotten past the interception point and had thus been to the south, off to McClusky's left, that "he would have heard about it." He was apparently referring to the fact that he knew that Midway-based Catalina PBY flying boats were out on patrol and that they would have reported any large body of ships nearing the atoll.[1]

---

[1]Telephone interview with Philip McClusky, December 18, 2016.

It is true that the PBY crews did an excellent job of scouting and reporting during the battle. They even did some attacking. One PBY crew spotted the troop-laden Japanese transport vessels 700 miles west of Midway on June 3. That night, Capt Cyril Simard, the naval commander on Midway itself, organized and dispatched a four-strong group of Catalinas with orders to make a torpedo attack against the approaching invasion fleet. As would be the case the following day, the fact that the Americans had recognized the value of radar much earlier than did the Japanese would bear fruit. These PBYs were radar-equipped and were thus able to locate the Japanese transports after midnight and after a long flight out from Midway. Later in the war, the PBY would become a formidable antisubmarine weapon, with crews trained to drop depth charges and acoustic torpedoes when they sighted enemy submarines on the surface. In mid-1942, however, most PBYs were used strictly for patrol: for finding the enemy so that combat aircraft could make an attack. It is therefore safe to say that these PBY crews barely knew one end of a torpedo from the other. Nevertheless, each plane now had a torpedo slung under one wing with a crude release mechanism rigged to the cockpit. This was another instance of the American willingness to improvise and showed a desire to win at all costs. The PBY piloted by Ensign Gaylord D. Propst made a good approach and a good drop. Propst had the satisfaction of watching his torpedo explode against the hull of the fleet oiler *Akebono Maru*. Damage, however, was modest and the ship survived, probably because the warhead struck near the bow, away from the ship's vitals.[1] Nevertheless, this attack should have been an early warning to Nagumo that his adversaries were more energetic and resourceful than he had been led to believe.

It had been another PBY that had spotted Nagumo's *Kido Butai* carrier striking force on the morning of June 4 – the sighting that

---

[1] Jonathan Parshall and Anthony Tully, *Shattered Sword: The Untold Story of the Battle of Midway* (Washington, DC: Potomac Books, 2007): p114.

had caused Adm Fletcher to order the American carriers to launch the attack. PBYs also rescued many downed American (and a few Japanese) pilots and aircrew during and after the battle. Thus, while the PBYs out of Midway provided yeoman service, it is by no means certain that they would have been broadcasting on a frequency that McClusky could have picked up. Task Forces 16 and 17 were operating under strict radio silence. Thus, it is doubtful that the *Enterprise* would have been broadcasting any course corrections to McClusky even if the staff had been aware of Nagumo's course change (which they were not). Therefore, while Wade believed he would have been informed had the Japanese been south of him, the reality may have been different if such a scenario had actually occurred.

12

JUNE 4, 1942 – THE ATTACK

At 10.22am (local time) on the morning of June 4, 1942, Wade McClusky pushed the nose of his SBD-3 Dauntless dive-bomber into a 70-degree dive and began to line up the rectangular shape of the flight deck of the Japanese aircraft carrier *Kaga* in the crosshairs of the telescopic bomb sight that extended through his windshield. The two squadrons of *Enterprise* dive-bombers that McClusky had led to the target were about to execute the pivotal event of the Battle of Midway: namely the destruction of the *Kaga* and its stablemate in IJN Carrier Division One, *Akagi*; the latter being Adm Nagumo's flagship. These two enormous aircraft carriers were the most important ships in the Imperial Japanese Navy and Wade McClusky's pilots would destroy them both. Over the years, unnecessary historical controversy has come to surround the manner in which McClusky directed this attack. This controversy can be easily put to rest when one examines the original source documents. The place to start is to continue with McClusky's search for a maddeningly elusive enemy.

After making the all-important decision that the Japanese were north of him somewhere, McClusky had to figure out exactly where to his north the Japanese lay: were they off to the northwest, due north, or northeast? At 9.35am, he began a box search by turning himself and his two squadrons of SBDs to the northwest to fly the reverse of the approach track of the Japanese. Twenty minutes later, McClusky spotted the Japanese destroyer *Arashi* far below speeding off to the northeast.

166

The *Arashi* had been ordered to do something about the troublesome American submarine USS *Nautilus*, whose captain, Lt Cdr William H. Brockman, had announced his presence by firing a torpedo that passed close to one of Nagumo's battleships – either the *Kirishima* or the *Haruna*. This attack took place just a few minutes before Nagumo turned 90 degrees to port at 9.17am to close with the American fleet. The *Arashi* had remained in the area for 15 or 20 minutes as the rest of Nagumo's ships headed off on their new heading to the northeast; long enough to drop a pattern of depth charges and to pick up a downed American pilot, Ensign Wesley F. Osmus of the *Yorktown*'s VT-3. Osmus had been forced to bail out of his badly shot-up torpedo plane. His rear-seat gunner, Aviation Radioman 3rd Class Benjamin R. Dodson, was already dead when the plane hit the water.[1] Wesley Osmus would share the fate of Aviation Machinist's Mate 1st Class Bruno Peter Gaido and Gaido's pilot, Ensign Frank O'Flaherty of VS-6, mentioned earlier, in being interrogated then executed by his Japanese captors.[2] As for the *Nautilus*, the submarine seemed to lead a charmed life, surviving this and several more depth charge attacks this day.

Now, the *Arashi*'s captain was making high speed to the northeast to catch up to the main force. Sighting the destroyer reassured McClusky that he had been correct to turn north. Now, he turned right again, on to a northeasterly heading, the *Arashi*'s heading. After ten minutes on that heading, at 10.05am, McClusky spotted the Japanese fleet. The ships were just tiny specks far ahead in the distance. Thus, what McClusky saw first were the wakes – the frothy white water churned up by propellers making high speed.[3] In a 1966

---

[1]Walter Lord, *Incredible Victory* (New York: Harper & Row, 1967): pp160–162, pp210–213.

[2]Robert E. Barde, "Midway: Tarnished Victory" *Military Affairs.* Vol. 47; No. 4. December 1983, pp188–192. Robert E. Barde, "The Battle of Midway: A Study in Command" PhD dissertation. University of Maryland, 1971. Pp420–433.

[3]Clarence E. Dickinson, with Boyden Sparkes, *The Flying Guns: Cockpit Record of a*

interview, Bombing Six pilot Wilbur E. (Bill) Roberts would tell Walter Lord that his first sighting of the wakes far ahead and far below looked to him like "curved white slashes on a blue carpet."[1] As the *Enterprise* dive-bombers got closer, Wade McClusky saw all four of the Japanese carriers surrounded by several cruisers, two battleships, and a number of destroyers. The fortunes of war were about to shift dramatically in favor of the United States.

For Wade McClusky, this was the payoff for a career marked throughout by quiet competence. It was a reward for keeping himself mentally and physically fit enough to still be flying combat missions at age 40. But the need for McClusky to make quiet, calm, accurate decisions unencumbered by panic or knee-jerk reactions was not over yet. Some of McClusky's pilots thought they had returned to the *Enterprise*; that this was the American fleet that had been spotted, especially since McClusky's SBDs were now flying in a northeasterly direction – the direction in which the American carriers lay.[2] McClusky knew it was the Japanese. He saw four aircraft carriers. The Americans had only three carriers on hand. He also saw the long, low silhouettes of two battleships, a type the Americans were not using in the Midway battle. Being certain that he saw four aircraft carriers was not as easy as it sounds. Aerial recognition from high altitude of ship types is extremely difficult, even for experienced naval pilots. From the air, ships always look larger than they really are. Even McClusky had initially thought that the *Arashi*, which had led him to the target, was a Japanese cruiser, not a

---

Naval Pilot from Pearl Harbor Through Midway (New York: Charles Scribner's Sons, 1942, 1943): p148. Craig L. Symonds, *The Battle of Midway* (New York: Oxford University Press, 2013): 297–298.

[1]Walter Lord notes from interview with Bill Roberts, April 19, 1966. Walter Lord Papers. Operational Archives. Naval History and Heritage Command (NHHC). Washington Navy Yard. Washington, DC. Also in Lord, *Incredible Victory*, p163.

[2]Lord, *Incredible Victory*, p163.

destroyer.[1] A cruiser is considerably larger than a destroyer, but on many occasions during the war American and Japanese pilots would mistake destroyers for cruisers. Even aircraft carriers, despite their large size, were often misidentified during the war when sighted from the air. During the Battle of the Coral Sea a month prior to Midway, for instance, the American fleet oiler *Neosho*, a tanker, along with its escorting destroyer USS *Sims*, had drawn a full-scale attack from three dozen Japanese dive-bombers because the Japanese pilots had mistakenly identified the two ships as an American "aircraft carrier" and a "cruiser," respectively. The *Neosho* was not a small ship, but at 553ft in length, it was only half the size of the Very Large Crude Carrier – VLCC – tankers that are common sights on the world's oceans in the 21st century and which do resemble aircraft carriers. *Neosho* lacked the width, length, and acres and acres of unobstructed flat deck space that do make a modern VLCC resemble an aircraft carrier.

McClusky examined the armada below him carefully through his binoculars until he was certain it was not American. The combination of euphoria, relief, excitement, and sheer disbelief experienced by the American pilots when they realized they had found the enemy and were in an excellent position to attack is perhaps most eloquently described by Edward Stafford in his biography of the *Enterprise*. Stafford writes (using Pacific Standard Time, not Local Time):

"At five minutes past noon McClusky found the enemy ... Down there, sliding across the blue sea, once in a while disappearing for a minute under a puff of cloud, were the narrow yellow flight decks of four Japanese carriers. Arranged haphazardly around the carriers were other big ships, two battlewagons with red disks painted on their forward turrets, several cruisers

[1] Wade McClusky Midway after action report, pp2–3. Courtesy National Naval Aviation Museum, Pensacola, Florida.

and smaller ships. But it was the carriers that fascinated the Dauntless pilots and made their hearts beat and their breath come short ... Here was Japan's elite force, the crack ships and pilots that had given her the confidence to attack America. Here they were under the wings of the Big E's bombers, wide open in the clear and open sea—and still no fighters."[1]

After satisfying himself that he had indeed found the Japanese and not his own task force, Wade McClusky made another crucial decision: he would not get carried away by trying to attack all four carriers. He knew that his 30 aircraft were simply not carrying enough bomb tonnage for that. Better to ensure the complete destruction of two of the carriers rather than inflict minor damage on all four. He chose the two nearest carriers, which turned out to be the *Kaga* and the *Akagi*.[2] In concentrating his attack in this way, McClusky was paying careful attention to dive-bombing doctrine as it was spelled out in Volume One of *Current Tactical Orders and Doctrine U.S. Fleet Aircraft (USF-74, Revised)*. This "Bible" of carrier-based aviation tactics had been prepared in March 1941 under the direction of then V Adm William F. Halsey, Jr in his capacity as commander, Aircraft, Battle Force. *USF-74* states that: "The guiding principles of aircraft attack on surface vessels are: (a) Concentration of sufficient strength to sink or completely disable individual vessels, rather than dispersal of attack so as to inflict less damage on a greater number."[3] In recent literature

[1]Edward P. Stafford, *The Big E: The Story of the USS Enterprise* (Annapolis: Naval Institute Press, 1962, 2002): pp100–101.

[2]Wade McClusky, Midway after action report, p2. Courtesy National Naval Aviation Museum, Pensacola, Florida.

[3]William F. Halsey, Jr, *Current Tactical Orders and Doctrine U.S. Fleet Aircraft—Volume One: Carrier Aircraft (USF-74, Revised)*. Hereinafter "Halsey, *USF-74, Revised*" (United States Pacific Fleet Aircraft, Battle Force Fleet Air Detachment. Naval Air Station, Pearl Harbor, T. H., March 1941): p100. Available online at: http://www.admiraltytrilogy.com/read/USF-74_Tact&Doct-Acft_V1-CV-Acft_194103.pdf.

on the Battle of Midway, Wade McClusky has been accused of not understanding dive-bombing doctrine – an accusation that falls flat when it is remembered that McClusky followed the instructions in the above quote to the letter.

McClusky now broke radio silence. He informed the *Enterprise* that he had sighted the Japanese. Then, he instructed his two squadron commanders as to targets. He told Lt Richard Best, the commander of Bombing Squadron Six, to attack the carrier on the right (*Akagi*), and Lt Earl Gallaher, commanding Scouting Squadron Six, to take the carrier on the left (*Kaga*). McClusky himself intended to lead the attack on Gallaher's left-hand carrier[1] and made that intention clear by saying over the radio: "Earl, follow me down."[2]

It is surprising that after successfully beating back numerous American air attacks that morning, the Japanese were not expecting the American dive-bombers that now appeared overhead. The attention of Japanese lookouts was focused down low since the most recent attacks by American aircraft had been from low-flying torpedo planes. Most crucially, the Japanese ships had no radar to warn them of approaching high-altitude aircraft. In fact, it appears that the Japanese did not even spot McClusky's *Enterprise* SBDs or a separate group of dive-bombers from the *Yorktown* until after the American SBDs were already in their dives.

The fact that none of Nagumo's ships were equipped with radar has to rank as a major factor in the Japanese defeat at Midway. The barriers to installing radar in Japanese warships were doctrinal, not technical. Japan's scientists and industry were certainly capable of getting radar out to the fleet at an early date if doing so had been made a priority. Among the many examples of the technical prowess of the Japanese armaments industry early

---

[1] Wade McClusky, Midway after action report, p2. Courtesy National Naval Aviation Museum, Pensacola, Florida.
[2] Stafford, *The Big E*, p101.

in the war are that the Japanese Type 93 torpedo was the finest torpedo in the world in 1942 and the high quality of Japanese naval aircraft such as the Mitsubishi Zero fighter plane, which came as a rude shock to the Americans. The Imperial Japanese Navy's tardiness in recognizing the value of radar is closely related to that Navy's emphasis on offense above all else. Unlike the American dive-bombers and fighter planes that were used in the Battle of Midway, Japanese naval aircraft had no armor plate behind the pilot's seat and no self-sealing for the fuel tanks. Protecting the lives of Japanese pilots was very much a secondary consideration for Japan's naval leaders.[1] Striking power was all that mattered. Without the safety features found in American aircraft, Japanese naval aircraft were lighter and thus had greater range and, in the case of the Nakajima B5N "Kate" torpedo plane and the Zero fighter, greater speed than their American counterparts at Midway.

Radar must have seemed cowardly and defensive to the Japanese naval high command, just as warm clothing for German soldiers seemed cowardly, defensive, and unnecessary to Hitler and his generals at the time of the German invasion of the Soviet Union on June 22, 1941. Hitler had refused to even consider the possibility that his troops would have to fight a winter campaign in Russia. The Japanese were likewise totally unprepared for a long war in which it might be necessary to at least temporarily go over on to the defensive in certain areas. The cavalier disregard for the value of radar within the IJN is a classic example of that sentiment.

The Americans, on the other hand, realized that, to juxtapose a popular phrase, defensive measures can be part of a good offense. A complete surrender to a defensive strategy, such as the French government building the Maginot Line along the Franco–German border in the late 1920s and early 1930s, is a

---

[1] Jonathan Parshall and Anthony Tully, *Shattered Sword: The Unknown Story of the Battle of Midway* (Washington, DC: Potomac Books, 2005, 2007): pp84–85, p248.

bad idea, but limited defensive measures are a good one. The Americans recognized that highly trained pilots are valuable and worth protecting with armored seat backs and self-sealing fuel tanks. They also realized that it was particularly important to equip aircraft carriers with radar. Carriers are constantly being approached by groups of aircraft and it is essential to know whether such aircraft are one's own getting ready to land or those of the enemy closing to attack. The *Yorktown*'s state-of-the-art CXAM radar system at Midway was able to differentiate between enemy and friendly aircraft due to its IFF (Identification; Friend or Foe) capability. During the first Japanese counterattack on the afternoon of June 4, 1942, *Yorktown* radar operators were able to confirm that the "hostiles" that the IFF had picked up at 65 miles out were indeed enemy dive-bombers when it could be seen on the radar screens that the aircraft were gaining altitude as they got closer – something enemy dive-bombers do as they approach a target preparing to attack. It was especially impressive that the Yorktown's IFF system identified the Japanese dive-bombers as hostile since there were American dive-bombers returning from the morning strike at the same time and from the same direction. The IFF transponders in each of the American aircraft properly identified those particular airplanes as "friendly" to the *Yorktown*'s radar operators.[1]

American naval leaders had not only put radar out with the fleet at the earliest possible date, but had also made sure that radar was used vigorously and not simply regarded as an amusing toy. On all three of the American aircraft carriers at Midway, a trained radar operator was on duty during every watch, carefully monitoring that ship's radar screen. The use of radar as a vital weapon of war had been thoroughly ingrained into the culture of the US Navy by the time of the Battle of Midway. That kind of acceptance, even welcoming, of radar into the *culture* of the US

---

[1] H. P. Willmott, *The Barrier and the Javelin: Japanese and Allied Pacific Strategies February to June 1942* (Annapolis: Naval Institute Press, 1983): pp436–437.

Navy was just as important as was the actual physical presence of radar sets aboard ships.

By way of contrast, the Japanese were still in the "amusing toy" stage in regard to radar. Japanese use of it in 1942 was extremely limited and still very much of an experimental process. The Japanese battleships *Ise* and *Hyuga* each carried a primitive radar set that had been hastily added only in May 1942. However, those two battleships were hundreds of miles north of Nagumo, participating in the wasteful and pointless Aleutians phase of the Battle of Midway. Even had *Ise* and *Hyuga* been with Nagumo, the fact that their respective radar sets had just been added makes it highly doubtful that the radar operators on those ships would have had the experience to accurately evaluate the data on their screens[1] – a skill that is just as important as having a radar antenna rotating overhead; failure to accurately evaluate radar data completely nullifies the advantages of the physical presence of radar equipment on board a ship. An inexperienced radar operator might mistake a flock of seagulls for an approaching aircraft. It is not enough to have radar, you have to appreciate what its exact purpose is and then take the time to learn how to accurately read what a radar screen is telling you.

Not only did Adm Nagumo lack radar, but he and his staff officers were also completely unaware of how vulnerable the absence of radar had made them. Nagumo would have been wise to divide his CAP fighters into high and low elements. The Japanese could have mitigated the risk of being jumped unawares by American dive-bombers if they had kept half a dozen fighter planes circling at 20,000ft above *Kido Butai* throughout the day with orders to ignore any low-level attacks, just in case American dive-bombers should appear from on high. The need for such a step was plainly demonstrated to Nagumo more than two hours before McClusky's *Enterprise* group of dive-bombers arrived overhead. At approximately 8.00am, a squadron of American

---

[1] Parshall and Tully, *Shattered Sword*, p136, p454.

Army Air Forces B-17 bombers commanded by Lt Col Walter Sweeney, having flown out from Midway, had unsuccessfully attacked Nagumo's carriers. In keeping with Army Air Forces policy governing the use of heavy bombers against land targets, Sweeney had ordered his crews to drop their bombs from 20,000ft. The Japanese carriers thus had plenty of time for evasive maneuvers and the Army planes scored no hits. This attack was, however, a stark warning of the danger the Japanese ships faced from American aircraft that approached at high altitude.[1] Nagumo's failure to maintain defensive fighters at high altitude must therefore be added to the lengthy list of errors made by the Japanese during the battle.[2] Such a critical error adds to the evidence supporting the conclusion that the Japanese were outgeneraled, and not simply unlucky, during the Battle of Midway.

Without any Japanese radar to pick them up, McClusky's *Enterprise* dive-bombers, as well as a separate squadron of SBDs from the *Yorktown*, were able to get to a point directly above the Japanese fleet without being spotted. Reaching their pushover points without being molested by fighters or by antiaircraft fire gave the pilots the leisure to set up their attacks carefully. In the span of ten minutes, beginning at 10.20am (local time) the exceptionally good aim of *Enterprise* and *Yorktown* dive-bomber pilots would send 500lb and 1,000lb bombs crashing through the flight decks of *Kaga*, *Akagi*, and *Soryu*. The blows delivered were mortal. Japanese mechanics had been frantically arming and fueling aircraft on all three ships. Thus, the American bombs set off a chain reaction of secondary explosions that transformed three of Japan's finest aircraft carriers into raging infernos of flame and smoke. In ten minutes, three-quarters of the aircraft carrier striking force that Adm Nagumo had had at his disposal was destroyed. If one factors in the *Shokaku* and *Zuikaku*, the

---

[1]Parshall and Tully, *Shattered Sword*, pp178–180.
[2]Parshall and Tully, *Shattered Sword*, p407.

two large and modern Japanese aircraft carriers that were not present at Midway, fully half of Japan's large fleet carriers were now blazing wrecks. That figure of destroyed tonnage would increase to two-thirds after the *Hiryu* was destroyed by the Americans a few hours later.

As for the *Kaga*, Wade McClusky dropped his 500lb bomb at 1,800ft. It was a near miss, landing in the water alongside *Kaga*.[1] The fourth SBD to dive, that of VS-6 commanding officer Lt Earl Gallaher, scored the first of the four direct hits sustained by *Kaga*.[2] Seeing his bomb hit *Kaga* – one of the carriers that had launched the Pearl Harbor attack – had special significance for Earl Gallaher, as noted by historian Stephen Moore: "Back on December 7, Gallaher had seen the destruction of the battleship *Arizona*, the first vessel he had served upon after graduation from the academy. Through his brain flashed the satisfying thought, *Arizona, I remember you!*"[3]

The attack led by Wade McClusky was a resounding success that had profound strategic implications for the war in the Pacific. After six months of stunning and unbroken success, the Imperial Japanese Navy was after Midway thrown on to the defensive, where it would remain for the remainder of the war. The two targets McClusky chose for destruction, the *Akagi* and the *Kaga*, were each destroyed. Nevertheless, there have been controversies and mysteries about that attack that have continued right up until the present day. Everyone agrees that it was an "unbalanced" attack. Having chosen to dive with Scouting Six on the left-hand carrier, which turned out to be *Kaga*, McClusky

---

[1] Lord, *Incredible Victory*, pp164–168.

[2] Dickinson, with Sparkes, *The Flying Guns*, p154. For confirmation of four hits, see postwar interview with Capt Amagai Takahisa, Air Officer of *Kaga*, in *United States Strategic Bombing Survey* (USSBS) (New York: Garland Publishing Co., 1976): *Pacific*. Vol. 1. Interrogations of Japanese Officials. Naval Analysis Division. (OPNAV-P-03-100), pp1–2.

[3] Stephen L. Moore, *Pacific Payback: The Carrier Aviators Who Avenged Pearl Harbor at the Battle of Midway* (New York: NAL Caliber, 2014): pp219–220.

dove first, followed by his two wingmen, Ensigns Bill Pittman and Dick Jaccard; then by Earl Gallaher and the rest of Scouting Six. For reasons that are still not entirely clear, a number of aircraft from Bombing Squadron Six, which McClusky had ordered to attack the carrier on the right, *Akagi*, ended up joining in the attack on the *Kaga* instead, leaving less than a full squadron of aircraft left over to attack the *Akagi*. The exact number of SBDs to dive on *Akagi* is still a subject of debate. Part of the reason for the less-than-perfect division of American dive-bombers to targets was undoubtedly due to overly enthusiastic young pilots getting carried away. (At age 40, McClusky was the "old man" of the group. Most of the *Enterprise* dive-bomber pilots were in their 20s.) There are other possible reasons for the mix-up. In recent literature about the Battle of Midway, the debate about how the morning attack by *Enterprise* dive-bombers became disorganized has taken on a life of its own. Partisans in this debate often seek to pit Wade McClusky against Lt Richard Best, the latter being the commander of Bombing Squadron Six, saying that one or the other of these men supposedly made some sort of mistake that violated dive-bomber doctrine. The bitterness of this debate is regrettable, completely unnecessary, and unfair to the respective legacies of both men. Wade McClusky and Dick Best were both heroes who performed brilliantly at Midway. In point of fact, the two men made an excellent team. Dick Best was the finest bomb aimer in the Navy and Wade McClusky seemed to be part bloodhound in his ability to locate an elusive enemy under extremely difficult conditions. As we will see, Wade McClusky and Dick Best both had an excellent understanding of dive-bombing doctrine and both followed that doctrine. It was the formal American dive-bombing doctrine itself, written out by other people, that contained flaws and inconsistencies that would bedevil both McClusky and Best during the battle.

During the flight out from the *Enterprise*, several pilots in Bombing Six reported having trouble with their oxygen supply. The *Enterprise* dive-bombers had climbed to 19,000ft after take-off. However, the difficulties with his pilots' auxiliary oxygen forced Dick Best to take Bombing Six down to 15,000ft, almost a mile below McClusky, so that the pilots could breathe without wearing their oxygen masks. Best could not break radio silence to tell McClusky what he was doing. In addition to flying lower, the pilots of Bombing Six were also trailing slightly behind McClusky and Scouting Six. Written doctrine, as presented in the aforementioned March 1941 edition of *Current Tactical Orders* (*USF-74*), failed to take account of such an unforseen situation.

That document places an extraordinarily high premium on the value of hand signals to be used by pilots, particularly by squadron and group leaders, so as to enable radio silence to be maintained. *USF-74* has a hand signal for just about everything. For instance, readers are instructed that "Leader pats self on head, points to number two plane, holds up one finger then blows a kiss" is the proper method of informing the squadron that "Leader shifting lead to number two plane."[1] None of these signals are of any use if squadrons become widely separated from each other – as VS-6 and VB-6 would be at Midway. Also, all of the directives written out in *USF-74*, including those for hand signals, were better suited to small formations of aircraft, such as the sections and divisions within a single squadron. A large formation of more than 30 dive-bombers was probably not what the authors of *USF-74* had in mind when they were writing. The document, although only a year old at the time of the Battle of Midway, was already badly out of date. For Dick Best to inform Wade McClusky without breaking radio silence that he had to take Bombing Six to a lower altitude would have necessitated Best leaving his squadron temporarily, speeding up to fly around the aircraft in Scouting Six, which were following just behind McClusky's three-plane leading element, and pull up next to McClusky in order to use a hand signal. Such a maneuver would have burned precious fuel that Best could not

---

[1]Halsey, *USF-74, Revised*, p3.

spare on such a long flight and also would have thrown both squadrons into confusion as pilots tried to figure out what was going on.

Some accounts of the battle, including a 1995 oral history interview Dick Best granted to William J. Shinneman, state that upon descending to 15,000ft, the SBDs of Bombing Six were briefly out ahead of the entire *Enterprise* dive-bomber formation,[1] which would imply that McClusky could see that Bombing Six was now far below himself and Scouting Six. However, McClusky's own after action report indicates that he did not find out until just before he pushed over into his dive that Bombing Six was so far below him, receiving this news via radio from Dick Best shortly before pushover.[2] Since McClusky was looking down, desperately scanning the surface for the enemy fleet, it seems unlikely he would have failed to see Bombing Six if that squadron had pulled out ahead, however briefly. It thus seems unlikely that Bombing Six was ever in the lead.

The problem of determining how and why who dove on which carrier is further complicated by other factors. The exact position of each Japanese ship in Nagumo's formation at the time the *Enterprise* dive-bombers appeared overhead has been a subject of intense debate ever since the battle. Richard Best saw the two nearest Japanese carriers as being the "near" one and the "far" one. Wade McClusky saw them as being on the "right" and the "left," respectively.[3] Historians critical of Wade McClusky feel that written US Navy dive-bombing doctrine at the time

---

[1]Moore, *Pacific Payback*, p209. Oral history memoir of Lt Cdr Richard Halsey Best, USN (Ret) as told to William J. Shinneman, 11 August 1995. (The interview took place in King of Prussia, Pennsylvania.) Courtesy of the National Museum of the Pacific War, Fredericksburg, Texas. P40.

[2]Wade McClusky. After action report. Available at website "U.S.S. Enterprise: The Most Decorated Ship of the Second World War" www.cv6.org/company/accounts/wmcclusky/.

[3]Moore, *Pacific Payback*, p217. Parshall and Tully, *Shattered Sword*, p228. Symonds, *The Battle of Midway*, 298–300.

clearly stipulated that in a scenario in which two squadrons of dive-bombers approached two enemy targets, the leading squadron was to overfly the nearer target and take the farthest target, leaving the near target for the trailing squadron, and that McClusky failed to obey this rule.[1] In point of fact, written doctrine for distribution of targets was highly contradictory and ambiguous on this very point. What to do if the two targets were equidistant from the approaching aircraft is not even discussed in *USF-74*, but the implication was that in such a case, the group commander would assign targets by either hand signal or radio after sizing up the situation on the spot.[2]

Secondary accounts written since 1990 almost all conclude that Dick Best was certain that the carrier that McClusky saw as being to the right was further away, and thus that Best's own target for VB-6 was the carrier McClusky saw as being on the left – ie the very *Kaga* that McClusky and Scouting Six had chosen to dive on; and that by leading Scouting Six in diving on *Kaga*, McClusky took the target that should have been for Best and Bombing Six. Dick Best's 1995 interview with William Shinneman does not add any clarity to the scenario. About the approach, Dick Best said in 1995, "What I saw very thin on my port bow, just slightly to the left of my engine, was the carrier, AKAGI. More to the left was another carrier, which turned out to be the KAGA. They were about five to seven miles apart. As we continued our course, McClusky steamed just to the right of the far one, it was clear to me what he was going to do."[3] So far so good. Best's own words have the *Kaga* as the far target and that Best knew that McClusky was out ahead and heading for it (*Kaga*), leaving the *Akagi*, which Best said was nearer to himself for his own Bombing Six squadron – exactly according to doctrine as Dick Best understood it. Why then would Best

[1]Moore, *Pacific Payback*, p217. Parshall and Tully, *Shattered Sword*, p228.

[2]Halsey, *USF-74, Revised*, pp143–144.

[3]Dick Best oral history interview with Bill Shinneman, 1995. P40.

always remain convinced that McClusky had, with Scouting Six, taken the target that should have been left for Best and Bombing Six?[1]

USF-74 supports both the idea that the closer of two targets should be left for whichever squadron was trailing *and* McClusky's actions regarding how to properly divide an attacking force when the target consisted of two or more ships. The book is not well organized. Before actual bombing tactics are even discussed, dozens of pages in *USF-74* are devoted to the intricacies of formation flying and in describing the circumstances and methods under which naval aircraft should lay down smoke screens. Attack doctrine only begins to be described two-thirds of the way through a very long document. How to attack should have been covered much earlier in the book since attacking the enemy is the *raison d'être* for all naval aircraft. Quite frankly, much of what is written in *USF-74* would have been useless to American pilots at Midway because the book was out of date. Its authors indicate that they thought that a purely air battle like Midway or Coral Sea in which opposing surface ships never sighted each other was far less likely than a combined arms battle in which naval aircraft would be used to supplement attacks by surface ships. For instance, *USF-74* states that in a torpedo attack, it is advisable to have American destroyers launch torpedoes from one side of the target while American torpedo planes launch torpedoes from the other side, so as to catch the target in an "anvil" attack – ie with nowhere to turn.[2] The combined destroyer/aircraft attack on an enemy fleet is an idea that was first developed for use in US Navy fleet maneuvers in the late 1920s, a time when the lack of any kind of electronic homing device and the fact that most naval aircraft were not yet equipped with radios meant that American naval aircraft rarely flew beyond visible sighting range of their home aircraft carrier for fear of getting lost over the trackless

[1]Moore, *Pacific Payback*, pp223–227.
[2]Halsey, *USF-74, Revised*, p140.

ocean.[1] During World War 2, on the other hand, American naval aircraft would routinely search and strike at distances of well over 100 miles from their home carriers. While *USF-74* does say that if an enemy surface ship is attacked by torpedo planes alone those aircraft should divide and endeavor to come in on both bows of the target, the authors clearly feel that for torpedo attacks, a combined destroyer and air attack against enemy ships is far more desirable.[2] What American aircraft carriers were supposed to do for antisubmarine protection and for plane guard duty while their destroyers have been detached to close with the enemy to conduct such torpedo attacks is not even mentioned in *USF-74*. The fastest American destroyers in World War 2 would still have required six hours to leave their task force, steam at full speed to close with an enemy fleet 100 miles distant, launch a torpedo attack, and then return to the American carrier(s) they were responsible for guarding.

Indeed, the authors of *USF-74* failed to realize that by vastly increasing the striking distance of a fleet, naval air power ensured that during World War 2 naval battles in the Pacific would almost always be either "all air" or "all surface," but only rarely a combination of the two. The Guadalcanal campaign featured several night-time surface battles involving cruiser and battleship gunfire at close quarters in which aircraft played no role whatsoever. Full deckload strikes by carrier-based aircraft, either American or Japanese, were almost all confined to the hours of daylight during the war. On the other hand, the occasions during the war in the Pacific when opposing surface fleets slugged it out during the daytime without air support, such as at the Battle of the Komandorski Islands in March 1943, were quite rare events in which Japanese and American fleets stumbled upon each

---

[1]Thomas Wildenberg, *Destined For Glory: Dive Bombing, Midway, and the Evolution of Carrier Airpower* (Annapolis: Naval Institute Press, 1998): pp55–56, pp85–87, pp173–175.

[2]Halsey, *USF-74, Revised*, p124, p140.

other by accident. A combined air and surface battle was a very rare event during the Pacific war. The most notable example of such an engagement is the Battle off Samar in October 1944, which unfolded as it did only because the Americans were caught completely off guard on that occasion.

Adm Halsey had supervised the preparation of *USF-74* in his capacity as Commander, Aircraft, Battle Force and he wrote a short preface for the volume. However, Halsey almost certainly delegated the actual writing of the document to his staff officers. Writing "by committee" is quite common for any type of bureaucratic technical manual. However, when this occurs, it is essential that whomever does the final edit eliminates contradictions and ensures that the finished book speaks with "one voice." *USF-74* fails miserably in that regard.

Among the many doctrinal shortcomings of *USF-74* is that the document makes no provision for communications breakdowns. Dick Best had not picked up Wade McClusky's radio message telling him to attack the right-hand carrier. After hearing McClusky break radio silence by reporting contact with the enemy back to the *Enterprise*, Best had radioed McClusky that Bombing Six would take the left-hand carrier. More specifically, Best said "I am attacking according to doctrine,"[1] which Best believed McClusky would understand as Best and the trailing squadron taking what Best saw as the nearer of the two carriers. Somehow, McClusky never heard that message, but he did hear a second message immediately afterward by which Best now informed McClusky of the oxygen problems in VB-6 and explained that, owing to this trouble, VB-6 was now at a lower altitude than was VS-6.[2]

---

[1] Best to Lord, March 7, 1967. Walter Lord Papers, Naval History and Heritage Command (NHHC). P2.

[2] Wade McClusky. After action report. Available at website "U.S.S. Enterprise: The Most Decorated Ship of the Second World War" www.cv6.org/company/accounts/wmcclusky/. Accessed May 20, 2015.

The passage of *USF-74* that supports Dick Best's belief that the leading squadron should take the far target states under the heading "Target Designation" that dive-bombing attacks should be characterized by "all airplanes of a *section bombing* the same target whether the dive is made by sections or by single airplanes." Immediately following is the sentence that motivates all of Wade McClusky's critics: "No. 1 target is the farthest away."[1] However, those critics would do well to note that elsewhere in the same document, under the heading "Distribution of Targets," *USF-74* contradicts everything that was said earlier about "near" and "far" and leaves everything up to the group commander's discretion instead:

> "(1) If the number of main objective targets to be attacked has not been specified by higher authority, the Group Commander will do so either before take-off *or prior to ordering the attack*. (2) Each squadron will normally divide planes equally among the main objectives assigned."[2]

Nothing here about "near" and "far" and this set of instructions was followed to the letter by Wade McClusky. He assigned targets when he was on the scene and could size up the situation for himself. Fourteen pages further on in *USF-74* are more instructions that support McClusky's actions: "Group commanders will determine and direct the distribution of targets to the squadrons of their respective groups. This will be dependent to a certain extent upon what targets have been attacked by the groups ahead."[3] This injunction would have been especially relevant at Midway if the dive-bombers, fighter planes, and torpedo planes of all three American carriers had formed up and proceeded to

---

[1]Halsey, *USF-74, Revised*, p105. Italics in original for "*section bomb*," at which point the line breaks. Italics added for "ing."

[2]Halsey, *USF-74, Revised*, pp143–144. Italics added.

[3]Halsey, *USF-74, Revised*, p158.

the target together.[1] But group commanders are seen as being the key element, and McClusky did his job in terms of assessing the results of the earlier American attacks; namely he realized that none of the Japanese ships had as yet been damaged. Wade McClusky had to decide how his group of 30 aircraft could do the most damage to a fleet containing four undamaged aircraft carriers. His choice – focusing exclusively on the two nearest (and largest) carriers – was undoubtedly correct.

In the face of such completely contradictory written instructions, the real problem lay in the fact that Dick Best never received McClusky's radioed instructions, which was nobody's fault. Both men were following doctrine. The contradictions regarding target distribution in the pages of *USF-74* are a classic example of the pitfalls of a document written by committee. Most likely, different officers wrote these contradictory sets of instructions, which appear in different sections of the document, and the final editor failed to reconcile the inconsistencies. All the information on target distribution should have been placed in one section of the document. Instead, target selection instructions are scattered across isolated parts of the *USF-74* manual. Forty pages of text on other subjects separate the "No. 1 target is the farthest away"[2] instruction followed by Dick Best and the injunctions that everything about target selection/distribution is up to the group commander's discretion once he has sized up the situation in person – the latter being the instructions Wade McClusky followed. Both Wade McClusky and Dick Best followed written dive-bombing doctrine. It was that written doctrine that was flawed and contradictory.

Several theories have been mentioned as to why Best did not pick up McClusky's radio signal assigning targets. The radio aerial on each SBD was a wire extending from a short mast

---

[1]Halsey, *USF-74, Revised*, pp157–158.

[2]Halsey, *USF-74, Revised*, p105. Italics in original for "*section bomb*," at which point the line breaks. Italics added for "ing."

sticking up from the fuselage just in front of, and to the left of, the cockpit to a grommet attached to the top of the tail. It has been suggested that since McClusky and Scouting Six were flying a mile above Bombing Six and slightly ahead, McClusky's own airplane was blocking his radio transmissions to Best and also blocking some of Best's return signals – ie that the two men were in each other's radio blind spots. It is also possible that each man may have keyed his radio transmitter at the same moment – ie they were talking over each other.[1] Dick Best himself offered a much simpler explanation in 1995: that his radio simply was not working properly that day.[2]

The radio blind spot theory is only valid if Best and VB-6 were aligned laterally with McClusky – ie if VB-6 was below and slightly behind, but still in exact *lateral* alignment with McClusky and VS-6. It is quite possible, however, that the two squadrons had diverged laterally as well as vertically well before reaching the pushover point. Most accounts agree that by the time the *Enterprise* dive-bombers reached their respective pushover points, Dick Best and Bombing Six were flying a mile below and somewhat behind Wade McClusky and Scouting Six. However, it is quite possible that in addition to flying a mile below McClusky, the SBDs of VB-6 may have also been quite some distance to McClusky's left; perhaps as much as a half mile or more at 10.22am (local time) when Wade McClusky himself initiated the first dive by an *Enterprise* SBD on the Japanese carriers at Midway. The evidence for this scenario is a map (see Figure 12.1) which is attached to the shorter of two Bombing Six action reports and that seems to have been drawn either by Dick Best or by Lt J. R. Penland, the latter having been the leader of the Second Division of Dick Best's Bombing Six squadron. J. R. Penland wrote the squadron's formal after action report, dated June 10, 1942 and covering VB-6 activities during the entire battle

---

[1]Moore, *Pacific Payback*, p217. Symonds, *The Battle of Midway*, pp300–301.
[2]Best oral history interview with Shinneman, 1995. P41.

because Dick Best had become seriously ill after inhaling soda ash from a defective oxygen bottle on June 4. Thus, while Best turned in superb performances in both American dive-bombing attacks on June 4 – landing a 1,000lb bomb on the *Akagi* in the morning attack and then putting another one through the flight

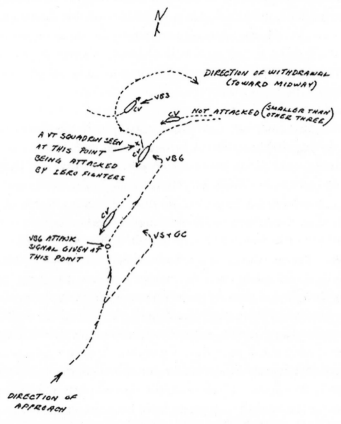

FIGURE 12.1 The map attached to the shorter of two Bombing Six Action Reports and that may have been drawn by Dick Best.[1]

[1]Bombing Squadron 6 Action Report, Battle of Midway, 4 June 1942. (Abbreviated report covering morning attack) National Archives and Records Administration (hereinafter NARA), College Park, Maryland. Record Group (hereinafter RG) 38. Records of the Office of the Chief of Naval Operations. World War II Action and Operational Reports. Box 387. Commander Bombing Squadron Six (VB-6) file.

deck of the *Hiryu* during the afternoon attack – he was quite ill by day's end. The soda ash had activated latent tuberculosis in his lungs and Best was taken directly to sick bay upon returning to the *Enterprise* after the attack on the *Hiryu*. Dick Best did survive his bout with tuberculosis, but he had to endure a long period of hospitalization that put an end to his career as a Navy pilot.

In this map, McClusky and VS-6 can be seen approaching *Kaga*, which is furthest south of the four Japanese carriers – his position labeled as "VS and GC" (scouting squadron and group commander). Next in line to the north of *Kaga* is *Akagi*, which on the map is being approached by those Bombing Six aircraft that had split off from McClusky.

Historians have not paid much attention to the Best/Penland map, perhaps because of the uncertainty as to which of the two men drew it. The original of the map resides in the US National Archives at College Park, Maryland and was drawn on the back side of a short VB-6 action report – one that describes the salient points of the morning attack only. There is some question as to who wrote this early, hurried report: Best or Penland? The full report referenced earlier dated June 10 was definitely written by Penland and is quite comprehensive. Such reports served as the official and comprehensive account of each squadron for the entirety of each battle that that particular squadron had been involved in. The earlier, summary, report detailing VB-6 activity in the morning attack only is much more brief; more like a set of talking points rather than a formal report. These summary reports had a "fill-in-the-blank" format in which squadron commanders were expected to provide data on certain specific issues under designated headings such as "Specific Objectives" and "Enemy Tactics." Squadron commanders were required to fill out these preliminary reports as soon as they landed after each combat mission. These initial action reports were typed on to pre-printed forms that under the heading "Instructions," stated in no uncertain terms:

"(a) To be filled out by unit commander immediately upon landing after each action or operation in contact with the enemy.

188

(b) Do not 'gun deck' this report--if data can not be estimated with reasonable accuracy enter a dash in space for which no data is available."[1]

The instructions are clear: no delay. J. R. Penland's name is typed at the bottom of this report, which also bears his signature.[2] Intriguingly, however, the report is dated June 4, a date that is impossible if Penland was its author. Penland ran out of fuel after the morning attack and had to make a water landing, and he and his gunner H. F. Heard were picked up from their inflatable raft the following day (June 5) by the destroyer USS *Phelps*. It was not until June 7 that, while the fleet was refueling at sea, the *Phelps* was able to transfer Penland and Heard as well as VS-6 pilot Clarence Dickinson and his gunner J. F. DeLuca to a tanker by high line. A few hours later the four men were transferred again, this time back aboard the *Enterprise*.[3] Dick Best was the commander of Bombing Six, but inhaling the soda ash meant that he was beginning to feel ill after the morning attack. He was able, however, to fly the afternoon strike against the *Hiryu*. If the abbreviated report was filled out immediately after the morning attack on June 4 as per the "do not gun deck

[1]Bombing Squadron 6 Action Report, Battle of Midway, 4 June 1942. (Abbreviated report covering morning attack) NARA RG 38. Records of the Office of the Chief of Naval Operations. World War II Action and Operational Reports. Box 387. Commander Bombing Squadron Six (VB-6) file.

[2]Bombing Squadron 6 Action Report, Battle of Midway, 4 June 1942. (Abbreviated report covering morning attack) NARA RG 38. Records of the Office of the Chief of Naval Operations. World War II Action and Operational Reports. Box 387. Commander Bombing Squadron Six (VB-6) file.

[3]Email communication, Thom Walla to me, March 12, 2015. Dickinson, with Sparkes, *The Flying Guns*, pp193–196. Bombing Squadron 6 Action Report, Battle of Midway, 4 June 1942. (Abbreviated report covering morning attack) NARA RG 38. Records of the Office of the Chief of Naval Operations. World War II Action and Operational Reports. Box 387. Commander Bombing Squadron Six (VB-6) file.

this report" instructions quoted above, it and the map that accompanies it would, it seems, have to have been written and drawn, respectively, by Dick Best. Lending credence to this idea is the fact that there is apparently no such abbreviated VB-6 action report for the afternoon strike against the *Hiryu*. By the time he landed back aboard *Enterprise* after the afternoon strike, Dick Best was far too ill to write anything and J. R. Penland was still at that time floating in a liferaft awaiting rescue. Indeed, in a 1967 letter he wrote to Walter Lord, Penland stated emphatically that he definitely had *not* drawn the map and that he, Penland, thought it must have been drawn by Dick Best.[1]

Why then does the brief report bear Penland's signature? There is no date beside Penland's signature at the end of that report. The June 4 date appears at the top of the document only. It thus seems highly likely that Dick Best wrote this brief report and drew the map before he fell ill, and that Penland merely signed the document as a formality a few days later so that it could be turned in as an official squadron record.[2]

For these reasons, it is perhaps best to refer to the highly revealing diagram in Figure 12.1 as "the Best/Penland map." The map shows McClusky as group commander and VS-6 swinging far out to the right long before the pushover point, while Best and VB-6 headed straight for the Japanese carrier that turned out to be *Kaga*. If the Best/Penland map is accurate, it goes far toward explaining why McClusky saw the two targets as being equidistant from him – one on the left and one to the right – while Dick Best saw the two carriers as being "near" and "far." If the Best/Penland map is accurate, it would seem that McClusky was completely unaware that VB-6 was not only a mile below

---

[1] J. R. Penland to Walter Lord, February 26, 1967. Walter Lord Papers, NHHC.

[2] Bombing Squadron 6 Action Report, Battle of Midway, 4 June 1942. (Abbreviated report covering morning attack) NARA RG 38. Records of the Office of the Chief of Naval Operations. World War II Action and Operational Reports. Box 387. Commander Bombing Squadron Six (VB-6) file.

him but also quite a ways off to his left. Not having received McClusky's radio message assigning targets, Best's cryptic "I am attacking according to doctrine"[1] message may indicate that Best worried that McClusky was going to allow each individual pilot to choose his own target. Perhaps being confused as to what McClusky's intentions were, Best's message was his way of letting the group commander know that Best intended for his own VB-6 to remain together as a unit and to take what Best saw as the "near" carrier.

McClusky's after action report indicates that by the time he pushed over into his dive, the group commander was aware that Best was below him but that McClusky also firmly believed that Best and the other planes of VB-6 had been directly behind McClusky and VS-6 right up to the pushover point. McClusky wrote that:

> "Picking the two nearest carriers in the line of approach, I ordered Scouting Six to follow my section in attacking the carrier on the immediate left and Bombing Six to take the right-hand carrier. These two carriers were the largest in the formation and later were determined to be the *Kaga* and the *Akagi*. As a point for later mention, LT Dick Best, skipper of Bombing Six, radioed that he was having oxygen trouble, had dropped to 15,000 feet and would remain at that altitude to commence the attack."[2]

McClusky's attack order as described above in his own words would not have made any sense if McClusky had been aware that VB-6 was far off to his left and not right behind him. If the Best/Penland map is accurate, McClusky must have believed that Best and VB-6 were directly behind himself and VS-6, when in fact VB-6 and VS-6 were quite possibly now widely separated

[1]Best to Lord, March 7, 1967. Walter Lord Papers, NHHC. P2.

[2]Wade McClusky. After action report. Available at website "U.S.S. Enterprise: The Most Decorated Ship of the Second World War" www.cv6.org/company/accounts/wmcclusky/. Accessed May 20, 2015.

laterally as well as vertically.[1] The Best/Penland map shows why McClusky saw the targets as being on the "right" and the "left," while Dick Best saw them as being "near" and "far."[2] Dick Best's own words, quoted above from his 1995 oral history, indicate that when he first spotted the Japanese carriers, *Akagi* was near to him – just to his left and slightly ahead of him. "More to the left" was the *Kaga* and the two carriers "were about five to seven miles apart." He saw that McClusky and VS-6 were "just to the right of the far one" (*Kaga*).[3] This lends credence to the idea that McClusky and Best had indeed become separated laterally, although Best puts McClusky and VS-6 some 5 miles *to the left* of Best and VB-6 whereas the Best/Penland map indicates that it was Best and VB-6 that were themselves off to the left of McClusky and VS-6.

While researching his *Incredible Victory*, Walter Lord interviewed Dick Best and many other veterans of the battle, both American and Japanese. Best and Lord also exchanged many letters in 1966 and 1967. In one of his letters to Lord, Dick Best recalls being directly behind and below McClusky: "I was flying approximately 5,000ft below and a quarter mile behind McClusky."[4] He makes no mention of being off to McClusky's left and thus that hypothesis cannot be considered proven fact. In the same letter to Lord and elsewhere, Best claims that he was left with five aircraft (ie the entire first division of Bombing Six) with which to attack the *Akagi*: "As I remember, then McCluskey [sic] took his three plane group leader section, eighteen planes of Gallaher's, and ten of my [fifteen] planes in on a carrier, never to be positively identified."[5]

---

[1]Email correspondence, Thom Walla to me, March 11, 2015.

[2]Moore, *Pacific Payback*, p217. Parshall and Tully, *Shattered Sword*, p228. Symonds, *The Battle of Midway*, 298–300.

[3]Best oral history interview with Shinneman, 1995. P40.

[4]Best to Lord, January 27 1966, p2. Walter Lord Papers, NHHC.

[5]Best to Lord, January 27, 1966, p3. Walter Lord Papers, NHHC.

1. Wade as an infant in 1903. Phil McClusky collection.

SENIOR CLASS

2. The Senior Class at South Park High in 1918. Wade stands third from right in the fourth row, near the center of the photo. *The Dial: 1917–1918* (yearbook). Courtesy of South Park High School.

3. The Nine High Hats in formation. U.S. Navy Photo. Phil McClusky collection.

4. The Nine High Hats performing on August 17, 1929. Note the ropes connecting each set of three aircraft. U.S. Navy Photo. Phil McClusky collection.

5. Another view of the High Hats on August 17, 1929. U.S. Navy Photo.
Phil McClusky collection.

6. Admiral Pettengill with his staff. Wade is standing, far right. U.S. Navy Photo.
Phil McClusky collection.

7. The first tour on Admiral Horne's staff. Wade is standing, center rear, behind Horne's right shoulder. U.S. Navy Photo. Phil McClusky collection.

8. A Douglas SBD Dauntless dive bomber as flown by Wade McClusky flies over Wake Island. Photo. Corbis/Getty Images.

9. Wartime publicity photo after Midway, standing next to an F4F Wildcat. U.S. Navy Photo. Phil McClusky collection.

10. Staff duty, 1943. U.S. Navy Photo.
Phil McClusky collection.

11. As a Commander in the
mid-war period. U.S. Navy Photo.
Phil McClusky collection.

12. More staff duty, 1946. U.S. Navy Photo. Phil McClusky collection.

13. As a captain in 1946. U.S. Navy Photo. Phil McClusky collection.

14. The house Wade designed at 1826 Circle Road, Ruxton, Maryland.
Phil McClusky collection.

15. Another view of the house. Phil McClusky collection.

16. Left to right: Admiral Spruance, McClusky, and Maxwell Leslie arrive in Hawaii for a 15-year reunion of Midway veterans, 1957. Phil McClusky collection.

17. Wade as a Civil Defense Shelter Officer for the state of Maryland, second from left, front row, 1963. Phil McClusky collection.

18. Wade tours *U.S.S. Yorktown* (CV-10), 1968. U.S. Navy Photo.
Phil McClusky collection.

19. Wade with Secretary of the Navy John H. Chafee, 1971. U.S. Navy Photo.
Phil McClusky collection.

20. Wade, Ruth, and Philip at the Pentagon with Secretary of the Navy John H. Chafee, 1971. Young Philip had actually cut his hair for the occasion. U.S. Navy Photo. Phil McClusky collection.

21. Wade, at right, in December 1975; six months before his death. Phil McClusky collection.

22. Relaxing after doing some yard work, 1975. Phil McClusky collection.

23. U.S.S. *McClusky*, FFG-41, at sea. U.S. Navy Photo. Phil McClusky collection.

24. Launch day for U.S.S. McClusky, FFG-41, September 18, 1982.
Todd Pacific Shipyards Co. Phil McClusky collection.

25. The family at the launching. Left to right: Wade Sanford (Pat) McClusky, Patricia, Carole, Philip, Ruth. Todd Pacific Shipyards Co. Phil McClusky collection.

26. Ruth breaks a champagne bottle against the bows at the launch. Todd Pacific Shipyards Co. Phil McClusky collection.

In his own communications with Walter Lord, Wade McClusky indicates that he too thought that Best and Bombing Six were directly behind him: "It *may* have been the unreliability of the radios that Best didn't get the word but he was having oxygen trouble and dropped down to 15,000 ft. However, Scouting Six was closely following me and Best, lagging behind, could see the pattern as it developed—and consequently took the right-hand carrier."[1]

If, as the Best/Penland map indicates, VB-6 and VS-6 diverged laterally by a considerable distance long before the pushover point, the question remains as to why? McClusky's after action report makes no mention of his ordering such a lateral split. It is feasible, but highly unlikely, that McClusky ordered the squadrons to diverge laterally as early as the map indicates and then forgot to mention that order in his own after action report. However, Wade McClusky was a careful man who was highly unlikely to neglect to include such an important detail. It is also possible that Dick Best sighted the Japanese ships before McClusky did and headed straight in, with McClusky passing south of the Japanese and then turning left when he sighted them. This also seems unlikely in that flying a mile higher than Best, McClusky would have had the better view, and McClusky was watching very carefully for any sign of the enemy, writing in his after action report that he was using a pair of binoculars "which were practically glued to my eyes."[2] It is more likely that McClusky, at the head of the leading element, saw the enemy ships before anyone else in the group did. His reason for swinging out to the right could well have been a desire to

---

[1]McClusky to Walter Lord, February 24, 1967. Walter Lord Papers, NHHC. Handwritten with squiggly line under "may" and a straight underline of "get".

[2]Wade McClusky. After action report. Available at website "U.S.S. Enterprise: The Most Decorated Ship of the Second World War" www.cv6.org/company/accounts/wmcclusky/. Accessed May 20, 2015.

get the sun behind him before he attacked.[1] If McClusky was trying to get up-sun, that too would be exactly according to doctrine as spelled out in *USF-74*, which states that "Diving directly out of the sun provides concealment from the vessel being attacked. It further hampers anti-aircraft fire control. To be effective all airplanes of the squadron must dive directly out of the sun."[2]

In addition to seeking to dive out of the sun, McClusky's swing out to the right, followed by a left turn that put *Kaga* and *Akagi* to his left and right, respectively, may have been prompted by another injunction in *USF-74*, which states: "When bombing four vessels the direction of dive must not coincide with the line of bearing. This precaution is necessary in order to avoid pulling out directly toward and over the target of following airplanes."[3] McClusky's route, as shown in the Best/Penland map, may have been prompted by his desire to be not only up-sun but also on the enemy's beam. That map and other sources indicate that when the American dive-bombers arrived, the four Japanese carriers were strung out in a line: – southwest to northeast.[4] McClusky may have wanted to ensure that his own and the other American aircraft that dove on *Kaga* did not pull out of their dives directly above the next ship in line, *Akagi*, thereby perhaps throwing off the aim of the pilots of Bombing Six, whom McClusky had ordered to attack the *Akagi*. As a superb air group commander,

---

[1] I am indebted to Thom Walla for making me aware of the existence of the Best/Penland map and for many other helpful suggestions, such as that Best may have spotted the enemy before McClusky did, and that a beam attack made the *Kaga* very difficult to hit. I am also indebted to George Walsh for suggesting that McClusky may have been trying to get "up-sun" of the enemy. Email communication, Thom Walla to me, March 11, 2015. Email communication, George Walsh to me, May 9, 2015.

[2] Halsey, *USF-74, Revised*, p101.

[3] Halsey, *USF-74, Revised*, p105.

[4] For another map that generally supports this scenario, see Parshall and Tully, *Shattered Sword*, p220.

McClusky was thinking about both of his squadrons, not just VS-6, to which he had attached himself.

McClusky's swing out to the right may have confirmed Dick Best in the latter's belief that McClusky was going to attack what Best saw as the "far" carrier and thus may explain why Best may have diverged laterally from McClusky well before the pushover point so as to bore straight in on what Best saw as the "near" carrier. In diverging laterally from McClusky well before the pushover point, Best would have been supported by a passage in *USF-74* that states that it is advantageous for a large group of attacking aircraft to break up into smaller groups as it nears the target.[1] This technique was seen as being particularly important when American naval aircraft were, as at Midway, attacking a group of enemy ships rather than just one vessel.[2]

Wade McClusky and Dick Best clearly misunderstood each other's intentions at the pushover point and Best was shocked to see McClusky and the SBDs of Scouting Six diving down past him toward the target Best had expected to attack with Bombing Six. If the Best/Penland map is accurate, McClusky and VS-6 came not just from above, but also from Best's right when diving past VB-6. Best and the other pilots in Bombing Six already had their dive brake flaps open and had been about to push over into their dives. With an admirable calmness similar to that displayed by McClusky himself when McClusky had to decide which way to turn during the search, Richard Best rapidly adjusted to a changed situation. He closed his dive brakes and signaled to his squadron to follow him as he headed toward the right-hand carrier, Nagumo's flagship *Akagi*.[3]

It is here that another of the great mysteries of the Battle of Midway surfaces. How many pilots in Bombing Six actually understood the change in plans and followed Best, and how many

[1]Halsey, *USF-74, Revised*, p142.
[2]Halsey, *USF-74, Revised*, p71.
[3]Moore, *Pacific Payback*, pp223–227.

dove with McClusky and Scouting Six on the *Kaga*? At the very least, Best and his two wingmen, Lt (junior grade) E. J. Kroeger and Ensign F. T. Weber, dove on the *Akagi* and it was Richard Best himself who scored a direct hit amidships with his 1,000lb bomb. One of the pilots with Best scored either a second hit or a near miss at the stern of the *Akagi*. The *Akagi*'s captain, Aoki Taijiro, stated in a postwar interview that two bombs struck the *Akagi*.[1] J. F. Murray, Dick Best's rear-seat gunner, told Walter Lord that there were at least two direct hits on *Akagi*, with a third bomb being either a hit or a very close near miss.[2] Each American dive-bombing squadron was divided into three divisions. What of the other two pilots in Best's First Division of VB-6, Ensign Delbert W. Halsey (no relation to Adm William F. Halsey, Jr) and Lt (junior grade) Wilbur E. (Bill) Roberts? Dick Best stated on numerous occasions after the war that Bill Roberts dove on the same target that he (Best) had attacked.[3] Likewise, Roberts claimed after the war that he dove with Best on a carrier that had a left-side island structure.[4] Of the three Japanese aircraft carriers destroyed in the morning attack, only *Akagi* had its island on the port side, indicating that at least a fourth airplane dove with Best and his wingmen on the Japanese flagship. Delbert Halsey did not survive the battle. He ran out of fuel after dropping his bomb. Halsey was heard on the radio saying he had to make a water landing. Each SBD carried a self-inflating liferaft. Halsey and his rear-seat gunner J. W. Jenkins did get their raft inflated and were seen to climb aboard it. As we have seen, at least three American aviators – Ensigns Wesley F. Osmus and Frank O'Flaherty and Aviation Machinist's Mate, 1st Class Bruno Peter Gaido – were

---

[1]Naval Analysis Division, *United States Strategic Bombing Survey* (hereinafter USSBS) (New York: Garland Publishing Co., 1976): *Pacific*. Vol. 1. Interrogations of Japanese Officials. (OPNAV-P-03-100): p13, p14.

[2]James F. Murray to Lord, February 26, 1967. Walter Lord Papers, NHHC.

[3]See, for instance, Barde, "The Battle of Midway: A Study in Command," p257.

[4]Lord notes from interview with Bill Roberts, April 19, 1966. Walter Lord Papers, NHHC.

interrogated, then executed by the Japanese after being unlucky enough to go down near the Japanese fleet.[1] It is possible that other downed American aviators were sighted by the crews of Japanese warships, plucked from the water, tortured, interrogated, and then executed. That could have been the fate of Halsey and Jenkins. For several days after the battle, American ships and PBY Catalina flying boats searched for and picked up survivors, American and Japanese, from the water in the battle zone. Despite the best efforts of the searchers, the Pacific Ocean is vast and it is almost certain that not all survivors were located. Thus, it is entirely possible that Halsey and Jenkins were simply missed in the search and eventually died of exposure, thirst, and/or starvation. Whichever way they met their deaths, the fact remains that nobody was ever able to interview Delbert Halsey or J. W. Jenkins to get their opinions as to which Japanese carrier Halsey dove on.

The fact that Bill Roberts, piloting the fourth or fifth aircraft in the First Division of Bombing Six, remained convinced that his target had a port-side island structure is a critical piece of evidence in determining how many American aircraft dove on *Akagi*. While he concluded that five American dive-bombers dove on *Akagi*, Walter Lord admits that Japanese witnesses on *Akagi*, including Adm Nagumo, saw only three of them.[2] Two of the four Japanese carriers, *Akagi* and *Hiryu*, had port-side island structures, something that was and is exceedingly rare (so rare that nowadays it is unheard of; every American aircraft carrier since the old *Lexington* and *Saratoga* of 1927 has had a starboard-side island structure.) The certainty of Bill Roberts, when he was interviewed by Walter Lord, that he (Roberts) had attacked a carrier with a port-side island provides compelling evidence that at least four American aircraft dove on the *Akagi*. Japanese aircraft carriers tended to have small island structures

---

[1] Robert E. Barde, "Midway: Tarnished Victory" *Military Affairs*. Vol. 47; No. 4. December 1983. Pp188–192.

[2] Lord, *Incredible Victory*, pp171–173.

because unlike American naval architects, Japanese designers generally did not incorporate a carrier's funnels into the island structure. Instead, most Japanese aircraft carriers sported odd-looking horizontal funnel trunks that vented boiler exhaust out the side of the ship rather than straight up. The *Akagi* had a particularly massive funnel trunk on its starboard side, which Richard Best apparently confused with a starboard-side island. However, there is no way that Bill Roberts could have mistaken funnel trunks for a left-side island for one simple reason: while *Akagi* and *Hiryu* differed from *Kaga* and *Soryu* in having port side islands, *the funnel trunks on all four of the Japanese carriers vented to starboard*. There was no major structural element on the left side of the *Kaga* that Roberts could have mistaken for a port-side island structure, which makes it quite difficult to avoid the conclusion that Bill Roberts dove on the *Akagi* – which did have a left-side island (and right-side funnel trunks). And it is worth repeating that the fifth pilot in Best's first division of VB-6, Delbert Halsey, was killed in the battle and thus was never able to tell anybody which carrier he dove on.

In recent years, many historians have insisted that only three American dive-bombers attacked the *Akagi*,[1] but the possibility that five or more did so cannot be discounted. Like the idea that Wade McClusky supposedly did not understand dive-bombing tactics, the "three-planes-only attacking *Akagi*" has become a prominent but unproven part of the post-1990 paradigm used by most Midway scholars. Older literature allows for the possibility of more American SBDs diving on *Akagi*. For instance, aviation historian Barrett Tillman wrote in 1976 that Dick Best's entire first section of Bombing Six (five aircraft) dove on *Akagi*. However, by 2011 Tillman had revised his estimate downward. In his biography of the *Enterprise*

---

[1] Moore, *Pacific Payback*, pp226–227. Barrett Tillman, *Enterprise: America's Fightingest Ship and the Men Who Helped Win World War II* (New York: Simon & Schuster, 2012): p74, pp76–77.

published that year, Tillman now claims that only Dick Best and his two wingmen dove on *Akagi*.[1]

In point of fact, the three-plane-only scenario has never been proven in regard to the attack on the *Akagi*. Indeed, there is considerable evidence available to challenge that very theory. The leader of a division is supposed to dive first. For only three aircraft to attack the *Akagi* would mean that Halsey and Roberts, the fourth and fifth SBDs in Richard Best's First Division of VB-6, would have had to begin their dives before Best himself dove. Since Dick Best was both their division leader and their squadron leader, for Halsey and Roberts to do that would have constituted a major breach of combat discipline. Walter Lord interviewed 400 veterans of the Battle of Midway including Dick Best, Wade McClusky, and Bill Roberts while researching *Incredible Victory*. Walter Lord concluded that five SBDs – ie the entirety of the Dick Best's first division of VB-6 – did in fact dive on the *Akagi*.[2]

Lord was undoubtedly influenced in concluding that five planes dove on *Akagi* by what Dick Best himself had told Lord. Walter Lord's papers at the Naval Historical and Heritage Command in Washington, DC contain a wealth of primary source data from the 1960s, when the Midway veterans were still active, middle-aged men, indicating that Dick Best and Bill Roberts were both convinced that they dove together and attacked the same carrier. Best told Lord in 1967 that "I must plead guilty myself to a firm conviction that my drop was a hit. I thought I was equally firm as to which side the island was on on my target. My certainty there is shaken by Bill Roberts' recollection of particularly noticing something which he had no reason to expect."[3] That something was *Akagi*'s port-side island.

[1] Tillman, *Enterprise*, p76.

[2] Lord, *Incredible Victory*, pp164–168. I am indebted to Mr. Thom Walla for reminding me of the protocol of combat discipline.

[3] Best to Lord, March 7, 1967. Walter Lord Papers, NHHC. P3.

Best clearly felt that Roberts, a fourth pilot, was with him. Best also felt that three of the five planes in his division scored hits: "My recollection of our target goes even further in that when I pulled it back on its tail to watch the bomb drop I observed six to twelve planes back near the fantail and saw two bombs drop among them right after mine."[1]

Further evidence that Bill Roberts dove with Best, Kroeger, and Weber on *Akagi* comes from a 1971 University of Maryland PhD dissertation by Midway scholar Robert Barde. While it was, sadly, never published, Barde's dissertation is an invaluable source for any historian researching the Battle of Midway. Doing his research in the late 1960s, contemporaneously with, but independently of, Walter Lord, Robert Barde spoke to many of the same Midway veterans that Lord did. What Barde learned is highly revealing about the attack on *Akagi*, yet Barde's views on this phase of the battle are ignored in books about the battle written since 1990.

Like Walter Lord, Robert Barde benefited greatly from the fact that although the Midway veterans he interviewed were no longer young, neither were they old enough for their memories to have dimmed much. Dick Best was 56 years old when he was interviewed by Barde at Best's home at 218 Twenty-First Street, Santa Monica, California on May 15, 1966.[2] Best told Barde that when he pulled out of his dive after scoring a hit on *Akagi* with his 1,000lb bomb, he noted that Bill Roberts was "still flying wing on him."[3] That means, in Dick Best's own words, that at least four SBDs dove on *Akagi* – Best, his regular wingmen Kroeger and Weber, *and* Bill Roberts. Robert Barde thus concluded that all five planes in Best's First Division of Bombing Six dove on *Akagi*. He even felt it was possible that at least one SBD from that squadron's Third Division also dove on *Akagi*, which would

[1]Best to Lord, March 7, 1967. Walter Lord Papers, NHHC. P4.

[2]Barde, "The Battle of Midway: A Study in Command," p232, *n.*

[3]Barde, "The Battle of Midway: A Study in Command," p257.

make a total of six American aircraft involved in the attack on the Japanese flagship; double the figure of three grudgingly allotted by Midway historians writing since 1990.[1]

In 1967 Walter Lord sent Dick Best a model of the *Akagi*, with its left-side island and enormous right-side funnel trunks, as the two men continued to ponder which carrier Best had attacked. In his reply to Lord, Best begins to doubt his earlier insistence that he had attacked a carrier with a right-side island. In this letter, Dick Best also reiterates his certainty that Bill Roberts, who always insisted that his target had a port-side island, dove with Best:

"The thing that caught my eye, both in the sketches and in the model you sent me, is the obtrusiveness of the stack on the starboard side that juts out horizontally. With the black boot topping painted around the smoky end, it is really a very noticeable piece of the superstructure. So much so that the small bridge superstructure on the port side isn't especially conspicuous. Do you suppose it possible that in the first excitement and thrill of exhilaration of seeinga [sic] Japanese carrier … I could have mistaken a stack structure for the carrier island I expected to find in that approximate location?

Either Bill Roberts is crazy; or I am. And, I am so fairminded I don't know which one to accuse. Instead, I have constructed and exucse [sic] by which I might be mistaken instead of merely crazy."[2]

In view of how firmly the "three planes only" attacking *Akagi* idea is entrenched into the post-1990 paradigm currently used by most Midway scholars, it cannot be stressed often enough that here again Dick Best clearly states that Bill Roberts, a fourth

[1] Barde, "The Battle of Midway: A Study in Command," pp244–247.
[2] Dick Best to Walter Lord, December 6, 1967. Walter Lord Papers, NHHC.

pilot, was with Best, Weber, and Kroeger in the attack on *Akagi*.
And there is still the very real possibility that Delbert Halsey
also dove on *Akagi*. The five aircraft in Best's First Division of
Bombing Six – Best himself, his wingmen Kroeger and Weber
as well as Roberts and Halsey – were flying close together, each
plane within 100ft of another, but the other two divisions in
Best's words "had pulled well out to either side." Best continues
in regard to signaling the other pilots in his division to abort
their attacks on the *Kaga* and to head over toward *Akagi*
instead: "My shaking elevators could clearly be seen by all *four*
of them and was an unmistakable and unambiguous signal to
close up."[1]

Bill Roberts himself never had the slightest doubt that he
A) dove on a carrier with a port-side island (which could only
have been *Akagi* since *Hiryu* was not attacked in the morning
attack by dive-bombers from *Enterprise*); B) that it was the same
carrier Dick Best dove on; and C) that he (Roberts) saw Dick
Best make his dive. Roberts adds at least a fourth aircraft to the
attack on *Akagi*, and there may have been several more. Walter
Lord interviewed Bill Roberts face-to-face on April 19, 1966.
In the Acknowledgments section of *Incredible Victory*, Lord
thanks his secretary and typist/transcriber Florence Gallagher,
who had worked with him on all of his books, for her continued
willingness to carry out the thankless task of "typing [Lord's]
scribbled foolscap."[2] The long-suffering Ms Gallagher deserves
all the credit Lord gives her, and then some. Walter Lord was a
superb historian but his handwriting was atrocious – bad enough
to make the worst scrawl on a doctor's prescription pad look
good. Lord's notes from his interview with Bill Roberts are quite
revealing but his hieroglyphic handwriting makes them difficult
to decipher. In the quote below, any word that is less than fully
legible in Lord's notes is set off in brackets:

---

[1] Best to Lord, March 7, 1967. Walter Lord Papers, NHHC. P2. My italics.

[2] Lord, *Incredible Victory*, p307.

"Best's group formed in column, & Robbie thought he was crazy. Seemed to invite enormous trouble from Zeros. Later realized how smart Best was—he had figured all Zeros down below fighting torp planes... Sure [illegible] target was Akagi.

Then suddenly Best pushed over—& no one dived more suddenly or steeply than Best. Group hurled down after him. Target had island on port—certain of this; noticed it at the time because so unusual... Feels sure Best's bomb hit right in middle of planes—wonders whether some one could have dropped a near miss from higher up, which reached water first—hence explains Jap accounts that 1st bomb a near-miss [abaft?] Akagi's bridge.

Own bomb—near miss—he thought off starboard bow."[1]

Bill Roberts *saw* Dick Best's bomb hit *Akagi*. How can anyone say, as many have, that Roberts himself did not dive on *Akagi*? And what about the "near miss" dropped "from higher up?" Could that bomb have been dropped by Delbert Halsey? That would make five American aircraft diving on Nagumo's flagship, not three.

And, there may have been even more than five. While most Midway historians have paid little attention to the Best/Penland map, Walter Lord clearly felt it to be an authentic and critical piece of evidence. Lord sent out copies of the Best/Penland map with a standard questionnaire he had prepared to American pilot veterans of the battle. Several *Enterprise* pilots made corrections to the map and returned their versions to Lord. From these corrections to the map – made by participants in the battle – it can be seen that Ensign George H. Goldsmith, from the Third Division of Dick Best's Bombing Six felt that he attacked the carrier whomever drew the original map had identified as *Akagi* – the carrier being attacked by those VB-6 aircraft that had split off from McClusky. The Best/Penland map,

---

[1] Lord notes from interview with Bill Roberts, April 19, 1966. Walter Lord Papers, NHHC.

as corrected by Goldsmith, is shown in Figure 12.2. Goldsmith's name in the upper right corner of the map was printed either by Walter Lord or by his secretary. Lord, or his secretary, also pasted in the typewritten note at lower right. The handwritten correction, altering the track and position of *Akagi*, and the handwritten comments about the "hard right turn" and "my section attack" were written by Goldsmith himself:

FIGURE 12.2 Best/Penland map as modified by George H. Goldsmith.[1]

[1]Walter Lord Papers. Operational Archives, Naval History and Heritage Command (NHHC). Washington Navy Yard. Washington, DC. Original map without alteration is referenced and sourced in Figure 12.1 above.

As indicated in his corrections to the map, Goldsmith thought his target had a right-side island; as for many years did Dick Best. In fairness to Goldsmith and to the confusion of that action-packed ten minutes in which the battle was decided, what Goldsmith wrote in a March 1966 letter to Walter Lord differed from what Goldsmith had drawn on his map – which he presumably drew at about the same time that he wrote the letter. In his letter, Goldsmith tells Lord that he dove on *Kaga* and retired with Bill Roberts (whom Best was certain dove with him on *Akagi*). Goldsmith doesn't say how he knew it was *Kaga* that he dove on and, unlike on his map where he states that his target had a right-side island, Goldsmith's letter to Lord says nothing about the island structure of the target he attacked.[1] So, Goldsmith's letter to Lord contradicts the corrections Goldsmith made to the map Lord had sent him. According to these corrections, Goldsmith felt that his entire section, which included his wingmen Lt (junior grade) J. J. Van Buren and Ensign N. F. Vandivier, dove on the same carrier as did Dick Best. In a letter to Robert Barde dated February 24, 1967, Goldsmith stated that the carrier he and Van Buren (both of the Third Division of Bombing Six) dove on was "just starting a hard right turn as he attacked her."[2] That would match the map Goldsmith modified for Lord, which has Goldsmith diving on *Akagi*. However, Goldsmith continues by telling Barde that he was "positive" that this ship "had her island structure on the right or starboard side."[3] Here it should be remembered that for many years, the memory of what turned out to be the massive funnel trunk on the right-hand side of *Akagi* had also fooled Dick Best into believing that the carrier he attacked had had a starboard-side island.

---

[1] G. H. Goldsmith to Walter Lord, March 1, 1966. Walter Lord Papers, NHHC.

[2] Barde, "The Battle of Midway: A Study in Command," pp246–247; see text on both pages and footnote on p247.

[3] Barde, "The Battle of Midway: A Study in Command," pp246–247.

A quick summary of Goldsmith's contradictory testimony, as presented in his letters to Lord and Barde respectively and in the map he modified for Lord, presents intriguing possibilities. Goldsmith wrote that he and Van Buren dove on *Kaga*, a view apparently based on Goldsmith's belief that the ship he dove on had a starboard-side island. Yet, Goldsmith modified the Best/Penland map sent to him by Lord in such a way as to indicate that he, Van Buren, and Vandivier actually dove on *Akagi*. Furthermore, Goldsmith wrote Lord that after he pulled out of his dive, he left the battle area with Bill Roberts – who Dick Best himself was certain dove with Best on *Akagi*! Taking into account Goldsmith's corrections to the map, it is therefore possible that eight American dive-bombers dove on *Akagi*.

There is other testimony supporting the idea that more than five aircraft dove on *Akagi*. Ensign Lewis A. Hopkins, of the Second Division of Bombing Six, felt that his entire division dove on *Akagi* and modified his copy of the Best/Penland map that Walter Lord had sent him accordingly. After the war, Hopkins told his daughters that he dove on *Akagi*.[1] The map, as modified by Lewis Hopkins, is shown in Figure 12.3 (opposite).

If Hopkins did dive on *Akagi*, he did not do so as part of a *six*-plane division, contrary to what he wrote on the map. First of all, his division comprised five aircraft total. Also, the leader of the Second Division of VB-6, Lt J. R. Penland, freely admitted that he (Penland) dove with Wade McClusky because he saw that the first few bombs dropped on *Kaga* (McClusky, Pittman, and Jaccard, respectively) were near misses and he wanted to add more weight to the attack on that ship. But, the corrections made by Hopkins to the map show that at least one aircraft from the second division of Bombing Six attacked *Akagi*.

[1]Email communication, Anne Hopkins to me, November 11, 2017.

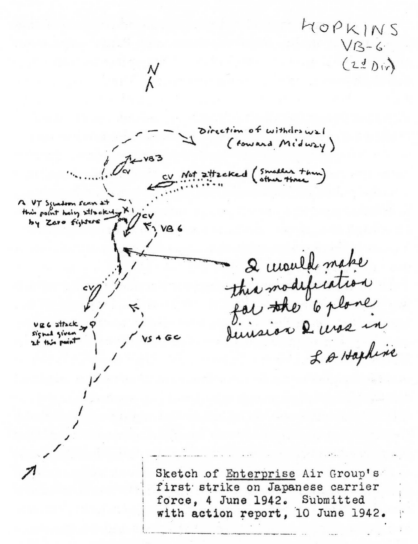

FIGURE 12.3 Best/Penland map as modified by Lewis A. Hopkins.[1]

[1]Walter Lord Papers. Naval History and Heritage Command. Original map without alteration is referenced and sourced in Figure 12.1 above.

Thus, perhaps Wade McClusky was correct in the way he described the attack in the first-person account that he wrote after the war, a copy of which is in the Walter Lord papers at the Naval History and Heritage Command:

"In the meantime, our bombs began to hit home. Scouting SIX obtained at least eight direct hits. The first division of Bombing SIX obtained at least three direct hits on their assigned target with 1,000 lb. bombs. Both carriers were then enveloped in masses of flames and smoke. The second and third divisions of Bombing SIX, in accordance with squadron doctrine, then divided their attack between both carriers, obtaining many hits. Violent explosions resulted."[1]

The process by which historians over the years have gradually whittled down the number of American dive-bombers that attacked *Akagi* to three is apparently based on one eyewitness account: that of Aviation Chief Radioman James F. Murray, who flew as Dick Best's rear-seat gunner. Murray was there and he was facing backward. His view that he saw no other aircraft behind Best's three-plane leading element during the dive is therefore not to be dismissed lightly. However, Bill Roberts, Lewis Hopkins, and George Goldsmith were also there and they were facing forward. Their views (in the case of Goldsmith, views that are admittedly somewhat contradictory) that they attacked the same target as did Dick Best should at least be given a fair hearing, instead of being utterly dismissed and ignored as they are in the current literature on the Battle of Midway. And there is also Delbert Halsey who, with Bill Roberts, brought up the rear as the fourth and fifth aircraft,

[1] Wade McClusky, "The Midway Story" Unpublished manuscript, p5. Walter Lord Papers, NHHC.

respectively, of the First Section of Bombing Six, and the fact that Halsey could never be interviewed because he did not survive the battle.[1]

If, as seems likely, more than three SBDs dove on the *Kaga*, J. F. Murray's observations must have been incorrect. His account differs from that of the other eyewitnesses to the attack on *Akagi* who spoke with Walter Lord – Roberts, Hopkins, Goldsmith (map version), and Dick Best himself. Dick Best was driving the airplane that Murray was riding in and Best was convinced that his five-plane division remained together and attacked *Akagi*. Granted, as the rear-seat gunner, Murray was facing backward and would thus seem to have had the best view of what was going on behind Best, Kroeger, and Weber. Perhaps Halsey and Roberts were off to the sides, out of Murray's line of vision? Or, perhaps Roberts, Hopkins, Goldsmith, and Halsey made shallower dives than did Best and were thus on a different trajectory below Best's aircraft? If so, Murray would not have been able to see them.[2] Dick Best was a veteran combat pilot and combat pilots usually do not live long if they fail to look behind them from time to time. It therefore strains credulity to believe that if Dick Best had only three planes in his formation instead of five, that he could have been completely unaware of such an elemental and critical factor – yet Best remained convinced that all five of the aircraft in his first division of Bombing Six attacked *Akagi*.

Interestingly, Earl Gallaher, the commander of Scouting Six (VS-6) did not like the map Walter Lord sent him and so he drew his own and returned that to Lord. Gallaher claimed the four Japanese carriers were in a box formation when he sighted them and that *Kaga* and *Akagi* were equidistant from the approaching American dive-bombers, to the left and the

[1]James F. Murray to Lord, February 26, 1967. Walter Lord Papers, NHHC.
[2]James F. Murray to Lord, February 26, 1967. Walter Lord Papers, NHHC.

right, respectively. Gallaher also saw American torpedo planes under attack by Japanese fighter planes. His map is shown in Figure 12.4:

Earl Gallaher did hear McClusky's attack order over the radio and Gallaher's version, as presented in his map, supports Wade McClusky's view of the manner in which the American dive-bomber attack unfolded.

As for Bill Roberts, after pulling out of his dive, Roberts left the battle area in company with Vandivier, Van Buren, and Goldsmith. This has been put forward as supposed proof that

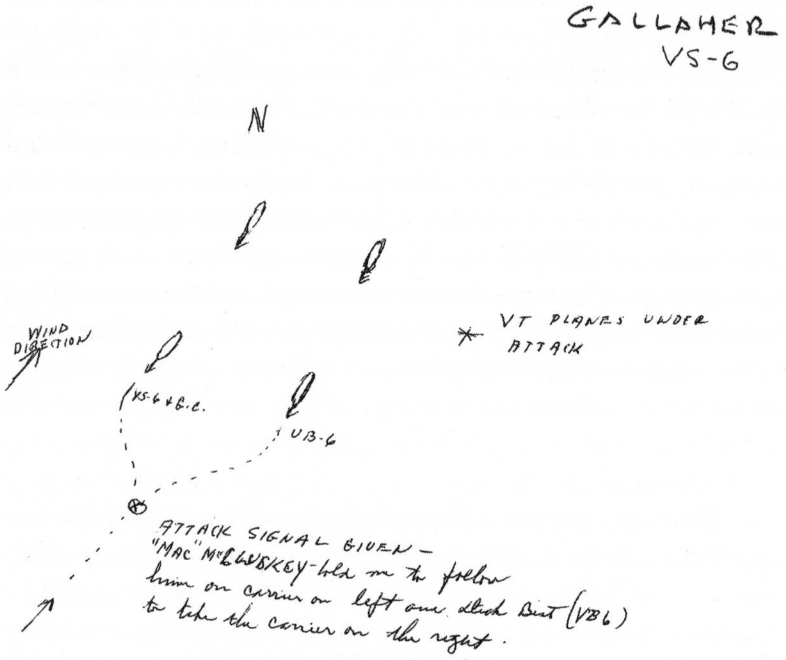

FIGURE 12.4 Map drawn by Earl Gallaher.[1]

---

[1]Walter Lord Papers, Naval History and Heritage Command. Original map without alteration is referenced and sourced in Figure 12.1 above.

Roberts had to have made his dive on *Kaga*[1] since the post-1990 paradigm used by Midway scholars has Vandivier, Van Buren, and Goldsmith supposedly diving with McClusky on *Kaga*. However, it could have been the other way around, especially in view of the manner in which Goldsmith and Hopkins updated the map Walter Lord sent them. It is quite possible that Vandivier, Van Buren, Goldsmith, and Halsey all dove with Best, Kroeger, and Weber on *Akagi*. After all, Van Buren and Vandivier were Goldsmith's section mates and Goldsmith wrote on his map that his *section* dove on the carrier that turned out to be *Akagi*. As for Bill Roberts, the evidence (presented above) that Bill Roberts dove with Best, Kroeger, and Weber on *Akagi* is overwhelming.

Whether it was three, four, five, or more aircraft that attacked the *Akagi*, the flagship was doomed. McClusky set out that morning with 33 SBDs, including his own. One from VS-6 had to turn back early on with engine trouble. Two more, from VB-6, ran out of gas just before the attack, forcing their pilots to make water landings. This left McClusky with 30 planes in all for the attack, including his own.[2] Historian John B. Lundstrom describes the attack on the *Kaga* and the *Akagi* as follows (and showing that as recently as 1984, the five planes diving on *Akagi* scenario still held sway among historians):

"McClusky at 1022 pushed over on the *Kaga*, the westernmost of the four carriers… Gallaher's Scouting Six followed McClusky down, and, by mistake, most of Bombing Six piled on as well. The *Akagi* commenced launching Zeros, holding course into the wind to launch aircraft. Best went after her with five SBDs from Bombing Six. Meanwhile, the first of

---

[1]Email communication, Mark Horan to me, March 6, 2015.

[2]John B. Lundstrom, *The First Team: Pacific Air Combat from Pearl Harbor to Midway* (Annapolis: Naval Institute Press, 1984): p348, p360.

four bombs slammed into the *Kaga*... Flaming aircraft and explosions soon turned the *Kaga*'s flight deck into an inferno and doomed the vessel. The *Akagi*'s time had also come. At 1025, the first Zero started down her flight deck, but Best's five SBDs already hurtled toward her. His pilots secured two 1,000-lb. bomb hits, one detonating in the midst of the eighteen carrier attack planes spotted aft on deck for launch. Like the *Kaga*, the fleet flagship had taken mortal damage."[1]

As for Japanese survivors of the *Akagi* seeing only three American dive-bombers, it is quite likely that Roberts and Halsey did become temporarily separated from Best, Kroeger, and Weber in the traffic jam that occurred as VS-6 airplanes, along with some from VB-6, jostled for position to follow Wade McClusky in his dive on *Kaga*. That does not in any way prove, however, that Halsey and Roberts then abandoned their division and squadron leader completely and dove on the *Kaga*. If, as seems more than likely, Halsey and Roberts dove on *Akagi*, they may have arrived over the Japanese flagship a bit later than did Best, Kroeger, and Weber. That could explain why the Japanese witnesses on *Akagi* saw only the first three Dauntlesses to attack. It could also explain why J. F. Murray, riding in the rear seat of Dick Best's SBD, did not see Roberts and Halsey. Most accounts of the battle agree that Dick Best scored a direct hit on *Akagi* with his 1,000lb bomb while his wingmen scored either near misses or a second hit and a near miss. If Halsey and Roberts also dove on *Akagi*, it would seem that their bombs missed by a considerable margin because the Japanese noticed only the first three bombs to fall. Another reason why Japanese witnesses on board *Akagi* did not see the fourth and fifth aircraft (ie Halsey and Roberts) was undoubtedly that the Japanese crew on *Akagi* stopped looking up once Richard Best's bomb landed amidships and began setting off catastrophic secondary explosions

[1] Lundstrom, *The First Team*, pp360–361.

fueled by the aviation fuel, the bombs, and the torpedoes that had been intended for loading into and on to Japanese aircraft.[1]

The Best/Penland map also helps to explain why McClusky and the pilots of VS-6 found the Kaga to be such a difficult target to hit. As many as 25 of the big 500lb and 1,000lb bombs were dropped, but there were only four direct hits on Kaga, plus a few hits with the small 100lb bombs that some of the VS-6 bombers were carrying.[2] The map confirms the wild nature of the evasive maneuvers that Nagumo's carriers had been making during the attacks by American torpedo planes; attacks that were just ending when the dive-bombers arrived. While Nagumo's intention at the time of McClusky's arrival overhead was to steam northeast to close with the American carriers so he could launch a strike, the Best/Penland map shows that Hiryu, Kaga, and Akagi were all steaming temporarily to the southwest when the dive-bombing attacks began, which placed McClusky and VS-6 off the Kaga's port beam. Attacking from the side gave the American pilots less of a target than they would have had if the attack had been made from either directly ahead or directly astern.[3] The scenario of the attack on Kaga coming from the port beam is supported in the memoir penned by VS-6 pilot Lt Clarence E. Dickinson. Ninth in line during the dive on Kaga, Dickinson agrees that Earl Gallaher dropped fourth overall and scored the first hit.[4] In describing his own dive, Dickinson lends support to the idea that McClusky attacked from the port beam, writing that: "I was coming a little abaft the beam on the port side on a course that would take me

---

[1] I am indebted to Mr Thom Walla of the Midway Roundtable organization for his insights on this matter.

[2 and 3] Email communication, Thom Walla to me, March 11, 2015.

[4] Clarence E. Dickinson and Boyden Sparkes, "The Target was Utterly Satisfying" as reprinted in S. E. Smith, ed., The United States Navy in World War II: The One-Volume History, from Pearl Harbor to Tokyo Bay—by Men Who Fought in the Atlantic and the Pacific and by Distinguished Naval Experts, Authors and Newspapermen (New York: William Morrow & Company, 1966): p279, p280.

diagonally across her deck to a point ahead of her island."[1] All three of Dickinson's bombs, his 500lb and his two 100 pounders, were direct hits.[2] Further evidence that the evasive maneuvers that Nagumo made while under attack by American torpedo planes had forced *Akagi* and *Kaga* to be heading south (at a time when Nagumo wanted to be heading northeast) by the time the American dive-bombers arrived is provided in the abbreviated Bombing Six report referenced earlier and written by either Dick Best or J. R. Penland. That report states: "Attack made westerly direction enemy course southerly."[3]

Some accounts of the Battle of Midway have claimed that Wade McClusky, as air group commander, should have been the last man to dive, not the first. The SBD of at least one of McClusky's two wingmen was equipped with cameras and Bill Pittman, on McClusky's wing, was surprised to see McClusky diving first, thinking instead that McClusky's three-plane leading element would dive last so that a photographic record could be made of the attack from on high. Actually, *USF-74* suggests that the best place for a group commander to fly is out in front in a separate element, just as McClusky did. As for order of diving, *USF-74* does not say whether the group commander is supposed to dive first, last, or at all:

"Position of the Group Commander in all formations is discretionary, being dependent to a certain extent upon the

[1] Dickinson and Sparkes, "The Target was Utterly Satisfying" as reprinted in S. E. Smith, ed. *The United States Navy in World War II.* p280.

[2] Dickinson and Sparkes, "The Target was Utterly Satisfying" as reprinted in S. E. Smith, ed. *The United States Navy in World War II.* p280.

[3] "Bombing Squadron 6, Action Report, Battle of Midway, 4 June 1942. U.S. Aircraft—Action with the Enemy." Naval History and Heritage Command (web). Available online at: http://web.archive.org/web/20150415070417/http://www.history.navy.mil/research/archives/organizational-records-collections/action-reports/wwii-battle-of-midway/bombing-squadron-6.html. Accessed July 10, 2020.

maneuver which is being conducted. Under normal cruising conditions it will be advantageous for the Group Commander to be leading in a separate section of planes with the remainder of the group following his movements. From this position the Group Commander can best control the movements of the group with minimum use of radio."[1]

The copyediting of *USF-74* is rather crude. The document is typewritten, but not professionally typeset. In those pre-computer days, that meant that cutting text could necessitate retyping an entire document to correct the pagination. Instead, in a few places, short passages in *USF-74* to be deleted are merely crossed out in ink. One of these crossed-out passages refers to the group commander's dive. The document states that at the beginning of a dive-bombing attack, the "Group Commander rolls wing in full view of group, then dives directly at target."[2] This set of instructions is complicated by the fact that the phrase "then dives directly at target" has been scratched out in ink and replaced by a period. The instructions then describe a series of hand signals the group commander is supposed to give, including one for "FOLLOW ME."[3] Indicative of the poor organization of the document, what the group commander is supposed to do next is not explained. The authors immediately move on to a new section on a different topic because this section of the manual is concerned only with visual signals to be used by the group commander. The author of this section of *USF-74* may have been influenced by an earlier section of the manual that sets out doctrine to be followed when a patrol aircraft sights an enemy submarine at or near the surface thus: "The location of the submarine should be indicated by repeated dives and by dropping

[1]Halsey, *USF-74, Revised*, p144.
[2]Halsey, *USF-74, Revised*, p152.
[3]Halsey, *USF-74, Revised*, p152.

float lights."[1] These dives to alert other aircraft and ships as to the location of an enemy submarine would presumably be made from low altitude. Perhaps the reason that somebody scratched out the reference to the group commander diving immediately to show his pilots where a target that may *not* be a submarine is located is that the author(s) realized that, unlike a patrol plane at low altitude, a dive-bombing group commander cannot make "repeated dives" to show his pilots where the target is. Once a dive-bombing pilot commits to a dive from 20,000ft, there is no going back. An aircraft on antisubmarine patrol would be flying much lower. Due to its ambiguity and crude editing, *USF-74* never makes clear exactly what a group commander is supposed to do once a dive-bombing attack commences. After he rolls his wings, then what? We are left to wonder.[2]

No account of the attack McClusky led on the morning of June 4, 1942 would be complete without paying tribute to the complementary and simultaneous actions of Bombing Squadron Three (VB-3) from the USS *Yorktown*. After first sighting the Japanese, it took McClusky's two squadrons of *Enterprise* dive-bombers 15 more minutes to reach their pushover points above the Japanese carriers, the moment when from directly above the pilots would activate their specially slatted dive brake wing flaps and plunge into 70-degree dives that would, in less than 60 seconds, bring them down from 4 miles up to an altitude of less than half a mile, all the while lining up the target in the crosshairs of their bomb sights. At 2,000ft, sometimes lower, the pilot would release his bomb and pull out of his dive. By the time the *Enterprise* pilots began their steep dives on the *Akagi* and the *Kaga*, McClusky's old Annapolis friend from the class of 1926, Lt Cdr Maxwell Leslie, had arrived with a squadron of

---

[1] Halsey, *USF-74, Revised*, p63.

[2] I am indebted to Mr Mark Horan regarding the ambiguity in the written doctrine regarding whether or not the group commander was supposed to participate in an actual attack. Email communication, Mark Horan to me, March 6 and 7, 2015.

17 dive-bombers from the *Yorktown*. McClusky's and Leslie's groups had arrived simultaneously, but Leslie was approaching from due east while McClusky's long and complex search meant that the *Enterprise* dive-bombers were approaching from the southwest. Leslie and McClusky were unaware of each other's presence. Coming from due east, Max Leslie ordered his group to attack a carrier that was further north and further east than were McClusky's two targets. Max Leslie's *Yorktown* pilots dove on the *Soryu* and destroyed that ship with three 1,000lb bomb hits. Thus, the *Enterprise* and *Yorktown* dive-bomber groups had accidentally coordinated their attacks brilliantly so that three Japanese aircraft carriers would be destroyed in the morning attack.[1]

Incidentally, the Best/Penland map also sheds valuable light on the attack by VB-3 on the *Soryu*. The Best/Penland map would appear to support two claims regarding Max Leslie's attack made in a recent history of the Battle of Midway. First, contrary to most accounts of the battle, during the morning attack it was the *Soryu*, not the *Hiryu*, that was furthest to the north among the four Japanese aircraft carriers, and that Max Leslie and VB-3 flew past the *Hiryu* to get at the more northerly *Soryu*. Second, that there were still a few American torpedo planes in the vicinity of the Japanese fleet when the *Enterprise* and *Yorktown* dive-bombers arrived at 10.20am. The torpedo planes were almost certainly the very few survivors of the *Yorktown*'s VT-3 squadron.[2] The Best/Penland map identifies the *Hiryu* as "CV not attacked (smaller than other three)."[3] In point of fact the *Hiryu* was not small, being almost the exact same size as the 19,000-ton *Soryu*.

---

[1] Gordon W. Prange, Donald M. Goldstein, and Katherine V. Dillon, *Miracle at Midway*. (New York: McGraw Hill, 1982): p271. Postwar interview with Capt Ohara, H., executive officer of Soryu, in *USSBS: Pacific*, Vol. 1, p167, p168.

[2] Parshall and Tully, *Shattered Sword*, pp219–226.

[3] See Figure 12.1.

As for McClusky's decision-making during the attack, Wade McClusky and Dick Best were both victims of an overly complex, poorly organized, and often contradictory set of written regulations. *USF-74* does indicate that group and squadron commanders were supposed to provide the pilots under their command with all available information, including a best estimate of how an attack should unfold once the enemy was located, prior to take-off.[1] What McClusky, Best and Gallaher did or did not discuss prior to take-off remains unknown for certain, although Dick Best hints in his 1995 oral history that there was no conference between the three men. After mentioning the leading squadron taking the far target aspect of dive-bombing doctrine, Best told Shinneman in 1995 that: "You don't go out and talk air attack [by which he means, perhaps, that one does not break radio silence for a lengthy discussion about targets while airborne], you've either been assigned before you take off, or you attack according to doctrine."[2] Best seems to be saying that there was no preflight conference between Wade McClusky and his two dive-bombing squadron leaders. In addition, "fog of war" factors such as the fact that *Enterprise* dive-bombers were acting on a contact report that was more than two hours old by the time McClusky reached the anticipated interception point; that *Hornet*'s entire dive-bomber group got lost and was unable to participate in the morning attack; that half of the *Yorktown*'s dive-bombers were kept aboard ship as a reserve; and that McClusky had no way of knowing the location of either his own fighter planes and torpedo bombers from the *Enterprise* or of any of the aircraft from the *Hornet* and *Yorktown*, respectively, would have made it impossible for any preflight discussion between McClusky and his two dive-bombing squadron commanders to

[1] Halsey, *USF-74, Revised*, pp66–67.

[2] Best oral history interview with Shinneman, 1995, pp 40–41. Quote on p41.

have accounted for all of the unusual and even bizarre events that the pilots would encounter once they were aloft.

While McClusky's own bomb was a near miss on *Kaga*, the American dive-bombing attack that destroyed Japan's two largest aircraft carriers never would have taken place without his calm leadership. It was Wade McClusky's refusal to panic when the interception coordinates he had been given prior to take-off from the *Enterprise* proved to be incorrect that made it possible for the dive-bombers to make a devastatingly successful attack. The late historian Gordon Prange rates "McClusky's decision to continue his search with an unconventional pattern"[1] very highly on the list of reasons for American victory in the Battle of Midway. By ignoring the temptation to turn south toward Midway, by turning north, and by continuing to search to the absolute limit of his pilots' fuel capacity (and even a bit beyond), McClusky was able to locate the Japanese fleet under extremely difficult circumstances. By doing that he put some of the best bomb aimers in the US Navy, such as Dick Best and Dusty Kleiss (the latter, of VS-6, landed a 500lb bomb on *Kaga*'s forward deck), in a position to do what they did best: landing bombs on a moving target. Contrary to suggestions made in some recent histories of the Battle of Midway, Wade McClusky, the former fighter pilot, did not "bungle" the attacks on *Kaga* and *Akagi*, nor was he "unfamiliar" with dive-bombing tactics, as already explained.[2] Most importantly, both of the Japanese carriers McClusky chose for destruction were indeed sent to the bottom of the ocean as a direct result of the attacks made by his two squadrons of dive-bombers. In assessing Wade McClusky's performance at Midway, it is difficult to argue with success.

[1]Prange, et al, *Miracle at Midway*, p271.

[2]Moore, *Pacific Payback*, p217. See also, Parshall and Tully, *Shattered Sword*, p228.

13

JUNE 4, 1942 – ESCAPE, A SHOT-UP AIRPLANE, AND TWO GALLONS OF GASOLINE

At 11.42am (local time) on the morning of June 4, 1942, Lt Robin M. Lindsey, the landing signal officer standing at his post on the port side at the extreme aft end of the flight deck of the USS *Enterprise*, watched as Wade McClusky's SBD made its final approach. Some accounts say the approach looked bad and Lindsey waved him off, but that Wade paid no attention to the wave-off and even thumbed his nose at Lindsey while bringing the plane in to land.[1] Whether or not that part is true, McClusky did make a safe landing. The SBD's wheels found the deck gently and the plane's tail hook caught a wire, bringing the aircraft to an abrupt halt. McClusky cut the engine, the propeller slowed to a stop, and the plane handlers moved in to push the aircraft forward to a parking spot so that other aircraft could land. As the "airedales" prepared to start pushing, McClusky and Chocalousek climbed out of the cockpit on to the plane's right wing and then hopped down on to the flight deck. Wade McClusky had just led the most important attack carried out by US Navy pilots in all of World War 2. He and Chocalousek had been in the air for four hours and 36 minutes which, in the days before in-flight refueling, was as long as one could possibly keep an SBD aloft.

[1]Walter Lord interview with McClusky, June 21, 1966. Walter Lord Papers, Operational Archives, Naval History and Heritage Command (NHHC). Washington Navy Yard. Washington DC.

During that time, the dive-bombers under McClusky's command had destroyed Japan's two largest aircraft carriers, the *Akagi* and the *Kaga*.[1] Meanwhile, *Yorktown* dive-bombers had set *Soryu* ablaze. The magnitude of what had been accomplished cannot be overstated. Code breakers and the wisdom of Adm Nimitz had put the American carriers in the right place at the right time. But carrier-versus-carrier battles were a new type of naval warfare and the two American flag officers present, Fletcher and Spruance, had not had time to engage in detailed planning before the battle. It was Wade McClusky and his Annapolis classmate Max Leslie, two officers of relatively low formal rank, who had restored order to a completely chaotic situation.[2]

McClusky almost hadn't made it back. The roller-coaster ride that was a World War 2 dive-bombing attack had taken McClusky's SBD from an altitude of 4 miles up down to the level of the mast head of his target, the *Kaga*, in just 30 seconds[3]. He had released his bomb as he passed the 1,800ft mark in a dive of 70 degrees. The bomb exploded in the water just 30ft from the carrier's hull. While the killing blows would be delivered by the pilots who followed McClusky and who scored direct hits, McClusky's near miss probably caused some damage to *Kaga*'s hull. After dropping his bomb and enduring the 9g pull-out from his dive, McClusky was flat on the deck, just 20ft above the water. Now level once again, he was able to push the plane to its maximum speed of 250mph since he was no longer encumbered by the 500lb weight of the bomb he had been carrying. Deliberately staying low probably

---

[1]Take-off time from Personal Report. Lt Cdr Wade C. McClusky. Air Group Commander. Enterprise Air Group. Battle of Midway, 4–6 June, 1942. National Naval Aviation Museum, Pensacola, Florida. (Also available online on several websites). Flight time from Wade McClusky personal logbook; courtesy Philip McClusky.

[2]Thomas B. Buell, *The Quiet Warrior: A Biography of Admiral Raymond A. Spruance* (Annapolis: Naval Institute Press, 1974, 1987): p151.

[3]Stephen L. Moore, *Pacific Payback: The Carrier Aviators Who Avenged Pearl Harbor at the Battle of Midway* (New York: NAL Caliber, 2014): p219.

made the antiaircraft gunners on the Japanese carriers and their escorting battleships, cruisers, and destroyers reluctant to fire at him for fear of hitting their own ships.[1] He did not immediately head east, back toward the *Enterprise*, but instead turned south. While it seems that there had been no preflight conference in which McClusky and his squadron leaders discussed exactly how an attack would unfold, it had been agreed before take-off that each dive-bomber, and presumably each torpedo plane if the latter had been able to avoid being massacred, would head south immediately after attacking. This tactic would be an effort to prevent Japanese aircraft from following the American planes back to the American carriers. Better yet, the Japanese might even think that the attacking aircraft had come from Midway itself and would hopefully remain unaware that American aircraft carriers were anywhere in the vicinity. Only after they had flown over the horizon on a southerly heading would the American planes turn east to head back to their respective carriers.[2]

If McClusky had headed east immediately after pulling out of his dive he would have been well beyond the outer ring of the Japanese combat air patrol fighter planes within five or ten minutes. His dogleg to the south before turning east, however, kept him in the battle area and thus still fair game for prowling Japanese fighter planes. He discovered this the hard way when, 15 minutes after pulling out of his dive, by which time he had turned east-northeast to head back to the *Enterprise*, McClusky's aircraft was jumped by two enemy Zeke fighter planes whose pilots took turns making passes in which they raked McClusky's SBD with machine gun fire as well as with 20mm cannon. As a former fighter pilot, McClusky knew that the best angle of attack for any fighter pilot is from

[1] Wade McClusky, "The Midway Story" Unpublished Manuscript, p5. Walter Lord Papers, NHHC. Also, podcast of Wade McClusky 1972 interview with radio station WMCA. Courtesy Philip McClusky.

[2] Robert J. Cressman, Steve Ewing, Barrett Tillman, Mark Horan, Clark Reynolds, and Stan Cohen, *A Glorious Page in Our History: The Battle of Midway, 4–6 June 1942* (Missoula, Montana: Pictorial Histories Publishing Co, Inc: 1990): p107.

behind and below one's quarry. Having remained just 20ft above the waves since pulling out of his dive, McClusky denied the Japanese pilots any opportunity to get below him. In his own variation of the "Thach Weave," McClusky proceeded to turn directly toward whichever of the two Japanese planes was making a strafing run. Heading straight for the attackers threw their aim off because they had less of a target to shoot at. It also allowed McClusky to bring his plane's two fixed, forward-firing .50 caliber machine guns to bear. Meanwhile, in the plane's rear seat, young Walter Chocalousek was far from idle. Enthusiastically engaging the enemy fighters with his swiveling twin .30 caliber machine guns, Chocalousek managed to shoot one down. Eventually, the other Japanese pilot gave up and turned away.[1] McClusky's earlier hunch that the eager young Chocalousek would turn out to be a good shot had been correct.[2]

McClusky was hit in the shoulder several times in this attack with bullets and shrapnel. The plane itself was hit 55 times – mostly with 7.7mm machine gun fire, but also with a few 20mm rounds, but the rugged SBD kept flying. There were also a few chunks of aluminum missing from the front of the tail fin. These extra hits had been inadvertently delivered by Chocalousek during his duel with the Zekes; in his enthusiasm, Chocalousek had tried firing at the Japanese fighters when they were directly astern, meaning that he damaged his own aircraft's tail. Chocalousek would not be the only American dive-bomber gunner to try this during the war. The 8in. separating the two barrels of the twin .30 caliber mount in the rear seat created the optimistic, but false, impression that one could fire straight astern and have the bullets pass harmlessly on either side of the tail.[3] Fortunately, the SBD Dauntless was a rugged and forgiving airplane.

[1]Edward P. Stafford, *The Big E: The Story of the U.S.S. Enterprise* (Annapolis: Naval Institute Press, 1962, 2002): p102. Podcast of Wade McClusky 1972 interview with radio station WMCA. Courtesy Philip McClusky.

[2]See Chapter 10.

[3]McClusky, "The Midway Story," p6. Walter Lord Papers, NHHC. Podcast of Wade McClusky 1972 interview with radio station WMCA. Courtesy Philip McClusky.

After the encounter with the Zekes, McClusky tried calling Chocalousek on the intercom, but got no answer. Fearing that Chocalousek had been killed, McClusky turned and looked back over his shoulder to find that Chocalousek was very much alive, hunched over the barrels of his guns, eagerly searching for more targets. While the enemy fighters had not hit any vital components, they had shot up the plane's intercom wires.[1]

Wade and every other *Enterprise* dive-bomber pilot who survived the Battle of Midway had flown to the extreme range limit of his aircraft. McClusky's SBD had only 2 gallons of 100 octane sloshing around in its fuel tank when his plane touched down on the Big E's flight deck.[2] It seemed especially cruel to McClusky that after his pilots had persevered in a very long search for the enemy and had then made an excellent attack, their trip home was lengthened unnecessarily because Adm Spruance and his staff aboard the *Enterprise* had made a mistake when calculating "Point Option," the estimated position of where the ship would be when the pilots returned; a position estimate that was supposed to take into account the planned course and speed of the ship while its strike aircraft were away. Given to pilots before take-off, the Point Option position was also supposed to take into account periodic delays as the ship deviated from its base course to turn into the wind to launch and recover its combat air patrol fighters. In those days, before the advent of GPS navigational systems, the preparation and distribution to pilots of an accurate Point Option position was a critical piece of staff work on any aircraft carrier. Adm Spruance's staff failed badly in this regard during the Battle of Midway.[3]

Each American dive-bomber did have a primitive electronic homing device on board, the ZD "Zed" Baker, which could pick up a signal broadcast from the home carrier. However, ZD Baker was a new technology in 1942 and was often unreliable.

---

[1]Cressman et al. *A Glorious Page in Our History*, p107.

[2]Stafford, *The Big E*, p103.

[3]Buell, *The Quiet Warrior*, pp148–149.

Even when it was working, it required a pilot to climb to at least 5,000ft in order to receive any kind of signal – something a pilot often could not do if, like McClusky, he was hugging the deck while dodging enemy fighter planes.[1] By the time McClusky arrived at Point Option he had escaped the Zekes and had climbed to 5,000ft. Even though he could look around a bit from that altitude, the situation was a repeat of that in the morning when, upon reaching the interception coordinates where he was told the Japanese fleet would be, he found only empty ocean – exactly what he saw now where he had been told the *Enterprise* would be upon his return. This angered McClusky greatly. He knew he had pushed his pilots well beyond the safe limit of their fuel endurance in order to carry out the morning attack. Now, due to events beyond his control – namely, bad staff work on the *Enterprise* – his pilots were essentially on their own when it came to finding the sanctuary of their home carrier. McClusky at this point made a plain language broadcast to his Annapolis classmate Lt Cdr Leonard "Ham" Dow, the *Enterprise* fighter director officer, requesting a corrected position report for the *Enterprise*. Dow's voice came back immediately, loud and clear, but all he said initially was "wait."[2] Just then McClusky began to get a homing signal on his ZD Baker receiver hinting at the ship's location. His anger at this extra and completely avoidable hurdle for himself and his pilots is evident in the postwar account he wrote:

"While orientating to this new course, 'Ham' Dow came in by radio giving a 'new' position for the Task Force. This proved to be about 60 miles south of where they were supposed to be. It has always been a mystery to me, why, after radio silence was broken, they hadn't enlightened us poor pilots on

[1]McClusky, "The Midway Story," pp6–7. Walter Lord Papers, NHHC.

[2]Stephen L. Moore, *Pacific Payback: The Carrier Aviators Who Avenged Pearl Harbor at the Battle of Midway* (New York: NAL Caliber, 2014): pp259–260.

their subsequent changes of courses or position. Who knows, maybe some of those lost due to running out of fuel might have returned!"[1]

McClusky headed south, as per Dow's instructions. After 20 minutes on that heading he saw American ships. *Enterprise*, *Yorktown*, and *Hornet* were all identical in outward appearance, having been built from the same plans, which explains why McClusky almost landed on the *Yorktown* by mistake. Having joined that ship's landing circle, he belatedly noticed that this was not the *Enterprise* while flying past the ship at low altitude headed toward the stern, beyond which he would bank around to come in for his landing. Perhaps he noted the large numeral "5" painted on the flight deck? He then saw a second carrier approximately 5 miles distant that did turn out to be the *Enterprise*. He would have known even from a distance that this second carrier was not the *Hornet*. Unlike her two sisters, *Hornet* was almost brand new and had only recently come from the United States. As such, *Hornet* sported the mottled "Measure 12" camouflage paint scheme that the Navy had begun to use in early 1942. *Enterprise*, like *Yorktown*, was still painted a uniform grey at the time of Midway. Although dangerously low on fuel, McClusky decided to head for the *Enterprise*. He did not bother about landing circles this time, but instead headed straight in.[2]

As for the story that has become entrenched in Midway lore that Wade thumbed his nose at Robin Lindsey while supposedly ignoring the latter's wave-off, McClusky himself is a bit inconsistent on this point. In his postwar expansion of his original action report, he said it was a bit less dramatic than that: "I made a straight-in approach on the ENTERPRISE and landed aboard. The Landing Signal Officer claims he waved me off, but I didn't see it and furthermore, figured I didn't have enough gas

---

[1]McClusky, "The Midway Story," pp6–7. Walter Lord Papers, NHHC.
[2]McClusky, "The Midway Story," p7. Walter Lord Papers, NHHC.

to go around again anyway."[1] However, in his 1966 interview with Walter Lord, McClusky claimed that he did see the wave-off but ignored it, complete with the ribald salute he is said to have delivered to Lindsey while landing.[2] A few SBDs had landed before McClusky. After he landed, they continued to arrive, one by one, not in any kind of formation. Within half an hour of Wade landing, all *Enterprise* dive-bombers that were coming home from the morning attack, less than half the number that had taken off, had landed back aboard.[3]

According to VS-6 pilot Dusty Kleiss, several other SBDs arrived back at the *Enterprise* at the same time McClusky did. Kleiss was disappointed that McClusky, rather than Earl Gallaher or Dick Best, had led the morning attack, and Kleiss agrees with the incorrect but prevalent post-1990 Midway paradigm for historians that McClusky bungled the morning attack and that as a result only three aircraft were left over to attack the *Akagi*.[4] Nevertheless, Kleiss does admit that McClusky cared about the well-being of the pilots under his command. Indeed, Kleiss shows his mixed feelings about, and some praise for, Wade McClusky when he writes of McClusky's behavior during the landing back aboard *Enterprise* when several fuel-starved SBDs were trying to land quickly after the morning strike:

"LCDR McClusky insisted on landing last. Although he was the air group commander and by all rights could have landed first, he begged that the others precede him. As it turned out, McClusky had received a shoulder wound when a Zero had

---

[1]McClusky, "The Midway Story," p7. Walter Lord Papers, NHHC.

[2]Lord interview with McClusky, June 21, 1966. Walter Lord Papers, NHHC.

[3]Deck Log. USS *Enterprise* (CV-6). NARA RG 24. Box 3334. January 1942 to June 1942. P15 of the entries for June 4, 1942.

[4]N. Jack "Dusty" Kleiss, with Timothy and Laura Orr, *Never Call Me a Hero: A Legendary American Dive-Bomber Pilot Remembers The Battle of Midway* (New York: William Morrow, 2017): pp200–201.

attacked his plane after its pullout. Unsure of his ability to land an unfamiliar plane while wounded, McClusky insisted on waiting until his other planes had trapped on deck before making his final approach. For all the mistakes he made during the morning mission, this selfless act more than made up for it, and I forever applauded McClusky afterward. When we examined his bullet-riddled plane, we discovered that he had less than five gallons of fuel remaining."[1]

This rather backhanded compliment from Dusty Kleiss probably sums up the feelings many of the dive-bomber pilots held toward Wade McClusky; a feeling that McClusky had not quite paid his dues as a dive-bomber pilot but they could not help admiring his selflessness, courage, and honesty.

Once he was back aboard the *Enterprise*, McClusky headed immediately for the carrier's island structure. Once inside, he climbed to the flag bridge to report to Capt Murray and Adm Spruance. The bullet wounds made his left shoulder ache, but he was eager to relate the amazing events of the morning to his superiors. As McClusky told the story of the attack and its very welcome results, *Enterprise* Executive Officer Commander Tom Jeter noticed that blood was dripping from the cuff of the left sleeve of McClusky's leather flight jacket to the deck. Jeter exclaimed "Mac, you've been shot!" It was quickly decided that McClusky's report could wait and he was ordered to sickbay.[2]

[1]Kleiss, *Never Call Me A Hero*, p208.
[2]Moore, *Pacific Payback*, p260.

14

JUNE 4, 1942 – THE AFTERNOON ATTACK

Although a great victory had been won in the morning attack on June 4, the day was far from over for American dive-bomber pilots. There was still one Japanese carrier out there. At 2.45pm (local time) *Yorktown* dive-bomber pilot Lt Samuel Adams, one of ten sent out by Adm Fletcher to find the remaining carrier, located the elusive *Hiryu* and radioed its position back to the American fleet. At almost the exact same time that this contact report was broadcast, the urgent need to destroy the *Hiryu* was emphasized when two torpedoes launched from "Kate" torpedo planes that had flown from that carrier slammed into the *Yorktown*'s port side below the waterline.[1]

The Japanese pilots on Adm Nagumo's four carriers were an elite group who proved their mettle when, with three of Nagumo's carriers transformed into blazing, exploding wrecks, *Hiryu*'s air group would strike back with impressive effectiveness. R Adm Yamaguchi Tamon, commanding Carrier Division 2 (*Hiryu* and *Soryu*) succeeded in getting off not one, but two, counter-attacks with *Hiryu*'s aircraft before his flagship succumbed to the second American dive-bombing attack of the day.[2] Both groups sent out

[1] Samuel Eliot Morison, *History of United States Naval Operations in World War II*. Vol. 4. *Coral Sea, Midway and Submarine Actions: May 1942–August 1942* (Boston: Little, Brown and Company, 1954; reissued in 2001 by Castle Books, Edison, NJ): pp135–136.

[2] Jonathan Parshall and Anthony Tully, *Shattered Sword: The Unknown Story of the Battle of Midway* (Washington, DC: Potomac Books, 2005, 2007): p262.

by Yamaguchi would draw blood; three bombs from *Hiryu*'s dive-bombers had struck *Yorktown* before the Japanese torpedo planes arrived. Adm Yamaguchi was a brilliant officer who, unlike Nagumo, did have the ability to improvise. Unfortunately for the Japanese, it took the sight of the destruction of the other three carriers to spur Yamaguchi's innovative talents. Earlier in the day, Yamaguchi had urged Nagumo to attack immediately when the heavy cruiser *Tone*'s search plane number 4 had radioed back a contact report after sighting American ships. Yamaguchi had a better understanding than did Nagumo of the critical fact the Americans had discovered during the mock "battles" fought between the *Lexington* and the *Saratoga* ten years earlier during the American Fleet Problem exercises described earlier: that in a carrier battle the side that strikes first is the side that wins.[1] However, in the morning Yamaguchi had reluctantly accepted Nagumo's decision to wait. Now, shutting the barn door after the horse had bolted, Yamaguchi acted quickly. Not waiting to launch a coordinated attack, Yamaguchi launched 18 dive-bombers and six protecting Zeke fighters from *Hiryu* immediately, because they were ready. The time was 10.54am, less than half an hour after the American dive-bombers had departed after striking their deadly blows against *Akagi*, *Kaga*, and *Soryu*.[2] *Hiryu*'s torpedo planes would be launched later.

At the time of Midway, the US Navy did not keep all of its carriers together during a battle, a practice that would become common later in the war for several reasons, not the least of which was the economies of scale that were realized when it became apparent that American CAP fighters from different carriers could easily be combined into one large group to protect the entire fleet from enemy air attack. Thus, as the Japanese dive-bombers attacked *Yorktown* at Midway, the fighter pilots from

[1]Thomas Wildenberg, *Destined for Glory: Dive Bombing, Midway, and the Evolution of Carrier Airpower* (Annapolis: Naval Institute Press, 1998): p84.

[2]Parshall and Tully, *Shattered Sword*, p263.

Task Force 16 (*Enterprise* and *Hornet*) were ordered to continue guarding the air space above their home carriers and could only watch from a distance as the *Yorktown*, further west and thus the first American carrier the Japanese pilots had spotted, absorbed the entire enemy attack. McClusky's old friend from his days leading the *Enterprise* fighter squadron, Lt Roger Mehle, was flying CAP over *Enterprise* in his Wildcat fighter as the leader of the Third Division of Fighting Six. Mehle found it unbearable that he was being held above the *Enterprise* and missing out on a scrap that was taking place just a few miles away and therefore decided to do a little improvising of his own, and ordered the other three *Enterprise* fighter pilots in his division, Ensigns Howard L. Grimmell, Jr, Thomas C. Provost III, and James A. Halford, Jr, to do likewise. According to Edward Stafford: "Mehle, stretching his protective circles (and his orders), swung over *Yorktown* at the last possible moment for a good shot at the incoming bombers. His gun solenoid failed and he could not fire, but Provost and Halford shot one down after its drop."[1] In a 1975 interview with historian John B. Lundstrom, Roger Mehle claimed that in reality his actions were a bit less insubordinate – that Mehle had begged for permission from McClusky's Annapolis classmate Leonard "Ham" Dow, fighter director officer on board *Enterprise*, with such persistence that Dow had finally relented and had radioed Mehle permission to take his division out of the protective "umbrella" above the *Enterprise* and go to the aid of *Yorktown*.[2]

Already damaged by three bomb hits in the first Japanese counter-attack, the torpedo damage caused *Yorktown* to take on a sharp list to port. Fearing that his ship was about to capsize, Capt Elliott Buckmaster ordered *Yorktown* abandoned

---

[1]Edward P. Stafford, *The Big E: The Story of the U.S.S. Enterprise* (Annapolis: Naval Institute Press, 1962, 2002): p104.

[2]John B. Lundstrom, *The First Team: Pacific Air Combat from Pearl Harbor to Midway* (Annapolis: Naval Institute Press, 1984): p473, pp483–484.

just before 3.00pm.[1] Maxwell Leslie's 17-strong group of SBDs (VB-3) had come through their attack on the *Soryu* unscathed and had plenty of fuel for the return flight to the *Yorktown* because their route to the Japanese fleet had been far less circuitous than had been McClusky's. The return of the *Yorktown*'s dive-bombers had also gone smoothly because Adm Fletcher's staff had given the *Yorktown* pilots a more accurate Point Option than that provided by the staff of Adm Spruance to McClusky and the other *Enterprise* pilots.[2] However, just as the *Yorktown* dive-bombers began to form up in a landing circle in preparation for coming aboard, they were vectored away when the *Yorktown*'s radar picked up approaching Japanese dive-bombers.

Most of Max Leslie's VB-3 pilots landed on the *Enterprise* after circling near the American fleet while the *Yorktown* was under attack. Leslie himself, however, ran so low on fuel while waiting for a friendly deck to land on that he was forced to make a water landing near the heavy cruiser USS *Astoria*, whose crew had already lowered a boat to pick up Leslie's wingman, Lt (junior grade) Paul "Lefty" Holmberg and his gunner, Aviation Machinist's Mate, 2nd Class George LaPlant, who had also landed in the water. With Holmberg and LaPlant safely aboard, the same boat quickly picked up Leslie and his rear-seat gunner, Aviation Radioman, 1st Class William Gallagher (not to be confused with Wilmer Earl Gallaher, the commander of Scouting Six).[3]

Although the SBD Dauntless was far less vulnerable to enemy attack than was the deathtrap TBD Devastator flown by American torpedo plane pilots at Midway, losses had still been quite heavy among *Enterprise* dive-bomber crews in the morning attack.

[1]Morison, *Coral Sea, Midway and Submarine Actions*, p135.

[2]Morison, *Coral Sea, Midway and Submarine Actions*, pp130–131.

[3]Stephen L. Moore, *Pacific Payback: The Carrier Aviators Who Avenged Pearl Harbor at the Battle of Midway* (New York: NAL Caliber, 2014): pp268–269.

Sixteen *Enterprise* dive-bombers either went down under the guns of Japanese fighter planes and antiaircraft fire or ditched after running out of fuel. Twelve of the crewmen were later recovered by American ships and by PBY Catalina flying boat aircraft, which could land on the water. Two *Enterprise* dive-bombers from VS-6 were so low on fuel upon their return that the pilots, Lt (junior grade) Bill Roberts and Ensign G.H. Goldsmith, opted to land on the most westerly and thus the closest of the American carriers: *Yorktown*.[1] Because the Japanese air attacks that crippled the *Yorktown*, rendering the big carrier incapable of further flight operations, began just minutes later, Roberts and Goldsmith were unable to play any further role in the battle. Twenty-two *Enterprise* dive-bomber pilots and gunners were dead, as were 18 of the pilots and gunners who had flown the torpedo planes of VT-6 from *Enterprise*. As mentioned previously, VS-6 pilot Frank O'Flaherty and his gunner, Bruno Peter Gaido, were taken prisoner by the Japanese when they ditched after the morning attack on June 4 and were both executed by their captors on June 15. Lt Samuel Adams of *Yorktown*'s VS-5, whose contact report on June 4 had sealed the fate of *Hiryu*, had landed on the *Enterprise* because the heavily damaged *Yorktown* was out of action. Adams duly took off from the *Enterprise* on June 5 as part of a 30-strong dive-bomber force whose mission was to find and destroy any Japanese ships remaining near Midway. Adams and his rear seat gunner, Aviation Radio Mechanic, 1st Class Joseph J. Karrol, were shot down and killed while attacking the Japanese destroyer *Tanikaze*, the only enemy ship the American strike force located on June 5. One more *Enterprise* dive-bomber crew – Ensign Clarence Vammen and his gunner, Aviation Machinist's Mate, 2nd Class Milton Clark – would be killed in the closing stages of the battle of June 6, while *Enterprise* dive-bombers were

[1]Robert J. Cressman, Steve Ewing, Barrett Tillman, Mark Horan, Clark Reynolds, and Stan Cohen, *A Glorious Page in Our History: The Battle of Midway, 4–6 June 1942* (Missoula, Montana: Pictorial Histories Publishing Co, Inc: 1990): p112.

attacking the Japanese heavy cruisers *Mogami* and *Mikuma*.[1] These were sobering losses indeed.

Three *Enterprise* dive-bombers that did return from the morning attack on June 4, including McClusky's own aircraft, were heavily damaged and would need extensive repair before they could fly again. Only 11 of the 14 *Enterprise* SBDs that had made it back safely to the ship after the June 4 morning attack were thus capable of being flown again in the afternoon. The good news was that the *Enterprise* and *Yorktown* air groups worked quite well together on June 4; by accident in the morning when dive-bombers from both carriers arrived over the Japanese fleet coincidentally at the same time, and by design in the afternoon when dive-bombers from the two carriers were launched together from *Enterprise* in a coordinated attack. That 15 undamaged *Yorktown* dive-bombers had landed aboard the *Enterprise* while their own ship was under attack allowed the *Enterprise* to field a reasonably powerful second strike.[2] A composite force of 24 dive-bombers from three different squadrons (VS-6, VB-6, and VB-3) was thus assembled and took off from the *Enterprise* at 3.30pm. Ten of these were *Enterprise* planes; the remainder comprised planes and pilots from *Yorktown*. While the *Hornet* did launch 16 dive-bombers for its own afternoon strike,[3] it

---

[1]Enterprise casualties are listed on the "USS Enterprise CV-6" website, at www.cv6.org/company/muster/casualty.asp?s=19420604&e=19420606. See also, Lundstrom, *The First Team*, p518, p532.

[2]Morison, *Coral Sea, Midway and Submarine Actions*, pp130–131. Thomas B. Buell, *The Quiet Warrior: A Biography of Admiral Raymond A. Spruance* (Annapolis: Naval Institute Press, 1974, 1987): p150. VS-6 Action Report, Midway. Available online at: www.cv6.org/ship/logs/action19420604-vs6.htm. "Bombing Squadron 6, Action Report, Battle of Midway, 4 June 1942. U.S. Aircraft—Action with the Enemy" Naval History and Heritage Command (web). Available online at: http://web.archive.org/web/20150415070417/http://www.history.navy.mil/research/archives/organizational-records-collections/action-reports/wwii-battle-of-midway/bombing-squadron-6.html.

[3]Parshall and Tully, *Shattered Sword*, p319.

would again be *Enterprise* and *Yorktown* dive-bombers that delivered the knockout punch.

Finding a commander for the second dive-bombing strike of the day to be launched from *Enterprise* had been a bit of a problem. Wade McClusky and his Annapolis classmate Max Leslie were out of the running. McClusky was in sick bay having the bullet wounds to his left shoulder treated while Leslie, after his ditching, was still stranded aboard the *Astoria*. As with the morning attack, there was no detailed coordination between the air groups and air staffs of *Enterprise* and *Hornet*, respectively. Again, that was just as well. With the exception of the valiant members of Torpedo Squadron Eight (VT-8), the *Hornet*'s air group continued to perform poorly. Many *Hornet* pilots were demoralized by the failure that morning of their air group commander, Stanhope Ring, to find the enemy at all. Not all of the *Hornet*'s difficulties were self-inflicted, though. *Hornet* was the only one of the three American carriers that did not have a flag officer on board. While Adm Spruance, aboard *Enterprise*, performed brilliantly during the battle, it must be admitted that he and his staff could have done a better job of keeping the *Hornet* informed as to Spruance's thinking and his plans. The messages that *Hornet* was receiving from the flagship *Enterprise* in the afternoon were vague and contradictory.[1]

Command of the afternoon strike launched from *Enterprise* fell to the talented and well-respected Lt Wilmer Earl Gallaher, the commander of VS-6 who had scored the first hit on *Kaga* in the morning attack.[2] After McClusky and Leslie, Earl Gallaher was the most senior pilot aboard the *Enterprise*. Wounded and a bit groggy from the medicinal brandy he had been given after landing, McClusky played no role in planning the afternoon attack on June 4. That work was carried out by Earl Gallaher; his two

[1]Parshall and Tully, *Shattered Sword*, p319.

[2]Morison, *Coral Sea, Midway and Submarine Actions*, pp130–131, 136. Stafford, *The Big E*, p103, p105.

divisional commanders, Dick Best of Bombing Six and DeWitt "Dave" Shumway of the *Yorktown*'s VB-3; and Adm Spruance's staff. This time the dive-bombers found the enemy carrier easily. Samuel Adams's contact report was highly accurate, pinpointing *Hiryu* at a distance of 110 miles due west of the *Enterprise*. Earl Gallaher initiated the attack on *Hiryu* by pushing over into his dive at 5.05pm (local time). Four pilots, including Dick Best and Dusty Kleiss of VB-6 and VS-6, respectively, scored direct hits on the forward half of *Hiryu*'s flight deck. Adm Nagumo's fourth and last carrier was finished. Best and Kleiss had gone two for two for the day, each man having scored a hit during the morning attack as well. Two American dive-bombers were shot down by Japanese fighters after pulling out of their dives, but with *Hiryu* now a blazing hulk, Japanese naval airpower in the vicinity of Midway had been completely eliminated.[1]

The 22 surviving SBDs had formed into a landing circle above the *Enterprise* at 6.15pm and all of them were safely aboard by 6.45pm.[2] Now it was time for American mechanics to repair damaged aircraft while Adm Spruance pondered his next move.[3] During the assault against *Hiryu*, Spruance had radioed Adm Fletcher to report that the fourth enemy carrier was under attack and to enquire about Fletcher's plans for future operations. Adm Fletcher had been forced to transfer to the cruiser *Astoria* when his flagship, the battle-damaged *Yorktown*, had been abandoned after the Japanese torpedo plane attack. Feeling that a carrier battle should be directed from an aircraft carrier, not a cruiser, Fletcher now selflessly turned tactical command over to Spruance.[4] To Spruance's enquiry, "Have you any instructions for further

---

[1]Stafford, *The Big E*, pp105–108. N. Jack "Dusty" Kleiss, with Timothy and Laura Orr, *Never Call Me a Hero: A Legendary American Dive Bomber Pilot Remembers the Battle of Midway* (New York: Morrow, 2017): pp217–222.

[2]Kleiss, et al, *Never Call Me a Hero*, pp221–222.

[3]Stafford, *The Big E*, p110.

[4]Buell, *The Quiet Warrior*, pp153–154.

operations?" Adm Fletcher replied, "Negative. Will conform to your movements."[1]

Most historians who study the Battle of Midway have nothing but praise for Adm Spruance for his refusal to get carried away in the flush of victory. At dusk on June 4, instead of pursuing the now retreating enemy, Spruance gave orders for Task Force 16 to retire to the east until midnight before turning around and heading west so as to close the range in time to launch an air strike against any Japanese ships that could be located after sunrise on June 5. Wade McClusky did not agree with this decision. He later wrote:

"What followed was anti-climatic [sic], a matter of wonderment and disappointment to our aviators. Here was a notable victory by air alone, all four enemy carriers put out of action and the remaining ships fleeing northward [actually *westward*]. Not a gun had been fired ship against ship! Great superiority then existed on our side. Yet our Task Forces retired to the eastward. Our ships were equipped with radar. It was assumed, and later developed to be true, the Japs were not so equipped. How simple it seemed to us to send out our heavy cruisers with destroyer escort and finish off the crippled fleeing enemy. It is my firm belief that if Admiral 'Bull' Halsey had been the Task Force Commander, he would have correctly analyzed the complete devastation caused by his aviators, and with his aggressiveness and initiative, would have immediately followed up for a total victory. Who knows, it might have shortened the war!"[2]

Wade's criticism here of Adm Spruance is a bit harsh, to say the least. American heavy cruisers were no match for Japanese battleships and the Japanese had the best cruisers in the world.

---

[1]Buell, *The Quiet Warrior*, p154.

[2]Wade McClusky, "The Midway Story" Unpublished manuscript, p8. Walter Lord Papers, Naval History and Heritage Command (NHHC).

Halsey probably would have acted just as McClusky surmised he would, and in doing so probably would have run into powerful Japanese surface forces composed of cruisers and battleships in the middle of the night. Later in 1942, the Japanese would demonstrate during the Guadalcanal campaign that, while their ships did indeed lack radar, the Japanese were in fact highly skilled and well trained in the art of night fighting.

According to Stafford: "From the northwest and southwest Yamamoto and Kondo stood in toward the battle, the bulging hulls of their battleships plowing the sea at 30 knots and the biggest naval guns in the world manned and trained out under the quarter moon. Either enemy force was capable of brushing aside the US cruisers, and against them the puny five-inch guns and the thin sides of the carriers were a ghastly joke."[1] Other historians, such as Spruance biographer Thomas Buell, agree with Stafford that Adm Spruance was undeniably correct to proceed with great caution on the night of June 4.[2] While Wade McClusky had proven himself to be a great tactical commander at Midway, his comments above seem to show that he was not fully aware of all the variables inherent in the grand strategy of the battle as a whole.

[1]Stafford, *The Big E*, pp108–109.
[2]Buell, *The Quiet Warrior*, p154.

15

June 5, 1942 – McClusky Versus Browning

The hitherto most well-documented aspect of Wade McClusky's life is the heated argument he got into with Adm Spruance's acting chief-of-staff, Cdr Miles R. Browning, on the flag bridge of the *Enterprise* on the afternoon of June 5. By then, Wade was up and around after spending the afternoon of June 4 in sick bay having his wounds treated. Those wounds meant it would be another week before McClusky could fly again.[1] Even though he could not fly on June 5, McClusky was deeply interested in the missions his pilots in Air Group Six would be flying as the battle continued.[2] Exploring the background of McClusky's clash with Miles Browning is useful for what it shows about the normally mild-mannered McClusky's leadership qualities.

Adm Spruance had not chosen Browning and the two men had had no time whatsoever in which to get used to one another. Miles Browning had been Adm Halsey's chief-of-staff and would go back to that role after the battle when Bill Halsey got out of hospital. It would be difficult to imagine two men more different in temperament than Raymond Spruance and Miles Browning. Adm Spruance was a calm, quiet, reticent man. By way of contrast, words like "controversial," "reckless," and

[1]Wade McClusky pilot logbook entries for June 1942. Philip McClusky collection.

[2]Robert E. Barde, "The Battle of Midway: A Study in Command" PhD dissertation. The University of Maryland, 1971. p354.

"hot tempered" have with considerable justification become indelibly attached to Miles Browning's reputation over the years. Earlier, in his regular post as chief-of-staff to Adm Halsey, Cdr Browning's performance had been adequate for the early hit-and-run strikes in the Marshalls and against Wake and Marcus Islands, respectively, but he showed during the Battle of Midway that he was not up to the task of coordinating all of the requisite activities involved in a major carrier battle. In fairness, it must be noted that carrier battles were an entirely new form of warfare that nobody had mastered completely in 1942, and regarding Adm Halsey himself, it has often been said that Halsey was a fighter, not a planner. Adm Halsey had never demanded detailed planning from Browning when the two men worked together. Halsey's usual instructions to Browning and the rest of the staff before an action probably went something like this: "Get me within range of the enemy and we'll launch an attack." What to do afterward and planning for contingencies were not priorities for Halsey.[1] Miles Browning had taken advanced courses at the Naval War College in Newport, Rhode Island during the 1936–1937 academic year; courses in which planning *was* heavily emphasized, but working for Bill Halsey was not a good way for any officer to keep his planning skills sharp.[2]

Incidentally, some accounts of the Battle of Midway state that Browning's rank during the battle was "commander" while others say "captain." In fact, while Adm Halsey had recommended Cdr Browning for promotion before the battle, the record shows that Browning's promotion to the rank of

[1]Thomas B. Buell, *The Quiet Warrior: A Biography of Admiral Raymond A. Spruance* (Annapolis: Naval Institute Press, 1974, 1987): p140.

[2]Robert J. Cressman, Steve Ewing, Barrett Tillman, Mark Horan, Clark Reynolds, and Stan Cohen, *A Glorious Page in Our History: The Battle of Midway, 4–6 June 1942* (Missoula, Montana: Pictorial Histories Publishing Co, Inc: 1990): p214.

temporary captain became effective on June 17, 1942, ten days after the battle.[1]

When Wade McClusky and the other pilots aboard the *Enterprise* had been awakened and gone to general quarters in the early hours of June 4, McClusky had presumed that Adms Fletcher and Spruance were working from a unified and coherent battle plan. As we have seen, however, as the morning of June 4 wore on, McClusky was at first concerned, then alarmed, then appalled that there was no coordination between the air groups of the three American carriers; that he had been told to proceed to the target with the *Enterprise* dive-bombers but without his torpedo planes or his fighters; that the target coordinates he had been given had proven to be inaccurate; and finally, that the *Enterprise* was not where he had been told it would be when his surviving aircrews returned from the attack.[2] Furthermore, if McClusky's claim, noted in Chapter 9, that he was never told whether it was Fletcher or Spruance who was in overall command of the American aircraft carriers at Midway is accurate, then there were indeed planning errors that went higher in the command hierarchy than Miles Browning.[3] In *A Glorious Page in Our History*, Robert Cressman et al use polite understatement about these planning errors when they write of the spectacular success achieved by the Americans on June 4 and of the situation facing the Americans on June 5 that: "It was obvious that the results achieved the previous day had been attained through the bravery

[1]Cressman et al, *A Glorious Page in Our History*, pp214–215. *Register of Commissioned and Warrant Officers of the United States Navy and Marine Corps.* July 1, 1944. (Washington, DC: Government Printing Office, 1944): p27. Available online at: www. ibiblio.org/hyperwar/AMH/USN/Naval_Registers/1944.pdf

[2]Personal Report. LCDR Wade C. McClusky. Air Group Commander. Enterprise Air Group. Battle of Midway, 4–6 June, 1942. P1. Courtesy National Naval Aviation Museum, Pensacola, Florida. See also, Chapter 12.

[3]Wade McClusky, "The Midway Story" Unpublished manuscript, p2. Walter Lord Papers, Operational Archives, Naval History and Heritage Command (NHHC), Washington Navy Yard, Washington DC.

and dedication of the pilots and radio-gunners—not the plan by which they had been sent out."[1]

Chief of naval operations, Adm Ernest J. King, considered Raymond Spruance to be the most brilliant officer in the United States Navy,[2] an assessment with which most naval historians have heartily agreed. But Spruance was not an aviator. Before his promotion to flag rank in 1939, Spruance, as a captain, had commanded the battleship USS *Mississippi*, but he had never commanded an aircraft carrier. He would need the advice of experienced aviators to carry out the orders he and Adm Fletcher had received from Adm Nimitz: to utilize Task Forces 16 and 17 to defend Midway and to do their best to destroy the enemy fleet, especially Nagumo's aircraft carriers. Thus, during the Battle of Midway, Adm Spruance was forced to rely on Adm Halsey's staff, particularly on Halsey's chief-of-staff, Miles Browning. Spruance brought only one member of his own staff with him from the *Northampton* – his flag lieutenant Robert J. Oliver – when he transferred himself and his flag to the *Enterprise*. Spruance apparently never seriously considered bringing his entire staff from the *Northampton* with him when he went aboard *Enterprise* since, like himself, they were not pilots and Spruance had also learned at the May 26 conference with Nimitz that his assignment to command Task Force 16 was to be temporary. Win, lose, or draw at Midway, Nimitz had told Spruance that when the battle was over Spruance would go ashore at Pearl Harbor to become chief-of-staff to Nimitz.

Even his many critics admit that Miles Browning was an intellectually brilliant officer, but that the brilliance was fatally flawed by the man's mentally unstable personality. A 1918 Annapolis graduate who completed his flight training in 1924, Miles Browning had forged a close bond with Adm Halsey first

---

[1]Cressman, et al, *A Glorious Page in Our History*, p149.

[2]Ernest J. King, with Walter Muir Whitehill, *Fleet Admiral King: A Naval Record* (New York: W. W. Norton, 1952): p491 *n*.

as Halsey's air tactical officer and since June 1941 as his chief-of-staff.[1] Much has been written about Browning's psychiatric issues. Adm Spruance's biographer, Thomas B. Buell, has described the bundle of nerves and contradictions that was Miles Browing thus: "A lean, hawk-like man, [Browning] was emotionally unstable and evil-tempered, becoming angry, excited, and irrational with little provocation. He drank too much, too often, and had a capacity for insulting behavior, especially when drunk."[2]

Browning's positive abilities tended to appear in flashes of brilliance that proved to be all too brief and increasingly infrequent. For instance, while his overall performance at Midway was poor, Browning did have a few good moments during the battle. According to Buell, Adm Spruance was deeply impressed by Browning's quick reaction to a submarine sighting on the night of June 5. By Buell's account, the cruiser "*Northampton* reported a submarine on the starboard bow. Browning ... immediately picked up the TBS (voice radio) and snapped an order to the force for an emergency left turn."[3] This quick decision by Browning to order, on his own initiative, a course change for the entire fleet may well have prevented one or more of the ships in Task Force 16 from being torpedoed. The question with Browning was always "Are such moments of brilliance worth the cost?" The cost being Browning's irascible, volatile, and self-destructive personality. Ultimately, the naval high command would decide that Miles Browning's negative characteristics outweighed his brilliance by too great a margin to justify keeping the man in a position of such importance as that of chief-of-staff to Adm Halsey.

Not surprisingly, the neat, tidy, mild-mannered Adm Spruance, with whom maintaining an even temper was an article of faith, gradually grew more and more disenchanted with Miles Browning the more time the two men spent together. As his relations with

---

[1]Cressman et al. *A Glorious Page in Our History*, p214.

[2]Buell, *The Quiet Warrior*, p140

[3]Buell, *The Quiet Warrior*, p159.

Browning deteriorated during the battle, Spruance began to place more and more trust in Wade McClusky instead. Indeed, McClusky and Spruance developed a high opinion of each other during the Battle of Midway. The two men had much in common; like Spruance, McClusky was a quiet man who got things done. Each was able to make decisions based solely on the merits of a given situation without being influenced by emotion; each knew when to be bold and when to be cautious; and each knew how to adapt rapidly to altered circumstances.[1]

While sometimes brilliant in an emergency, Miles Browning, on the other hand, seemed to have difficulty with even the most mundane of day-to-day tasks. The man who showed such skill in ordering Task Force 16 to make that emergency left turn at Midway displayed extremely poor ship-handling skills when he was given a ship of his own to command. Browning was still with Adm Halsey as chief-of-staff when Halsey took command of the South Pacific Area in October 1942. Halsey did quite well in his new billet, earning a fourth star by providing the vigorous leadership required for American forces to wrest control of Guadalcanal from the Japanese. Adms Nimitz and King, however, as well as Secretary of the Navy Frank Knox, gradually became convinced that Halsey's success in the South Pacific was occurring in spite of, not because of, the presence of Miles Browning at Halsey's headquarters in Noumea.[2] By early 1943, Adm King was convinced that Browning was a bad influence on Halsey and was determined that Browning should be relieved. The late naval historian Clark G. Reynolds, an admirer of Browning, expressed chagrin that "after the war, [Adm] King recalled that Browning was 'no damn good at all.' [King] rated Browning as handsome, an adequate pilot, but lacking brains and understanding."[3] As commander-in-chief, US fleet and chief of naval operations, King

---

[1] Buell, *The Quiet Warrior*, pp157–158.

[2] E. B. Potter, *Bull Halsey* (Annapolis: Naval Institute Press, 1985): p199, p244.

[3] Cressman et al., *A Glorious Page in Our History*, p215 *n*.

could simply have ordered the change. Instead, he decided to salve Halsey's feelings; rather surprising since Ernest J. King was not known for either tact or personal warmth and it is open to question if he actually "liked" anyone except his own children. He did, however, respect Adm Halsey and King knew that Halsey wanted to keep Browning.[1]

Because of the urgency of the situation, and showing a level of delicacy quite rare for him, Adm King resorted to bribery to get Browning away from Halsey. According to Halsey's biographer: "At last King lured Browning away with a bait so attractive that Halsey would no longer stand in his way."[2] That bait was that in July 1943, King arranged for Miles Browning to be named as the first commanding officer of the brand new *Essex* Class carrier USS *Hornet* (CV-12). With this wonderful assignment handed to him, Browning proved almost immediately to be disastrous as a carrier commander. By contrast, when Wade McClusky got command of the small aircraft carrier USS *Corregidor* (CVE 58) in late 1944, he proved to be a highly capable and popular commanding officer. The same could never be said of Miles Browning's tenure aboard *Hornet*. Just as he had been unable to be a team player with other officers on Halsey's staff, Browning proved to be completely incapable of forging any kind of effective bond with the crew of his new ship. Indeed, the *Hornet* was a very unhappy ship while Miles Browning was in command and constantly teetered on the brink of disaster. Browning's string of mishaps included narrowly avoiding a collision with a tanker, and almost tearing the carrier's bottom out by passing much too close to a coral reef. The last straw as far as the naval high command was concerned came in May 1944. Browning flew into a rage when a small CO_2 canister exploded on *Hornet*'s hangar deck. Browning's ensuing temper tantrum caused a stampede in which two men fell overboard. Browning then ignored the good

[1]Cressman, et al., *A Glorious Page in Our History*, p215.
[2]Potter, *Bull Halsey*, p244.

advice of R Adm J. J. "Jocko" Clark, who was on board, that a muster call of attendance should be taken at once. Consequently, the fact that two men were missing was not discovered until the next day. By then, both men had drowned. Browning was relieved of his command shortly after and sent as an instructor to the Command and General Staff College at Fort Leavenworth. It was no accident that the disgraced Browning was sent to an *Army* base in *Kansas* – the geographic center of the United States. Adm King wanted Miles Browning to spend the remainder of the war as far from salt water as it was possible for a man to be.[1]

Similarly, the quick, brilliant, decisive side of Miles Browning's personality was definitely not the aspect that Wade McClusky saw during the Battle of Midway. Instead, Wade was to experience the full measure of Miles Browning's mentally unstable streak on the afternoon of June 5. It was probably not a total surprise to Wade that Browning would quickly become unraveled during the battle. McClusky had certainly gotten to know Browning well since both men had been aboard the *Enterprise* for some time prior to Midway. By the time McClusky took over as commanding officer of Fighting Six in April 1941, if not earlier, his seniority would have required his frequent presence at meetings with Adm Halsey and with the admiral's staff. As such, McClusky had had plenty of time to observe Browning's behavior prior to the battle and he had not liked what he had seen. McClusky's immediate objection to the attack plan Browning devised on June 5 indicates that he had by then acquired a deep distrust of the chief-of-staff, a distrust that had to have been strengthened by mistakes made by Spruance's staff the previous day.

It would be unfair to blame Miles Browning for all of the mishaps and miscommunications that had plagued the Americans on June 4, the decisive day of the battle. The plain fact of the matter was that carrier battles were an entirely new form of warfare in 1942. Both the Americans and the Japanese had trained for such battles during

---

[1] Cressman, et al., *A Glorious Page in Our History*, pp215–216. Potter, *Bull Halsey*, p244.

the 1930s, but actually fighting one proved to be far more complex than anyone had imagined. When planning the afternoon attack against *Hiryu* on June 4, Adm Spruance's neat and tidy mind had been appalled by the wild and unpredictable nature of an all-out carrier battle as events had played out in the highly successful but costly morning attack by the American dive-bombers. Spruance's biographer writes of the admiral's decision to delay launching the attack against *Hiryu* until he had a precise contact report:

> "Why, then his decision to wait? Spruance's analysis of the morning attack highlighted the hazards of finding an elusive enemy based upon an hours-old contact report. His planes had wandered about the ocean in scattered groups, and the *Hornet* dive-bombers had missed the Japanese entirely. The American attacks had been haphazard and piecemeal, allowing the Japanese to demolish the torpedo planes. Other American planes had been lost at sea, having wasted their fuel in futile searches. The morning attack could have been a fiasco. Its success was owed to Wade McClusky of *Enterprise*, Lieutenant Commander M. F. (Max) Leslie, . . . —and luck."[1]

Like good doctors, Spruance and McClusky knew that *preventing* a disease from occurring is much easier than curing one once it hits. Both men knew that it had been the quick thinking and adaptability of Wade McClusky and Max Leslie that had restored order out of chaos on June 4. They were determined to have a better plan at the outset *before* any dive-bombers took off for the attack on June 5.

By early afternoon of June 5, Adm Spruance knew that the Japanese were retreating and he had ordered Task Force 16 to pursue. While Spruance knew that the tide of the battle had turned in favor of the Americans, he thought that at least one of the Japanese carriers might still be afloat. A series of sporadic

---

[1]Buell, *The Quiet Warrior*, p151.

contact reports from PBYs flying from Midway indicated that a burning carrier might be drifting off to the northwest of Midway. (In fact, the last of the four Japanese carriers, *Hiryu*, had gone down early that morning after having burned all night.) Eager to finish off this, and any other crippled Japanese ships he could find, Spruance ordered an early afternoon attack.[1] It was the plan prepared by Browning for this attack that led to the legendary showdown between McClusky and Browning; a confrontation in which McClusky objected vehemently to Browning's attack plan and Adm Spruance sided with McClusky.

The plan Browning presented to Adm Spruance at noon on June 5, 1942 showed that Browning's mind lacked the flexibility shown by McClusky and Spruance. Browning seemed not to understand that the battle was won and that the only question now was what the actual extent of the American victory would be. Browning was still in the mindset that the Americans needed to strike first with maximum strength regardless of the risks. Spruance and McClusky knew by this point that even if the *Hiryu* was still afloat (it was not), it was no longer capable of launching or recovering aircraft. In short, any attack the Americans made would be that all-important "first strike" because the Japanese didn't have any air power in the vicinity to strike with.

Spruance's order for an afternoon attack had been based on a late-morning contact report that detailed several Japanese ships, presumably cripples, still in the vicinity. Browning proceeded to produce an unbelievably bad and unrealistic plan, a plan that called for Task Force 16 dive-bombers to be armed with 1,000lb bombs and launched when the enemy ships were 275 miles away. That meant a round trip of 550 miles.[2] A day earlier, McClusky had flown approximately 400 miles in total and he had had barely enough fuel to make it back to the *Enterprise* – and he had carried only a 500lb bomb, not one of the half-tonners that

[1]Buell, *The Quiet Warrior*, p157.

[2]Cressman et al., *A Glorious Page in Our History*, p149.

Browning ordered for the June 5 strike. Because of the enormous range and heavy bomb load involved, Browning's June 5 attack plan seemed certain to end in disaster. Even Adm Spruance, while not a pilot, should have seen the fallacy of it, but he instead accepted the scheme and preparations were underway to arm and fuel the planes when McClusky first heard the details.

The Browning plan was brought to Wade's attention by Lts DeWitt "Dave" Shumway and Wallace Short, respective commanders of the *Yorktown*'s VB-3 and VS-5 squadrons, both of which had sought refuge on *Enterprise* after *Yorktown* was put out of action on the afternoon of June 4. Shumway had participated in the respective attacks against *Soryu* and *Hiryu* on June 4 and had been tapped to lead the strike force that *Enterprise* would launch on June 5. Max Leslie was still aboard the *Astoria* and Earl Gallaher, who had led the attack against *Hiryu*, was now himself out of action. During his dive on *Hiryu* the day before, Gallaher had been dismayed to find that the angle of his dive was not quite right and that his bomb was going to fall a bit short of the target. He tried an unorthodox and dangerous countermeasure in that he attempted to "throw" his bomb by jerking the nose of his aircraft up just as he released it. Jerking the nose up so sharply severely strained Gallaher's back (and his bomb missed anyway). In agonizing pain, Gallaher had barely been able to fly his airplane during the return trip to the *Enterprise*, and he was in no condition to fly on June 5.[1]

Shumway and Short decided to bring their objections to Browning's plan to Wade McClusky's attention.[2] Usually a quiet, unassuming man, there was nothing reserved about the way

---

[1]Stephen L. Moore., *Pacific Payback: The Carrier Aviators Who Avenged Pearl Harbor at the Battle of Midway* (New York: NAL Caliber, 2014): p287, pp295–296, pp306–307. Barde, "The Battle of Midway: A Study in Command," pp353–355. Cressman, et al., *A Glorious Page in Our History*, pp137, 149. Craig L. Symonds, *The Battle of Midway* (New York: Oxford University Press, 2013): p333.

[2]Cressman et al., *A Glorious Page in Our History*, p149.

McClusky reacted. Incredulous upon hearing what Shumway and Short had to say, Wade needed little prompting to act. The events of the previous day had convinced McClusky that he should take a more active role in planning operations prior to take-off to ensure that they were realistic, contact information was accurate, and most importantly, that Point Option was calculated accurately. In the first-person account of the battle that he completed after the war, McClusky describes his reaction when he heard about Browning's plan:

"When I heard this, I immediately went to the Flag Bridge to object to the distance and related bomb load. I said it couldn't be done. The Chief of Staff [ie Browning] argued that it could and stated he knew more about flying an SBD than I did. I merely asked if he had ever flown the plane with self-sealing tanks which reduced the gas capacity, armor plated seats which increased the weight, and a 1,000 pound bomb, under combat conditions. Many of us had the day before. Following in my footsteps were Leslie, skipper of Bombing THREE and Gallagher [sic], skipper of Scouting SIX. Admiral Spruance listened a minute or two, turned to me and said, 'I'll do whatever you pilots want to do.'

I suggested we reload with a 500 pound bomb, wait until 1700 before launching in order to close the enemy as much as possible. Remember, this was a cold contact and I believe no one really thought it was worth while. That recommendation was carried out."[1]

Wade is mistaken here about Max Leslie being with him during the confrontation with Browning. In point of fact and as noted earlier, Max Leslie had been forced to make a water landing on June 4 and had been picked up the cruiser USS *Astoria*. While he would succeed McClusky as *Enterprise* air group commander after the battle, Leslie was never on the Big E during the battle,

[1]Wade McClusky, "The Midway Story," p9. Walter Lord Papers. Operational Archives, Naval History and Heritage Command (NHHC). Washington Navy Yard. Washington, DC.

although some 20 *Yorktown* dive-bombers did land on the *Enterprise* when the *Yorktown* was left damaged and dead in the water after being attacked by Japanese dive-bombers and torpedo planes from the *Hiryu* on June 4.[1] Although he was eager to rejoin his squadron, and therefore very much to his own personal chagrin, Max Leslie was still aboard the *Astoria* on the afternoon of June 5.

Miles Browning did not take kindly to being publicly overruled by Adm Spruance. According to Spruance biographer Thomas Buell: "Hurt and humiliated, Browning stormed off the shelter and fled below to the bridge. There he lost all control; he wept and raged and screamed. Finally he went to his cabin where he sulked until a staff officer persuaded him to return to the flag shelter."[2] Taking McClusky's side in the argument on the afternoon of June 5 shows that Adm Spruance was deeply disappointed with Browning's overall performance at Midway. Losses of American aircrew had been relatively light during the early hit-and-run raids in the Marshalls and in the Battle of the Coral Sea.[3] Midway was a great American victory. But unlike the earlier engagements involving American aircraft carriers, this time the butcher's bill had come due with a vengeance. To the pilots like Wade McClusky who survived the battle, American losses seemed shockingly high; higher than they had needed to be. As air group commander, McClusky was in charge of all *Enterprise* aircrews: those that flew torpedo planes and fighters, as well as those of the dive-bombers. The torpedo squadrons of all three of the American carriers had been essentially wiped out. Thirty-seven of the 41 torpedo planes launched by the Americans were lost. Their slow speed making them easy targets for Japanese fighter pilots and antiaircraft gunners, the TBD Devastators had

[1] Max Leslie to Thaddeus V. Tuleja. July 21, 1958, p7. Walter Lord Papers, NHHC.
[2] Buell, *The Quiet Warrior*, p157.
[3] Edward P. Stafford, *The Big E: The Story of the U.S.S. Enterprise* (Annapolis: Naval Institute Press, 1962, 2002): p113.

been shot to pieces. Most of those were shot down in the battle area, and a few ditched on the return due to battle damage and/or fuel exhaustion. Every one of the 15 aircraft in *Hornet*'s Torpedo Squadron Eight (VT-8) had been shot down. Of the 30 men who rode in those planes, only one, Ensign George Gay, survived. Ten of the 14 planes in the *Enterprise* Torpedo Squadron Six (VT-6) were lost with 20 men killed. Included among the dead aircrew from VT-6 was the squadron commander, Lt Cdr Eugene E. Lindsey, with whom McClusky had eaten breakfast on the morning of June 4. Ten of the 12 torpedo planes from *Yorktown*'s VT-3 were shot down. Twenty-one pilots and gunners from the downed VT-3 planes perished.[1] Altogether, 70 aircrewmen out of the 82 who were launched from the three American carriers in the 41 torpedo planes were killed. Adding to the poignancy of the wholesale slaughter of the American torpedo planes at Midway is that while their low-level attacks did distract the crews of the enemy carriers and the Japanese fighters pilots flying CAP, thereby aiding the American dive-bombers to approach from on high without being detected, none of the American torpedo pilots who got close enough to drop a torpedo succeeded in scoring a hit. Everybody knew that the TBD Devastator torpedo plane was obsolete, but the true level of the plane's deficiencies – that the plane was in fact a deathtrap – had not been apparent at Coral Sea, where American torpedo pilots had scored hits against the carrier *Shoho* without loss to themselves.

At the forefront of McClusky's concerns was his lack of confidence in the accuracy of the contact reports that had been

---

[1] *Yorktown* after action report (written by Capt Elliott Buckmaster), June 18, 1942. Available online at: https://www.history.navy.mil/research/archives/digitized-collections/action-reports/wwii-battle-of-midway/uss-yorktown-action-report.html. *Enterprise* Action Report (Serial 0133), written by Capt George D. Murray, June 8, 1942. Available online at: www.midway42.org/Midway_AAR/USSEnterprise1.aspx. I am indebted to Mr Thom Walla of "The Midway Roundtable" for his encyclopedic knowledge of American aircrew losses at Midway. Email correspondence, Thom Walla to me, December 23 and December 24, 2017.

received on the morning of June 5. He was acutely aware of just how quickly a contact report could become out of date – something he had learned the hard way the previous day. Spruance and Browning should have ordered that cruiser floatplanes from Task Force 16 be used to aid in the search for Nagumo's carriers and then to shadow the Japanese fleet once it had been located on the morning of June 4. Continuous shadowing would have allowed Nagumo's course change to be detected and reported to McClusky in a timely fashion so that his search would have been far less arduous and his pilots would have had more fuel left over for the return light. That American cruiser floatplanes were not so used, and in fact remained sitting atop their catapults aboard ship, is probably more the fault of Spruance than of Browning. As a former cruiser division commander, Adm Spruance was well aware of the value of the scouting aircraft carried by American cruisers. Why Spruance ignored such a precious asset on June 4 remains a mystery.

Even though he flew with the dive-bombers, Wade no doubt felt keenly the loss of so many torpedo plane crews. Closely related to this feeling was that the failure of Browning and the rest of Spruance's staff to accurately calculate Point Option on June 4 was still unfinished business as far as Wade was concerned. Wade's calculated risk of taking the *Enterprise* dive-bombers beyond the safe limit of fuel endurance had been justified by the potential to achieve spectacular results, but it was a decision he had taken in the belief that the Spruance's staff aboard *Enterprise* and the ship's senior officers had all the mundane matters such as calculating Point Option well in hand. McClusky was enraged that the Big E had not been where it was supposed to be when surviving pilots returned – a situation he was convinced had cost additional American lives.[1] In addition to feeling badly that he had been compelled to push his dive-bomber pilots beyond the limit of safe fuel endurance during the long search on June 4,

[1] Wade McClusky, "The Midway Story," pp6–7. Walter Lord Papers. Operational Archives, Naval History and Heritage Command (NHHC). Washington Navy Yard. Washington, DC.

Wade also knew that the TBD Devastator torpedo plane had considerably less range than did the SBD Dauntless. It is safe to say that McClusky was incensed about the Point Option fiasco. His bitterness that the *Enterprise* had not been where it was supposed to be upon the return of the surviving pilots had not diminished in the 24 hours since he had returned from leading the decisive attack. Wade was therefore in no mood for more poor planning on the part of Miles Browning. But poor planning was exactly what McClusky was confronted with on the afternoon of June 5, 1942.

Wade's account of the dispute with Browning, and the predicament that argument placed Adm Spruance in, is borne out by other historians. Spruance, a non-aviator, was faced with a bitter dispute between his senior pilot and his chief-of-staff – also an experienced pilot. Robert Barde, who interviewed McClusky on June 30, 1966 at Wade's home at 1826 Circle Road, Ruxton, Maryland,[1] wrote of the McClusky-Browning shouting match that:

"From the side of the small room, Admiral Spruance ... was quietly listening and observing the discussion which, by this time, had become quite heated. He was in a different and very difficult position as a surface officer running an air war. Browning was his primary assistant, his right hand, and a man with years of experience in almost every phase of aviation. On the other hand, the stocky, red-faced McClusky had presented a sound argument with reasoning that even a surface, 'black shoe,' officer could understand with abundant clarity. Spruance stepped up to the chart covered table in the center of the room and, without a word to Browning or anyone else on his staff, said to McClusky, 'I'll do whatever the pilots want.' The planes took off with the lighter bombs an hour later."[2]

[1]Barde, "The Battle of Midway: A Study in Command," p176, *n*.
[2]Barde, "The Battle of Midway: A Study in Command," pp354–355.

Barde here refers to Spruance as a "black shoe" officer because in the World War 2 US Navy, the only difference in the uniforms of officers who were pilots and those who were not was their shoes: the aviators wore brown shoes, surface officers wore black ones. All accounts of the Browning-McClusky argument agree on the principal items: 1) Browning's plan was wildly impracticable; 2) McClusky urged a much better alternative; 3) Browning told McClusky to keep quiet and follow orders; 4) the argument became a shouting match between Browning and McClusky; 5) Spruance had had enough of Miles Browning by then and publicly sided with McClusky; 6) the then humiliated and enraged Browning threw a temper tantrum upon being overruled.

Subsequent events proved Wade to have been entirely correct to urge caution in this instance. On the June 5 mission, the American dive-bombers were only able to find one target, the Japanese destroyer *Tanikaze*, a speedy little ship that managed to dodge every bomb the Americans dropped. A lone enemy destroyer was certainly not a target worth anything like the risks that Browning was prepared to have the pilots undertake. On June 4, Wade had been willing to take the chance of leading his squadrons in a search that extended beyond the safe fuel range of the aircraft involved. The results achieved had fully justified the risk. June 5 was a different story. All four Japanese aircraft carriers had been destroyed. The battle was won. Any additional Japanese ships destroyed would be icing on the cake but not worth the kind of risks that had been fully justified a day earlier when Nagumo's carriers were still intact.

16

McClusky and Historians

In a recent volume on naval leadership, Captain Chris Johnson praises Wade McClusky's leadership ability by writing: "when the nation desperately needed heroes and victories, a man of courage, commitment, and intuition, leading his flight of bombers into battle, answered that call superbly."[1] Johnson's praise of McClusky is a rare exception in recent literature about the Battle of Midway. Wade McClusky's treatment in the secondary literature written prior to 1990 is uneven and rather scanty. After 1990, mentions of McClusky in written accounts of the battle are more plentiful – and almost uniformly hostile. The early histories mention only the bare outlines of his actions during the battle; the later ones often accuse him of incompetence. Indeed, since the late 1980s the idea that Wade McClusky was supposedly unfamiliar with dive-bombing doctrine, particularly in the matter of target selection, has become the new paradigm for Midway scholars and has remained essentially unchanged to the present day. Wade McClusky continues to be blamed for the fact that his two squadrons, Scouting Six and Bombing Six, did not divide evenly and that more *Enterprise* dive-bombers dove on the *Kaga* than on Nagumo's flagship, *Akagi*. For instance, one recent history

---

[1]Captain Chris Johnson, "Clarence W. McClusky: Intuition" in Joseph J. Thomas, ed., *Leadership Embodied: The Secrets to Success of the Most Effective Navy and Marine Corps Leaders*. 2nd Edition. (Annapolis: Naval Institute Press, 2013): p82.

claims that in regard to McClusky and the proper manner of assigning targets during a dive-bombing attack, that "such doctrine was apparently unknown to *Enterprise*'s new air group commander, whose background was that of a fighter pilot."[1] In point of fact, because McClusky had gained experience flying more than a dozen different types of aircraft in the 1930s, as already explained, it would be far more accurate to say that his background was that of an *everything* pilot. The fact that both targets chosen by McClusky for destruction were in fact destroyed by *Enterprise* dive-bombers is de-emphasized in the currently accepted paradigm used by most historians who write about the Battle of Midway and who seem determined to eviscerate Wade McClusky. These critics are preoccupied with the *way* the battle was fought rather than with results. Instead, one could argue thus: who cares whether it was three, five, or ten American dive-bombers that dove on *Akagi*? Wade McClusky had ordered his pilots to destroy the *Akagi* and the *Kaga*, and those pilots did just that – sending both carriers to the bottom. The desired result was achieved.

Why would a man like Wade McClusky, who exhibited superb leadership in combat coupled with personal characteristics of selflessness and modesty, somehow become the target of jealousies and controversy? The fact that he never really told his side of the story may have hurt him in this regard; McClusky did not write a full-scale memoir. His first-person article-length account of the Midway battle, mentioned earlier, was circulated in such a limited fashion that it cannot be considered to be a "published" document. "Shy" might be the wrong word to describe him, but Wade McClusky was a quiet man whose personality was completely antithetical to any effort at self-promotion. In the secondary literature, there are sometimes hints that his role in the battle was pivotal. Even when he is so recognized, his feat is

---

[1]Stephen L. Moore, *Pacific Payback: The Carrier Aviators Who Avenged Pearl Harbor at the Battle of Midway* (New York: NAL Caliber, 2014): p217.

still usually only described in a few brief sentences. For instance, Edward Stafford's high praise for McClusky quoted in Chapter 2 is found in a book that is devoted to chronicling the career of the *Enterprise* throughout the war in 20 major naval battles, not just at Midway. This biography of *Enterprise* has sold well ever since it first appeared in 1962 and Stafford obviously admired McClusky, but the book is a biography of a ship, not of a man. Stafford's admirable purpose was to pay tribute to all of the men who served on "the Big E" during the war by describing all of the battles that they and their ship fought in.

In contrast to Stafford, most other histories written prior to 1990 portray Wade McClusky as just an ordinary pilot, as if the decisions he made on June 4, 1942 were the ordinary ones that any moderately competent Navy pilot would have made. The early accounts of the Battle of Midway lack the hostility toward McClusky that is evident in more recent literature on the battle. Even in Stafford's account, however, Wade remains a two-dimensional character. No history has as yet succeeded in bringing him to life as a person. In fact, there was nothing ordinary about Wade McClusky and the superb leadership he displayed at Midway.[1] This was recognized by his immediate superiors at the time, but much less so in the years since. In the after action report following the battle, *Enterprise* captain George D. Murray stated that McClusky's cool, calm decision-making was the most important single factor in the American victory at Midway.[2] Similarly, in his report to Chief of Naval Operations Adm Ernest J. King after the battle, Pacific Fleet Commander-in-Chief Adm Chester W.

---

[1]Johnson, "Clarence W. McClusky: Intuition" in Thomas, ed. *Leadership Embodied*, pp81–82.

[2]USS *Enterprise* Action Report, June 13, 1942. Air Battle of the Pacific, June 4–6, 1942. Action Report (Serial 0137) — 4–6 June, 1942. Available online at website of *USS Enterprise CV-6: The Most Decorated Ship of the Second World War*. Available at www.cv6.org/ship/logs/action19420604.htm.

Nimitz wrote of McClusky, using typical naval understatement, that "the *Enterprise* Group Commander, proceeding separately decided to turn north to search, estimating that enemy must have reversed course. This was one of the most important decisions of the battle and one that had decisive results."[1] Indeed it did. This book is an effort to prove Murray and Nimitz to have been undeniably correct in their respective assessments of Wade McClusky's performance.

While praising McClusky in his report to Adm King, Nimitz inadvertently did McClusky, and all the Navy pilots who flew at Midway, a disservice in his public pronouncements about the battle. Just after the battle, Adm Nimitz was in a public-relations bind. He and King well knew that the killing blows in the battle had been delivered exclusively by US Navy dive-bombers. Nevertheless, Nimitz was a theater commander responsible for, and to, all Allied forces in the Pacific Theater. How then to include the efforts and sacrifices of Marine fighter pilots, many of whom were flying obsolete Brewster Buffalo aircraft, who rose from Midway's airstrip to attack the Japanese aircraft that bombed Midway? Nimitz also had to acknowledge the Marines who flew out from Midway to attack the Japanese fleet. Then there were the Army Air Forces B-17s that dropped heavy bomb loads from high above the Japanese carriers but scored no hits.

One of the reasons why Chester Nimitz was such a superb fleet and theater commander was that he was a healer, not a divider. He truly wanted all three services in his theater – land, air, and naval – to cooperate and get along together. Thus, in his messages to the press after the battle, Nimitz compounded the understatement he had used when communicating with King by placing the Navy's efforts at Midway very much in the

---

[1] Adm Chester W. Nimitz. Battle of Midway After Action Report. Cincpac File No.A16 01849. Available online at www.ibiblio.org/hyperwar/USN/rep/Midway/Midway-Cin CPac.html. Accessed December 20, 2015. See paragraph 30.

passive voice. Nimitz's biographer explains the public relations predicament Nimitz faced after the battle:

"Distributing proper credit now became something of a problem. The Army flyers were the first to return to Pearl and had given representatives of the press their version of the Battle of Midway ... None of these [Army] flyers was more than dimly aware that the Navy had been involved in the battle...

Admiral Nimitz, recognizing that the [Army] aviators made up in gallantry what they lacked in aim and damage-assessment, declined to contradict the Army's extravagant pretensions. His spokesman merely claimed for the Navy a share in the victory. Later ... Nimitz issued a statement that went a little further: 'The performance of officers and men was of the highest order, not only at Midway and afloat, but equally so among those at Oahu not privileged to be in the front line of battle. I am proud to report that the cooperative devotion to duty of all those involved was so marked that, despite the necessarily decisive part played by our three carriers, this defeat of the Japanese arms and ambitions was truly a victory of the United States' armed forces and not of the Navy alone.'"[1]

Nimitz was a generous man; perhaps a bit too generous. "Despite the necessarily decisive role played by our three carriers" was far too vague and passive a statement and it helped to prevent the average newspaper reader in the United States in the weeks following the battle from gaining any clear idea of how the Battle of Midway was actually won. Typical of the wildly inaccurate newspaper accounts immediately following the battle is a July 15, 1942 story in the *Salt Lake Tribune* entitled "Midway Cost Foe 20 Ships, Navy Reveals," which claims that American Army B-17s, Navy torpedo planes,

---

[1] E. B. Potter, *Nimitz* (Annapolis: Naval Institute Press, 1976, 1987): pp104–105.

dive-bombers, and PBY Catalinas all scored hits against Japanese ships (and multiplies the total number of Japanese ships actually sunk by a factor of four).[1]

Returning to the theme of how historians have treated Wade McClusky, both approaches, that of the older histories that mention him only in passing and the newer histories that vilify him, help explain why he has remained such an obscure figure in the years since the Battle of Midway. The authors of the older histories who present only the outlines of McClusky's actions were writing "great man" history in which the actions of admirals are front and center. More recent histories of the battle spend more time discussing the activities and personalities of individual players of lower formal rank. Wade McClusky gets plenty of attention from these authors, almost all of it negative.

The postwar literature on the Battle of Midway is often thought to begin with Samuel Eliot Morison's 15-volume *History of United States Naval Operations in World War II*. Morison describes the Battle of Midway in Volume Four of that series, published in 1949. Convinced that history could be written to read like great literature, Morison set out to write it that way – and succeeded brilliantly; Samuel Eliot Morison has few, if any, equals when it comes to writing military history that flows effortlessly with the page-turning appeal of an adventure novel.[2] If Morison had a flaw as a historian, it is that he places too much emphasis on the role of admirals when explaining how and why naval battles are won and lost. In his top-down writing style, Samuel Eliot Morison almost never mentions an enlisted man by name. Ship's captains and air squadron

---

[1]"Midway Cost Foe 20 Ships, Navy Reveals" *Salt Lake Tribune*. July 15, 1942. Pp1–2. Available online at: www.newspapers.com/image/13035962. Accessed September 18, 2017.

[2]*Encyclopædia Britannica Online*, s. v. "Samuel Eliot Morison", accessed December 28, 2015. Available online at www.britannica.com/biography/Samuel-Eliot-Morison.

leaders are about as low as Morison goes in the command hierarchy when describing the contributions to a given battle of individual American naval personnel. In his account of the Battle of Midway, Morison writes approvingly of the actions of Wade McClusky, but he is primarily interested in what Adms Nimitz, Fletcher, Spruance, Nagumo, and Yamamoto did or did not do.[1] Wade McClusky is mentioned on fewer than a dozen pages in a 300-page volume. Granted, Samuel Eliot Morison was writing a broad strategic overview of the battle, but the lack of emphasis on the individual initiative of pilots is disappointing. The aforementioned Norman "Dusty" Kleiss, a pilot not even mentioned by Morison, flew a dive-bomber in Wade McClusky's *Enterprise* group at Midway scoring a hit on the *Kaga* in the morning attack and another hit on the *Hiryu* in the June 4 afternoon attack and, two days later, he probably scored yet another bomb hit, this time on the Japanese heavy cruiser *Mikuma*.[2] Historians Timothy Orr and Laura Orr interviewed Dusty Kleiss on several occasions beginning in 2011 as they helped him prepare his memoir.[3] In these interviews, Kleiss lamented what he saw as a lack of recognition accorded to pilots in general by Midway historians. According to the Orrs, Kleiss "hopes that Americans might well remember the effective service rendered by the dive-bomber pilots. It was they

---

[1]Samuel Eliot Morison, *History of United States Naval Operations in World War II*. Vol. 4. *Coral Sea, Midway and Submarine Actions: May 1942–August 1942* (Boston: Little, Brown and Company, 1954 – reissued in 2001 by Castle Books, Edison, NJ): passim.

[2]Capt Jack "Dusty" Kleiss, USN (Ret), "History from the Cockpit: Reflections of a World War II U.S. Navy Dive Bomber Pilot" *The Daybook*. Vol. 15. Issue 4. A publication of the Hampton Roads Naval Museum, 2012. P6. Available online at www.history.navy. mil/museums/hrnm/files/daybook/pdfs/volume15issue4.pdf. Accessed February 14, 2016.

[3]Email correspondence, Laura L. Orr to me, February 8, 2016.

who delivered in the Navy's hour of need, not the admirals."[1] Indeed they did.

Like most early histories of the Battle of Midway, Samuel Eliot Morison's account also gets a few points of detail wrong. Morison has the *Enterprise* strike group containing 37 dive-bombers instead of the correct figure of 33. Morison also claims erroneously that of the Japanese aircraft carriers, the *Akagi* was the westernmost and the *Hiryu* furthest north at the time McClusky arrived overhead.[2] More recent research has shown that *Kaga* was westernmost and *Soryu* was furthest north.[3] Edward P. Stafford, in *The Big E*, correctly states that McClusky was leading 32 dive-bombers (not including his own), although there are still factual errors in Stafford's book. For instance, Stafford has Earl Gallaher taking Scouting Six down to 15,000ft due to oxygen problems when in fact it was Dick Best and Bombing Six that ended up at 15,000ft due to defective oxygen bottles. Earl Gallaher and Scouting Six remained right behind McClusky's leading element at 19,000ft.

Thaddeus V. Tuleja's *Climax at Midway*, first published in 1960, is a straightforward account of the battle in which Wade McClusky fares well as regards assessment of his performance. Unfortunately, the book contains no information on McClusky's

---

[1] Timothy Orr, PhD, and Laura Orr, 'Jack "Dusty" Kleiss and the Battle of Midway' *The Daybook*. Vol. 15. Issue 4. A publication of the Hampton Roads Naval Museum, 2012. P11. Available online at www.history.navy.mil/museums/hrnm/files/daybook/pdfs/volume15issue4.pdf. Accessed January 3, 2015.

[2] Morison, *Coral Sea, Midway and Submarine Actions*, pp122–124.

[3] Map drawn by either J. R. Penland or Dick Best. Bombing Squadron 6 Action Report, Battle of Midway, 4 June 1942. (Abbreviated report covering morning attack) NARA RG 38. Records of the Office of the Chief of Naval Operations. World War II Action and Operational Reports. Box 387. Commander Bombing Squadron Six (VB-6) file. See Figure 12.1 in Chapter 10. See also, Jonathan Parshall and Anthony Tully, *Shattered Sword: The Untold Story of the Battle of Midway* (Washington, DC: Potomac Books, 2007): pp224–233.

personal characteristics. Tuleja interviewed many Midway veterans and corresponded with others. Tuleja had no bias either for or against McClusky, but his book presents only the bare outlines of his contribution to the battle. Tuleja errs in claiming that the *Enterprise* dive-bombers destroyed *Akagi* and *Soryu*, saying that Max Leslie's *Yorktown* group destroyed *Kaga*. While working on his book, Tuleja formed a close bond with Maxwell Leslie. Until the day he died in 1985, Leslie mistakenly believed *Hiryu* and *Soryu* to be small ships (they were not) and was adamant that *Yorktown* dive-bombers had sunk one of the big carriers, either *Kaga* or *Akagi*.[1] Tuleja found Leslie's argument convincing and wrote his account of the battle accordingly.

Historians agree that it was Walter Lord who, for his superb 1967 account of the battle, *Incredible Victory*, did the lion's share of the painstaking research necessary to determine the basic outline of how the battle unfolded. Historian Steve Ewing has written that Walter Lord's "meticulous research on what squadrons hit what ships that morning has withstood the test of time."[2] Indeed it has. The only major error in Walter Lord's account of the morning attack on June 4 is that Lord felt that *Hiryu*, not *Soryu*, was furthest to the north among the Japanese carriers.

The idea that Wade McClusky somehow bungled the June 4, 1942 morning attack first began to gather steam in the late 1980s and has continued on almost unabated into the 21st century. One of the first, perhaps even the first, written account to put forth this "McClusky as bungler" scenario is *A Glorious Page in Our History: The Battle of Midway: 4–6 June 1942*, written by a group of scholars headed by Robert J. Cressman and published in 1990. This book, and others written since 1990, seems to pit

---

[1] Thaddeus V. Tuleja, *Climax at Midway* (New York: Jove/Norton, 1960/1983): passim.

[2] Steve Ewing, "Personalities and Perspectives" Appendix in Robert J. Cressman, Steve Ewing, Barrett Tillman, Mark Horan, Clark Reynolds, and Stan Cohen, *A Glorious Page in Our History: The Battle of Midway: 4–6 June 1942* (Missoula, Montana: Pictorial Histories Publishing Co, Inc, 1990): p193.

Dick Best, the commander of Bombing Squadron Six, against his commanding officer, Wade McClusky. Cressman et al write that Dick Best was "an expert dive-bomber pilot (unlike McClusky, who had, up until recently, flown fighters)."[1] In point of fact Dick Best and Wade McClusky were both expert dive-bomber pilots and both had begun their respective pilot careers flying fighter planes. The authors of *A Glorious Page in Our History* and their adherents ignore the uncomfortable fact that Wade McClusky was trained in, and had wide experience flying, every type of aircraft in the naval inventory. This included dive-bombers, fighters, torpedo planes, and catapult-launched observation aircraft. None of the literature on the Battle of Midway, even that written by Walter Lord and Samuel Eliot Morison, neither of whom had any particular grudge against McClusky, mentions that prior to June 4, 1942 Wade McClusky had put in more than 400 hours flying three different types of dive-bombing aircraft.

Recent literature on the Battle of Midway has McClusky violating dive-bombing doctrine and causing confusion by leading Scouting Squadron Six (VS-6) in diving on the "near" target (said to be *Kaga*) rather than the "far" target (said to be *Akagi*), the latter supposed to have been left for the trailing squadron, Dick Best's Bombing Six (VB-6).[2] As we have seen, the dive-bombing doctrine studied by US Navy pilots early in the war was in fact poorly written, quite vague, and highly contradictory in the matter of target selection. Also, the exact angle of approach of the *Enterprise* dive-bombers as they neared the Japanese fleet is still a matter of some debate. The latter point means that it is possible that when Wade McClusky pushed over into his dive, the *Kaga* and *Akagi* may have been equidistant to his right and left as opposed to being "near" and "far" targets.[3]

[1]Cressman, et al. *A Glorious Page in Our History*, p101.

[2]Cressman, et al. *A Glorious Page in Our History*, pp101–102.

[3]Craig L. Symonds, *The Battle of Midway* (New York: Oxford University Press, 2011, 2013): p300.

McClusky's critics take for granted that Bombing Squadron Six was definitely directly behind (albeit at a lower altitude than) McClusky and Scouting Squadron Six when the pushover point was reached; and that *Akagi* was definitely further away from McClusky than was *Kaga* at pushover. In fact, the Midway map discussed in Chapter 12 shows that it is quite possible that Dick Best and VB-6 may have been a half mile or more to the left of McClusky and VS-6 at the time of pushover.[1] If accurate, that evidence would explain why Best saw the enemy carriers as being the "near" one and "far" one while McClusky saw them as being equidistant to his "right" and "left," respectively.

Second in intensity only to their conviction that McClusky bungled in the matter of target selection, McClusky's critics seem to feel that it was unusual for a fighter pilot to transition to dive-bombers. They also soft pedal the fact that other American dive-bomber pilots who would perform brilliantly at Midway, such as Dick Best, Earl Gallaher, and Maxwell Leslie, had also flown fighters before transitioning to dive-bombers.[2]

Dick Best wrote to Walter Lord in 1967: "As you may recall, I always thought that the foul up over the target resulted from McClusky's lack of familiarity with bomber doctrine, and from what seemed a likelihood that my radio was not working except on intercom."[3] An honest opinion, honestly expressed. However, while Dick Best thought that McClusky might have gained a few hours in dive-bombers in the 1930s, he definitely was not aware that he had logged 400 hours in dive-bombers prior to Pearl Harbor.[4]

Actual time in dive-bombers was not the only variable in the recipe that resulted in either great or poor performances by

---

[1]See Chapter 12.

[2]See Moore, *Pacific Payback*, p34, p35, for very brief mention of Gallaher and Best, respectively, starting out in fighter planes.

[3]Richard Best to Walter Lord, March 7, 1967. Walter Lord Papers. Operational Archives, Naval History and Heritage Command (NHHC). Washington Navy Yard. Washington, DC. p2.

[4]Richard Best to Walter Lord, March 7, 1967. Walter Lord Papers, pp1–2.

American pilots at Midway. Dusty Kleiss of VS-6 turned in a stellar performance at Midway, and yet he had qualified as a pilot only in spring 1941, barely a year prior to Midway.[1] Fourteen years younger than McClusky, Kleiss performed brilliantly at Midway because he had trained hard and was a born pilot. The aircraft in which American pilots would deliver the winning blows at Midway, the Douglas SBD Dauntless dive-bomber, was new to every pilot in the Navy. The first combat-ready version of the Dauntless, the SBD-2, began to join the fleet only in December 1940.[2] Thus, there was not a single pilot in the US Navy who had more than 18 months of experience flying the Dauntless dive-bomber prior to the Battle of Midway. A Navy pilot flying full time at the time of Pearl Harbor was likely to be in the air 40 hours per month. Given the newness of the SBD, even at 40 hours a month, it is unlikely that any Navy pilot was even close to attaining 1,000 hours in an SBD prior to Midway. The idea that there were dozens of American pilots who had accrued hundreds, or even thousands, of hours at the controls of an SBD by the time of Midway, and were therefore more suited than McClusky to lead the attack, is quite erroneous.[3] Earlier dive-bombers used by Navy pilots, such as the Northrop BT-1, had nothing like the capabilities of the SBD Dauntless.

In their well-received 2007 account of the battle, historians Jonathan Parshall and Anthony Tully continue the idea of "McClusky as bungler" when describing his actions upon finding the enemy fleet:

"Doctrine dictated that each squadron should attack one carrier, and McClusky radioed instructions to that effect. However, as mentioned previously, doctrine also said that

---

[1]Moore, *Pacific Payback*, pp48–49, p140, pp216–219.

[2]Thomas Wildenberg, *Destined for Glory: Dive Bombing, Midway, and the Evolution of Carrier Airpower* (Annapolis: Naval Institute Press, 1998): p161.

[3]I base my estimate of 40 hours per month as being full-time flying from an analysis of Wade McClusky's pilot logbooks.

when two squadrons attacked together, the leading squadron should take the further target.

However, Wade McClusky, despite being an excellent group leader, was also a former fighter pilot and had only recently transferred to dive-bombers. Not surprisingly, he was not as studied in attack doctrine as were his subordinates and consequently overlooked this guiding principle, with spectacular results."[1]

By "spectacular," Parshall and Tully do not mean "good." They feel that McClusky attacked the wrong target, Dick Best's target, thereby causing great confusion.[2] Again, no mention is made of the 411 hours and 21 minutes that Wade McClusky had logged flying three different types of dive-bomber prior to Midway.[3] The erroneous impression that is given is that, since earning his wings at Pensacola in 1929, McClusky had flown nothing but fighter planes until a few weeks prior to Midway. As we have seen, such an impression is quite inaccurate. Parshall and Tully also fail to mention that the most current written doctrine available to American pilots who flew at Midway, the aforementioned *USF-74* document, was riddled with contradictions. *USF-74* does contain one sentence stating that the leading squadron should attack the further target, but elsewhere in the same document, it is also stated with equal emphasis that the group commander is free to set up an attack however he sees fit once he arrives on the scene and assesses the progress of a battle for himself, on the spot.[4]

[1] Parshall and Tully, *Shattered Sword*, p228.

[2] Parshall and Tully, *Shattered Sword*, p228.

[3] McClusky's flight hours in dive-bombers are from his logbooks. Email correspondence, Philip McClusky to me, March 5, 2016 and March 14, 2016; and Wade McClusky logbook entries for June 1942. All courtesy of Philip McClusky.

[4] V Adm William F. Halsey, Jr, *Current Tactical Orders and Doctrine U.S. Fleet Aircraft— Volume One: Carrier Aircraft (USF-74, Revised)* (Naval Air Station, Pearl Harbor, T. H. United States Pacific Fleet Aircraft, Battle Force Fleet Air Detachment, March 1941): passim.

Honest mistakes in the way participants remembered the battle could have helped to form the dim view that historians have generally adopted toward McClusky. Errors of memory were apparent even in the 1960s when the Midway veterans were telling their stories to Walter Lord at a time when the surviving veterans were not yet old men. Wade McClusky himself remembered a few aspects of the battle incorrectly, such as his mistaken belief that Maxwell Leslie had been with him on the flag bridge of the *Enterprise* during his own confrontation with Miles Browning on June 5, 1942.

Dick Best told Walter Lord in 1967 that he (Best) had eaten breakfast with "Jimmy" Thach on June 5, 1942.[1] That was almost certainly an error of memory on the part of Best. After returning to the *Enterprise* following the afternoon attack that destroyed the *Hiryu* on June 4, Best was deathly ill and was taken directly to sick bay. It would have been impossible for him to have made his way to the wardroom for breakfast with anyone. It is possible that Thach, the commander of the *Yorktown*'s VF-3 who did land his F4F Wildcat fighter plane aboard the *Enterprise* on June 4 after the *Yorktown* was crippled,[2] visited Best in the *Enterprise* sick bay, but it is doubtful that Best was feeling well enough to eat anything for breakfast on June 5.

McClusky takes a lot of heat from his critics for being promoted from command of a fighter squadron to the post of air group commander; and for deciding to switch back to flying dive-bombers as group commander. Interestingly, no such criticism has ever been attached to Oscar Pederson who, like Maxwell Leslie, was a 1926 Annapolis classmate of McClusky and who was promoted in late April 1942 from commander of the *Yorktown*'s Fighting Squadron 42 (VF-42) to become the *Yorktown*'s air group

---

[1]Richard Best to Walter Lord, March 7, 1967, Walter Lord Papers. Naval History and Heritage Command. p3.

[2]John B. Lundstrom, *The First Team: Pacific Naval Air Combat from Pearl Harbor to Midway* (Annapolis: Naval Institute Press, 1984): p519.

commander – the exact same promotion that McClusky received aboard the *Enterprise* at approximately the same time.[1] Perhaps the reason for Pederson not being criticized by historians for his performance as air group commander is that *Yorktown*'s captain, Elliot Buckmaster, refused to allow Pederson to fly in either the Coral Sea or Midway battles – preferring to keep Pederson on board as air advisor and as the fighter director officer who would coordinate the activities of the *Yorktown*'s CAP fighter planes.[2] It is equally interesting that Wade's immediate predecessor as *Enterprise* air group commander, "Brigham" Young, attracts no criticism whatsoever from historians for switching back to dive-bombers from fighters upon *his* elevation to command of Air Group Six and for personally leading the attacks in the Marshalls and at Marcus – in an SBD dive-bomber.

In being obsessed with *process* instead of results, historians critical of Wade McClusky fall into the trap that would bedevil the Kennedy and Johnson administrations, respectively, in regard to the manner in which the United States fought the Vietnam War. Of the basic tenets of the Kennedy/Johnson strategy of "Flexible Response," a strategy characterized by politicians and diplomats attempting to exercise total control over the way American military forces fight a war, Cold War historian John Lewis Gaddis writes:

> "These assumptions in turn reflected a curiously myopic preoccupation with process—a disproportionate fascination with means at the expense of ends—so that a strategy designed to produce a precise correspondence between intentions and accomplishments in fact produced just the opposite."[3]

Gaddis's point: too much attention paid to *how* things are done causes one to lose sight of results, or in the case of the Vietnam

---

[1]Lundstrom, *The First Team*, p161.

[2]Lundstrom, *The First Team*, p66, p199, p209, pp427–428, p472.

[3]John Lewis Gaddis, *Strategies of Containment: A Critical Appraisal of American National Security Policy During the Cold War* (New York: Oxford University Press, 1982, 2005): p236.

War, of the lack thereof. Winston Churchill suffered from a similar obsession with process regarding the war against Japan. He rejected the idea of simply defeating Japan via the quickest and easiest strategy, namely the Central Pacific Drive by which American forces had by the end of 1944 either seized or bypassed and isolated all of the Japan's island possessions in the Central Pacific's Gilbert, Marshall, and Caroline island chains. By January 1945, the Americans had taken control of the Mariana Islands in the western Pacific and had developed Guam, Tinian, and Saipan into major air and naval bases that would have made excellent jumping-off points for an invasion of the Japanese home islands. American submarines had by then ravaged the Japanese merchant shipping fleet to such an extent that it was now nearly impossible for Japan to import any oil from the Dutch East Indies. The destruction of its merchant fleet also made it very difficult for Japan to send reinforcements or supplies to the threatened outposts of its rapidly shrinking empire.

Churchill seemed unimpressed by these overwhelming successes. At least until the time of the Allied second Quebec Conference in September 1944, he was opposed to the plan of his own chiefs-of-staff to place a British battle fleet with the American Pacific Fleet in the Central Pacific Area. This opposition to the most obvious and direct method for Britain to contribute to the final defeat of Japan was part of Churchill's conviction that it was essential that the war against Japan be ended in a ritualistic fashion, not necessarily in the fastest and most expedient fashion. The ritual was to be the restoration of British prestige by having British forces recapture from the Japanese the Far Eastern outposts of the British Empire, such as Malaya, Singapore, and Hong Kong *before* Japan itself surrendered.[1] Regarding his thinking at the time of the second Quebec Conference, Churchill wrote in his memoirs that: "We had to regain on the field of battle our rightful

[1]David Rigby, *Allied Master Strategists: The Combined Chiefs of Staff in World War II* (Annapolis: Naval Institute Press, 2012): pp84–87.

possessions in the Far East, and not have them handed back to us at the peace table."[1] He also related that he "had always advocated an advance across the Bay of Bengal and operations to recover Singapore, the loss of which had been a grievous and shameful blow to British prestige and must be avenged."[2] The fact that recapturing Hong Kong or Singapore would have done absolutely nothing to hasten the defeat of Japan did not seem to bother Churchill.

Wade McClusky's critics likewise seem to be hung up on process. They seem to place great weight on something Samuel Eliot Morison (who incidentally liked McClusky) wrote regarding the American air operations in the Midway battle: "The tactical performance of the three American carrier air groups [at Midway] would have been considered ragged later in the war." McClusky's critics would do better to heed what Morison wrote next: "Yet they had won, through courage, determination and the quick seizure of opportunities."[3] Morison's point: they may have lacked parade-ground finesse, but the Navy's dive-bomber pilots got the job done at Midway. Sadly, each new book about Midway that adheres to the current paradigm downplays McClusky's contributions a bit more. The manner in which historians following this paradigm are gradually writing Wade McClusky out of the Midway script is reminiscent of the fate of another forgotten American military hero: Maj Gen George Gordon Meade, who led the Union Army of the Potomac to victory at Gettysburg in July 1863 only to find in the months to follow that his role was being either ignored by or criticized in the press. The parallels between the way Maj Gen Meade was treated by the press after

[1]Winston S. Churchill, *The Second World War*. Vol. 6. *Triumph and Tragedy* (Boston: Houghton Mifflin Company, 1953): p147.

[2]Churchill, *Triumph and Tragedy*, p152.

[3]Morison, *Coral Sea, Midway and Submarine Actions*, p158.

Gettysburg and the way Wade McClusky is currently treated by historians are striking:

"In a letter to his wife in December 1863, Meade wryly noted that 'I see the *Herald* is constantly harping on the assertion that Gettysburg was fought by the corps commanders and the common soldiers, and that no generalship was displayed. I suppose after awhile it will be discovered I was not at Gettysburg at all.'"[1]

[1]Maj Gen George Gordon Meade to his wife, December 1863, as quoted in David Rigby, *No Substitute for Victory: Successful American Military Strategies from the Revolutionary War to the Present Day* (New York: Carrel Books/Skyhorse Publishing, Inc, 2014): p34.

17

THE MIDWAR PERIOD – TRAINING PILOTS
AND A DESK IN WASHINGTON

It was June 13, nine days after his decisions and actions helped to win the Battle of Midway, before his wounds had healed enough to enable Wade to fly again. As the *Enterprise* prepared to enter Pearl Harbor to a very warm welcome, McClusky, in an SBD-3, led the air group as the planes took off from the ship and headed for NAS Ford Island. That day, Wade was carrying his regular rear-seat gunner, John O'Brien, whom Wade had been glad to exchange for the sharpshooting Walter Chocalousek during the battle. The flight lasted two hours and 42 minutes. The air group took off just before noon and the Big E entered the harbor at 3.25pm.[1] In the weeks and months following the battle, every *Enterprise* dive-bomber pilot who participated in the morning attack on June 4, 32 men in all, would be awarded the Navy Cross for their actions.[2]

---

[1]Wade McClusky. Pilot logbook entries for June 1942. Philip McClusky collection. Deck Log; U.S.S. *Enterprise* (CV-6). January 1942 to June 1942. NARA RG 24. Box 3334. Entries for June 13, 1942 on p57 and p59.

[2]The Battle of Midway Honor Roll, at website "Their Finest Hour." Available online at http://theirfinesthour.blogspot.com/2012/06/battle-of-midway-honor-roll.html. Accessed July 13, 2020. *Register of Commissioned and Warrant Officers of the United States Navy and Marine Corps*, July 1, 1943, p54. Available online at: https://babel.hathitrust.org/cgi/pt?id=mdp.39015036626284&view=1up&seq=66&size=150. Accessed July 13, 2020. McClusky's name is followed by "(B) (F)", indicating that he was a fully qualified dive-bomber pilot as well as a fighter pilot.

Thus, Wade's Navy Cross can be seen as part of a group award celebrating the exploits of the entire *Enterprise* air group during the battle. Wade was formally recommended for the Navy Cross by *Enterprise* captain George D. Murray on June 12, 1942. The citation written by Murray reads:

"For gallantry in action. Lieutenant Commander Clarence W. McClusky, U.S. Navy, Commander, Enterprise Air Group, lead his Air Group against four aircraft carriers and protecting vessels of the Japanese Invasion Fleet with great boldness, determination, and utter disregard of personal safety, and thereby contributed by his example and leadership in an extraordinarily large degree to the magnificent victory of our air forces in the Battle of Midway. His courage and tenacity in the face of overwhelming enemy fighter and anti-aircraft opposition were superlative and in keeping with the highest traditions of the Naval Service."[1]

Wade was formally detached from the *Enterprise* on June 22, 1942 when he was relieved as *Enterprise* Air Group commander by his friend, fellow Midway hero and Annapolis 1926 classmate, Maxwell Leslie.[2] Promotion followed quickly; Wade was promoted full commander on August 15, 1942.

By then he had been transferred to California and tasked with training replacement pilots for the Pacific Fleet.[3] The need for

---

[1]Capt George D. Murray to Adm Chester W. Nimitz, June 12, 1942. Philip McClusky collection. For the text of the final version of Wade's Navy Cross citation, see Appendix B.

[2]Deck Log; U.S.S. *Enterprise* (CV-6). January 1942 to June 1942. NARA RG 24. Box 3334. P118-A1.

[3]*Register of Commissioned and Warrant Officers of the United States Navy and Marine Corps*, July 1, 1943, p54. Wade McClusky pilot logbook entries for August 1942. Philip McClusky collection. Orders, dated October 1, 1942, from R Adm Randall Jacobs, chief of naval personnel, to McClusky ordering McClusky to report to "Commander Carrier Replacement Squadrons, Pacific Fleet" to help establish "Carrier Replacement Group Twelve." Philip McClusky collection.

new pilots was great. Losses had to be replaced and new aircraft carriers were nearing completion. The Navy and the yard workers at Newport News, Virginia were determined to get the USS *Essex*, first and name ship of a new class of fleet carriers (CV), completed before the end of 1942. This goal was achieved when the new carrier was commissioned into naval service on New Year's Eve day, December 31, 1942, many months ahead of schedule. The *Essex* and her sister carriers still under construction would each need an entirely new air group. In addition to the *Essex* Class carriers that were being built, there were even more flight decks in the pipeline as well, and thus even more demand for trained aviators. In November 1942, construction began at the Kaiser shipyard in Washington State on the first of 50 small *Casablanca* Class escort carriers (CVE) – one of which, USS *Corregidor*, Wade would command late in the war.

As a pilot instructor, Wade worked mostly at NAS Alameda, but continued in his now familiar role as roving troubleshooter, traveling up and down the West Coast to check up on and put out "fires" at San Diego and other West Coast naval installations. For instance, in mid-October 1942, Wade was sent from Alameda to NAS San Diego for a brief stint helping to get new carrier squadrons into shape.[1] He was back at Alameda within a month, continuing to train pilots there.[2] Just after Christmas he was on the move again: on December 27, 1942, R Adm W. K. Harrill, Commander, Fleet Air, Alameda, sent McClusky on a brief trip to San Diego to attend a conference. The particular subject(s) of this conference have not been recorded but whatever the purpose

---

[1] Orders to McClusky from Commander, Fleet Air, Alameda, October 13, 1942. Philip McClusky collection.

[2] "LIEUTENANT COMMANDER CLARENCE W. MCCLUSKY, JR., USN" – a brief career summary prepared by the Navy Department after Midway and dated November 12, 1942, pp1–2. From the McClusky "Jacket" on file at the Nimitz Library, US Naval Academy. "McClusky, Clarence Wade, Jr." Jacket Number 8306. Special Collections & Archives Department, Nimitz Library, United States Naval Academy.

of the conference was, it was urgent. Wade's orders stated that if he was unable to get a seat on a Navy plane, he had "Priority Class ONE" for a seat on a commercial aircraft.[1] These West Coast naval air stations where Wade worked were Advanced Carrier Training Group (ACTG) bases. This meant that the pilots Wade was training had already completed ground school and basic flight training at either Pensacola or NAS Glenview, Illinois – the latter a station Wade would command after the war. What the fledgling pilots needed Wade to teach them were how to make the short-distance take-offs and landings that would be necessary on the deck of an aircraft carrier and how to put bombs and torpedoes on to or into a target.[2]

Wade continued to fly a variety of different aircraft types while he was stateside during the midwar period. These included an F4F-4, an SBD-3, and most often, North American SNJ-3s and SNJ-4s.[3] The SNJ series were the Navy version of the ubiquitous AT-6 Texan, an advanced trainer that bore a superficial resemblance to an SBD. Wade may even have hauled some cargo during this period. His wartime logbook shows that on December 30, 1942 he flew a Lockheed R-50 Lodestar from San Diego to Alameda. The Lodestar was a medium-sized twin-engine, twin-tail transport aircraft that could carry a dozen passengers. For this flight, Wade's always terse log lists himself as the only passenger with no name in the "pilot" column, so he may or may not have had another pilot with him to share the flying duties. It seems unlikely that at the height of the war the Navy would

---

[1] Orders: Jacobs to McClusky, October 1, 1942. Harrill to McClusky, October 13, 1942 and December 27, 1942, respectively. Philip McClusky collection.

[2] N. Jack "Dusty" Kleiss, with Timothy and Laura Orr, *Never Call Me a Hero: A Legendary American Dive Bomber Pilot Remembers the Battle of Midway* (New York: Morrow, 2017): pp67–68, pp241–242, pp244–245.

[3] Wade McClusky pilot logbook entries, August 1942 to January 1944. Philip McClusky collection.

allow a fairly large transport plane to be flown from San Diego to San Francisco without loading it up with some kind of cargo.[1]

On May 10, 1943, Wade was detached from his duties training pilots on the West Coast and ordered to Washington. His old friend and mentor, V Adm Frederick J. Horne, wanted McClusky back in his old post as Horne's aide. By now the two men knew each other well. Horne had been captain of the *Saratoga* back in 1929 when Wade, then a newly minted Navy pilot, had reported aboard as part of the Nine High Hats squadron. Wade had served as Horne's aide from 1935–1938 when Horne had been successively: commander, aircraft, base force, and then commander, aircraft, battle force. In March 1942, Adm Horne had been appointed to the post of vice-chief of naval operations.[2] Wade would now be chief-of-staff as well as aide to Horne. As vice-chief of naval operations, Adm Horne now reported directly to Adm Ernest J. King, the commander-in-chief, US Fleet (COMINCH) and chief of naval operations (CNO). Working in such exalted company at "Main Navy," the Navy Department's headquarters on Constitution Avenue in Washington meant that McClusky got to sit in on many meetings of the joint and combined chiefs-of-staff. As such, McClusky was involved in the planning for upcoming military campaigns such as the Central Pacific Drive and the *Overlord* cross-channel invasion of western Europe. With this new duty came promotion to captain. The official date of promotion was April 27, 1944, but it was made retroactive to August 1, 1943.[3]

---

[1]Wade McClusky pilot logbook entry for December 30, 1942. Philip McClusky collection.

[2]Orders from R Adm William W. Smith, Commander, Fleet Air, Alameda (with the concurrence of V Adm Randall Jacobs, Chief of the Bureau of Personnel) to McClusky, May 10, 1943. Philip McClusky collection.

[3]*Register of Commissioned and Warrant Officers of the United States Navy and Marine Corps,* July 1, 1944. (Washington, DC: Government Printing Office, 1944): p40. Available online at: www.ibiblio.org/hyperwar/AMH/USN/Naval_Registers/1944.pdf. Appointment letter from James Forrestal as acting secretary of the Navy to McClusky,

For these midwar meetings of the joint and combined chiefs-of-staff, Wade and Adm Horne would repair to the Public Health Building directly across Constitution Avenue from Main Navy. This building had been appropriated as the wartime headquarters of the British-American combined chiefs-of-staff. At meetings in the cramped Octagon room on the second floor of the Public Health Building, Adm Horne sat on the American side of the conference table with the joint chiefs-of-staff – Gens George C. Marshall and Henry H. Arnold and Adms William D. Leahy and Ernest J. King. McClusky and other aides, American and British, sat in chairs ranged against the walls. This high-level duty in Washington was partly a reward for McClusky's services at Midway and partly due to Adm King's policy during the war of constantly rotating the staff officers who worked in the Navy Department building in Washington into and out of combat duty so that King and his senior staff would always have fresh perspectives from the fighting front available to them.[1]

Adm Horne and his new chief-of-staff were heavily involved in naval logistics. In fact, getting any items the Navy needed and transporting them to where they were needed was Adm Horne's main responsibility.[2] Adm King was COMINCH and CNO, but in reality, he spent almost all his time dealing with strategic planning, which were his responsibilities as COMINCH. His responsibilities as CNO were to coordinate all of the support functions that made it possible to implement strategic plans. King delegated all of

April 27, 1944; with an endorsement from V Adm Horne dated May 12, 1944. Philip McClusky collection.

[1] Thomas B. Buell, *Master of Sea Power: A Biography of Fleet Admiral Ernest J. King* (Boston: Little, Brown and Company): p227. Ernest J. King and Walter Muir Whitehill. *Fleet Admiral King: A Naval Record* (New York: W. W. Norton & Company, Inc, 1952): pp358–359.

[2] Samuel Eliot Morison, *History of United States Naval Operations in World War II.* Vol. 7. *Aleutians, Gilberts and Marshalls: June 1942–April 1944* (Boston: Little, Brown and Company, 1951): p101.

these support functions to Adm Horne.[1] Specifically, according to Adm King's biographer: "[King] relied upon Vice Adm Horne as surrogate CNO to handle all congressional liaison, procurement, logistics, and administration."[2] Wade's arrival in Washington in spring 1943 coincided with the decision by the combined chief-of-staff that American forces would conduct an advance through the Central Pacific Area beginning in November. McClusky thus would have been almost immediately thrust into the role of helping Adm Horne solve the enormous logistical difficulties the Central Pacific Campaign would bring. The first targets for American forces in the Central Pacific Drive would be the coral and sand atolls Tarawa and Makin in the Gilbert Islands. The marines and infantry that were to seize these Japanese-held atolls would have to operate some 2,000 miles west of Hawaii.[3]

The Navy had grown quite a bit during the months that Wade had been ashore. By the time the Gilberts campaign began on November 20, 1943, there were four new *Essex* Class carriers available, as well as the older *Enterprise* and *Saratoga*. In addition to these six fleet carriers, several of the fast new light carriers (CVL) had joined the fleet, as had a number of the small, slow escort carriers (CVE). The carriers would be screened by no fewer than 65 destroyers. Hundreds of aircraft – both shore- and carrier-based – would be used in the Central Pacific Campaigns. All of them would need trained pilots, 100-octane aviation fuel, mechanics, and spare parts either at forward bases or afloat aboard aircraft carriers.[4] The story of how this mighty fleet was supplied with fuel oil, spare parts, food, ammunition, medicine, and trained crews and pilots deserves a book of its own – and in fact has one: Worrell Reed Carter's delightful 1953 account

---

[1] Buell, *Master of Sea Power*, p227. King and Whitehill, *Fleet Admiral King*, pp573–574.

[2] Buell, *Master of Sea Power*, p227.

[3] Morison, *Aleutians, Gilberts and Marshalls*, pp80–84

[4] Thomas B. Buell, *The Quiet Warrior: A Biography of Admiral Raymond A. Spruance* (Annapolis: Naval Institute Press, 1974, 1987): p188.

Beans, Bullets, and Black Oil: The Story of Fleet Logistics Afloat in the Pacific During World War II.

Carter writes that the Gilberts campaign was "the first time in the Central Pacific that large numbers of fleet units remained away from permanent bases for long periods."[1] Indeed it was. The Gilbert and Marshalls operations were not walkovers by any means; 1,000 American marines were killed in the taking of Tarawa from a very determined Japanese defending force, and roughly 400 American marines and infantry were killed in the subsequent seizure of Kwajelein, Roi-Namur, and Eniwetok in the Marshall Islands in early 1944.[2] In addition to enemy defenders, the logistical problems involved in projecting American military power so far away from friendly fixed bases were immense. The success of the island-hopping campaigns of the Central Pacific Drive was due to the grit of American combat troops, sailors, and pilots, and to the fact that under Adm Horne's direction, the US Navy during the war transformed logistics into a science.

A few statistics shed light on the logistical problems that Horne and Wade, as Horne's chief-of-staff, were facing as the Central Pacific Drive unfolded. One-hundred-seventy-nine American combatant vessels were involved in the Gilberts campaign. They all needed fuel oil. By the end of 1942, the US Navy was already quite proficient in the technical aspects of refueling at sea, but now that kind of fueling would be done on a much larger scale. Thirteen fleet oiler vessels were constantly employed during the Gilberts campaign. The fuel problems would only get bigger as American forces moved westward. Three-hundred-fifty-nine American ships would participate in the Marshalls campaign

---

[1] Worral R. Carter, *Beans, Bullets and Black Oil: The Story of Fleet Logistics Afloat in the Pacific During World War II* (Newport, Rhode Island: Naval War College Press, 1998. Originally published in 1953 by the Government Printing Office, Washington, DC, on behalf of the Navy Department): p98.

[2] Buell, *The Quiet Warrior*, p246. Morison, *Aleutians, Gilberts and Marshalls*, p278.

– an operation that would require the services of 17 fleet oilers as well as nine commercial tankers.[1]

Oil was only one part of the logistical problems involved in the Central Pacific Campaign. Combat troops and the sailors on the ships that escort them and cover their landings also need food and fresh drinking water. In an example from later in the Central Pacific Campaign, Worral Carter writes that while large naval vessels such as aircraft carriers and battleships were able to produce enough fresh drinking water from their own distillation equipment to supply their crews, their evaporators could not make enough extra water to supply small ships without such equipment or the transports that were packed with combat troops.[2] Thus, selected cargo ships had to be turned into giant water tankers whose sole reason for being was to bring fresh water from Hawaii, the West Coast of the United States, or from Australia and New Zealand forward to the combat zone in the Central Pacific Area. Carter writes that: "In the comparatively short Iwo Jima operation 22,000,000 gallons of [fresh] water were supplied to the participating vessels."[3]

The obvious reason for American success in the Gilbert and Marshalls operations is that growing American power had enabled the Americans to bring greater forces to bear than the enemy could muster in return. But it can also be said that the Japanese had failed to make the logistical arrangements necessary to maintain these isolated Central Pacific Area outposts of its empire. American victory in the Central Pacific Campaigns was due in no small part to the fact that the Americans had taken the time and effort to figure out such seemingly mundane matters such as that, according to Samuel Eliot Morison, "it takes one ton (70 cubic feet) of shipping space to keep one soldier supplied

[1]Carter, *Beans, Bullets and Black Oil*, p87, p115, p117. Morison, *Aleutians, Gilberts and Marshalls*, pp107–108.

[2]Carter, *Beans, Bullets and Black Oil*, pp100–101.

[3]Carter, *Beans, Bullets and Black Oil*, pp100–101.

with food, fuel, clothing, ammunition and small stores for one month."[1] The Americans did not just figure out such matters as an academic exercise; they acted on solving these problems. They made it their business to obtain that 70 cu ft of shipping space per person so that American combat troops had what they needed to fight and win. Indeed, the American system of a mobile logistics apparatus was so successful that, after the Marshalls campaign, the bulk of the American Pacific Fleet was able to remain at sea until the end of the war, more than a year later. Advanced bases were used during this time, such as the lagoons at Majuro and Eniwetok in the Marshalls and at Ulithi in the Caroline Islands – each of which made a fine natural harbor sheltered from Ocean waves. However, unless a ship was damaged beyond the ability of the repair ships and mobile floating dry docks at the advanced bases to repair, there was no longer any need to return to Pearl Harbor.[2]

Working on a set schedule in an office in Washington must have taken some getting used to for Wade, after the excitement of flying combat missions. But in this war, logistical problems were so immense that solving them required the same kind of hard-driving efficiency, stamina, and planning skills that were required of the best combat commander. Thus, working as Horne's chief-of-staff during the midwar period must have provided Wade with plenty of excitement. On the importance of logistics to the war in the Pacific, Adm Spruance's biographer writes that:

> "Before the war, logistics was a dull subject that the Navy largely had ignored—no fleet staff had included a 'logistics officer.' But the war in the Pacific painfully demonstrated that logistics controlled nearly every naval operation. In order for fleets to roam the broad Pacific, thousands of miles from fixed

[1]Morison, *Aleutians, Gilberts and Marshalls*, p110.
[2]Carter, *Beans, Bullets and Black Oil*, p125.

bases, the Navy had to devise methods to provide logistical support: fuel, food, ammunition, repair parts, consumable supplies, and the means to repair damaged ships and to replace lost aircraft and pilots."[1]

That the Japanese failed to make the proper logistical support of its Central Pacific island garrisons a priority was only one factor in the Japanese defeat in the Central Pacific Area. Supply lines have to be protected. Wade himself would be involved in protecting American supply lines in the Pacific when he returned to seagoing duty in 1944 as the commanding officer of a small aircraft carrier. The Japanese high command regarded the Gilberts and Marshalls as an outer defensive perimeter to which the Japanese were unwilling to commit the bulk of their fleet to defending. The only outside assistance the Japanese garrisons at Tarawa and Makin in the Gilberts received was from some land-based torpedo planes that flew down from bases in the Marshalls and from half a dozen Japanese submarines that were deployed to the waters around the Gilberts. The main Japanese surface fleet stayed away.

Being back in Washington enabled Wade to be with Millicent and young Wade Sanford. The couple then either owned or rented a house at 6706 Hillandale Road in Chevy Chase, Maryland.[2] Wade probably did not spend much time at home, however, being kept very busy at work. It was at about this time that Wade's marriage to Millicent began to unravel. By now, and as with many wartime couples, the uncertainties and prolonged separations they had endured coupled with the long hours McClusky was now working in Washington were taking a heavy toll on the bond between them. Although the couple were still living together when Wade joined Adm Horne's staff, Wade and

[1]Buell, *The Quiet Warrior*, p190.
[2]NARA. USS *Corregidor* (CVE-58/CVU-58) Deck Logs 1941–1950. RG 24. Box 2484; September 1944 to August 1945.

Millicent had separated by war's end.[1] Their divorce would be finalized in 1952.

Despite the intensity and excitement of the work involved in helping to solve logistics problems for mammoth operations such as the Central Pacific Drive and *Overlord*, Wade's deteriorating marriage probably made it a blessing that in late August 1944, after 15 months in Washington, he was ordered to proceed to San Diego to take command of the escort carrier USS *Corregidor* (CVE-58).[2]

[1]Email correspondence, Philip McClusky to me, March 1, 2015.

[2]Orders, from Randall Jacobs at the Bureau of Personnel to McClusky, August 21, 1944. Philip McClusky collection.

18

CVE 58

She was small, slow, cramped, and ugly. Such might have been among Wade McClusky's first thoughts in late September 1944 when he got his first look at his new command, the *Casablanca* Class escort carrier USS *Corregidor* (CVE 58).[1] As captain of *Corregidor*, Wade would be taking command of a ship that, although it was then barely a year old, had already seen extensive action in the Pacific. Wade had arrived in California on August 7, 1944, having flown out, with Adm Horne along for the ride, in a Douglas R-5D-4, the naval version of the Douglas C-54. The R-5D was an enormous four-engined transport plane – undoubtedly the largest plane Wade ever flew. His logbook lists the length of the flight as five hours and 12 minutes. In fact, a cross-country flight in a propeller plane must have taken twice that long. It can thus be surmised that there were other pilots on board and the time Wade listed was only the time he personally spent at the controls.[2]

Old hands in the naval aviation community like Wade McClusky were a precious commodity late in World War 2, even if they were no longer flying from carriers. Most obviously, the experience possessed by Annapolis graduates from the 1920s who

---

[1] On CVEs as ugly; see David Rigby, *No Substitute for Victory: Successful American Military Strategies from the Revolutionary War to the Present Day* (New York: Carrel Books, 2014): p159.

[2] Wade McClusky logbook entries for August 1944. Philip McClusky collection.

had become pilots and were by the late-war period now seasoned combat veterans was essential for the training and mentoring of new pilots. But the prewar naval aviators like McClusky also had other skills that were exceedingly valuable: namely, they knew how ships worked and they knew how to navigate. As noted in Chapter 5, young Navy pilots who earned their wings after Pearl Harbor were well trained in the art of flying one particular type of combat aircraft but these youngsters knew nothing about driving ships.

As the entire Navy expanded dramatically during the war, pilots from the prewar Navy were desperately needed to command the new aircraft carriers entering service in 1943 and 1944. In addition to being veteran naval aviators – a prerequisite dating from the days of the Morrow Board for command of an aircraft carrier – Navy pilots of Wade McClusky's generation had all spent at least two years as general duty officers aboard surface ships after graduating from Annapolis but before they had begun their formal flight training. Even earlier, the summer training cruises that the older pilots had made with the battleship squadron during their Academy days had provided invaluable training in the intricacies of surface ship operation. American warships in World War 2 were more modern than were those in the fleet during McClusky's Annapolis days, being now equipped with radar and burning oil instead of coal as fuel. Nevertheless, all that coal that McClusky and his fellow midshipmen had loaded aboard and then shoveled into boilers, the gunnery exercises they had participated in, and the navigational skills they had learned aboard the dreadnoughts of the battle fleet during the summer cruises back in the 1920s were experiences instrumental in providing those men with the all-round knowledge of how a warship works. Navy pilots who were Annapolis graduates of McClusky's vintage would put this stored knowledge to good use during World War 2 when they were tapped to command aircraft carriers. In fact, Wade McClusky became one of no fewer than 38 members of the Naval Academy class of 1926 who would command escort carriers during the war.[1] These men had the seniority for important commands, while still being young enough for front-line duty in combat zones. They were in their prime. This combination of seniority and relative youth ensured that McClusky and his Annapolis classmates would have a very busy war.

An escort carrier (CVE) was a mass-produced wartime hybrid stopgap. Escort carriers were much smaller and slower than the World War 2 fleet carriers of the *Yorktown* and *Essex* Classes. A typical CVE weighed less than 10,000 tons, was approximately 500ft in length, carried two dozen aircraft, and steamed at a stately 18 knots. An *Essex* Class fleet carrier (CV), on the other hand, was 820ft in length, displaced 27,000 tons, carried 90 aircraft, and could steam at over 30 knots. The large fleet carriers were designed and built as aircraft carriers from the keel up. Early escort carriers on the other hand were built quickly by placing a small flight deck atop the hull of a cargo vessel. Beginning with the *Casablanca* Class, CVEs also began to be *designed* as aircraft carriers but their hulls were still modeled very closely on those used for cargo vessels. That none of the small escort carriers had the armored, hydrodynamic hull of a true warship would prove very costly when CVEs were sent out to the front lines of the war in the Pacific.[2]

Because they were far less expensive and much easier to build than were the large fleet carriers, escort carriers made up the bulk of the roughly 100 aircraft carriers being operated by the United States by the end of the war. The American carrier fleet by summer 1945 boasted 19 large fleet carriers (CV) – the only true thoroughbreds in the American wartime carrier fleet;

[1]Anonymous, *Aloha: Class of 1926: United States Naval Academy*. Written by an unnamed 1926 class member or members to commemorate the 55th class reunion. (Privately printed, 1982): pp24–26.

[2]David Rigby, *Allied Master Strategists: The Combined Chiefs of Staff in World War II* (Annapolis: Naval Institute Press, 2012): pp187–188. Rigby, *No Substitute for Victory*, pp159–160.

the only ones that would still qualify as true aircraft carriers by 21st-century standards. Joining the big carriers on the US Navy's roster by August 1945 were roughly 80 CVEs as well as nine *Independence* Class light carriers (CVL). The *Independence* Class had in common with the CVEs that both types were hybrids. The CVLs, however, were far more valuable ship for ship than were the CVEs. The *Independence* and its eight sister light carriers were built on the hulls of *Cleveland* Class light cruisers. With cruiser hulls and cruiser machinery (ie high-pressure steam turbines), the CVLs were fast and could thus operate with the big carriers. And since they had warship hulls, the CVLs also had some armor plate for protection. Although still smaller than the fleet carriers, the CVLs were each 100ft longer than a CVE.

While he must have been glad to get out of Washington and be back at sea, it seems unfortunate that McClusky did not get a better command than a CVE. Escort carriers played a critical role in the war effort in both the Atlantic and the Pacific, but it was a supporting role. Aircraft from escort carriers hunted U-boats in the Atlantic and provided close air support for US marines and infantry in the island campaigns of the Central Pacific Drive. However, the small, slow escort carriers were not intended to launch strikes against an enemy battle fleet. That more glamorous duty was left to the *Essex* Class fleet carriers (CV) and to the *Independence* and her sister CVL light carriers.[1] It could be argued that Wade McClusky should have been given command of an *Essex* Class carrier, or at least one of the cruiser-hulled light carriers. That Miles Browning got to command an *Essex* and Wade McClusky did not has to rank as one of the great ironies of World War 2. Most of the *Essex* Class carriers had excellent commanders during the war, but none of those men had made a greater contribution to victory against Japan than had Wade McClusky. That he was relatively young by naval standards for his rank – having just turned 41 when he was promoted captain in

[1] Rigby, *Allied Master Strategists*, pp187–188.

August 1943 – perhaps militated against McClusky in terms of his being considered for command of a large fleet carrier.[1] Regarding his reaction to getting a CVE instead of an *Essex* Class carrier, as always, Wade accepted his new assignment without complaint. He never lobbied for a better billet than the one he was assigned.

Built at the Kaiser shipyard in Vancouver, Washington State, *Corregidor* was completed in the summer of 1943 and was commissioned into naval service on August 31, 1943. The *Casablanca* Class differed from the preceding *Bogue* and *Sangamon* Class CVEs in that the *Casablanca*s were designed as aircraft carriers rather than being conversions. The *Bogue*s had been built on cargo hulls while the *Sangamon*s had originally been intended as fleet oilers. Despite being designed as small aircraft carriers, the hulls of the *Casablanca* Class CVEs were still essentially those of cargo ships, with high sides sheathed in plates of $^1/_4$in. steel. No precious armor plate could be spared for these mass-produced workhorses. Protection and speed were very much secondary considerations in their design. An unfavorable length-to-beam ratio, being short and stubby rather than long and narrow, gave all CVEs poor hydrodynamic lines. This, coupled with very modest shaft horsepower guaranteed that escort carriers would be slow. Weighing in at 7,800 tons, *Corregidor* was 512ft in length with a maximum width of 65ft. While the *Bogue*s and *Sangamon*s had low-pressure steam turbine engines, *Corregidor* and the other *Casablanca* Class CVEs each had to make do with two five-cylinder reciprocating engines to drive the ship's twin screws, delivering a maximum speed of 19 knots.[2] Steam turbines, especially the high-pressure type necessary to give a warship high speed, were generally reserved for warships deemed more valuable: destroyers, fleet carriers, cruisers, and battleships.

---

[1] I am indebted to Philip McClusky for pointing out to me how his father's relative youth may have worked against him in this instance.

[2] William T. Y'Blood, *The Little Giants: U.S. Escort Carriers Against Japan* (Annapolis: Naval Institute Press, 1987; 1999): pp17–18, pp34–35.

The engines used in the CVEs built by Henry Kaiser were manufactured by the Skinner Engine Co of Erie, Pennsylvania and were of a type known as "Uniflow" because most of the steam was exhausted through ports located halfway down the length of the cylinders, after pushing the piston down, rather than being exhausted at the top of the cylinder as the piston returned from its downstroke. The Uniflow design was more efficient than other types of reciprocating steam engines such as the triple-expansion type because by not pushing steam back up the cylinder during what would be the exhaust stroke, the intake end of a cylinder in a Uniflow engine was kept constantly hot, thereby greatly reducing condensation on the cylinder walls.[1] Such in-cylinder condensation was the cause of the greatest loss of energy in conventional piston-driven steam engines, in which a considerable amount of the incoming steam's heat energy was wasted in reheating the cylinder walls.[2] By reducing condensation, the Uniflow design thus marked a considerable advance in steam-engine technology. Nevertheless, the engines used in the Kaiser CVEs were still reciprocating engines and thus could never develop the power of a high-pressure steam turbine; the turbine being the ultimate steam engine. Nineteen knots was, and is, about the limit for speed that reciprocating engines linked directly to propeller shafts can give to a ship. Unfortunately, in addition to being less powerful, piston engines also have far more moving parts than do steam turbines. Therefore, *Corregidor*'s engines were subject to excessive wear and tear requiring a great deal of maintenance. Of the reciprocating engines used in the *Casablanca* Class CVEs, historian William T. Y'Blood writes that:

---

[1] Richard L. Hills, *Power from Steam: A History of the Stationary Steam Engine* (Cambridge: Cambridge University Press, 1989): pp258–278.

[2] The Babcock & Wilcox Co, *Steam: Its Generation and Use* (New York: The Knickerbocker Press, 1906): p87. William Barnet Le Van, *The Practical Management of Engines and Boilers* (Philadelphia: Philadelphia Book Co, 1900): pp147–149.

"These old-fashioned engines used superheated steam, which presented several problems in cylinder lubrication and the filtering system. The engines were never quite up to the task of day in, day out, hard-charging operations. Exorbitant piston ring wear was a malady of these engines that drove many a chief engineer to near despair."[1]

Marine diesel engines might have been able to give the Kaiser CVEs the same speed as did the Uniflow engines without requiring anywhere near as much maintenance, but diesels were reserved for small ships that did not have enough internal space to carry boilers, such as submarines. American submarines in World War 2 utilized diesel power when surfaced and power from storage batteries when submerged. The diesels enabled American submarines to make 18 knots when running on the surface. Thus, with their Uniflow piston engines, the *Casablanca* Class CVEs were at the very bottom of the Navy's priority list when it came to engine allocation.

Corregidor carried approximately two dozen aircraft: fighters and Grumman TBF Avenger torpedo planes. Escort carriers usually did not carry a dive-bombing squadron.[2] The wings of the SBD Dauntless did not fold, which increased the space needed to park each one – a serious handicap on a small CVE, particularly when the aircraft were stored below on the hangar deck. The SBD's 42ft wingspan was also a very tight fit on either of a CVE's two elevators. Dive-bombers were primarily an antishipping weapon and so really belonged on the fleet carriers that, unlike CVEs, were expected to engage the enemy fleet in battle. Most CVEs carried a small composite air group similar to that of *Corregidor*, consisting of one squadron of Grumman TBF Avenger torpedo planes and a squadron of fighter planes.

Sometimes referred to as "Jeep Carriers" or simply "Jeeps," perhaps because like their wheeled namesakes the escort carriers

[1] Y'Blood, *The Little Giants*, p35.
[2] Y'Blood, *The Little Giants*, p64.

performed difficult, unglamorous but essential jobs without fanfare but with great reliability, the primary tasks of a CVE were to hunt for enemy submarines and to provide air support to ground troops above recently established beachheads. Because escort carriers were not intended to engage an enemy battle fleet, *Corregidor*'s Avengers usually carried bombs for close air support or depth charges for antisubmarine work rather than torpedoes.[1]

For fighters, most escort carriers, *Corregidor* included, had to make do with cast-offs. The Navy's best fighter planes, the Grumman F6F Hellcat and the Vought F4U Corsair, went to the big fleet carriers. *Corregidor*'s fighter squadron was equipped with the FM-2, an improved version of the Grumman F4F Wildcat built by General Motors under a licensing agreement with Grumman. The FM-2 addressed some of the deficiencies of the F4F-4 version of the Wildcat that Wade had flown in his days as the commander of Fighting Six. The FM-2 Wildcat had the four .50 caliber machine gun armament of the F4F-3, rather than the ill-advised six-gun layout of the F4F-4. With fewer guns to feed, the FM-2 carried significantly more ammunition per gun, a situation greatly preferred by pilots. The FM-2 also had a more powerful engine than did earlier versions of the Wildcat.

American full-sized fleet carriers in World War 2 are often referred to as the "fast" carriers – high speed being one of the many ways in which the big carriers differed from the CVEs. Although each *Essex* Class fleet carrier had two catapults in the bow, most American carrier-based aircraft on fleet carriers in World War 2 took off under their own power by making a run down the flight deck. During launching and landings, a carrier would turn into the wind – something still done on modern aircraft carriers. In periods of low wind, the fast carriers could make their own wind across the deck by steaming at high speed. This was a luxury not available to the slow escort carriers. *Corregidor* and its sister CVEs each had one catapult in the bow. They could have used

[1]Rigby, *No Substitute for Victory*, 159–160.

two since CVEs tended to make far more catapult launches than did the fleet carriers. If there was no wind, 19 knots simply was not enough speed and 500ft not enough deck to enable the big Grumman Avengers to fly off the deck of a CVE under their own power, although the smaller FM-2s could just manage it. In low-wind situations, the solitary catapult was the only way to get an Avenger airborne from the deck of a CVE.[1]

While there is no doubt that escort carriers played a critical role in winning the war at sea in both the Atlantic and the Pacific Theaters, there is also no denying that CVEs were second-rate ships, built quickly and cheaply in order to get more flight decks out to the fleet as quickly as possible in an emergency situation. Since Wade had previously served on big, thoroughbred carriers such as *Saratoga* and *Enterprise*, which were literally worth their weight in gold, the limitations of *Corregidor*'s design – in speed, size, striking power, and overall value to the fleet – must have taken some getting used to.

Under its first captain, R. L. Bowman, *Corregidor* had seen extensive service during the island-hopping campaigns of the Central Pacific Drive, providing close air support for American marines and infantry during the amphibious landings in the Gilbert, Marshall, and Marianas campaigns. In addition, *Corregidor*'s aircraft also carried out antisubmarine patrols during those invasions. The necessity for these patrols became rudely apparent very early in the Central Pacific Campaign, when American invasion fleets operating near atolls in the Central Pacific presented inviting targets for prowling Japanese submarines. *Corregidor*'s crew witnessed a horrifying demonstration of this unpleasant fact during Operation *Galvanic*, the invasion of Gilbert Islands in November 1943 – the operation that kicked off the Central Pacific Drive and marked *Corregidor*'s combat debut.

[1]Y'Blood, *The Little Giants*, p116. "The Saga of the Mighty C" Unpublished manuscript written by an unnamed member (or members) of the wartime crew of USS *Corregidor* (CVE 58). P14. Philip McClusky collection.

For *Galvanic*, *Corregidor* was assigned to the northern attack force that landed and covered the 27 Infantry Division's invasion of Makin Atoll. Off Makin on the morning of November 24, 1943 *Corregidor* was steaming just 1 mile away from its sister carrier, the USS *Liscome Bay*, another *Casablanca* Class CVE, when the latter was rent by a horrific explosion – the result of a torpedo fired by the Japanese submarine *I-175*.[1] Just after the explosion of the torpedo against the ship's hull, the *Liscome Bay* was torn apart by a massive secondary explosion – caused by the torpedo having struck aft on the starboard side, exactly where the bombs for the *Liscome Bay*'s own aircraft were stored, in unarmored shell rooms.[2] The burning, exploding wreck of the *Liscome Bay* went down in just 23 minutes. Casualties were shockingly high: 644 members of the doomed ship's crew were killed. Among those was Mess Steward Dorrie Miller, who had been awarded the Navy Cross on May 27, 1942 in the same ceremony at which McClusky was awarded the Distinguished Flying Cross. A full-sized fleet carrier, or even one of the cruiser-hulled light carriers, would have been better able to withstand the damage from a single torpedo hit. Indeed, just four days earlier the light carrier *Independence* had survived a torpedo hit. As hybrid stopgaps, escort carriers were too slow to run away from trouble and they had no armor plating to insulate the ordnance they carried. Neither was there any armor augmenting the thin steel plating that formed the ship's hull. In fact, CVEs were no better protected against torpedoes than were passenger ships. The fate of the *Liscome Bay* was a sobering reminder to all who sailed in escort carriers that the naval high command considered CVEs to be expendable.[3] Indeed, resorting to gallows humor, crews of escort carriers used to say that instead of "Aircraft Carrier; Escort," the designator letters "CVE" really stood for "Combustible,

[1] "The Saga of the Mighty C," pp2–4. Philip McClusky collection.

[2] Y'Blood, *The Little Giants*, pp2–3. Rigby, *No Substitute for Victory*, p160.

[3] Rigby, *No Substitute for Victory*, pp158–160. Y'Blood, *The Little Giants*, p96.

Vulnerable, Expendable."[1] "Kaiser Coffins" was another popular sobriquet reserved for *Casablanca* Class CVEs, all of which had been built at Henry Kaiser's Vancouver, Washington shipyard.

Between the Marshalls and Marianas campaigns, *Corregidor* was sent on a brief detour to the South Pacific. There, in early April 1944, along with its sister carrier USS *Coral Sea* (CVE 57) – not to be confused with the large fleet carrier *Coral Sea* (CV 43) that joined the fleet in 1947 after *Coral Sea* the escort carrier had been decommissioned – it began providing air support for part of the Third Marine Division that had been landed on Emirau in the St Mathias Islands in the Bismarck Archipelago near New Guinea on March 20. This proved to be quiet duty as the Emirau landings went uncontested by the Japanese. Emirau was a classic example of the benefits of island-hopping done correctly. By seizing Emirau, the Americans were able to bypass Kavieng in New Ireland, which *was* a heavily defended Japanese air and naval base.[2] Before returning to the Central Pacific Area, *Corregidor* helped in late April to provide air support for the landing of US infantry on the northern shores of New Guinea at Aitape and Hollandia, respectively.[3] In June 1944, as the flagship of Carrier Division 24, *Corregidor*, flying the flag of R Adm Felix Stump, had supported American forces during the respective invasions of Guam, Tinian, and Saipan in the Mariana Islands. The ship itself came under attack by Japanese aircraft during the Marianas campaign but escaped with no damage.[4]

Corregidor had thus been a very busy ship by the time Wade McClusky relieved Capt Bowman as commanding officer on September 21, 1944 while the little carrier was docked at Pier Number 4 at the Naval Repair Base in San Diego, having just

[1]Y'Blood, *The Little Giants*, p9, p37.

[2]Rigby, *Allied Master Strategists*, p81. E. B. Potter. *Bull Halsey.* (Annapolis: Naval Institute Press, 1985): p267. "The Saga of the Mighty C," pp6–7. Y'Blood, *The Little Giants*, p95.

[3]Y'Blood, *The Little Giants*, pp97–98.

[4]"The Saga of the Mighty C", pp8–10.

completed an overhaul.[1] Including the ship's air group, Wade was now in command of a crew of approximately 900 men. The difficulties of managing any large body of people were brought home to Wade as soon as he stepped aboard. In its brief life *Corregidor* had already steamed thousands of miles and had seen a great deal of action. Consequently, the crew had been enjoying their stateside visit a bit too much and Wade was immediately confronted with disciplinary problems. In fact, disciplinary matters figure prominently in the ship's deck log for the first several weeks of Wade's command. For instance, just two days after Wade stepped aboard, the log records that at "0100 – Munk, C. AMM3c, 381-84-12, picked up by Shore Patrol for drunkenness, brought back to ship by Lt. (jg.) A. ODDIE, A-V (S), USNR. Time picked up 2215, released 0000."[2] There was more to come. Wade held his first captain's mast on Tuesday, October 10. No fewer than 36 men were masted that day. Initially, Wade seems to have been rather lenient during his mast sessions, his preferred punishment being extra duty, as shown by the following log entry: "Ogle, R.M., S1c, AWOL for 14 hours and 15 minutes, 10 hrs. extra duty."[3] More serious offenses were handled the following day when Wade's air officer, Cdr G. M. Clifford, presided over a number of "Deck Court" trials, which were in effect miniature courts martial. The cases heard and sentences issued by Clifford were more severe than those dealt with in a captain's mast. One man found guilty of disobeying an order and of "shirking duty" was sentenced to 15 days' solitary confinement on a diet of bread and water, with regular meals to

---

[1]"The Saga of the Mighty C," p14. USS *Corregidor*, War Diary. NARA. RG 38. Records of the Office of the Chief of Naval Operations. World War II War Diaries. Box 760. Entries for September 1944.

[2]NARA. USS *Corregidor* (CVE-58/CVU-58) Deck Logs 1941–1950. RG 24. Box 2484; September 1944 to August 1945. P606.

[3]NARA. USS *Corregidor* (CVE-58/CVU-58) Deck Logs 1941–1950. RG 24. Box 2484; September 1944 to August 1945. P652.

be given every third day. This unfortunate sailor was also docked $36 in pay – an amount equal to what many Americans earned in a week in those days.[1]

As captain, Wade had the most spacious accommodations aboard *Corregidor*. His quarters, located on the starboard side of the gallery deck just below the flight deck and just forward of the island structure, consisted of a suite of four rooms. The captain's main cabin measured approximately 15ft by 8ft. A door in the forward bulkhead led to an adjoining sitting room, which in turn adjoined a small bathroom. Also adjoining Wade's main cabin was a small pantry. Although Wade's quarters were spacious, the ship's forward elevator being quite close by probably made that part of the ship noisy as aircraft were raised and lowered to and from the flight deck at all hours of the day and night. The ship's Air Plot and Combat Information Center were both close by Wade's cabin. Wade's executive officer, Cdr M. W. Williamson, was also nearby, berthed in a stateroom on the opposite side of the gallery deck from Wade's cabin. While the ship was at sea, Wade most likely slept in the captain's sea cabin, a small space large enough for a bunk and not much else, located at the rear of the base of the island structure just below the bridge.[2] To maintain his status – and extra pay – as a naval aviator, Wade put in his obligatory four hours of flying for the month of September 1944 by taking one of *Corregidor*'s FM-2s on a flight around the San Diego area on September 27, a few days after he had assumed command of the ship.[3] Even when

---

[1]NARA. USS *Corregidor* (CVE-58/CVU-58) Deck Logs 1941–1950. RG 24. Box 2484; September 1944 to August 1945. P656 and p118-A1.

[2]Deck Plans, USS *Thetis*, CVE 90 [*Casablanca* Class sister ship to *Corregidor* CVE 58]. *Booklet of General Plans*. Blueprints drawn by the Industrial Command; US Naval Repair Base, San Diego, CA, May 31, 1945. Available online at: https://maritime.org/doc/plans/cve90.pdf. See also, USS *Corregidor* (CVE-58/CVU-58) Deck Logs 1941–1950. NARA. RG 24. Box 2484; September 27, 1944 to August 1945. P118-A1.

[3]Wade McClusky logbook entry for September 1944. Philip McClusky collection.

it was difficult to work his flying time into his schedule, such as when he had staff duty ashore or while he was commanding officer of *Corregidor*, Wade always saw himself as a pilot first and a sailor second.[1]

The Central Pacific Drive was still underway when Wade took command of *Corregidor*. Instead of covering more amphibious landings on islands in the Central Pacific Area, however, *Corregidor* had now been designated the heart of a "Hunter-Killer" Group which, in company with destroyer escort (DE) vessels, would concentrate on hunting for Japanese submarines. *Corregidor* had done some antisubmarine work before Wade took command, but now the ship and its crew were expected to specialize in and become expert at this form of warfare. *Corregidor* and her escorts would eventually be designated Task Group (TG) 12.3. Adm Stump had moved on to other duty by then, meaning that *Corregidor* was no longer a "flagship" per se. Nevertheless, Wade would now have as many as half a dozen ships under his command. Task Groups are usually commanded by a rear admiral, which means that Wade would be doing an admiral's job on a captain's pay.

Corregidor and its escorts departed San Diego alone on October 6, 1944 heading west, and docked at Pearl Harbor on the 12th.[2] There, *Corregidor* exchanged Composite Air Group 41 (VC-41), which had been with the ship since its commissioning, for the 12 Avengers and 12 FM-2 fighters of Composite Air Group 83 (VC-83), an air group led by Lt Cdr Bill Gates.[3] From Pearl Harbor, *Corregidor* conducted training exercises with destroyers and destroyer escorts (DEs) as Task Group 19.1. For instance, in mid-October, the group conducted "qualification

[1] Interviews with Philip McClusky, December 27 and December 29, 2016.

[2] "The Saga of the Mighty C," pp14–20. USS *Corregidor*, War Diary. NARA. RG 38. Records of the Office of the Chief of Naval Operations. World War II War Diaries. Box 760. Entries for October 1944.

[3] "The Saga of the Mighty C," pp1–2, pp14–15.

and refresher air operations with VC-83 ... Conducted anti-aircraft firing practice at towed sleeves."[1] Wade's first escorts as part of Task Group 19.1 were the destroyers *Calhoun* and *Williamson*, the latter of which would have been familiar to Wade as the destroyer he had served on as a young officer in the 1920s.

Hunting submarines would require Wade's pilots to fly at night, the best time to catch a submarine on the surface. World War 2 submarines had to surface at least once every 24 hours to replenish the air supply and to use the diesel engines that provided propulsion when surfaced to recharge the batteries that were used when submerged. Submarine captains also preferred running on the surface whenever possible because they could make better speed. The hours of darkness were the safest times to do that, but nothing about serving in submarines was, or is, completely safe. Many German and Japanese submarines, and some American, were destroyed by air attack when they were thus caught on the surface. In late October 1944, while TG 19.1 and its new air group were practicing the respective and complementary arts of submarine hunting and night-time carrier landings in the waters off Hawaii, Wade received orders to return to Pearl immediately. The outfit was to be given its first job as a Hunter-Killer unit. The SS *Johnson*, a Liberty Ship cargo vessel traveling between Pearl Harbor and San Francisco, had just been torpedoed and sunk by a Japanese submarine. Wade was ordered to find and destroy the offending submarine. After staying at Pearl just long enough to refuel and reprovision, *Corregidor* and its escorts headed east to search. At the outset of this mission, Wade's little fleet adopted the designation Task Group 12.3 on November 1, 1944 upon its departure from Pearl to hunt the submarine.[2] Wade and

---

[1]USS *Corregidor*, War Diary. NARA. RG 38. Records of the Office of the Chief of Naval Operations. World War II War Diaries. Box 760. Entries for October 15, 1944.

[2]USS *Corregidor*, War Diary. NARA. RG 38. Records of the Office of the Chief of Naval Operations. World War II War Diaries. Box 760. Entries for October and November 1944.

Corregidor had left port accompanied by three DEs and picked up two more along the way.[1]

The ideal scenario for any Hunter-Killer unit was to launch radar-equipped Avengers at night. A pilot who thus located a surfaced submarine could then switch on a searchlight to illuminate the target for a bombing attack. But a Hunter-Killer unit such as Wade's had other options as well. During the hours of daylight, a submarine was likely to remain submerged. To launch a torpedo attack against a surface ship while submerged, however, a World War 2 submarine could go no deeper than periscope depth – about 50ft beneath the surface. At that depth the outline of a submerged submarine was visible from the air on a clear day. Aircraft could and did take advantage of this fact to drop either depth charges or acoustic torpedoes against such shallowly submerged submarines. Also, escort vessels such as the DEs that accompanied *Corregidor* were equipped with sonar, which could sound the depths to locate submarines that were running deep. Once located by sonar, a submarine down deep would be subjected to depth charge attacks; the depth charges being launched from the escort vessels or dropped by aircraft flying from an escort carrier. Wade's task group did locate an enemy submarine in the vicinity where the *Johnson* had been torpedoed and *Corregidor*'s aircraft duly attacked it on November 2 and again two days later. Nevertheless, the submarine escaped unscathed.[2]

In the first attack against the submarine, a radar contact was made by a *Corregidor* TBM at 0422 on November 2. A sonobuoy was dropped but the contact disappeared quickly from the plane's radar screen, presumably by submerging. A depth charge was dropped by a TBM but it failed to explode. Two other TBMs also

---

[1]USS *Corregidor* "Report of Antisubmarine Action by Aircraft," p3 of Section G: Narrative. NARA. RG 38. Records of the Office of the Chief of Naval Operations. WW II Action and Operational Reports. Box 932. World War II Action Report; Serial 0007. November 19, 1944.

[2]"The Saga of the Mighty C," p15. Y'Blood, *The Little Giants*, pp248–249.

dropped depth charges, but only one exploded. The result of the air attack, according to Wade's official report, was disappointing: "No oil or debris found on surface."[1] After daybreak, the planes landed back on deck and two of Wade's escorts – the USS *O'Flaherty* (DE-340) and USS *Kendall C. Campbell* (DE-443) – moved in with the intention of: "Circling to keep contact and hold sub down."[2] Wade's plan was to use his destroyer escorts to keep the submarine submerged and to use his aircraft to make the kill.

During the air attack, several sonobuoys had been dropped by four different TBMs and a few of these picked up "cavitation sounds," but the depth charges dropped by the first two planes failed to explode.[3] The charge dropped by a third TBM did explode, but the propeller noises continued to be audible by sonobuoy so the target was not destroyed.[4] Wade wrote that the depth charges were the contact type and so the one that exploded must have hit something, perhaps the submarine or

[1]USS *Corregidor* "Report of Antisubmarine Action by Aircraft," pp1–4 NARA. RG 38. Records of the Office of the Chief of Naval Operations. WW II Action and Operational Reports. Box 932. World War II Action Report; Serial 0007. November 19, 1944. The quote is on one of several pages bearing the number 4. See also p1 of a Narrative, which has a Chronology in the same box, RG 38, Box 932. World War II Action Report; Serial 0007. November 19, 1944.

[2]USS *Corregidor* "Report of Antisubmarine Action by Aircraft," p5. NARA. RG 38. Records of the Office of the Chief of Naval Operations. WW II Action and Operational Reports. Box 932. World War II Action Report; Serial 0007. November 19, 1944.

[3]USS *Corregidor* "Report of Antisubmarine Action by Aircraft," p3 of the Section G: Narrative. NARA. RG 38. Records of the Office of the Chief of Naval Operations. WW II Action and Operational Reports. Box 932. World War II Action Report; Serial 0007. November 19, 1944.

[4]USS *Corregidor* "Report of Antisubmarine Action by Aircraft," p4 of the Section G: Narrative. NARA. RG 38. Records of the Office of the Chief of Naval Operations. WW II Action and Operational Reports. Box 932. World War II Action Report; Serial 0007. November 19, 1944.

a countermeasure projectile or object used by the submarine to draw off depth charges. Wade also wondered if the submarine was employing some sort of radar detection device that enabled it to submerge quickly as his aircraft approached.[1]

The second unsuccessful attack, in the small hours of the morning of November 4, 1944, was also based on a radar contact from a TBM. Sonobuoys were dropped, cavitation sounds were picked up, and two depth charges were dropped. Only one exploded. Wade again surmised that the submarine may have been using a noise-making machine towed behind the submarine to draw off the aim of the attackers.[2]

Although blessed with an expert manager's ability to delegate responsibility, Pacific Fleet commander Adm Nimitz at Pearl Harbor had been watching this particular mission closely, perhaps because it was *Corregidor*'s first formal foray into antisubmarine warfare as the heart of a designated Hunter-Killer group. Nimitz and his staff were disappointed that McClusky's pilots had been unable to make the kill, particularly since the offending submarine was practically in American home waters, well to the east of Hawaii and far from the front lines of the war in the Pacific.[3] In memos to Adm King written for him by his

[1] USS *Corregidor* "Report of Antisubmarine Action by Aircraft," pp5–6 of the Section G: Narrative. NARA. RG 38. Records of the Office of the Chief of Naval Operations. WW II Action and Operational Reports. Box 932. World War II Action Report; Serial 0007. November 19, 1944. USS *Corregidor* "Report of Antisubmarine Action by Aircraft," pp5–6 of the Narrative. NARA. RG 38. Records of the Office of the Chief of Naval Operations. WW II Action and Operational Reports. Box 932. World War II Action Report; Serial 0008. November 19, 1944. Pp3–6 of Section G: Narrative.

[2] USS *Corregidor* "Report of Antisubmarine Action by Aircraft," pp5–6 of the Narrative. NARA. RG 38. Records of the Office of the Chief of Naval Operations. World War II Action and Operational Reports. Box 932. World War II Action Report; Serial 0008. November 19, 1944. P3–6 of Section G: Narrative.

[3] E. B. Potter, *Nimitz* (Annapolis: Naval Institute Press, 1976, 1987): p253. Y'Blood, *The Little Giants*, pp248–249.

chief-of-staff, R Adm Charles "Soc" McMorris, for both of these actions, Adm Nimitz felt that McClusky's planes had wasted too much time between the dropping of the sonobuoys and the dropping of depth charges. Via McMorris, Nimitz does praise Wade's ship-handling, blaming everything about this failure on the inexperience of Wade's air group.[1]

Captains of aircraft carriers are held responsible for the performance of the ship's air group. But in this case, the powers that be concluded that Wade himself was not the problem. Instead, prodded by McMorris, Adm Nimitz decided that *Corregidor* needed a more experienced air group if the ship was going to be successful in the Hunter-Killer role. Accordingly, Nimitz ordered that Wade's air group, VC-83, be replaced by VC-42 – an air group that had gained experience hunting U-boats from an escort carrier as part of a Hunter-Killer outfit in the Atlantic. Wade had thus hardly had time to get acquainted with the pilots and aircrew of VC-83 when, back at Pearl Harbor, the planes of VC-83 were flown ashore and those of VC-42 brought aboard. The orders for this change were dated December 12. The exchange of air groups actually took place on December 14.[2] Wade's new air group commander was Lt Cdr A. C. Hall.

The exchange of air groups complete, *Corregidor* and its escorts departed Pearl on December 19, 1944 with orders to conduct antisubmarine patrols north of Oahu. That duty necessitated spending Christmas at sea, but TG 12.3 was back at Pearl in time for New Year's celebrations. By January 1945 the front line of the war in the Pacific was now rapidly moving westward. As such, Eniwetok Atoll in the western Marshall Islands was now a major

---

[1]Memo prepared by McMorris, from Nimitz to King. December 9, 1944 (date of report), pp1–2. World War II Action Report; Serial 0007. November 19, 1944 (date on folder in archive); and December 15, 1944 (date of report), pp1–2. World War II Action Report; Serial 0008. November 19, 1944 (date on folder in archive). NARA RG 38, Box 932.

[2]Y'Blood, *The Little Giants*, p249. "The Saga of the Mighty C," p16. USS *Corregidor*, War Diary. NARA. RG 38. Records of the Office of the Chief of Naval Operations. World War II War Diaries. Box 760. Entries for December 1944.

advanced American fleet and air base. Consequently, *Corregidor* departed Pearl in early January and spent that month hunting for prowling Japanese submarines along the now vital Oahu–Eniwetok line of supply and communication.[1]

Corregidor was given a special mission in late February 1945. The plane carrying Army Air Forces Lt Gen Millard F. Harmon had vanished on February 26. Gen Harmon was one of the most senior Army Air Forces field commanders. Nimitz ordered Wade to use *Corregidor*, then at Pearl Harbor, and its aircraft to search for survivors along the route Harmon's plane would have taken. Undoubtedly, Nimitz hoped for a repeat of the happy ending to a search for another VIP whose plane had gone down in the Pacific earlier in the war; in October 1942 the legendary American World War 1 ace fighter pilot and since 1935 the President of Eastern Airlines Eddie Rickenbacker and six other men had survived for three weeks drifting in liferafts after their B-17 bomber had run out of fuel and had made a water landing southwest of Hawaii.

When his plane, a Consolidated Aircraft C-87 cargo version of the famed B-24 bomber, disappeared, Gen Harmon had been on his way from Guam to Washington for discussions with Gen Henry H. "Hap" Arnold, the commanding general of the US Army Air Forces (USAAF) and a member of the joint and combined chiefs-of-staff. The Army Air Forces command structure in the Pacific had become hopelessly complex. Until late 1944, the numbered Army Air Forces operating in the Pacific Theater had been under the command of theater commanders. Thus, the Seventh and Thirteenth Air Forces were under the control of Adm Nimitz, while the Fifth Air Force in the southwest Pacific was controlled by Gen MacArthur. The arrival in the Pacific Theater of the new, gigantic Boeing B-29 Superfortress bombers in autumn 1944 changed all that.

Hap Arnold had pushed hard to get the B-29 into production. When enough of these huge aircraft with trained crews became available for deployment in early 1944, Gen Arnold was unwilling to put the new planes under the control of any one

---

[1]Y'Blood, *The Little Giants*, p249. "The Saga of the Mighty C," p16.

theater commander. By retaining control of the B-29s himself, Arnold introduced a level of complexity into the American theater command structure in the Asia and the Pacific that was unfortunate and probably unnecessary – and that would place Gen Harmon in a very difficult position. At Arnold's urging, the joint chiefs-of-staff approved in late March and early April 1944 the establishment of the Twentieth Air Force as the administrative unit under which the B-29s would operate.[1] Arnold himself was named commanding officer of the Twentieth Air Force. Being based in Washington, however, meant that Arnold would rely on trusted deputies to manage B-29 operations on a day-to-day basis in the field. Foremost among these trusted deputies was Gen Harmon, who was appointed deputy commander, under Gen Arnold, of the Twentieth Air Force – that is, of the B-29s.[2]

Initially based in India at Kharagpur in Bengal province, B-29s began their bombing campaign against the Japanese home islands with a raid against the Yawata Steel Works on Kyushu on the night of June 15/16, 1944. Even with a 1,500-mile combat radius, the great distance involved in these flights necessitated that the B-29s use airfields at Chengtu in China as staging bases, landing there to refuel on their way to and from Japan. Permanently basing the B-29s at Chengtu was out of the question because Japanese troops were still occupying all of coastal China and Chengtu was under constant threat of Japanese air and ground attack. Using India and China as bases for the B-29s was a logistical nightmare of the first magnitude. American military equipment sent to the China–Burma–India (CBI) Theater first arrived by ship at Calcutta on the Hooghly River a short distance upstream from the Bay of Bengal. From there, American war materiel would be shipped a short distance by rail to airfields in the Assam region of northeast India.

---

[1]Wesley Frank Craven and James Lea Cate, *The Army Air Forces in World War II*. Vol. 5. *Matterhorn to Nagasaki: June 1944 to August 1945* (Chicago: The University of Chicago Press, 1953): pp19–23, pp35–39, p49.

[2]Craven and Cate, *Matterhorn to Nagasaki*, pp510–511.

Then, in the famous "Hump" airlift, supplies destined for China would be flown over the Himalaya mountains to Kunming.

The need to find a better base than India for the B-29s was a major reason for the American invasion of Guam, Tinian, and Saipan in the Mariana Islands in the western Pacific in the summer of 1944. Even with a refueling stop at Chengtu, the B-29s based in India could barely reach southern Kyushu. The Marianas on the other hand were closer to the Japanese home islands and, being islands themselves, could have all the supplies the B-29s and their crews needed brought in relatively easily by ship. B-29s flying from Guam and Tinian would be able to reach the southern half of Honshu, which meant that with the Mariana Islands in American hands Tokyo would for the first time be within range of American land-based bombers.

On March 10, 1944, while the joint and combined chiefs-of-staff were planning the American invasion of the Mariana Islands, another layer was added to the Army Air Forces command structure in the Pacific when Gen Harmon was appointed to command the new Army Air Forces, Pacific Ocean Areas (AAFPOA) organization. In this role, Harmon would oversee the use of all American land-based aircraft in the Pacific Ocean Areas Theater except the B-29s. As such, Harmon would report directly to Nimitz. Harmon's situation was rapidly becoming more than what any one man could handle; his appointment to command AAFPOA coincided with his being made deputy commander of the Twentieth Air Force just at the time when it became clear that the B-29s would be moving their bases from India to the Mariana Islands.[1]

By early January 1945, Gen Harmon's overlapping responsibilities and the continuing ambiguity regarding the exact nature of his command were making his position increasingly untenable. For instance, as commanding general, AAFPOA, Harmon had overall control of the Seventh Air Force based in Hawaii. The primary job of the Seventh Air Force was to provide land-based air power to supplement the striking power provided by the aircraft carriers of

[1]Craven and Cate, *Matterhorn to Nagasaki*, pp510–511.

the Pacific Fleet during the Central Pacific advance. As such, the Seventh moved west with the advancing Central Pacific Drive, operating four-engined B-24 bombers from newly captured Central Pacific atolls, such as Kwajelein in the Marshall Islands. Supervising the Seventh Air Force was a full-time job in and of itself, but Gen Harmon himself had to spend most of his time in the western Pacific since his job as deputy commander of the Twentieth Air Force meant that he needed to be in the Marianas where the B-29s were based. The mission of the Twentieth Air Force was completely different from that of the Seventh. The Twentieth did not support the Central Pacific advance but was instead focused almost exclusively on bombing Japan proper. Maj Gen Curtis Lemay had arrived in the Marianas on January 18, 1945 and two days later, Lemay formally took command of the XXI Bomber Command, a subunit of the Twentieth Air Force that would handle day-to-day operations of B-29s flying from the Marianas. Although an undeniably brilliant and courageous officer, Curtis Lemay was a difficult subordinate and supervising Lemay was now Harmon's problem. The cigar-chomping Lemay was a hard-driving and talented commander who had definite opinions of his own as to how the B-29s should be used. Although he was subordinate in rank to Harmon, Lemay's position commanding XXI Bomber Command practically guaranteed that there would be tension between himself and Gen Harmon. Another of Harmon's subordinates who needed to be handled with care was Maj Gen Willis Hale, the day-to-day commander of the Seventh Air Force. Hale was less than delighted with the establishment of AAFPOA and the installation of Gen Harmon into the Central Pacific command structure. Gen Hale correctly foresaw that the activation of the Gen Harmon's AAFPOA command would erode his, Hale's, own authority.[1]

[1]Craven and Cate, *Matterhorn to Nagasaki*, pp507–510, pp534–536.

Nelson, Commander Christopher, U.S. Navy, "Win With The Second Best Weapon: Lessons from Operation Starvation Against Japan" Proceedings: U.S. Naval Institute. November 2018, pp60–64

As for Harmon's superiors, Adm Nimitz and Gen Arnold were both even-tempered men, but Lt Gen Robert C. Richardson, the commander of US Army Forces in the Pacific Ocean Areas and nominally Harmon's immediate superior, was a different kettle of fish altogether. Gen Richardson was a difficult personality who was jealous of what he perceived as any attempt to downgrade his own authority – and he perceived many such attempts, more than in fact actually existed. Gen Harmon thus had too many responsibilities, too many bosses, and some difficult subordinates.[1]

Harmon's proposed trip to Washington in late February would, therefore, provide a much-needed opportunity for him to sit down with Hap Arnold and attempt to streamline the USAAF command structure in the Pacific. Bringing two staff officers with him, Harmon boarded his plane and made the first leg of the journey from Guam in the Marianas to Kwajalein in the Marshall Islands on February 25. The plane was refueled on Kwajalein, where Harmon's party spent the night. On the morning of the 26th, the plane departed Kwajalein and headed for its next stop – an airstrip on Johnston atoll that lies approximately 1,400 miles east-northeast of Kwajelein and some 850 miles southwest of Pearl Harbor. The plane never arrived at Johnston, news that was quickly transmitted to Pearl Harbor. Wade received orders on February 27 from Adm Nimitz to depart Pearl immediately and steam to Eniwetok in the Marshalls, a distance of 2,000 miles west-southwest from Hawaii. Wade's orders were to conduct air searches for any survivors from Harmon's plane along the entire route. It was hoped that Harmon's pilot might have been able to make a water landing, so *Corregidor*'s pilots were told to search for a liferaft. This they would do, but to no avail.

By April 1945, Japanese naval and air power in the vicinity of the Marshall Islands had been completely destroyed. It is thus unlikely that Harmon's plane was brought down by enemy action. Mechanical failure or bad weather are far more likely

---

[1]Craven and Cate, *Matterhorn to Nagasaki*, p157, pp510–511, p530, pp533–534.

culprits. The B-24 was a superb airplane that, along with the Boeing B-17, was the workhorse American heavy bomber in both the European and Pacific Theaters during the war. The extremely long range of the B-24 made unarmed versions of the plane, such as Harmon's, popular as VIP transports. Winston Churchill had been flown in a B-24 to Moscow for his first meeting with Stalin in August 1942. In March 1943 British Foreign Secretary Anthony Eden used the same plane and the same pilot to fly to Washington, DC. The longest leg of that journey, from Prestwick in Scotland to Gander in Newfoundland, required the plane to remain airborne for more than 13 hours, which shows that even by 21st-century standards, the B-24 had impressive fuel capacity.[1]

Whatever happened to Harmon's plane remains entirely speculative, but the B-24 did have one weakness that could have come into play if a sudden rain squall or some sort of mechanical problem had forced the pilot to attempt a wheels-up water landing. The B-24 wing attached to the top of the fuselage, which had the advantage of getting the wing root up and out of the way so that the body of the airplane could accommodate a large bomb load. Being a high-wing aircraft, however, made the B-24 a very difficult airplane to land in the water. The lack of structural strength at the bottom of the fuselage meant that during emergency water landings, B-24s almost always broke in half as soon as the belly of the airplane hit the water.[2] Breaking up quickly on the surface would have left little time for Harmon's crew to deploy the plane's liferafts. The B-17, on the other hand, was a low-wing airplane with great structural strength at the bottom of the fuselage; much better for water landings. Eddie Rickenbacker may well have owed his life to the fact that his

---

[1] Rigby, *Allied Master Strategists*, p147.

[2] See, for instance, the film *B-24 Liberator: 'Ditching of a B-24 Airplane into the James River'* 1944 NACA World War II. Available online at: https://www.youtube.com/watch?v=tG4nm2atjZI. Accessed July 13, 2020.

B-17 had *not* broken up upon hitting the water, giving that crew time to deploy three liferafts.

Task Group 12.3 was a bit smaller than usual for this hastily prepared rescue mission. When *Corregidor* departed Pearl Harbor on February 27 to begin the search, the carrier's only escorts were the DEs USS *Roberts* and USS *Bright*. Wade would need at least one of them for plane guard duty – stationed half a mile ahead of the carrier during launches and astern during landings to pick up crews of any planes that went into the water during these two most dangerous of aviation maneuvers: taking off from and landing on a ship. The lack of extra escorts for antisubmarine patrol around the carrier is indicative of the hastily planned nature of this particular mission. Despite having a huge area to search, Wade planned for a best-case scenario and ordered his pilots to search for a liferaft or rafts. On February 28, Wade launched nearly his entire air group, eight Avengers and eight FM-2s, to begin the search. That day, *Corregidor*'s pilots searched a grid pattern 250 miles out ahead of the carrier and 120 miles wide.[1] Each day for the next two-and-a-half weeks *Corregidor*'s pilots searched a similar-sized area. The grid to be searched each day was carefully planned with reference to how the prevailing winds and currents might have affected the drift pattern of a raft. By the time Adm Nimitz called off the search for Gen Harmon and his companions on March 17, *Corregidor*'s air group had searched an area of almost 650,000 square miles. They found nothing but some debris deemed to be unrelated to Harmon's aircraft, such as some packing crates that had probably fallen off a passing cargo ship.[2]

---

[1] USS *Corregidor* War Diary, February 27–28 and March 1, 1945. NARA RG 38: World War II War Diaries. Box 760.

[2] "The Saga of the Mighty C," pp16–17. The veracity of "The Saga of the Mighty C" as a source is backed up by the fact that the size of the grid searched on February 28 matches exactly with the account of the search given in the *Corregidor*'s War Diary. See *Corregidor* War Diary, February 27 and March 1, 1945. NARA RG 38: World War II War Diaries. Box 760.

Corregidor now went back on antisubmarine duty. Using Eniwetok and Majuro, the latter another newly won anchorage in the Marshalls, as a base, *Corregidor* spent the remainder of March and the first half of April on antisubmarine patrol in and around the Marshall Islands. Maloelap and Wotje, two atolls with which Wade was intimately familiar from the days of Halsey's hit-and-run raids two years earlier, still held Japanese garrisons – troops that were now completely cut off from Japan. Wade's pilots were hoping to catch one of the submarines the increasingly desperate Imperial Japanese Navy was now using to bring supplies to such beleaguered and blockaded island garrisons that could no longer be supplied by air or by surface ship. They came up empty. The attendant danger that night-time carrier operations entail was, however, brought home to *Corregidor*'s crew in early April when a night launch of an Avenger went terribly wrong, the plane going into the water shortly after take-off. The pilot and one crewman were rescued, but the radio operator, Aviation Radioman 2nd Class Claude H. Lebow, was killed.[1]

On April 14, 1945, Wade ordered that *Corregidor*'s flag be lowered to half mast for the next 30 days to honor President Roosevelt, who had died on April 12 at Warm Springs, Georgia. At this time, either Wade was becoming more strict in his captain's mast sessions or the disciplinary problems were becoming worse. On April 16, a sailor was brought up before Wade on a charge of "Disrespectful language to his superior officer."[2] The record does not indicate if this offense was committed against Wade himself or against one of the ship's other officers. The offending sailor was demoted, given a bad conduct discharge, and sentenced to one year in prison. However, Wade did leave room for redemption. The sentence stipulated that if the man behaved for two months he would be released from confinement and subjected to a six-month

[1] "The Saga of the Mighty C," p18.

[2] NARA RG 24. *Corregidor* (CVE-58/CVU-58 Deck Logs September 1944 to August 1945. Box 2484, p1,080.

probationary period, after which he might be reinstated into full naval service with his record clear.[1]

On April 19, while *Corregidor* was on antisubmarine patrol west of Eniwetok, the ship's aerologist or weather officer warned that a typhoon was brewing. Indeed one was. Beginning in the early evening of the 20th, *Corregidor* and its crew spent two miserable and dangerous days being battered by the enormous rollers kicked up by the typhoon's winds. Years later, Wade told his son Philip that the mountainous waves and the incessant pitching and rolling of the ship terrified one enlisted man to the extent that the man had to be restrained and tied up because, crazed with fear, he had tried to jump overboard. To ride out the enormous waves, Wade had to slow the ship to a maximum of 10 knots. The crew lashed each aircraft to the deck.[2]

Escort carriers were not good sea boats in bad weather. Like all aircraft carriers, CVEs had a high center of gravity. In view of its top-heaviness and short, stubby lines, it is surprising that *Corregidor*'s maximum roll during the typhoon was "only" 22 degrees. Bad, yes, but it could have been worse. The little carrier handled the violent storm better than anyone had a right to expect. No lives were lost, but after the ship limped into the anchorage in the lagoon at Eniwetok on April 23, an examination by repair experts revealed that the hull plates had been strained beyond what could be repaired at a forward base. The ship was ordered back to Pearl Harbor. *Corregidor* departed Eniwetok alone on April 27, headed east.[3]

---

[1]NARA RG 24. *Corregidor* (CVE-58/CVU-58 Deck Logs September 1944 to August 1945. Box 2484, p1,080.

[2]"The Saga of the Mighty C," p18. Philip McClusky interviews, December 27 and December 29, 2016. NARA RG 38, Box 760. War Diary, USS *Corregidor*, entry for April 19, 1945. NARA RG 24. Corregidor (CVE-58/CVU-58 Deck Logs September 1944 to August 1945. Box 2484, p1,088, p1,090. Walter E. Skeldon, *Escort Carriers in the Pacific: A History of All Escort Carriers in the Pacific* (Victoria, BC, Canada: Trafford, 2002): p235.

[3]"The Saga of the Mighty C," pp18–19.

Corregidor was in dry dock at Pearl Harbor having its hull repaired for two weeks, from May 13 to May 27. After this work was completed, *Corregidor* on June 3 began the last phase of its World War 2 career. This was to be extremely quiet duty conducting carrier qualification landings for young newly minted naval aviators in Hawaiian waters.[1] World War 2 Navy pilot training programs provided thorough and comprehensive training for new pilots. However, their training was not complete until they had each made five landings on an aircraft carrier. The largest Navy pilot training centers during the war were NAS Pensacola, where Wade himself had learned to fly in 1928 and 1929, as well as the newer NAS Glenview Illinois – a station Wade would command after the war. After completing ground school and mastering basic flight tactics at Pensacola or Glenview, pilots in training would be sent to an Advanced Carrier Training Group (ACTG) base for advanced training.[2] Pilots training at such bases in the southeastern United States could make their qualification landings on any new carrier that happened to be traversing the Gulf of Mexico en route to the Panama Canal and the Pacific Theater.

For pilots training in the midwest, an ingenious solution was devised for the problem of how the Navy pilots there could get their qualification deck landings completed. Two old Great Lakes passenger ships were converted into small carriers and renamed USS *Sable* and USS *Wolverine*, respectively. Sailing from their home port of Chicago out into Lake Michigan for flight operations, *Sable* and *Wolverine* were unique among US Navy aircraft carriers in that they were the only carriers during the war that still burned coal and that used side-mounted paddlewheels

---

[1] "The Saga of the Mighty C," p19. Skeldon, *Escort Carriers in the Pacific*, p247.

[2] N. Jack "Dusty" Kleiss, with Timothy and Laura Orr, *Never Call Me a Hero: A Legendary American Dive-bomber Pilot Remembers the Battle of Midway* (New York: Morrow, 2017): pp67–68, pp241–242, pp244–245.

instead of screw propellers for propulsion. With some claim to being the most unusual aircraft carriers in history, *Sable* and *Wolverine* nevertheless provided yeoman service during the war, providing the platforms on which several thousand young Navy pilots made their first carrier landings.

Despite these efforts to enable Navy pilots to make their qualification deck landings before they left the United States, by the spring of 1945 Pensacola and Glenview were turning out such a high number of new pilots that many were being sent out to Pearl Harbor with their required number of flying hours complete but without having had the chance to make their carrier landings; hence the need to press *Corregidor* into service as a qualification carrier. Between June 11 and June 26, 1945 some 1,000 landings were made on *Corregidor*'s deck, meaning that approximately 250 pilots were qualified during this time, after which they could be assigned to the air group of a fleet carrier or of another escort carrier. As a pilot training ship, *Corregidor* would spend five or six days at sea and then return to Pearl for two days for crew rest and reprovisioning of the vessel.[1]

Wade's tour of duty aboard *Corregidor* ended on July 28, 1945, when he was relieved by Capt S. G. Mitchell. Despite the disciplinary problems Wade had encountered, he had succeeded in running a very happy ship. *Corregidor*'s unofficial history records that regarding Wade's departure: "Truly everyone hated to see him leave. He had been 'tops' with all hands."[2]

[1] "The Saga of the Mighty C," pp19–20.
[2] "The Saga of the Mighty C," p20.

19

THE END OF THE WAR AND THE
TRANSITION TO PEACE

The very welcome transition from war to peace was accompanied by unavoidable administrative confusion in America's armed forces.[1] It is difficult to avoid the conclusion that McClusky's career suffered as a result of this. Before and during the war, Wade's career had been characterized by assignments of steadily increasing responsibility. After the war, Wade's assignments, while mostly good, did not involve the kind of quantum increases in responsibility that would have been necessary in order for him to attain flag rank while still on active duty. Wade's promotion to rear admiral in 1956 was thus a going-away present from the Navy on the occasion of his retirement. He would never get to exercise command as an admiral.

Part of the reason that Wade's career became stalled at the rank of captain is that the Navy's future needs were far from clear at war's end.[2] The United States had during the war built up the largest Navy in world history, and yet demobilization began almost immediately upon Japan's surrender on August 14, 1945. For example, to implement this rapid demobilization, several *Essex* Class carriers were pressed into service as troop transports in late 1945 as part of Operation *Magic Carpet*, the repatriation

[1]Thomas B. Buell, *The Quiet Warrior: A Biography of Admiral Raymond A. Spruance* (Annapolis: Naval Institute Press, 1974, 1987): p415.
[2]Buell, *The Quiet Warrior*, p415.

of American servicemen from bases in the western Pacific and Europe back to the United States.

Upon being relieved of command of *Corregidor*, Wade spent a few weeks in Hawaii before learning in late July that he had been assigned as chief-of-staff and aide to R Adm Donald Duncan, who had just been named commander of Carrier Division Four. It seems that Adm Duncan had met and formed a favorable impression of McClusky while the two of them held down staff jobs in Washington during the midwar period. That he was glad to have McClusky as his chief-of-staff is shown by the fact that in early November 1945, when Duncan moved on from Carrier Division Four to command Carrier Division Five, he took McClusky with him.[1]

Donald Duncan had been the first captain of the USS *Essex* (CV-9) and had commanded the big new carrier during Operation *Galvanic*, the invasion of the Gilbert Islands in late November 1943, which campaign formed the opening of the Central Pacific Drive.[2] Just after the Gilberts had been secured, Duncan had been transferred stateside. By the end of 1943 Duncan was in Washington, where he would hold down a number of administrative posts over the next 18 months. By August 1944, Duncan had "made flag" as a rear admiral and was serving on the Joint Planning Staff. Duncan was planning officer on Adm King's staff from October 1944 to July 1945. He also worked closely with King's deputy, V Adm Richard S. Edwards during this time.[3]

---

[1] Orders; R Adm R. E. Jennings, Commander, Carrier Training Squadron, Pacific Fleet to McClusky, July 28, 1945. Philip McClusky collection. Commander Carrier Division Four to McClusky, November 3, 1945, ordering McClusky to go with Duncan as chief-of-staff and aide in Carrier Division Five. Philip McClusky collection. See also, Clark G. Reynolds, *The Fast Carriers: The Forging of an Air Navy* (New York: McGraw-Hill, 1968): p362, pp376–377, p390.

[2] Samuel Eliot Morison, *History of United States Naval Operations in World War II*. Vol. 7. *Aleutians, Gilberts and Marshalls: June 1942–April 1944* (Boston: Little, Brown and Company, 1984): p339.

[3] Reynolds, *The Fast Carriers*, p214, pp216–217, p245, p352, p359.

Donald Duncan excelled at staff work and was a superb seagoing commander – two qualities that he and McClusky shared.[1] The reason Duncan and McClusky got along well together may have been that each could sympathize with the other in that their administrative skills had marooned each man in Washington during the midwar period when they would rather have been at sea.

Characteristic of the frenetic pace of activity during the final weeks of the war, there was some administrative confusion at the beginning of Wade's tour as Duncan's chief-of-staff; duty that was beginning just as the war was ending.[2] At the outset of this new duty, Wade traveled out to the western Pacific to join Duncan, but this trip turned out to be a bit premature. On August 18, four days after Japan's surrender, Wade flew in an R5-D from Pearl Harbor to Eniwetok. Eniwetok is some 2,500 miles from Pearl Harbor and the flight would have lasted at least 12 hours. The R5-D could carry 50 passengers. Apparently there were several pilots on board. Wade flew the plane himself for four hours – getting in his required flight time for the month of August. On August 20, Wade departed Eniwetok as a passenger aboard the carrier USS *Intrepid* (CV-14) for a five-day trip to join the massive Pacific fleet assembled in Japanese coastal waters, where *Intrepid* arrived on August 25.[3] Riding in *Intrepid* was Wade's first close look at an *Essex* Class carrier. Early in

---

[1]Reynolds, *The Fast Carriers*, p362, pp376–377, p390.

[2]Orders; R Adm R. E. Jennings, Commander, Carrier Training Squadron, Pacific Fleet to McClusky, July 28, 1945. Philip McClusky collection. See also, Reynolds, *The Fast Carriers*, p362, pp376–377, p390.

[3]Wade McClusky logbook entry for August 1945. Philip McClusky collection. Letter from Capt G. E. Short, commanding officer of *Intrepid*, stating that McClusky was aboard as a passenger from August 20–25, 1945. I am indebted to Mr Thom Walla for his encyclopedic knowledge of the movements of every *Essex* Class carrier for any given day during the war. Email correspondence, Thom Walla to me, December 29 and December 30, 2016 and December 29, 2017. Reynolds, *The Fast Carriers*, p362.

the morning of the 25th, Wade was transferred to the destroyer USS *Sumner*,[1] from which he was subsequently transferred to the carrier USS *Randolph* (CV-15), which was to have been Adm Duncan's flagship.

Being his usual reticent self, Wade wrote only the barest details of this trip to the western Pacific in his pilot logbook.[2] Any hopes Wade may have had of witnessing the surrender ceremonies that took place on September 2, 1945 in Tokyo Bay would be dashed. American battleships and cruisers did anchor in Tokyo Bay for the surrender ceremonies, but the big *Essex* Class carriers were kept outside the harbor, patrolling just off the coast of Japan instead. Many naval aviators took this exclusion as a severe insult since it was the fast carriers that had made possible the war-winning strategy of an American drive across the Central Pacific Area. After playing such a vital role in winning the Pacific War, it seemed quite unfair to leave the big carriers milling around outside Tokyo Bay while the "Gun Club" had all the fun inside the harbor. Added to which, that the surrender documents were signed aboard a battleship, the USS *Missouri*, instead of aboard a carrier, did not go over well with the aviators.[3] In point of fact, Adms Nimitz and Halsey meant no insult to the aviators when they ordered the carriers to remain outside Tokyo Bay. They worried that the Japanese might have a last-minute change of heart and decide not to surrender after all, so they did not want all US naval strength confined within Tokyo Bay, making it a convenient target for any type of attack. Keeping the fast carriers outside the harbor gave Nimitz insurance against any surprises. In fact, Adm Nimitz even kept some of his battleships and some high-ranking surface officers

---

[1]Deck Log, USS *Intrepid*, entry for August 25, 1945. NARA. RG 24. Records of the Bureau of Naval Personnel. Deck Logs, 1941–1950. Box 4863: P118–A1.

[2]Wade McClusky, pilot logbook entries for August and September 1945. Philip McClusky collection.

[3]Reynolds, *The Fast Carriers*, pp377–378.

far away from Tokyo on September 2 to ensure that the United States would have naval power and naval leadership even if, say, the Japanese had launched a mass kamikaze attack against the ships anchored in Tokyo Bay. For instance, the battleship USS *New Jersey* was anchored at Okinawa on the big day, 350 miles from Tokyo – and was flying a four-star flag at its truck because Adm Raymond Spruance was aboard.[1]

Adm Duncan boarded his would-be flagship *Randolph* on August 24, 1945 with orders to relieve R Adm Gerald Bogan as commander of Carrier Division Four.[2] *Randolph* was also Adm Bogan's flagship, but for some reason, Bogan was not quite ready to relinquish his command just yet. In fact, it would be more than a month later before the transfer of command actually took place,[3] which means that Wade might as well have waited in Hawaii for a few more weeks before heading out to the western Pacific. McClusky had reported aboard *Randolph* on August 27, 1945 with the title of "Aide and Chief of Staff." He was thereby thrust into a situation that was more than a bit awkward, in which there were two admirals aboard *Randolph*. Adm Duncan was listed in the ship's log as "Relief for ComCarDiv 4" (ie Bogan) but Bogan was not yet ready to be relieved and Bogan's chief-of-staff, Capt R. C. Morehouse was also still aboard when Wade arrived. Morehouse departed on August 31, but Bogan seems to have stayed on longer and so Wade may have spent a few days serving

---

[1]E. B. Potter, *Nimitz*, (Annapolis: Naval Institute Press, 1976, 1987): p389. Buell, *The Quiet Warrior*, p399. Reynolds, *The Fast Carriers*, p377.

[2]Reynolds, *The Fast Carriers*, p362, pp376–377, p390. USS *Randolph* Deck Logs, August 1945 to September 1946. List of Officers for the period August 1–31, 1945 and for September 1–30, 1945, respectively. NARA. RG 24 Records of the Bureau of Naval Personnel. Box 7756.

[3]Kristi Johnson, ed., *History of the U.S.S. Antietam: CV/CVA/CVS 36* (Paducah, Kentucky: Turner Publishing Co, 2001): p19. I am indebted to Thom Walla for digging up this information.

as chief-of-staff to both admirals.[1] Why this mix-up occurred is not clear from the records, but by October 1, *Randolph* was no longer a flagship; Duncan, Bogan, and Wade had all departed the ship by then.[2] After this premature trip to the western Pacific, McClusky was back at Pearl Harbor by September 12. His logbook entries for this period do not make clear whether he made the return trip by air or by sea. If he flew back to Pearl, it was as a passenger. The only piloting Wade did between August 1 and September 12 was those four hours at the controls of the R5-D on August 18.[3]

Wade was back in the western Pacific by October 8, 1945, the date on which Adm Duncan formally took command of Carrier Division Four. Duncan's flagship was the brand-new carrier USS *Boxer* (CV-21). A few weeks later, Duncan transferred temporarily to *Boxer*'s sister carrier USS *Antietam* (CV-36) at Tsingtao in China in early November so that *Boxer* could briefly return to Guam to restock provisions. Wade traveled with *Boxer* back to Guam. His pilot logbook shows that he flew an F6F Hellcat at Tsingtao on November 4. Then, just over a week later, he flew an SNJ at Guam on November 13 and again on the 14th. After completing her reprovisioning, *Boxer* was back on station two-and-a-half weeks later. Accordingly, Adm Duncan, now commanding Carrier Division Five, moved back aboard *Boxer* on November 23. In late December, *Boxer* was in Japan and Wade flew an F6F out of Yokosuka.[4]

---

[1] USS *Randolph* Deck Logs, August 1945 to September 1946. List of Officers for the period August 1–31, 1945 and for September 1–30, 1945, respectively. NARA. RG 24 Records of the Bureau of Naval Personnel. Box 7756.

[2] USS *Randolph* Deck Logs, August 1945 to September 1946. List of Officers for the period October 1–31, 1945. NARA. RG 24 Records of the Bureau of Naval Personnel. Box 7756.

[3] McClusky pilot logbook entries, August and September 1945. Philip McClusky collection.

[4] Johnson, ed., *History of the U.S.S. Antietam*, p19. Wade McClusky, pilot logbook entries, November 1945–December 1945. Philip McClusky collection. Commander Carrier Division Four to McClusky, November 3, 1945, ordering McClusky to go with Duncan as chief-of-staff and aide in Carrier Division Five. Philip McClusky collection.

Regarding Wade's fruitless trip out to the western Pacific and back to Hawaii in August and early September 1945, this kind of false start/stop-start activity would become characteristic of McClusky's post-World War 2 career: orders that sent him rushing out to the western Pacific only to find that he was not needed just yet were a metaphor of sorts for his postwar life in the Navy. The reason was that when the fighting stopped and the guns fell silent on August 14, 1945, the Navy descended almost immediately into administrative chaos.[1] The war had ended suddenly, with no invasion of the Japanese home islands (the planning for which had been well underway) being necessary after all. With no protracted invasion of the Japanese home islands, many questions arose: Should the Navy be kept at its wartime strength or should demobilization begin? Should the Armed Forces of the United States be unified? (The Navy had not yet moved into the new Pentagon building at war's end.) Would it be possible to continue the wartime alliance with Russia, or would Russia become an adversary? What was to be the Navy's role in the postwar world?[2] These and other questions demanded immediate consideration.

[1] Buell, *The Quiet Warrior*, p415. Reynolds, *The Fast Carriers*, p376.
[2] Potter, *Nimitz*, pp405–414. Buell, *The Quiet Warrior*, p415.

20

POSTWAR

The war-weary American people, via their elected representatives in Congress, opted for immediate demobilization once the war was won. "Bringing the boys home"[1] became the order of the day. Accordingly, the Pacific Fleet was rapidly reduced in size in the months after Japan's surrender. In the midst of this demobilization, Wade was detached from Adm Duncan's staff in late February 1946 and ordered first to Washington, then, in April 1946, Wade was assigned to be executive officer of a General Line postgraduate program located at and affiliated with the Naval War College at Newport, Rhode Island – Newport at that time still being a full service naval base.[2] This duty for Wade almost certainly had something to do with the fact that Adm Raymond Spruance had become president of the Naval War College a month earlier.[3]

In addition to duty at the Naval War College, Wade was, almost as soon as he stepped ashore, thrust back into his now

---

[1]As quoted in E. B. Potter, *Nimitz* (Annapolis: Naval Institute Press, 1976, 1987): p413.

[2]Orders; Duncan to McClusky, February 26, 1946. Philip McClusky collection. "Rear Admiral C. Wade McClusky, Jr. United States Navy, Retired" P2. Navy Biographies Section, OI-440, May 23, 1957. Courtesy National Naval Aviation Museum, Pensacola, Florida. Also, see *The Reminiscences of Rear Admiral James D. Ramage*. Interviewed by Robert L. Lawson and Barrett Tillman. (Annapolis: U.S. Naval Institute, 1999): pp1–129.

[3]Thomas B. Buell, *The Quiet Warrior: A Biography of Admiral Raymond A. Spruance* (Annapolis: Naval Institute Press, 1974, 1987): p415.

familiar role as roving troubleshooter for the Navy. For instance, in mid-April, he was loaned out from the Naval War College to Washington for one week of temporary duty with the Navy's Bureau of Personnel, probably to help untangle problems involving the Navy's rapid postwar demobilization. Although the orders were for only a week's duty, Wade apparently spent the next several weeks shuttling between Newport and Washington. For instance, he flew himself in an SNJ-6 from NAS Quonset Point (near Newport) to NAS Anacostia, the latter just outside Washington, DC, on April 18, and flew back to Quonset later the same day. On May 10, he flew to Anacostia again, returning to Newport on May 13. Interspersed with these flights recorded in his logbooks, he may well have done some additional shuttling between Newport and Washington by rail as well.[1]

The Naval War College was in the middle of tumultuous changes in the year following the war. Wade's assignment as executive officer of the General Line program had to have been challenging. Of the situation that existed when Adm Spruance took up his duties as President of the Naval War College in March 1946, Spruance biographer Thomas B. Buell writes that:

"the Navy was in turmoil owing to a stampeding demobilization. Hundreds of ships were being scrapped or placed in mothballs, shore installations were being reduced in size or totally shut down, and hundreds of thousands of officers and men were returning to civilian life. The demobilization had acquired a disorderly momentum, and no one could confidently predict the future composition and missions of the United States Navy."[2]

[1]Orders; Commanding Officer, Newport Naval Base to McClusky, at the behest of the Bureau of Personnel, April 16, 1946. Philip McClusky collection. Wade McClusky logbook entries for April and May 1946. Philip McClusky collection.
[2]Buell, *The Quiet Warrior*, p415.

For the next 18 months, Wade's duties kept him primarily at Newport. For his occasional trips to Washington, he would whenever possible continue to get in his monthly required flying time by flying himself down and back, sometimes in one day. Nevertheless, his duties in Newport kept him behind a desk most of the time and his flying time was reduced to four or five hours per month.[1]

Perhaps the biggest challenge McClusky and Spruance would face at the Naval War College was to oversee the development and implementation of a new curriculum – one that would reflect the realities of the postwar world and the beginnings of the Cold War. Not surprisingly, naval aviation and logistics, two of the most important aspects of American victory in the Pacific, were subjects that would feature prominently in the new curriculum.[2]

Wade was a good academic administrator and so after 18 months at the Naval War College he was assigned to perform the same tasks at what was becoming the Navy's other postgraduate institution: the US Naval School (General Line) in Monterey, California. Wade thus spent the 1947–1948 academic year as executive officer in Monterey. The Naval School in Monterey did not officially become accredited as a "postgraduate" institution until 1951, but the General Line program based there in the late 1940s did in fact provide postgraduate study and training for rising young naval officers. The curriculum at Monterey during McClusky's time as executive officer there included strategy and tactics, communications, naval law, aviation, and ordnance and gunnery.[3]

[1]Orders; Commanding Officer, NAS Newport to McClusky, May 22, 1946. Philip McClusky collection. Wade McClusky logbook entries from April 1946 to September 1947. Philip McClusky collection

[2]Buell, *The Quiet Warrior*, pp416–419.

[3]"Rear Admiral C. Wade McClusky, Jr. United States Navy, Retired" May 23, 1957; pp2–3 Courtesy of the National Naval Aviation Museum, Pensacola, Florida. J. J. "Jocko" Clark, with Clark G. Reynolds, *Carrier Admiral* (New York: David McKay Company, Inc,

In August 1948, Wade was ordered back to the fleet as the chief-of-staff to the commander of Carrier Division Five, R Adm Dixwell Ketcham. The duty with Carrier Division Five was extremely quiet – restricted to coastal waters off California. The Division was in a stateside rotation. Thus, Wade seems to have spent much of his time ashore. All of Wade's logbook entries for this period show that he flew into and out of West Coast naval air stations such as Alameda and San Diego and that he made no carrier landings during this period.[1]

1967): p258. Orders from R Adm Thomas L. Sprague, Chief of the Bureau of Personnel to McClusky, March 11, 1949. Philip McClusky collection. Wade McClusky, logbook entries, July 1948–July 1949. Philip McClusky collection. Email communication to me from Eleanor Uhlinger, university librarian, Naval Postgraduate School, Monterey, CA, October 24, 2017. Catalog from 1948; US Naval School (General Line), Monterey, California. George Dennis, Jr, LCDR, USN, ed., *All Hands: The Bureau of Naval Personnel Information Bulletin.* No 380, October 1948, p36. Available online at: www.navy.mil/ah_online/archpdf/ah194810.pdf. Photo caption for NH95745. USS *Valley Forge* (CV 45). NHHC. Available online at: www.history.navy.mil/our-collections/photography/numerical-list-of-images/nhhc-series/nh-series/NH-95000/NH-95745.html. See also, photo caption for NH 95744. R Adm Dixwell Ketcham, Commander, Carrier Division Five. Available online at: www.history.navy.mil/our-collections/photography/numerical-list-of-images/nhhc-series/nh-series/NH-95000/NH-95744.html.

[1] "Rear Admiral C. Wade McClusky, Jr. United States Navy, Retired" May 23, 1957; pp2–3 Courtesy of the National Naval Aviation Museum, Pensacola, Florida. Clark, *Carrier Admiral,* p258. Orders from R Adm Thomas L. Sprague, Chief of the Bureau of Personnel to McClusky, March 11, 1949. Philip McClusky collection. Wade McClusky, logbook entries, July 1948–July 1949. Philip McClusky collection. Email communication to me from Eleanor Uhlinger, university librarian, Naval Postgraduate School, Monterey, CA, October 24, 2017. Catalog from 1948; US Naval School (General Line), Monterey, California. George Dennis, Jr, LCDR, USN, ed., *All Hands: The Bureau of Naval Personnel Information Bulletin.* No 380, October 1948, p36. Available online at: www.navy.mil/ah_online/archpdf/ah194810.pdf. Photo caption for NH95745. USS *Valley Forge* (CV 45). NHHC. Available online at: www.history.navy.mil/our-collections/photography/numerical-list-of-images/nhhc-series/nh-series/NH-95000/NH-95745.html. See also, photo caption

Wade's tour with Carrier Division Five officially ended in March 1949, when he was ordered to duty as a student at the National War College in Washington, DC, but Wade's pilot logbooks show that he remained in California through July 1949.[1] Founded in 1946 on the grounds of the Washington Arsenal, soon to be renamed Fort Lesley J. McNair, the National War College was, according to Cold War historian John Lewis Gaddis, "the nation's first institution devoted to the study of politico-military affairs at the highest level."[2] George Kennan, the architect of "Containment" as a Cold War strategy, had been one of the first faculty members of the National War College, but had moved on to head the Policy Planning Staff at the State Department by the time McClusky arrived. Wade spent the 1949–1950 academic year studying at the National War College. Upon completing his studies in the spring of 1950, Wade was ordered in May 1950 back to high-level staff duty, this time in the office of Chief of Naval Operations Adm Forrest P. Sherman, where Wade was assigned as director of long-range planning in the Aviation Planning Division.[3] McClusky had probably met Sherman during the war when the latter served as deputy chief-of-staff to Adm Nimitz.

for NH 95744. R Adm Dixwell Ketcham, Commander, Carrier Division Five. Available online at: www.history.navy.mil/our-collections/photography/numerical-list-of-images/nhhc-series/nh-series/NH-95000/NH-95744.html.

[1] Orders from R Adm Thomas L. Sprague, Chief of the Bureau of Personnel to McClusky, March 11, 1949. Philip McClusky collection. Wade McClusky, logbook entries, July 1948–July 1949. Philip McClusky collection. Wade McClusky 1956 resumé, p2. Philip McClusky collection.

[2] John Lewis Gaddis, *Strategies of Containment: A Critical Appraisal of American National Security Policy During the Cold War*, (New York: Oxford University Press, 1982, 2005): p24.

[3] "Rear Admiral C. Wade McClusky, Jr. United States Navy, Retired" May 23, 1957. P3. Courtesy National Naval Aviation Museum, Pensacola, Florida. Wade McClusky 1956 resumé, p2. Philip McClusky collection.

Wade saw himself portrayed on film for the first time in the 1949 Warner Bros film *Task Force*, starring Gary Cooper and Jane Wyatt, Wade's character being played by the actor Bruce Bennett. The real Wade hated the film because it incorrectly has him landing on the *Yorktown* after leading the Midway attack. The actor Christopher George would portray McClusky in the 1976 film *Midway*. Wade's son Philip feels that the most accurate film portrayal of his father thus far was that turned in by actor Earl Hindman in the 1988 television miniseries *War and Remembrance*, based on the Herman Wouk novel of the same name. The *War and Remembrance* portrayal is the first film treatment that seeks to develop McClusky's character as a person, primarily by portraying the legendary argument between McClusky and Miles Browning on the flag bridge of the *Enterprise* on June 5, 1942.[1]

Wade's home life was unsettled during the late 1940s. He and Millicent had separated by the time Wade began his studies at the National War College, but Millicent was still living in Washington, DC in 1949. Wade's assignment to the National War College meant that his son, Wade Sanford, nicknamed "Pat" by his parents to differentiate him in conversation from his father, was able to spend time visiting with both of his parents. Pat had been enrolled as a boarding student since his Eighth Grade year at the elite Principia school in St Louis. Thus, the break-up of his parents' marriage did not affect him as severely as it might have done because Pat had gotten into the habit of spending his school vacations at the homes of friends he met at Principia.[2] Young Pat resembled his father in many ways. Quiet and shy, Pat was the type of person who had a few close friends rather than an array of casual acquaintances. Tall and handsome, he was a nice person blessed with a good sense of humor. He was also

---

[1]Interview with Philip McClusky, December 27, 2017.

[2]Telephone conversation with Carole McClusky-Pewthers, September 28, 2017.

a gifted athlete who played basketball and tennis at Principia – and played them well.[1]

After his graduation from the Principia School in 1949, Pat enrolled at Stanford University. He was a little late arriving for his freshman year, however. At the beginning of the long drive out to Stanford, Pat was arrested in mid-September after being involved in an automobile accident near Frederick, Maryland. He had misjudged the distance when trying to pass a car traveling in front of him and ended up striking a car that was coming from the opposite direction. Fortunately, Pat struck the side of the oncoming vehicle instead of hitting it head on – a fact that probably explains why the drivers of both vehicles were uninjured. While nobody was hurt, the police deemed Pat to be at fault.[2] He was fined $11.45 in Traffic Court for "passing when way ahead not clear."[3]

At Stanford, Pat joined the Phi Kappa Psi fraternity and majored in Economics. He spent his college summers working as a lifeguard at beaches in Ocean City, Maryland. Upon his graduation from Stanford in 1953, Pat joined the Navy with the intention of following his father's example by becoming a naval aviator. Like his father, however, Pat had to perform some surface fleet duty before beginning his flight training. His first assignment after completing his officer candidate training and being commissioned an ensign was as a surface officer aboard an LST. Pat McClusky won the golden wings of a naval aviator at Pensacola in 1956 and flew a North American FJ4 fighter jet as part of squadron VA 151 from the USS *Ticonderoga* (CV-14). Pat made a Far Eastern cruise aboard *Ticonderoga* in late 1958 and early 1959. Pat liked the Navy, but unlike his father he ultimately

---

[1] Telephone conversation with Carole McClusky-Pewthers, September 28, 2017.

[2] *The News* (Frederick, MD). September 14, 1949. P1

[3] Traffic Court notices. *The News* (Frederick, MD). September 22, 1949. Available online at: https://www.newspapers.com/image/8882547/.

decided not to make the Navy his career. He served only one tour of six years.[1]

Honorably discharged from the Navy in 1959 at the rank of lieutenant, Pat remained active in the Naval Reserve for some years. After his discharge from the Navy, Pat returned to Stanford, where he earned an MBA degree in 1962 in preparation for a career in finance. During his time in the Stanford MBA program Pat met his future wife, a Stanford graduate named Carole McCarthy who was working as a systems engineer at IBM, at a time when there were not many female engineers. Carole shared an apartment with another young woman in Menlo Park. Pat and Carole met on a blind date in 1959. The wedding took place in the spring of 1963. Although there was no known tension between father and son, the fact that Pat had settled in California made it difficult for Wade to visit his son; Wade, Sr was unable to get to California for Pat's wedding and he did not meet his daughter-in-law Carole for the first time until 1965 or 1966 when Pat and Carole came East for a visit.[2] California agreed with Pat and Carole. Carole's roommate had moved out of the apartment by the time of the wedding, so the newlyweds settled into Carole's apartment in Menlo Park. Pat and Carole would have one daughter, Patricia. In addition to her work at IBM, Carole was active in the American

---

[1]Obituary, *Baltimore Sun*. August 30, 1986. P9A. Email communication, Philip McClusky to me, September 10, 2017. *The Times* (San Mateo). December 5, 1962. P19. *Los Angeles Times*. "Fellowship Dessert to Feature Fashion Talk" January 31, 1971. P12 of Orange County Classified Section. Available online at: www.newspapers.com/image/164656149/?terms=Wade%2BS.%2BMcClusky. Accessed September 14, 2017. *The Times* (San Mateo). December 5, 1962. P19. Available online at: www.newspapers.com/image/52107904/?terms=Wade%2BS.%2BMcClusky. Accessed September 14, 2017. Email communication, Daniel Hartwig, Stanford University archivist, to me, September 21, 2017. Telephone conversations with Carole McClusky-Pewthers, September 28, 2017 and November 29, 2017.

[2]Telephone conversation with Carole McClusky-Pewthers, September 28, 2017.

Association of University Women. Pat sold avionics for Regency Avionics, an Indianapolis-based aircraft instrument company. Pat's job came with an airplane, a small Moony single-engine machine that was fitted out with Regency's latest avionics kit for Pat to show to potential customers. Compared to the jets he had flown in the Navy, Pat found flying a single-engined propeller plane to be a bit slow and dull. He was also appalled at the bad manners of the civilian pilots of other small planes with whom he now shared landing circles and glide paths; Pat found these civilians to be distressingly lacking in the Naval discipline he was accustomed to. [1]

Pat later worked as a stockbroker for Merrill Lynch. For this job, the couple relocated first to an apartment in Corona Del Mar near Irvine in southern California. A year later, they purchased a house in Costa Mesa, a few miles from Corona Del Mar. Pat eventually grew disenchanted with selling stocks because he was the kind of person who needed to believe in anything he was selling, and as a stockbroker he was sometimes compelled to push the stocks of companies in which he did not have complete confidence. Thus, he eventually gave up the Merrill Lynch job to take an accounting position with the Orange County government. Pat McClusky died prematurely in California at

---

[1]Obituary, *Baltimore Sun*. August 30, 1986. P9A. Email communication, Philip McClusky to me, September 10, 2017. *The Times* (San Mateo). December 5, 1962. P19. *Los Angeles Times*. "Fellowship Dessert to Feature Fashion Talk" January 31, 1971. P12 of Orange County Classified Section. Available online at: www.newspapers.com/image/164656149/?terms=Wade%2BS.%2BMcClusky. Accessed September 14, 2017. *The Times* (San Mateo). December 5, 1962. P19. Available online at: www.newspapers.com/image/52107904/?terms=Wade%2BS.%2BMcClusky. Accessed September 14, 2017. Email communication, Daniel Hartwig, Stanford University archivist, to me, September 21, 2017. Telephone conversations with Carole McClusky-Pewthers, September 28, 2017 and November 29, 2017. Email communication, Philip McClusky to me, September 10, 2017.

age 55 of non-Hodgkin's lymphoma on August 26, 1986.[1] He is
buried in Forest Lawn Memorial Park in Hollywood Hills, in the
same plot where his mother had been laid to rest after her death
on November 15, 1972.[2]

As for Wade, Sr, the outbreak of the Korean War in June
1950 eventually brought sea duty. In June 1951 he was detached
from the Pentagon with orders to become chief-of-staff to V
Adm Arthur D. Struble, the commander of the First Fleet, which
operated in the western Pacific. The First Fleet's task in the Korean
conflict was battle training; specifically ships, crews, and aviators
destined for combat duty with the Seventh Fleet, which operated
directly off the coast of Korea, and would first be assigned to
the First Fleet for a period of rigorous training. Adm Struble
was well qualified to oversee this battle training since he himself
had commanded the Seventh Fleet in Korean waters during the
first nine months of the Korean War. Wade himself was duly
transitioned from the First to the Seventh Fleet when in the spring
of 1952 he was assigned as chief-of-staff first to V Adm Robert
P. Briscoe and then to V Adm J. J. "Jocko" Clark, successive
commanders of the Seventh Fleet. Briscoe and Clark used as their
flagship the battleship USS *Iowa*, spacious and comfortable, but

---

[1]Obituary, *Baltimore Sun*. August 30, 1986. P9A. Email communication, Philip
McClusky to me, September 10, 2017. *The Times* (San Mateo). December 5, 1962. P19.
Los Angeles Times. "Fellowship Dessert to Feature Fashion Talk" January 31, 1971.
P12 of Orange County Classified Section. Available online at: www.newspapers.com/
image/164656149/?terms=Wade%2BS.%2BMcClusky. Accessed September 14, 2017.
The Times (San Mateo). December 5, 1962. P19. Available online at: www.newspapers.
com/image/52107904/?terms=Wade%2BS.%2BMcClusky. Accessed September 14, 2017.
Email communication, Daniel Hartwig, Stanford University archivist, to me, September
21, 2017. Telephone conversations with Carole McClusky-Pewthers, September 28, 2017
and November 29, 2017. Email communication, Philip McClusky to me, September 10,
2017.

[2]https://findagrave.com/memorial/135785397, via Ancestry.com. Accessed July 13,
2020.

an unfamiliar environment for two aging carrier pilots like Wade McClusky and Jocko Clark.[1] Adm Clark had qualified as a naval aviator in 1925 and had been a hard-charging carrier division commander in World War 2. Like Wade, Jocko Clark was a pilot first and a sailor second. Therefore, living on a battleship was a unique experience for both men. In fact, serving as chief-of-staff to Adms Briscoe and Clark was probably the first time Wade had set foot on a battleship since his days as a junior officer on the *Pennsylvania* back in the 1920s.

Wade would have assisted Adm Clark in the planning of a spectacular carrier air strike against power plants located at the Suiho hydroelectric dam in North Korea on the Yalu river, which forms the border between North Korea and China. The attack, carried out on June 23, 1952 by Douglas Skyraiders, successors to the legendary SBD, and Grumman F9F Panthers, the Navy's first jet fighters, flying from four different American aircraft carriers, was highly successful.[2]

The Suiho raid was difficult for the pilots because the rules of engagement set down by President Truman and the US joint chiefs-of-staff in the Korean conflict required American pilots to refrain from overflying Chinese territory or from attacking targets on Chinese soil even though China had been a full-fledged combatant in the war since October 1950. Thus, although there were enemy antiaircraft batteries on both sides of the river, the Americans were only allowed to attack those on the North Korean side. Similarly, pilots of US Air Force F-86 Sabrejets that had been tasked with protecting the Navy planes during the attack could see dozens of Russian-built MIG-15

---

[1] "Rear Admiral C. Wade McClusky, Jr. United States Navy, Retired." Navy Biographies Section, OI-440, May 23, 1957. P3. Courtesy of National Naval Aviation Museum, Pensacola, Florida. Orders, Bureau of Personnel to McClusky, May 9, 1951. Philip McClusky collection. William G. Smedburg and Joshua W. Cooper, *Cruise Book: U.S.S. Iowa: 1951–1952* (Tokyo: Toppan Printing Co, Ltd, 1952): pp32–33. Clark and Reynolds, *Carrier Admiral*, pp281–282, p284, p292.

[2] Clark and Reynolds, *Carrier Admiral*, pp285–287.

fighter jets parked on airfields at Antung, near the dam site, but were prohibited from attacking them because Antung lies on the Chinese side of the river. Indeed, the dam's power plants were fair game as targets only because they were located on the North Korean side of the dam.[1]

Wade's duty with Briscoe and Clark was rather brief. He was detached in late July 1952 and ordered to report to Glenview Illinois to take command of the Naval Air Station there. His tenure at NAS Glenview was also brief, just six months.[2] Indeed, Wade's career since the end of World War 2 seems to have suffered due to the chaos brought on by postwar demobilization; the unification of the armed forces in 1947; and the outbreak of a completely unexpected war in Korea. The Navy seemed not to know quite what to do with him. Being sent as a student to the National War College in 1949 was an indication that Wade was being groomed for promotion to flag rank. His successful tours of high-level staff duty during the Korean War also put him in line for promotion. However, unlike World War 2, Korea was a limited war in which the American economy and armed forces were never fully mobilized. By the time Wade was rotated stateside in the summer of 1952, the Korean War was in stalemate and it had become apparent to the US naval high command that the number of slots for flag officers in the postwar era would be limited. Suddenly, Wade was no longer on the flag officer track. His assignments during the last four years preceding his retirement were time-serving appointments designed to keep him busy until he could be retired at his present rank of captain.

Wade took command of NAS Glenview in August 1952. He was by now an old hand at training pilots. The biggest change

[1]Malcolm W. Cagle and Frank A. Manson, *The Sea War in Korea* (Annapolis: Naval Institute Press, 1957): pp443–447.

[2]Clark and Reynolds, *Carrier Admiral*, p282. "Rear Admiral C. Wade McClusky, Jr. United States Navy, Retired" May 23, 1957. P3. National Naval Aviation Museum, Pensacola Florida.

for Wade in this assignment was that the student pilots under his command were now learning to fly jets, although Wade himself seems to never have flown a jet himself; he mainly flew SNJ-5s and SNJ-6s during this period and for the remainder of his time in the Navy. The SNJs were adequate for the task of getting in his required flying time each month.[1] Wade marked time in Glenview until February 1953.

While Wade's career was winding down, his personal life was picking up. Wade married Ruth Goodwin Mundy on August 9, 1952 just after his divorce from Millicent was finalized. He was 50, Ruth was 28. The marriage took place in Montgomery County, Maryland.[2] They would have one son, Philip, who was born in 1953. Philip's view as to his mother being so much younger than his father is "Go dad!"[3] Ruth was from the aristocracy of old Virginia, where the Mundy family had arrived prior to 1700. One of Ruth's grandfathers had served in an artillery battery in Lt Gen James Longstreet's First Corps of the Confederate Army of Northern Virginia during the Civil War.[4]

Wade's final two assignments in the Navy were definitely dead-end jobs. From Glenview, Wade was sent to Washington for a job he must have hated – assistant director of the Production Division in the Office of Naval Material. It was during this tour in Washington that Ruth gave birth to their son Philip at the Bethesda Naval Hospital on October 27, 1953. Wade's final assignment was a little more interesting, but still a dead end. In June 1954 he became commander of the units of the Atlantic Reserve Fleet that

[1]Wade McClusky logbook entries, September 1945 to June 1956. Philip McClusky collection.

[2]From the McClusky "Jacket" on file at the Naval Academy. "McClusky, Clarence Wade, Jr." Jacket Number 8306. Special Collections & Archives Department, Nimitz Library, United States Naval Academy. Also, "Wade McClusky" entries at Ancestry.com: http://trees.ancestry.com/tree/32878307/person/18347961652/fact/88092160165.

[3]Email communication, Philip McClusky to me, March 1, 2015.

[4]Email communication, Philip McClusky to me, March 8, 2015.

were based in Boston.[1] This appointment automatically made him the commandant of the Boston Navy Yard. During Wade's tenure, the Boston Navy Yard was still a functioning naval base but the Charlestown, Massachusetts facility was primarily being used to store a number of surplus World War 2 destroyers. Japan, now a staunch US ally, needed ships for its postwar Self Defense Force. Wade must have thus found it highly ironic when Japanese naval personnel arrived in Charlestown to take possession of four destroyers. It had to have been difficult for Wade to hand over these destroyers to representatives of a nation that had been a mortal enemy less than ten years earlier.[2]

Wade was put on the retired list on July 1, 1956 and in the words of a Navy department biographical sketch prepared shortly thereafter, was promoted "Rear Admiral on the basis of combat awards."[3] This was a "tombstone promotion," however, in that Wade was entitled to wear the uniform of a rear admiral but his retirement pay was that of a captain, and he never exercised command as an admiral. Wade's flying skills remained sharp right up until the end of his naval career. His last flight at the controls of a naval aircraft occurred on June 5, 1956 in an SNJ-5 when he was then 54 years old.[4]

Upon Wade's retirement, he and Ruth purchased a plot of land at 1826 Circle Road in Ruxton, Maryland and Wade designed the house that they had built there – a rather odd-looking Cape, half of which had a second floor and with an attached garage. Phil McClusky describes the house as being quite comfortable: "The house at 1826 was defined as a story and a half. It was a good

[1]"Rear Admiral C. Wade McClusky, Jr. United States Navy, Retired" May 23, 1957. P3. National Naval Aviation Museum, Pensacola, Florida.

[2]Interviews with Philip McClusky, December 27 and December 29, 2016.

[3]"Rear Admiral C. Wade McClusky, Jr. United States Navy, Retired" May 23, 1957. P3. National Naval Aviation Museum, Pensacola, Florida.

[4]Email communication, Philip McClusky to me, March 1, 2015. Wade McClusky pilot logbook entries for 1956. Philip McClusky collection.

sized house by 1950/60s standards with a large living room, a large dining room, a den/library, 3 bedrooms, 2 ½ baths, finished basement and an oversized 1 car garage. It was on a 1 ½ [acre] wooded lot in a very upscale part of Baltimore called Ruxton."[1] The suburbs of Baltimore was a logical choice given Ruth's family ties to the aristocracy of old Virginia. The location also enabled Wade, and later Wade and Philip, to attend every Navy home football game. Bringing Philip to Navy football games, and to the parties with Wade's old academy friends that followed each game, was part of Wade's gentle effort to nudge Philip toward a career in the Navy. Wade never pushed too hard, however, and he harbored no animosity when Philip chose to attend the University of Maryland rather than apply for an appointment to Annapolis. The real reason for the move to Ruxton, though, is that Wade's first civilian job after his retirement from the Navy in 1956 was as a senior engineer at Martin Co in Baltimore. There, Wade probably worked on the PGM SeaMaster, a large jet-powered flying boat bomber that Martin was developing for the Navy. The Navy invested some money and a dozen prototypes were built, but the jet seaplane was cancelled in 1959.[2]

The resumé Wade put together when applying for civilian jobs is a concise and orderly four-page document. In it, Wade gives a brief outline of his different postings in the Navy. He mentions, but does not dwell on, Midway and his Navy Cross. As an objective, the resumé simply states that he had spent the past 30 years as a naval officer and was now seeking a management position in the private sector. It is rather touching that Wade presumed nothing. He did not assume that any potential employers would have heard

[1] Email communication, Philip McClusky to me, January 7, 2017.

[2] Interviews with Philip McClusky, December 27 and December 29, 2016. Questionnaire filled out by Wade McClusky in January 1960 for the Naval Academy's "Alumni Register and History Record." From the McClusky "Jacket" on file at the Naval Academy. "McClusky, Clarence Wade, Jr." Jacket Number 8306. Special Collections & Archives Department, Nimitz Library, United States Naval Academy.

of him. It is rather sad that a man like Wade McClusky actually had to apply for jobs as opposed to being actively recruited based on his record.[1]

A Naval Academy education was and is an excellent background for a career in engineering but Wade was dissatisfied with working as an engineer. Part of this probably stemmed from the fact that the PGM SeaMaster was the last fixed-wing aircraft designed by Martin. After the SeaMaster was cancelled, Martin focused exclusively on designing and building rockets and missiles, which evidently had no appeal for Wade. He was a pilot and he wanted to design airplanes. Thus, after three years at Martin, Wade decided to get a teaching job, something that was a natural enough choice since he had taught at Annapolis for two years just before World War 2 and had later served as an academic administrator in Newport and Monterey, respectively. In the fall of 1959, Wade began teaching math at the elite Bryn Mawr school in Baltimore.[2] Ruth also worked at Bryn Mawr as a part-time playground supervisor. An all-girl private academy, Bryn Mawr was quite a new experience for Wade. The girls there quickly discovered something that Wade's son Philip already knew: namely, that while Wade had had no difficulties or compunctions when it came to disciplining sailors under his command in the Navy, he was absolutely incapable of disciplining children. Wade's students at Bryn Mawr consequently got away with a lot. Nevertheless, the girls liked and respected their lenient new teacher. Students, faculty, and staff all paid Wade the courtesy of addressing him as "Admiral."[3]

---

[1]Wade McClusky 1956 resumé. Philip McClusky collection.

[2]Questionnaire filled out by Wade McClusky in January 1960 for the Naval Academy's "Alumni Register and History Record." From the McClusky "Jacket" on file at the Naval Academy. "McClusky, Clarence Wade, Jr." Jacket Number 8306. Special Collections & Archives Department, Nimitz Library, United States Naval Academy.

[3]Interviews with Philip McClusky, December 27 and December 29, 2016 and December 27, 2017.

In preparation for teaching, Wade had enrolled in the Masters in Education degree program at the Johns Hopkins University during the 1957–1958 school year, but had not yet completed his MA when he began teaching at Bryn Mawr.[1] Wade spent three years teaching at the Bryn Mawr School. He enjoyed the work greatly, but it was a part-time position. In 1962, the school got a new headmistress who decided to get rid of all part-time faculty. Consequently, Wade was let go that year. He had his Navy pension, but he was not yet ready to retire. Thus, he took a civil defense job with the state of Maryland. The Cold War was at its height, and just about every public building had a nuclear fallout shelter. Wade's title was "Shelter Officer". He spent a great deal of time inspecting shelters in the basements of public schools, town halls, and other public buildings, and supervised the maintenance of existing shelters as well as the design of new ones, using a state car to drive from shelter to shelter.[2] According to his son Philip, Wade "was responsible for every aspect of the state shelters. I used to joke that Maryland Civil Defense was an officers [sic] club disguised as a state agency. It was headed by a retired Air Force General and everyone in the office was a retired military officer O-6 or above!"[3] He held the job for ten years. It would be Wade's last job before his retirement in 1972.

Wade and Ruth enjoyed a happy marriage. In a way, they were a case of opposites attracting. Ruth, a socialite in the best sense of the word, was far more outgoing than was Wade. Under her management of the family social calendar, Ruth and Wade

---

[1] Questionnaire filled out by Wade McClusky in January 1960 for the Naval Academy's "Alumni Register and History Record." From the McClusky "Jacket" on file at the Naval Academy. "McClusky, Clarence Wade, Jr." Jacket Number 8306. Special Collections & Archives Department, Nimitz Library, United States Naval Academy.

[2] Email communication, Philip McClusky to me, November 7, 2017. Interview with Philip McClusky, December 27, 2017.

[3] Email communication, Philip McClusky to me, November 7, 2017.

became regular fixtures in the society pages of Baltimore area newspapers, attending cocktail parties and Steeplechase events. Almost every weekend there was a dinner party either at their home, the home of friends, or at a local restaurant. Ruth and Wade also went Basseting, which must have been Ruth's idea. Basseting has old Virginia written all over it, and is an activity ostensibly devoted to using a pack of Basset hounds to hunt a rabbit or rabbits that usually takes place in the fall. The leaders of the "hunt," such as the "Whips" who are supposed to keep the hounds under control, wear formal outfits similar to those worn during a fox hunt. Basseting is slightly less aristocratic than fox hunting, however – it does not involve horses and the vast majority of the "hunters" who walk behind the pack dress in casual clothing suitable for hiking. No weapons are used – none of the hunters is armed with anything more powerful than a Thermos bottle full of hot cocoa or perhaps a flask of brandy. Basset hounds are good trackers and are much faster on their feet than they look. Nevertheless, the hounds in a Basseting event almost never catch a rabbit. It is really an excuse for a group of people to take a pleasant walk through the countryside on a Sunday afternoon. When the hunt ends in late afternoon, the guests enjoy high tea, and sometimes cocktails, at the home of the host before heading home.[1] While it was almost certainly Ruth who introduced Wade to Basseting, Wade grew to enjoy the meets. Ruth liked the social aspects of Basseting, such as conversation with the other guests, whereas Wade liked the

---

[1] Interviews with Philip McClusky, December 27 and December 29, 2016. Also see Edwin A. Peeples, "The Genteel Sport of Basseting: Hunting with the Skycastle Thirty Years Ago As Seen Through the Discerning Eye of Edwin A. Peeples" (Chester Springs, PA: Skycastle French Hounds, 2005): pp1–14. Originally published as "The Genteel Sport of Basseting" by Edwin A. Peeples in the *Philipadelphia Inquirer* Sunday magazine *Today*, December 21, 1975. Available online at: http://skycastlefrenchhounds.com/wp-content/uploads/2012/01/GenteelSport1.pdf.

exercise. Sometimes Ruth remained at the hunt's base, a country club or a private home, to chat with other guests while Wade always went for the walk, following the hounds.[1]

Perhaps because they were a staple of the Baltimore area society pages, Wade and Ruth sometimes received a little more publicity than they wanted. Phil McClusky has a framed clipping from an October 1953 edition of a Washington DC area newspaper. A reporter assigned to the Washington, DC District Court beat who was having a slow news day stumbled across a lively tidbit about the tension between Ruth and Millicent and wrote this extract which appeared in the paper:

> "Mrs. Millicent K. McClusky, of 4201 Massachusetts – av NW, today asked District Court to order her former husband to quit sending her alimony checks marked 'Ex-Wife's Alimony.'
>
> Her complaint said the $250 monthly checks were made out by his wife."[2]

Something about this little spat between Wade's current and former wives intrigued newspaper editors. The story was picked up by a wire service – International News Service – and began to appear all over the country. The wire service version is a little more polished. It appeared in the October 22 edition of *The Courier-Post* of Camden, New Jersey in an excerpt datelined "Washington":

> "The former wife of Navy Capt. C. Wade McClusky claims she's embarrassed cashing her $250-a-month alimony checks because they're marked 'ex-wife's alimony.'

[1]Interviews with Philip McClusky, December 27 and December 29, 2016.

[2]Clipping from a Washington, DC newspaper, undated, but almost certainly from October 1953. Page number and exact newspaper not known. Philip McClusky collection.

Mrs. Millicent King McClusky told the court McClusky's
'new' wife has been writing the checks for the officer's signature.
She asked the court to put a stop to it."[1]

The wire service version appeared the same day in the *Miami News*
under the headline "No. 2 Labels Alimony Checks 'Ex-Wife,' and
No. 1 Resents It."[2] The wire story also appeared almost verbatim
without a headline in the *Minneapolis Star*.[3]

Ruth did indeed have a stubborn streak. Phil McClusky recalls
that during his childhood Millicent's name was never mentioned
in the house. In keeping with Wade's inability to discipline a
child, all matters disciplinary regarding Philip's upbringing were
handled by Ruth. When Philip was in high school, he and Ruth
engaged in all of the arguing common between a teenager and
a parent. Wade remained aloof from all of these disputes. On one
occasion, a friend and/or a colleague asked Wade in the late 1960s
why he allowed his son to go around with the long hair common
at the time, to which Wade replied that Phil "is his own person."
While always keeping his own hair cut short, Wade himself in his
later years grew a mustache and allowed his sideburns to grow
down to the level of his earlobes in keeping with the style of the
early 1970s.[4]

While she was definitely the disciplinarian in the household,
Ruth was not without a sense of humor. Shortly before the
wedding, her way of signing articles was to write the following

<hr />

[1] "'Ex' Says New Wife Writes Alimony" *Courier-Post* (Camden, NJ), October 22, 1953.
P26. Available online at: www.newspapers.com/image/180425649/?terms=Wade%2
BMcClusky. Accessed September 18, 2017.

[2] *Miami Daily News*. October 22, 1953. P6-B. Available online at: www.newspapers.com/
image/298956054/?terms=Wade%2BMcClusky. Accessed September 18, 2017.

[3] *Minneapolis Star*. October 22, 1953. P38. Available online at: www.newspapers.com/
image/187586476/?terms=Wade%2BMcClusky. Accessed September 18, 2017.

[4] Interviews with and photos shared by Philip McClusky, December 27 and December 29,
2016.

missive: "I hereby promise to marry Capt. C. Wade McClusky as soon as his divorce is final — be a wonderful wife, love him always — and strangle him if he doesn't behave — I also promise to stay fairly sober and try to keep him the same way —".[1]

World War 2 had provided Wade with all of the excitement that he ever needed or wanted. After his retirement from the Navy and the move to Ruxton, what Wade seemed to want most of all was peace and quiet. While Ruth kept their social calendar full on the weekends, Wade's weekday routine was extremely subdued. During the years in Ruxton, Wade would arrive home from work at around 5.30p.m. He and Ruth would discuss the events of the day over cocktails, then the family would have dinner. After dinner, Wade was content to watch prime-time television for an hour or two before retiring. He was highly literate; the brief account he wrote of the Battle of Midway and the letters he wrote to Walter Lord read quite well. Nevertheless, he was not a big reader. Nor did he play chess or do crossword puzzles – activities that would seem natural for someone of his cerebral temperament.[2] Although he did not play chess, Wade did enjoy other board games. Indeed, in the early 1960s Wade earned a modest stipend for serving as the expert consultant for the Baltimore-based Avalon Hill company's board game "Midway," which first appeared in 1964. Avalon Hill's military board games were extremely complex but highly popular in the 1960s and 1970s.

Wade and Philip would often play each other in the Midway game and in "*Bismarck*," another Avalon Hill game. While Wade could always beat Philip on the tennis court, it was Philip who ruled the game board. As a teenager always open to fresh perspectives, Philip would improvise during the board game matches in a manner that should have made Wade proud, but instead turned into a source of mild frustration. For instance, when playing "*Bismarck*," Philip would hide the German

---

[1]Handwritten note by Ruth McClusky. Philip McClusky collection.

[2]Interviews with Philip McClusky, December 27 and December 29, 2016.

battleship in unconventional places like the straits of Dover. Meanwhile Wade, cast in the role of the British Home Fleet, would be fruitlessly hunting for the *Bismarck* in the North Atlantic. After being defeated, Wade would complain about his son's tactics, saying for instance that it was unfair to hide the *Bismarck* in the English Channel, a place the German battleship never actually went. Philip would reply to the following effect: "Dad, it's a game. You don't have to follow the historical record; you just have to win!"[1]

The man who had in real life played the pivotal role in the American victory in the Battle of Midway would be similarly brought to ruin by his son when he and Philip squared off against each other in the "Midway" board game. Graciously allowing his father to be the Americans, Philip would reverse history by beating Wade. While playing the Midway game in the role of the Japanese, Phil would do things that Adm Nagumo should have, but did not, do in the actual battle. Phil would divide *Kido Butai*, sending two Japanese carriers north and placing the other two far to the south, close to Midway. Wade, on the other hand, would play the game the way the battle was actually fought. His son's machinations on the game board would negate moves that Wade had actually made in the battle, such as his decision to search to the north instead of the south.[2]

The Avalon Hill games were wildly popular. Wade was interviewed for a 1969 *Wall Street Journal* article on the subject. This article, entitled "Tabletop War Games Are Luring Battalions of Would-Be Generals" by Michael Stern, shows that the Avalon Hill military board games were a precursor to the video and computer war games that would begin to appear in the mid-1970s. In the article, after noting the popularity of the games, Stern writes (getting McClusky's rank at the time of the battle wrong) of the frustration that could result from their complexity:

[1]Interviews with Philip McClusky, December 27 and December 29, 2016.
[2]Interviews with Philip McClusky, December 27 and December 29, 2016.

"Take C. Wade McCluskey [*sic*], for instance. Mr. McClusky occasionally takes on his son Phillip [*sic*], age 16, in the war game of 'Midway,' based on the 1942 triumph of U.S. Navy planes over the Japanese fleet around Midway Island. Mr. McClusky says he's not too fond of the game; Phillip, taking the part of the Japanese, usually trounces him. And that's a little odd, since in 1942 C. Wade McCluskey was *at* Midway— as the rear admiral who led the Navy aircraft to a smashing victory."[1]

The article goes on to state that some people, and some game manufacturers, stayed away from military board games because of the unpopularity of the Vietnam War, which was then at its height.[2] While the Vietnam War undoubtedly deterred some people from playing these games, the unpopularity of that conflict may actually have boosted the popularity of Avalon Hill games that dealt with battles from wars in which the issue of right and wrong were more clearly defined than in Vietnam. For instance, "Midway," "The Battle of the Bulge," and "Waterloo" were three of Avalon Hill's most popular games. The company made a great effort to achieve historical accuracy, which is why participants like Wade McClusky were sought out as consultants. Retired Army General Anthony McAuliffe, the hero of Bastogne, worked with Avalon Hill in a similar capacity to develop the company's Battle of the Bulge board game.[3]

The popularity of the Avalon Hill military board games shows that in that pre-computer era, games were less isolating; you had to have at least one other person in the room with you to play

---

[1]"Tabletop War Games Are Luring Battalions of Would-Be Generals," by Michael Stern. *The Wall Street Journal*, Oct. 30, 1969. P1.

[2]"Tabletop War Games Are Luring Battalions of Would-Be Generals," by Michael Stern. *The Wall Street Journal*, Oct. 30, 1969. P1.

[3]"Tabletop War Games Are Luring Battalions of Would-Be Generals," by Michael Stern. *The Wall Street Journal*, Oct. 30, 1969. P1.

one. Also, these games required patience. Unlike computer games, the solution to an Avalon Hill military board game was never just one mouse click away. The *Wall Street Journal* article notes that: "Since the games are realistic and complex, it can take up to 10 days to play through to the end of some. The rule book for '1914' runs 40 pages." This level of complexity was a definite turn-off for some, "but the real fans love the complexity." Because of their historical accuracy, the Avalon Hill board games were even used as teaching tools in high school and college classes.[1]

Just about the only type of excitement Wade actively sought out after the war resulted from his fondness for fast driving. Legally mandated speed limits for automobiles have always been a problem for combat pilots and Wade was no exception. After the war, he drove as fast, or faster, than any teenager. He also fought every speeding ticket he received, and he seems to have received quite a few. His practice was to don his uniform before he headed to court. He seemed to enjoy arguing with traffic court judges. How many of those judges were actually moved to dismiss the fines owed by the disputatious captain has not been recorded.[2]

While Wade had enjoyed good health for most of his life, one day in November 1975 he suddenly woke up feeling confused. There had been no warning – he had felt fine upon going to bed the previous evening. Nobody knew it at the time, but this was the beginning of Wade's final illness, which would last eight months until his death at the Bethesda Naval Hospital on June 27, 1976. Exactly what Wade McClusky died of remains something of a mystery. While the official cause of death was cirrhosis of the liver, his son Philip believes that what really killed Wade was retirement. As a career naval officer, Wade had lived by schedules, duties, and orders, and it thus transpired that retirement was far

[1] "Tabletop War Games Are Luring Battalions of Would-Be Generals," by Michael Stern. *The Wall Street Journal*, Oct. 30, 1969. P1 and p26.
[2] Interviews with Philip McClusky, December 27 and December 29, 2016, and December 27, 2017.

too quiet a lifestyle for him. He did not have enough hobbies to take up his time, especially when an ankle injury forced him to give up playing his beloved game of tennis a few years before his death.[1]

Typical of an old Navy pilot, Wade had always enjoyed having a couple of drinks in the evening. He had actually been diagnosed with cirrhosis of the liver several years before he died, but he never told this to Ruth or Philip. The Naval Academy still had a full-service hospital in 1975 and Ruth took Wade there to see his primary care physician, who coincidentally had just recently given Wade a physical. Because the cirrhosis was getting worse, Wade's doctor had told him at the time of the physical to cease drinking, which Wade did. Upon being told that Wade was now feeling disoriented, the doctor's diagnosis was that Wade was experiencing alcohol withdrawal. This was almost certainly not accurate. After his initial diagnosis of cirrhosis, Wade had given up alcohol for short periods of time with no ill effects – making it highly unlikely that his present distress was due to withdrawal. In later years, Philip and his mother would become convinced that Wade's symptoms – sudden onset disorientation – were far more consistent with those of a stroke or some other neurological event rather than with alcohol withdrawal.[2]

Wade remained at the Annapolis hospital for a week before returning home, after which time he continued to be treated at the Academy as an outpatient for alcohol withdrawal, but not for any neurological conditions. He never really recovered.[3] According to Phil McClusky:

"For several months [Wade] would have periods of confusion and disorientation. In April [1976] he became jaundice [sic] and we decided to take him to Bethesda Naval Medical Center

[1]Email communication, Philip McClusky to me, March 1, 2015 and November 10, 2017.

[2]Email communication, Philip McClusky to me, November 10, 2017.

[3]Email communication, Philip McClusky to me, November 10, 2017.

bypassing Annapolis. Bethesda immediately began treating him for Cirrhosis, not alcohol withdrawal. Unfortunately, by than [sic] it was too late, his other organs had started to fail. He remained in Bethesda until his death."[1]

Phil and his mother came to regret that they had initially taken Wade to the Academy hospital instead of to Bethesda. They felt that if they had gone immediately to the latter, the treatment Wade received there for his cirrhosis might have enabled him to recover, or at least to stabilize and live longer.[2]

Wade McClusky has been memorialized to some extent by the Navy. In 1971 the Navy instituted a "C. Wade McClusky" Award given to the carrier-based squadron of aircraft that turns in the best performance in a given year.[3] In December 1983 a *Perry* Class frigate named the USS *McClusky* (FFG-41) was commissioned into naval service in Long Beach California, not far from the Todd shipyard in San Pedro where the ship had been built. Wade Sanford (Pat), Carole, their daughter Patricia, Philip, and Ruth had all attended the launching of the as-yet incomplete hull in September 1982 as well as the commissioning. Pat and Patricia carried out the laying of the mast ceremony by placing coins below the base of the mast as it was lowered into place. As the new ship's sponsor, Ruth did the honors during the launch of breaking a bottle of champagne against the bows just before the hull slid down the ways. Ruth and Philip donated the binoculars Wade had used at Midway as a gift to the new ship's crew.[4] The

[1]Email communication, Philip McClusky to me, November 10, 2017.

[2]Email communication, Philip McClusky to me, November 10, 2017.

[3]"Navy Pilot Gets Awards" *Casa Grande Dispatch* (Arizona). January 19, 1973. P7. Available online at: www.newspapers.com/image/2555236/?terms=Wade%2BMcClusky. Accessed September 18, 2017. Wade McClusky obituary. *The Baltimore Sun*, June 29, 1976. PA13. Available online at: https://www.newspapers.com/image/377700178/.

[4]Email communication, Philip McClusky to me, November 15, 2017. Telephone conversation with Carole McClusky-Pewthers, November 29, 2017. Interviews with

launching and commissioning events were among the relatively rare occasions when the two half-brothers, Wade Sanford and Philip, got to see each other. Wade Sanford was already a young adult when Phil was born and they lived on opposite sides of the country from each other. As for the ship, in a naval career that would span three decades, the USS *McClusky* would serve all over the world in assignments as varied as participating in the first Gulf War in 1991 to conducting drug interdiction patrols in the eastern Pacific.[1] A handsome, workmanlike ship, the USS *McClusky* was decommissioned in January 2015 after 32 years of hard service. Decommissioning the frigate has freed up the McClusky name to be used for a new ship. A frigate was nice, but a carrier would be a better and more appropriate namesake for one of the finest pilots the US Navy has ever produced.

There has been an effort in recent years to have the Navy Cross Wade McClusky was awarded for his actions in the Battle of Midway upgraded to a posthumous Medal of Honor. Those efforts have so far failed. One of the stumbling blocks has apparently been that as the *Enterprise* air group commander, McClusky was simply doing his job by leading his pilots to the enemy on June 4, 1942, which militates against the "above and beyond the call of duty" requirement for a Medal of Honor. While he was never bitter about not receiving a Medal of Honor, as the years went by and the true significance of the Battle of Midway became more and more apparent, Wade would in the words of his son Philip "not have been averse to the idea" had a Medal of Honor been bestowed upon him.[2]

Philip McClusky, December 27 and December 29, 2016.

[1] USS McClusky deploying in support of counter Illicit-trafficking. [USS] McClusky Public Affairs Office. January 3, 2012. Available at: www.public.navy.mil/surfor/ffg41/Pages/USSMcCluskydeployinginsupportofcounterIllicit-trafficking.aspx#.WgpVW8anGM8. Accessed November 13, 2017.

[2] Telephone interview with Philip McClusky, December 18, 2016.

A good way to conclude this account is with the summation found in USS *Enterprise* commanding officer Capt George D. Murray's after action report on the Battle of Midway. In his official report to Adm Nimitz dated June 13, 1942 and describing the part played by the *Enterprise* and its air groups in the recent battle, Capt Murray wrote:

"CONCLUSION: ENTERPRISE Air Group, both pilots and gunners, displayed a spirit of utter fearlessness, resolution and determination throughout all air actions. This spirit, though shared by pilots and gunners alike, found its highest expression in the person of the Air Group Commander, LtComdr C.W. McClusky, Jr. U.S.N. On June 4, prior to intercepting the main enemy forces, it was his decision, and his decision alone, that made the attack possible which lead to the destruction of a major part of the enemy forces. It is the considered opinion of the Commanding Officer that the success of our forces hinged upon this attack. Any other action on the part of LtComdr McClusky would inevitably have lead to irreparable loss to our forces."[1]

[1]USS Enterprise Action Report, June 13, 1942. Air Battle of the Pacific, June 4-6, 1942. Action Report (Serial 0137) — 4–6 June, 1942. Available online at website of *USS Enterprise CV-6: The Most Decorated Ship of the Second World War*. www.cv6.org/ship/logs/action19420604.htm.

Appendix A

Annapolis Class of 1926 Alumni at Midway

There was something special about the Naval Academy class of 1926, just as there was about the West Point class of 1915 – the latter producing 59 generals including Dwight Eisenhower and Omar Bradley. According to Wade's son Philip, "the Class of '26 was all over Midway."[1] Indeed they were; more than 20 members of that class figured prominently in the Battle of Midway. Being then 16 years into their respective careers, classmates of Wade McClusky who served at Midway were then at the perfect rank, lieutenant commander (unless indicated otherwise here), to hold senior positions at the tactical level as squadron commanders, air group commanders, or as the commanding officers of destroyers or submarines. The following brief histories are arranged alphabetically in sections according to which type of duty the particular classmate of McClusky performed during the Battle of Midway:

PILOTS

Leonard James "Ham" Dow:

Ham Dow served as *Enterprise* fighter director officer during the battle. Monitoring the radar and coordinating the activities of the *Enterprise* combat air patrol (CAP) fighter aircraft, Dow

[1]Interviews with Philip McClusky, December 27 and 29, 2016.

was responsible for protecting the *Enterprise* from aerial attack. Dow has been described as "an expert in radar,"[1] which was a very new technology in 1942. Wade McClusky would contact Dow by radio upon his return flight on June 4, 1942 to receive corrected coordinates for the location of *Enterprise*.

Lofton Henderson:

A Marine pilot with movie-star good looks, Lofton Henderson would lead 16 Marine SBD dive-bombers of Squadron VMSB-241 out from Midway itself to attack the Japanese carriers on June 4, 1942. A major in the Marine Corps, Henderson held the rank equivalent to his classmates who in 1942 were lieutenant commanders in the Navy. Henderson was experienced in dive-bomber tactics, but the young pilots of VMSB-241 that he was leading were not. Thus, Henderson opted for a shallow-dive attack against the *Hiryu*, a tactic easier than true dive-bombing but one that unfortunately negated all the advantages of dive-bombing.[2] Shallow dives beginning at low altitude made the Marine SBDs vulnerable to Japanese fighter planes throughout their approach. Shallow dives also rendered the SBD's telescopic bomb sight useless. Instead of lining up the target in the crosshairs of the bomb sight while diving almost straight down, Henderson's pilots would have had to guess when to release their bombs. VS-6 dive-bomber pilot "Dusty" Kleiss would write of his own efforts to use a shallow dive to bomb a small Japanese patrol boat in the February 24, 1942 strike against Wake Island: "It's not so easy to hit a small target when you're making a shallow dive and the target is a moving ship. The path of your bombs covers too much horizontal distance, and

---

[1]Anonymous, *Aloha: Class of 1926: United States Naval Academy*. Written by an unnamed 1926 class member or members to commemorate the 55th class reunion. (Privately printed, 1982): p34.

[2]Samuel Elliot Morison, *History of United States Naval Operations in World War II*. Vol 4. *Coral Sea, Midway and Submarine Actions: May 1942–August 1942* (Boston: Little, Brown and Company, 1954. Reissued in 2001 by Castle Books, Edison, NJ): p110.

the target can change course."[1] Despite this difficulty, Henderson's Marines came close with some near misses, but the *Hiryu* was not hit during this attack and Lofton Henderson was killed. His family was later presented with a posthumous Navy Cross. Later that summer, the airfield captured by other American marines on Guadalcanal in August 1942 would be named after Henderson.[2]

Robert Ruffin Johnson and Walter F. Rodee:

Both of the USS *Hornet*'s dive-bomber squadrons at Midway, Bombing Eight (VB-8) and Scouting Eight (VS-8), were commanded by Annapolis '26 alumni: Robert Ruffin Johnson and Walter F. Rodee, respectively.

Maxwell Leslie:

The commander of Bombing Squadron Three (VB-3) from the *Yorktown*, Max Leslie led the dive-bombing attack that destroyed the Japanese aircraft carrier *Soryu* on June 4, 1942 at almost the exact same time that Wade McClusky's dive-bombers from the *Enterprise* were attacking the *Akagi* and the *Kaga*.

Wade McClusky:

Enterprise air group commander.

Gordon Alexander "Scotch" McLean:

McLean was a scout plane pilot serving on the heavy cruiser *Astoria*, one of the *Yorktown*'s escorts in Task Force 17. After the first Japanese counterattack against *Yorktown* in the early afternoon of June 4, McLean climbed into his Curtiss SOC-1 floatplane and

---

[1] N. Jack "Dusty" Kleiss, with Timothy and Laura Orr, *Never Call Me a Hero: A Legendary American Dive-Bomber Pilot Remembers the Battle of Midway* (New York: William Morrow, 2017): p159.

[2] Morison, *Coral Sea, Midway and Submarine Actions*, p110. *Aloha: Class of 1926*, p16.

was launched from *Astoria*'s midships catapult with orders to fly to Midway to request land-based fighter cover for the beleaguered *Yorktown*, which had just been struck by three bombs.[1]

Oscar Pederson:

Max Leslie's immediate superior at Midway, *Yorktown* Air Group Commander Oscar Pederson was ordered by *Yorktown* Capt Elliott Buckmaster to remain aboard ship as Buckmaster's air advisor and as fighter director officer, and so did not fly during the battle.[2]

DECK OFFICERS

Robert G. Armstrong:

Assistant air officer on *Yorktown* (CV-5) during the battle.[3]

Daniel T. Birtwell:

By the time of Midway, Daniel T. Birtwell had undoubtedly witnessed more death and destruction than had any other member of the class of 1926. Birtwell had been eating breakfast with his wife at their home in Honolulu when the Pearl Harbor attack began on December 7, 1941. He had worked the previous evening shift in the engine room of the USS *Arizona*, of which he was chief engineer. Wracked with survivor's guilt after 1,177 of his shipmates perished in the attack, Birtwell "was never the same afterwards" according to his granddaughter Susan Fry. At Midway, Birtwell was serving as chief engineer of the heavy cruiser USS *Portland* (CA 33), part of the protective screen for *Yorktown* in Task Force 17.[4]

---

[1]Anonymous, *Aloha: Class of 1926*, pp17–18, p27.

[2]Stephen L. Moore, *Pacific Payback: The Carrier Aviators Who Avenged Pearl Harbor at the Battle of Midway* (New York: NAL Caliber, 2014): p196.

[3]Anonymous, *Aloha: Class of 1926*, p27.

[4]Telephone conversation with Ms Susan Fry, granddaughter of Daniel T. Birtwell, Jr, May 10, 2017.

John G. Foster:

Air officer on *Hornet* (CV-8) during the battle.[1]

Wendell Fischer Kline:

Wendell Kline commanded the USS *Thornton* (AVD-11), a World War 1-vintage *Clemson* Class destroyer that had been converted into a seaplane tender.[2] *Thornton* and another tender, USS *Ballard*, took turns keeping watch at French Frigate Shoals during May and June 1942. A small, low-lying atoll of sandbars and coral outcroppings with a lagoon in the middle, French Frigate Shoals lies roughly 500 miles northwest of Pearl Harbor and about halfway between Pearl and Midway. Making French Frigate Shoals a temporary base for American patrol aircraft prevented the Japanese from doing the same thing. Namely, it forced the Japanese to abandon Operation *K*, a plan to stage large four-engined Kawanishi H6K "Emily" seaplanes through French Frigate Shoals on their way to reconnoiter Pearl Harbor. Even with its very long range of 4,000 miles (and indicative of the vast distances involved in the war in the Pacific), a Kawanishi would still not have enough fuel to fly from Japanese bases at Jaluit and Wotje atolls in the Marshall Islands to Pearl Harbor and back again without refueling. Operation *K* involved loading aviation fuel aboard two Japanese submarines, *I-121* and *I-123* so that the submarines could rendezvous with the flying boats in the lagoon at French Frigate Shoals so that the aircraft could be refueled. By using this technique, the Japanese had managed to put a Kawanishi over Pearl Harbor on at least two previous occasions in March 1942. Adm Nimitz was aware of this and he and his staff correctly guessed that French Frigate Shoals had been the staging/refueling stop used by the Japanese aircraft on those earlier overflights. Nimitz was determined to prevent the Japanese

[1] Anonymous, *Aloha: Class of 1926*, p37.

[2] Morison, *Coral Sea, Midway and Submarine Actions*, p93.

from gathering any further Intelligence data on the comings and goings of American warships to and from Pearl. Thus, when the two Japanese submarines assigned to tanker duty for Operation *K* duly arrived at French Frigate Shoals in late May, the presence there of at least one of the two American seaplane tender vessels as well as some American PBY Catalina flying boats forced the Japanese to cancel their planned last-minute aerial reconnaissance over Pearl Harbor. Such reconnaissance, if it had been carried out on May 31 as planned, would have informed the Japanese that the American aircraft carriers were not at Pearl Harbor.[1] Had Operation *K* gone forward as planned, the Japanese might even have been able to track the American carriers to their location northeast of Midway, where the Americans were waiting to ambush the Japanese fleet.

Therefore, while duty at French Frigate Shoals was undoubtedly dull and lonely, Wendell Kline and the crew of *Thornton* did play a vital role in the Battle of Midway simply by the fact that their presence at French Frigate Shoals forced the Japanese to cancel Operation *K*. Incidentally, that Adm Nimitz, during the very busy month of May 1942, had remembered a small but very important detail such as sending a little force to lonely, desolate French Frigate Shoals shows that the American Pacific Fleet Commander was one step ahead of his opposite number Adm Yamamoto at every stage of the Battle of Midway.

Orin Livdahl:

Gunnery officer on the *Enterprise* during the battle.[2]

---

[1] *History of United States Naval Operations in World War II.* Vol 4. *Coral Sea, Midway and Submarine Actions: May 1942–August 1942,* (Boston: Little, Brown and Company, 1954. Reissued in 2001 by Castle Books, Edison, NJ): p85, pp93–94. Parshall, Jonathan and Anthony Tully, *Shattered Sword: The Untold Story of the Battle of Midway* (Washington, DC: Potomac Books, 2007): p50, p99.

[2] NARA. RG 24. Box 3334. *Enterprise* Deck Log, June 1942.

Earl K. Olsen:

Engineering officer of the heavy cruiser USS *Pensacola*, which was screening *Enterprise* and *Hornet* in Task Force 16.

Ralph E. Patterson:

Ralph Patterson served as assistant first lieutenant aboard the *Yorktown*. At the time, Patterson held the rank of lieutenant commander. The term "first lieutenant" aboard an aircraft carrier refers to the officer or officers, whatever their rank, who are in charge of all activities on the flight deck and the hangar deck, respectively.

Hubert E. Strange:

Wade McClusky's roommate at the Naval Academy, "Hubie" Strange was the *Yorktown*'s weather officer at Midway.[1]

SUBMARINERS

William Girard Myers, Jesse Lyle Hull, and Howard Walter Gilmore:

A number of class of 1926 alumni had gone into submarines and three of these men commanded submarines that were part of the group of 19 that Nimitz, a former submariner himself, had hoped would wreak havoc on the approaching Japanese armada. William Girard Myers, commanding the submarine USS *Gato*, had a disappointingly quiet patrol in the vicinity of Midway during the battle. Two other submarines that tried unsuccessfully to find enemy targets during the Aleutians phase of the battle

---

[1] On Hubert Strange being Wade McClusky's roommate; interviews with Phil McClusky, December 27 and December 29, 2016.

were commanded by two other class of 1926 alumni: USS *Finback* (Jesse Lyle Hull), and USS *Growler* (Howard Walter Gilmore).[1]

Howard Gilmore would later win a posthumous Medal of Honor when in February 1943 he gave his life to save his crew and the *Growler*. Wounded during a surface action with a Japanese gunboat, Gilmore realized that he would not be able to make it off the bridge and get below without assistance, which would mean delay. Knowing that the *Growler*, already damaged, would be sunk by enemy gunfire unless it submerged immediately, Gilmore ordered his executive officer, Lt Cdr Arnold Schade, to close the hatch and dive the boat immediately.[2]

1926 ANNAPOLIS GRADUATES IN THE ALEUTIANS PHASE OF THE BATTLE OF MIDWAY

Half of the destroyers that had been sent north in the cruiser and destroyer force commanded by R Adm Robert A. Theobald that was tasked with trying to intercept the Japanese invasion force headed for the Aleutian Islands during the Midway battle were commanded by '26 alumni. John J. Greytak commanded the USS *Kane* (DD 235); Herman O. Parish the USS *Gilmer* (DD 233); John K. Wells the *Humphreys* (DD 236); Charles T. Singleton, Jr the *Brooks* (DD 232); while Paul H. Tobelman commanded USS *Dent* DD-116. Incidentally, four of these destroyers were of the then 20-year-old *Clemson* Class, with which Wade McClusky was intimately familiar from his days serving aboard the *Williamson* (DD 244) in the late 1920s. *Dent* was of the slightly older *Wickes* Class. James S. Russell was a Catalina pilot commanding Patrol Squadron 42 (VP-42) based in the Aleutians.[3]

---

[1] Anonymous, *Aloha: Class of 1926*, pp116–117.

[2] Anonymous, *Aloha: Class of 1926*, pp119–120.

[3] Morison, *Coral Sea, Midway and Submarine Actions*, pp173–174. Anonymous, *Aloha: Class of 1926*, p54.

Appendix B

Wade McClusky Navy Cross Citation

The final version of the citation for Wade's Navy Cross was signed by then Secretary of the Navy Frank Knox and reads as follows:

"For extraordinary heroism and conspicuous devotion to duty as Commander, ENTERPRISE Air Group in the Battle of Midway on June 4, 1942. Pursuant to the report of an enemy Japanese invasion fleet in the vicinity, Lieutenant Commander McClusky led his Air Squadron in a thorough and dogged search flight, maintained until the objective was sighted, and followed by a bold, determined attack against four enemy Japanese carriers in complete disregard of heavy enemy anti-aircraft fire and fierce fighter opposition, with the result that such severe damage was inflicted on enemy carrier flight decks as to effectively put them out of action. In this engagement, in which Lieutenant Commander McClusky suffered a shoulder wound from enemy shrapnel, his courage and inspiring leadership in the face of overwhelming opposition and great danger were in keeping with the highest traditions of the United States Naval Service."[1]

---

[1] Text of the final version of Wade's Navy Cross citation, which was signed by Secretary of the Navy Frank Knox. Philip McClusky collection.

BIBLIOGRAPHY

Please note all URL links were current as of November 2020.

ARCHIVES VISITED:

National Archives and Records Administration (NARA), College Park, Maryland.
Special Collections & Archives Department, Nimitz Library, United States Naval Academy, Annapolis, Maryland.
Walter Lord Papers. Operational Archives, Naval History and Heritage Command (NHHC), Washington Navy Yard, Washington, DC.

ARCHIVES I RECEIVED DOCUMENTS FROM:

National Naval Aviation Museum, Pensacola, Florida.
National Museum of the Pacific War, Fredericksburg, Texas.

UNPUBLISHED PRIMARY SOURCES:

Biography of Frederick J. Horne prepared by the Navy Department's Office of Public Relations and dated January 31, 1945, a copy of which is in the Horne "Jacket" on file at the Naval Academy. "Horne, Frederick J." Alumni Jacket, Special Collections & Archives Department, Nimitz Library, United States Naval Academy.
Biographical materials in a file known as the McClusky "Jacket" on file at the Naval Academy, "McClusky, Clarence Wade, Jr." Jacket Number 8306. Special Collections & Archives Department, Nimitz Library, United States Naval Academy.
Bombing Squadron 6 Action Report, Battle of Midway, 4 June 1942. (Abbreviated report covering morning attack) NARA RG 38. Records of the Office of the Chief of Naval Operations. World War II Action and Operational Reports. Box 387. Commander Bombing Squadron Six (VB-6) file.
Deck Logs. USS *Corregidor* (CVE-58/CVU-58) 1941–1950. For period September 1944 to August 1945. NARA. RG 24. Box 2484.

Deck Log. USS *Enterprise* (CV-6). January 1942 to June 1942. NARA. RG 24. Box 3334.

Email communication, Philip McClusky to me, March 5, 2016; March 6, 2016; and March 14, 2016.

"McClusky, Clarence Wade, Jr." Jacket Number 8306. Special Collections & Archives Department, Nimitz Library, United States Naval Academy.

Memo prepared by R Adm Charles McMorris, from Nimitz to King in regard to the performance of *Corregidor*'s Air Group. December 9, 1944 (date of report), pp1–2. World War II Action Report; Serial 0007. November 19, 1944 (date on folder in archive); and December 15, 1944 (date of report), pp1–2. World War II Action Report; Serial 0008. November 19, 1944 (date on folder in archive). NARA. RG 38. Box 932.

NARA. RG 38. Records of the Office of the Chief of Naval Operations. WWII Action and Operational Reports. Box 966. Wade McClusky Action Report as CO of Fighting Six During the Marshalls Raid. Enclosure D.

National Archives and Records Administration, College Park, MD: NARA. RG 24. Records of the Bureau of Naval Personnel. Deck Logs, 1941–1950.

National Archives and Records Administration, College Park, MD: NARA. RG 38. Records of the Office of the Chief of Naval Operations. World War II War Diaries.

Naval Academy acceptance letter to Wade McClusky, May 17, 1922. Philip McClusky collection.

Navy Department; Bureau of Navigation letter to Wade McClusky, Jr. March 30, 1922. Philip McClusky collection.

Personal report. LCDR Wade C. McClusky. Air Group Commander. Enterprise Air Group. Battle of Midway, 4–6 June, 1942. National Naval Aviation Museum, Pensacola, Florida. (Also available online on several websites).

"Rear Admiral C. Wade McClusky, Jr. United States Navy, Retired" Navy Biographies Section, OI-440, May 23, 1957. Courtesy National Naval Aviation Museum, Pensacola, Florida.

"The Saga of the Mighty C." Unpublished manuscript written by an anonymous member (or members) of the wartime crew of USS *Corregidor* (CVE 58). Philip McClusky collection.

US Naval Air Station: Pensacola, Florida. "Final Report of Training for MCCLUSKY, Clarence W., Jr.", June 1929. Philip McClusky collection.

USS *Corregidor* "Report of Antisubmarine Action by Aircraft" NARA.
  RG 38. Records of the Office of the Chief of Naval Operations.
  WW II Action and Operational Reports. Box 932. World War II
  Action Report; Serial 0007 and Serial 0008. November 19, 1944.
USS *Corregidor*, War Diary. NARA. RG 38. Records of the Office of
  the Chief of Naval Operations. World War II War Diaries. Box 760.
Wade McClusky. After action report. Available at website "U.S.S.
  Enterprise: The Most Decorated Ship of the Second World War"
  http://www.cv6.org/company/accounts/wmcclusky/.
Wade McClusky binder containing copies of the assignment orders he
  received while on active duty. Philip McClusky collection.
Wade McClusky commission as ensign, 1926. Philip McClusky
  Collection.
Wade McClusky nomination letter from the Naval Academy, 1922.
  Philip McClusky collection.
Wade McClusky pilot logbooks covering the years 1926–1956. Philip
  McClusky collection.
Wade McClusky, "The Midway Story" Unpublished manuscript. Walter
  Lord papers. Operational Archives. Naval History and Heritage
  Command (NHHC), Washington Navy Yard, Washington, DC.
Wade McClusky, "The Midway Story." Unpublished manuscript,
  Washington, DC: Naval History and Heritage Command (NHHC).
Walter Lord Papers at Naval History and Heritage Command,
  Washington Navy Yard, Washington, DC.
X-ray of Wade McClusky's left shoulder, showing bullet and fragment
  wounds. Philip McClusky collection.

PUBLISHED PRIMARY SOURCES:

www.ancestry.com
*Annual Register of the United States Naval Academy: Annapolis,
  MD: 1923–1924.* (Washington, DC: Government Printing
  Office, 1923). Available online at: https://archive.org/details/
  annualregiste19231924unse/page/n5.
*Annual Register of the United States Naval Academy: Annapolis,
  MD: 1924–1925.* (Washington, DC: Government Printing
  Office, 1924). Available online at: https://archive.org/details/
  annualregiste19241925unse/page/n5.
*Annual Register of the United States Naval Academy: Annapolis,
  MD: 1925–1926.* (Washington, DC: Government Printing

Office, 1925). Available online at: https://archive.org/details/annualregiste19251926unse/page/n5.

Annual Register of the United States Naval Academy: : Annapolis, MD: 1926–1927. (Washington, DC: Government Printing Office, 1926). Available online at: https://archive.org/details/annualregiste19261927unse/page/n7.

Bland, Larry I., ed., Ritenour Stevens, Sharon, associate ed., *The Papers of George Catlett Marshall,* Vol 4. *Aggressive and Determined Leadership: June 1, 1943–December 31, 1944* (Baltimore: Johns Hopkins University Press, 1996).

The Battle of Midway Honor Roll, at website "Their Finest Hour" http://theirfinesthour.net/2012/06/battle-of-midway-honor-roll/.

Battle of Midway: 4–7 June 1942, Online Action Reports: Commander, Task Force SIXTEEN, Serial 0144A of 16 June 1942. Commander, Task Force SIXTEEN to Commander-in-Chief, U.S. Pacific Fleet, June 16, 1942. Archives of Naval History and Heritage Command, Washington, DC. Available online at: www.midway42.org/Midway_AAR/RAdmiral_Spruance.aspx.

"Bombing Squadron 6, Action Report, Battle of Midway, 4 June 1942. U.S. Aircraft—Action with the Enemy" Naval History and Heritage Command (website). http://web.archive.org/web/20150415070417/http://www.history.navy.mil/research/archives/organizational-records-collections/action-reports/wwii-battle-of-midway/bombing-squadron-6.html.

Catalog from 1948. US Naval School (General Line), Monterey, California.

California, Passenger and Crew Lists, 1882-1959 [database online]. Provo, UT, USA: Ancestry.com Operations Inc, 2008. Original data: *Selected Passenger and Crew Lists and Manifests.* National Archives, Washington, DC.

Casualties figures sustained by USS *Enterprise* at Midway from the "USS Enterprise CV-6" website, at www.cv6.org/company/muster/casualty.asp?s=19420604&e=19420606.

Deck plans, USS *Thetis*, CVE 90 [*Casablanca* Class sister ship to *Corregidor*, CVE 58]. *Booklet of General Plans.* Blueprints drawn by the Industrial Command; US Naval Repair Base, San Diego, CA, May 31, 1945. Available online at: https://maritime.org/doc/plans/cve90.pdf.

Deck plans, USS *Yorktown* [sister ship of USS *Enterprise*, CV-6], from *Booklet of General Plans*, Newport News Shipbuilding and

Drydock Company, Newport News, VA. Final blueprints drawn in 1939 and 1940 to accurately reflect the completed ship. Available online at: https://maritime.org/doc/plans/cv5.pdf.

Dennis, George, Jr, LCDR, USN, ed., *All Hands: The Bureau of Naval Personnel Information Bulletin.* No 380, October 1948. Available online at: www.navy.mil/ah_online/archpdf/ah194810.pdf.

Halsey, Jr, V Adm William F., *Current Tactical Orders and Doctrine U.S. Fleet Aircraft—Volume One: Carrier Aircraft (USF-74, Revised).* Naval Air Station, Pearl Harbor, TH United States Pacific Fleet Aircraft, Battle Force Fleet Air Detachment, March 1941. Available online at: http://www.admiraltytrilogy.com/read/USF-74_Tact&Doct-Acft_V1-CV-Acft_194103.pdf.

Honolulu, Hawaii, Passenger and Crew Lists, 1900-1959 [database online]. Ancestry.com. Provo, UT, USA: Ancestry.com Operations, Inc, 2009. National Archives and Records Administration (NARA); Washington, DC; *Passenger Lists of Vessels Departing from Honolulu, Hawaii, compiled 06/1900 - 11/1954*; National Archives Microfilm Publication: *A3510*; Roll: *098*; Record Group Title: *Records of the Immigration and Naturalization Service, 1787–2004*; Record Group Number: *RG 85*. Original data: Passenger Lists of Vessels Arriving or Departing at Honolulu, Hawaii, 1900–1954. NARA Microfilm Publication A3422, 269 rolls; A3510, 175 rolls; A3574, 27 rolls; A3575, 1 roll; A3615, 1 roll; A3614, 80 rolls; A3568 & A3569, 187 rolls; A3571, 64 rolls; A4156, 348 rolls. Records of the Immigration and Naturalization Service, Record Group 85. National Archives, Washington, DC.

Knox, Cdre Dudley W., USN (Ret), "The United States Navy Between World Wars" – printed as the Introduction to Samuel Eliot Morison. *History of United States Naval Operations in World War II.* Vol 1. *The Battle of the Atlantic, September 1939–April 1943.* (Boston: Little, Brown and Company, 1947).

McClusky, Wade, After action report, Midway. Available at website "U.S.S. *Enterprise*: The Most Decorated Ship of the Second World War" Available online at: www.cv6.org/company/accounts/wmcclusky/. Also available from the National Naval Aviation Museum, Pensacola, Florida.

McClusky, Wade, "The Midway Story" Unpublished manuscript. Philip McClusky collection.

Navy Department, brief biographical essay of McClusky, May 25, 1957. National Naval Aviation Museum, Pensacola, Florida.

Navy Directory: Officers of the United States Navy and Marine Corps: July 1, 1929. (Washington, DC: Government Printing Office, 1929): p51. Available online at: https://archive.org/stream/navydirectoryof1929unit_1#page/50/mode/2up.

Navy Directory: Officers of the United States Navy and Marine Corps: October 1, 1929. (Washington, DC: Government Printing Office, 1929): p50. Available online at: https://archive.org/stream/navydirectoryoff19294unit#page/50/mode/2up.

Navy Directory: Officers of the United States Navy and Marine Corps: October 1, 1930. (Washington, DC: Government Printing Office, 1930): p52. Available online at: https://archive.org/stream/navydirectoryof1930unit_1#page/52/mode/2up.

Nimitz, Adm Chester W., Battle of Midway after action report. Cincpac File No.A16 01849. Available online at: www.ibiblio.org/hyperwar/USN/rep/Midway/Midway-CinCPac.html.

Photo caption for NH 95744. R Adm Dixwell Ketcham, Commander, Carrier Division Five. NHHC. Available online at: www.history.navy.mil/our-collections/photography/numerical-list-of-images/nhhc-series/nh-series/NH-95000/NH-95744.html.

Photo caption for NH95745. USS *Valley Forge* (CV 45). NHHC. Available online at: www.history.navy.mil/our-collections/photography/numerical-list-of-images/nhhc-series/nh-series/NH-95000/NH-95745.html.

Podcast of Wade McClusky 1972 interview with radio station WMCA. Courtesy of Philip McClusky.

Register of the Commissioned and Warrant Officers of the United States Navy and Marine Corps. January 1, 1934. (Washington, DC: Government Printing Office, 1934). University of Michigan copy available online at: https://babel.hathitrust.org/cgi/pt?id=mdp.39015036626334&view=1up&seq=152.

Register of Commissioned and Warrant Officers of the United States Navy and Marine Corps, July 1, 1936. (Washington, DC: Government Printing Office, 1936): p14, p22. Available online, courtesy of the University of Michigan, at: https://babel.hathitrust.org/cgi/pt?id=mdp.39015036626326;view=1up;seq=7.

Register of Commissioned and Warrant Officers of the United States Navy and Marine Corps, July 1, 1941. (Washington, DC: Government

Printing Office, 1941). Available online at: https://babel.hathitrust.org/
cgi/pt?id=mdp.39015036626284&view=1up&seq=66&size=150.

*Register of Commissioned and Warrant Officers of the United
States Navy and Marine Corps. July 1, 1943.* (Washington,
DC: Government Printing Office, 1943): p10, p54 for
the title of Wade's post graduate courses of instruction.
Available online at: https://babel.hathitrust.org/cgi/
pt?id=mdp.39015036626284;view=1up;seq=62;size=150.

*Register of Commissioned and Warrant Officers of the United
States Navy and Marine Corps. July 1, 1944.* (Washington, DC:
Government Printing Office, 1944). Available online at: www.
ibiblio.org/hyperwar/AMH/USN/Naval_Registers/1944.pdf.

Scouting Squadron Six action report: 4–6 June 1942. Available online
at: www.cv6.org/ship/logs/action19420604-vs6.htm.

SS *Calawaii* brochure, available online at: http://cruiselinehistory.
com/wp-content/uploads/2012/10/Screen-shot-2012-10-
10-at-11.47.49-AM1.png. National Archives and Records
Administration (NARA); Washington, DC; *Passenger Lists of
Vessels Arriving at Honolulu, Hawaii, compiled 02/13/1900 -
12/30/1953*; National Archives Microfilm Publication: *A3422*;
Roll: *114*; Record Group Title: *Records of the Immigration and
Naturalization Service, 1787–2004*; Record Group Number:
RG 85.

"Their Finest Hour." Available online at: http://theirfinesthour.
blogspot.com/2012/06/battle-of-midway-honor-roll.html.

The Reminiscences of Rear Admiral James D. Ramage. Interview
conducted by Robert L. Lawson and Barrett Tillman. (Annapolis:
U.S. Naval Institute, 1999).

United States Strategic Bombing Survey (USSBS): *Pacific.* Vol 1.
Interrogations of Japanese Officials. Naval Analysis Division.
(OPNAV-P-03-100). (New York: Garland Publishing Co., 1976).

Enterprise casualties at "USS Enterprise CV-6" website: http://www.
cv6.org/company/muster/casualty.asp?s=19420604&e=19420606.
Accessed July 12, 2020.

USS *Enterprise* action report (Serial 0133), written by Capt George
D. Murray, June 8, 1942. Available online at: www.midway42.org/
Midway_AAR/USSEnterprise1.aspx.

USS *Enterprise* action report, June 13, 1942. Air Battle of the Pacific, June 4-6, 1942. Action Report (Serial 0137) — 4–6 June, 1942. Available at website of *USS Enterprise CV-6: The Most Decorated Ship of the Second World War.* Available online at: www.cv6.org/ship/logs/action19420604.htm.

USS *Yorktown* action report; Battle of Midway. Available online at Naval History and Heritage Command website: www.history.navy.mil/research/archives/digitized-collections/action-reports/wwii-battle-of-midway/uss-yorktown-action-report.html.

"Wade McClusky" entries at Ancestry.com: http://trees.ancestry.com/tree/32878307/person/18347961652/fact/88092160165.

Watts, Franklin, ed., *Voices of History: Great Speeches and Papers of the Year 1941* (New York: Franklin Watts, Inc, 1942).

SECONDARY SOURCES:

Books

Anonymous, *Aloha: Class of 1926: United States Naval Academy,* Written by an unnamed 1926 class member or members to commemorate the 55th class reunion (Privately printed, 1982).

Babcock & Wilcox Co, the, *Steam: Its Generation and Use* (New York: The Knickerbocker Press, 1906).

Buell, Thomas B., *Master of Sea Power: A Biography of Fleet Admiral Ernest J. King* (Boston: Little, Brown and Company, 1980).

Buell, Thomas B., *The Quiet Warrior: A Biography of Admiral Raymond A. Spruance* (Annapolis: Naval Institute Press, 1974, 1987).

Burnside, J. L., and Greenwald, J. A., *The Lucky Bag: Nineteen-Twenty-Six. The Annual of the Regiment of Midshipmen* (Rochester, NY: The Du Bois Press, 1926).

Cagle, Malcolm W., and Manson, Frank A., *The Sea War in Korea* (Annapolis: Naval Institute Press, 1957).

Childers, Erskine, *The Riddle of the Sands* (Mineola, New York: Dover Publications, 1903, 1976, 1999).

Clark, J. J. "Jocko", with Reynolds, Clark G., *Carrier Admiral* (New York: David McKay Company, Inc, 1967).

Craven, Wesley Frank and Cate, James Lea, *The Army Air Forces in World War II. Vol 5. Matterhorn to Nagasaki: June 1944 to August 1945* (Chicago: The University of Chicago Press, 1953).

Cressman, Robert J., Ewing, Steve, Tillman, Barrett, Horan, Mark, Reynolds, Clark, and Cohen, Stan, *A Glorious Page in Our History: The Battle of Midway, 4–6 June 1942* (Missoula, Montana: Pictorial Histories Publishing Co, Inc, 1990).

Churchill, Winston S., *The Second World War*. Vol 6. *Triumph and Tragedy* (Boston: Houghton Mifflin Company, 1953).

Dennis, George, Jr, LCDR, USN, ed., *All Hands: The Bureau of Naval Personnel Information Bulletin*. No 380, October 1948. Available online at: www.navy.mil/ah_online/archpdf/ah194810.pdf.

Dickinson, Clarence E., with Sparkes, Boyden, *The Flying Guns: Cockpit Record of a Naval Pilot from Pearl Harbor Through Midway* (New York: Charles Scribner's Sons, 1942, 1943).

Dickinson, Clarence E., and Sparkes, Boyden, "The Target Was Utterly Satisfying" in Smith, S. E., ed., *The United States Navy in World War II: The One Volume History, from Pearl Harbor to Tokyo Bay — by Men Who Fought in the Atlantic and the Pacific and by Distinguished Naval Experts, Authors and Newspapermen* (New York: William Morrow & Company, 1966): pp277–283.

Encyclopædia Britannica Online, s. v. "Samuel Eliot Morison". Available online at: http://www.britannica.com/biography/Samuel-Eliot-Morison.

Gaddis, John Lewis, *Strategies of Containment: A Critical Appraisal of American National Security Policy During the Cold War* (New York: Oxford University Press, 1982, 2005).

Groom, Winston, *1942: The Year that Tried Men's Souls* (New York: Atlantic Monthly Press, 2005).

Hills, Richard L., *Power from Steam: A History of the Stationary Steam Engine* (Cambridge: Cambridge University Press, 1989).

Hough, Frank O., Shaw, Henry I, and Ludwig, Verle E., *U.S. Marine Corps Operations in World War II*. Vol 1. *Pearl Harbor to Guadalcanal* (Washington, DC: Historical Branch, G-3 Division, Headquarters, US Marine Corps, 1958). Available online at: www.ibiblio.org/hyperwar/USMC/I/USMC-I-II-3.html.

Johnson, Captain Chris, "Clarence W. McClusky: Intuition" in Thomas, Joseph J., ed. *Leadership Embodied: The Secrets to Success of the Most Effective Navy and Marine Corps Leaders*. 2nd Edition (Annapolis: Naval Institute Press, 2013): pp79–83.

Johnson, Kristi, ed., *History of the U.S.S. Antietam: CV/CVA/CVS 36* (Paducah, Kentucky: Turner Publishing Co, 2001).

King, Ernest J., with Whitehill, Walter Muir, *Fleet Admiral King: A Naval Record* (New York: W. W. Norton, 1952).

Kleiss, N. Jack "Dusty," with Orr, Timothy and Laura, *Never Call Me a Hero: A Legendary American Dive Bomber Pilot Remembers the Battle of Midway* (New York: Morrow, 2017).

Kuehn, John T., *Agents of Innovation: The General Board and the Design of the Fleet that Defeated the Japanese Navy* (Annapolis: Naval Institute Press, 2008).

Le Van, William Barnet, *The Practical Management of Engines and Boilers* (Philadelphia: Philadelphia Book Co, 1900).

Lord, Clifford and Turnbull, Archibald, *History of United States Naval Aviation* (New Haven: Yale University Press, 1949).

Lord, Walter, *Incredible Victory* (New York: Harper & Row, 1967).

Lord, Walter, *The Night Lives On* (New York: Avon Books, 1986, 1987).

Lundstrom, John B., *The First Team: Pacific Air Combat from Pearl Harbor to Midway* (Annapolis: Naval Institute Press, 1984).

Macintyre, Donald, *Aircraft Carrier: The Majestic Weapon* (New York: Ballantine Books, 1968).

Moore, Stephen L., *Pacific Payback: The Carrier Aviators Who Avenged Pearl Harbor at the Battle of Midway* (New York: NAL Caliber, 2014).

Morison, Samuel Eliot., *History of United States Naval Operations in World War II*. Vol 1. *The Battle of the Atlantic, September 1939–April 1943* (Boston: Little, Brown and Company, 1947).

Morison, Samuel Eliot, *History of United States Naval Operations in World War II*. Vol 3. *The Rising Sun in the Pacific, 1931–April 1942* (Boston: Little, Brown and Company, 1948, 1954).

Morison, Samuel Eliot, *History of United States Naval Operations in World War II*. Vol 4. *Coral Sea, Midway and Submarine Actions: May 1942–August 1942* (Boston: Little, Brown and Company, 1954. Reissued in 2001 by Castle Books, Edison, NJ).

Morison, Samuel Eliot, *History of United States Naval Operations in World War II*. Vol 7. *Aleutians, Gilberts and Marshalls: June 1942–April 1944* (Boston: Little, Brown and Company, 1951).

Overy, Richard, *Why the Allies Won* (New York: Norton, 1995, 1997).

Parshall, Jonathan and Tully, Anthony, *Shattered Sword: The Untold Story of the Battle of Midway* (Washington, DC: Potomac Books, 2007).

Pogue, Forrest C., *George C. Marshall*. Vol 2. *Ordeal and Hope: 1939–1942* (New York: Viking, 1966).

Potter, E. B., *Bull Halsey* (Annapolis: Naval Institute Press, 1985).

Potter, E. B., *Nimitz* (Annapolis: Naval Institute Press, 1976, 1987).

Prange, Gordon W., Goldstein, Donald M., and Dillon, Katherine V., *Miracle at Midway* (New York: McGraw-Hill, 1982).

Reynolds, Clark G., *The Fast Carriers: The Forging of an Air Navy* (New York: McGraw-Hill, 1968).

Rigby, David, *Allied Master Strategists: The Combined Chiefs of Staff in World War II* (Annapolis: Naval Institute Press, 2012).

Rigby, David, *No Substitute for Victory: Successful American Military Strategies from the Revolutionary War to the Present Day* (New York: Carrel Books/Skyhorse Publishing Co, 2014).

Shepard, Alan, Slayton Deke, with Jay Barbreem, *Moon Shot: The Inside Story of America's Apollo Moon Landings* (New York: Open Road, 2011).

Skeldon, Walter E., *Escort Carriers in the Pacific: A History of All Escort Carriers in the Pacific* (Victoria, BC, Canada: Trafford, 2002).

Smedburg, William G. and Cooper, Joshua W., *Cruise Book: U.S.S. Iowa: 1951–1952* (Tokyo: Toppan Printing Co, Ltd, 1952).

Smith, S. E., ed., *The United States Navy in World War II: The One-Volume History, from Pearl Harbor to Tokyo Bay—by Men Who Fought in the Atlantic and the Pacific and by Distinguished Naval Experts, Authors and Newspapermen* (New York: William Morrow & Company, 1966).

Spennemann, Dirk H. R., "The Japanese Seaplane Base on Wotje Island, Wotje Atoll" 2000. Available online at: http://marshall.csu.edu.au/Marshalls/html/WWII/Wotje.html.

Stafford, Edward P., *The Big E: The Story of the USS Enterprise* (Annapolis: Naval Institute Press, 1962, 2002).

Sun Tzu, *The Art of War* Lionel Giles, trans. (New York: Barnes & Noble, 2012).

Sweetman, Jack, and Cutler, Thomas J., *The U.S. Naval Academy: An Illustrated History* Second ed. (Annapolis: Naval Institute Press, 1979, 1995).

Symonds, Craig L., *The Battle of Midway* (New York: Oxford University Press, 2011, 2013).

Tillman, Barrett. *Enterprise: America's Fightingest Ship and the Men Who Helped Win World War II* (New York: Simon & Schuster, 2012).

Tillman, Barrett, *The Dauntless Dive Bomber of World War Two* (Annapolis: Naval Institute Press, 1976).

Tuleja, Thaddeus V., *Climax at Midway* (New York: Jove/Norton, 1983, 1960).

Walsh, George J., *The Battle of Midway: Searching for the Truth* (Createspace Independent Publishing Platform, 2015).

Watts, Franklin, ed., *Voices of History: Great Speeches and Papers of the Year 1941* (New York: Franklin Watts, Inc, 1942).

Wildenberg, Thomas, *Destined for Glory: Dive Bombing, Midway, and the Evolution of Carrier Airpower* (Annapolis: Naval Institute Press, 1998).

Willmott, H. P., *The Barrier and the Javelin: Japanese and Allied Pacific Strategies February to June 1942* (Annapolis: Naval Institute Press, 1983).

Wragg, David, *The Escort carrier in World War II: Combustible, Vulnerable, Expendable!* (Barnsley, South Yorkshire: Pen & Sword Maritime, 2005).

Y'Blood, William T., *The Little Giants: U.S. Escort Carriers Against Japan* (Annapolis: Naval Institute Press, 1987, 1999).

Oral histories

Oral History Memoir of Lt Cdr Richard Halsey Best, USN (Ret) as told to William J. Shinneman, 11 August 1995. (The interview took place in King of Prussia, Pennsylvania.) Courtesy of the National Museum of the Pacific War, Fredericksburg, Texas.

Journal articles

Barde, Robert E., "Midway: Tarnished Victory" *Military Affairs* Vol 47; No 4. December 1983, pp188–192. doi:10.2307/1987858.

Hodge, Carl Cavanagh, "The key to Midway: Coral Sea and a culture of learning" *Naval War College Review* 68.1 (Winter 2015): pp119–127.

Horne, V Adm Frederick J., "Naval Logistics in World War II," in Whitman, Leroy, ed., *United States at War: Army and Navy Journal: December 7, 1943—December 7, 1944* (Washington, DC: 1944).

Kleiss, Jack "Dusty," Capt, USN (Ret), "History from the Cockpit: Reflections of a World War II U.S. Navy Dive Bomber Pilot" *The Daybook* Vol 15. Issue 4. A publication of the Hampton Roads

Naval Museum, 2012. Pp12–16. Available online at: www.history. navy.mil/museums/hrnm/files/daybook/pdfs/volume15issue4.pdf.

Nelson, Commander Christopher, U.S. Navy, "Win With The Second Best Weapon: Lessons from Operation Starvation Against Japan" *Proceedings: U.S. Naval Institute* November 2018, pp60–64.

Orr, Timothy, PhD, and Orr, Laura, 'Jack 'Dusty' Kleiss and the Battle of Midway." *The Daybook* Vol 15. Issue 4. Pp8–11. A publication of the Hampton Roads Naval Museum. Available online at: www.history.navy.mil/museums/hrnm/files/daybook/pdfs/ volume15issue4.pdf.

Peeples, Edwin A., "The Genteel Sport of Basseting: Hunting with the Skycastle Thirty Years Ago As Seen Through the Discerning Eye of Edwin A. Peeples" (Chester Springs, PA: Skycastle French Hounds, 2005): pp1–14. Originally published as "The Genteel Sport of Basseting" by Edwin A. Peeples in the *Philadelphia Inquirer* Sunday magazine *Today*, December 21, 1975. Available online at: https:// docs.skycastlefrenchhounds.com/GenteelSport1.pdf.

Robinson, Walton L., "*Akagi*: Famous Japanese Carrier", in *U.S. Naval Institute Proceedings*, Vol 74: May 1948, pp579– 595. Available online at: https://www.usni.org/magazines/ proceedings/1948/may/akagi-famous-japanese-carrier.

USS *McClusky* deploying in support of counter Illicit-trafficking. [USS] McClusky Public Affairs Office. January 3, 2012. Available online at: www.public.navy.mil/surfor/ffg41/Pages/USSMc CluskydeployinginsupportofcounterIllicit-trafficking.aspx#. WgpVW8anGM8.

Newspapers
Baltimore Sun. June 4, 1926. Available online at: http://www. newspapers.com/image/215712119/?terms=Wade%2BMcClusky.

Baltimore Sun. June 29, 1976. Available online at: https://www. newspapers.com/image/377700178/. Accessed June 27, 2020.

Baltimore Sun. August 30, 1986. Available online at: https://www. newspapers.com/image/378000012/. Accessed July 6, 2020.

(Buffalo) *Courier Express*. October 8, 1928.

Buffalo Evening News. October 8, 1928.

The Buffalo News. June 4, 2017. Michel, Lou. "Son Surprises Officials with Battle of Midway Hero's WWII War Medals" Available online at: https://buffalonews.com/2017/06/04/long-last-native-son-honored-instrumental-role-winning-wwii-midway-battle/

The Buffalo News. May 29, 2016. Michel, Lou. "South Buffalo Native's Mettle Turned the Tide in Battle of Midway" Available online at: https://buffalonews.com/2016/05/29/south-buffalo-pilots-mettle-turned-the-tide-in-battle-of-midway/

Casa Grande Dispatch (Arizona). January 19, 1973. Available online at: www.newspapers.com/image/2555236/?terms=Wade%2BMcClusky

Courier-Post (Camden, NJ). October 22, 1953. Available online at: www.newspapers.com/image/180425649/?terms=Wade%2BMcClusky

Honolulu Star-Bulletin. March 19, 1932. Available online at: www.newspapers.com/image/274956584/?terms=Wade%2BS.%2BMcClusky

Honolulu Star-Bulletin, April 2, 1932. Available online at: www.newspapers.com/image/275042117/?terms=Wade%2BMcClusky

Honolulu Star-Advertiser. April 3, 1932. Available online at: www.newspapers.com/image/259238238/?terms=Wade%2BMcClusky

Honolulu Star-Bulletin, June 11, 1932. www.newspapers.com/image/274960635/?terms=Wade%2BMcClusky

Los Angeles Times. January 31, 1971.
Available online at: www.newspapers.com/image/164656149/?terms=Wade%2BS.%2BMcClusky

Miami Daily News. October 22, 1953. Available online at: www.newspapers.com/image/298956054/?terms=Wade%2BMcClusky

Minneapolis Star. October 22, 1953. Available online at: www.newspapers.com/image/187586476/?terms=Wade%2BMcClusky

The News (Frederick, MD). September 14, 1949. Available online at: https://www.newspapers.com/image/8878580/.

The News (Frederick, MD). September 22, 1949. Available online at: https://www.newspapers.com/image/8882036/.

New York Times. February 3, 1985. Available online at: http://www.nytimes.com/1985/02/03/us/non-academy-graduates-get-to-navy-jobs.html?mcubz=1

Philadelphia Inquirer Sunday magazine *Today*, December 21, 1975. Available online at: https://docs.skycastlefrenchhounds.com/GenteelSport1.pdf.

Salt Lake Tribune. July 15, 1942. Available online at: www.newspapers.com/image/13035962.

South Buffalo News. June 15, 1944.

The Times (San Mateo). December 5, 1962. Available
  online at: https://www.newspapers.com/
  image/52107904/?terms=Wade%2BS.%2BMcClusky.
The Wall Street Journal. October 30, 1969.

Dissertations, correspondence, films, blogs, interviews
Barde, Robert E., "The Battle of Midway: A Study in Command" PhD
  dissertation. The University of Maryland, 1971.
B-24 Liberator: 'Ditching of a B-24 Airplane into the James River.'
  1944 NACA World War II. Available online at: https://www.
  youtube.com/watch?v=tG4nm2atjZI. Accessed July 13, 2020.
Email communications between myself and Mr Mark Horan.
Email communications between myself and Mr Philip McClusky.
Email communications between myself and Mr Barrett Tillman.
Email communications between myself and Mr Thom Walla.
Email communications between myself and Mr George Walsh.
Interviews with Philip McClusky, December 27 and December 29,
  2016; December 27, 2017.
Lt Cdr George G. Walsh USNR (Ret.), "Lt. Cmdr. Wade McClusky
  Hero of the Battle of Midway". Available online at: http://
  mccluskymidwayhero.blogspot.com/.
MGM Studio Tour 1925. Silent short film. Available online at:
  https://www.youtube.com/watch?v=Trni2JBzDaE&t=60s.
Telephone interviews with Carole McClusky-Pewthers, September 28,
  2017 and November 29, 2017.
Telephone interview with Philip McClusky, December 18, 2016.
US Navy training film "Landing Crashes of 1940: U.S.S. *Enterprise*"
  Available online at: www.youtube.com/watch?v=ZriGDd0RtFo.
Wade McClusky, undated post-World War 2 manuscript criticizing the
  Navy's method of promoting officers. Philip McClusky collection.

ACKNOWLEDGMENTS

First and foremost, I would like to thank Phil McClusky, without whose assistance this book could not have been written. Phil shared all of his father's papers and pilot logbooks with me, as well as several photographs. He even let me take over his dining room table to go through the material. Phil's enthusiasm about having his father's story told has been of enormous assistance to me and his large collection of his father's papers was an indispensable resource. Carole McClusky-Pewthers was kind enough to share her memories of her late husband, Wade Sanford McClusky, with me. I am indebted to Betty Beason and Anne Hopkins for allowing me to use the Midway diagram as modified by their father, Lewis Hopkins. Similarly, I am indebted to Wayne Goldsmith for allowing me to use the same diagram as modified by his father, George H. Goldsmith.

I exchanged emails with several Midway scholars, whose insights have been most helpful. In this regard, I would like to thank Barrett Tillman, Mark Horan, Thom Walla, Timothy and Laura Orr, and George Walsh. Matt Parsons was kind enough to scan and send me some photographs.

I would like to thank Lisa Thomas at Bloomsbury UK for believing in this project and for being a pleasure to work with.

I would like to thank the staff of the National Archives at College Park, Maryland as well Adam Minakowski, Reference & Special Collections Librarian at the Nimitz Library at the United States Naval Academy. The Staff of the Naval History and Heritage Command kindly allowed me to review the Walter Lord collection of papers at the Washington Navy Yard. The staff of the National Naval Aviation Museum sent me McClusky's Midway after action report, a short Navy Department biographical sketch of Wade McClusky, and a photograph. Eleanor Uhlinger, the University Librarian at the Dudley Knox Library at the Naval Postgraduate School in Monterey sent me some excellent background material dealing with Wade McClusky's time at Monterey. Monica Holland and Rachelle Rennagel provided me with excellent legal advice. Christophe Marchal provided an excellent preliminary cover design.

Any errors or omissions remain my responsibility alone.

INDEX